Best of
Taste of Home

The First 10 Years

Best of Taste of Home—
The First 10 Years

Editor: Faithann Stoner

Art Director: Kristin Bork

Food Editor: Janaan Cunningham

Associate Food Editor:
Diane Werner

Associate Editors: Heidi Reuter Lloyd,
Kristine Krueger, Julie Schnittka,
Jean Steiner

Production: Ellen Lloyd,
Catherine Fletcher

Art Associate: Jami Zewen

Taste of Home®

Executive Editor: Kathy Pohl
Food Editor: Janaan Cunningham
Associate Food Editors: Diane Werner,
Coleen Martin
Senior Recipe Editor: Sue A. Jurack
Test Kitchen Director: Karen Johnson
Managing Editor: Ann Kaiser
Assistant Managing Editor: Barbara Schuetz
Copy Editor: Kristine Krueger
Associate Editors: Sharon Selz, Faithann Stoner
Test Kitchen Home Economists:
Patricia Schmeling, Sue Draheim,
Peggy Fleming, Julie Herzfeldt, Joylyn Jans,
Kristin Koepnick, Mark Morgan,
Wendy Stenman, Karen Wright
Test Kitchen Assistants: Kris Lehman,
Megan Taylor
Editorial Assistants: Barb Czysz,
Mary Ann Koebernik
Design Director: Jim Sibilski
Art Director: Emma Acevedo
Food Photography: Rob Hagen, Dan Roberts
Food Photography Artists: Stephanie Marchese,
Vicky Marie Moseley
Photo Studio Manager: Anne Schimmel
Production: Ellen Lloyd, Catherine Fletcher
Chairman and Founder: Roy Reiman
President: Tom Curl

Taste of Home Books
©2002 Reiman Media Group, Inc.
5400 S. 60th St., Greendale WI 53129

International Standard Book Number:
0-89821-353-3
International Standard Serial Number:
1094-3463

PICTURED AT RIGHT. Clockwise from upper left:
Italian Cheese Twists (p. 121); Chocolate Malted
Cookies (p. 128); Slow-Cooked Vegetable Soup (p.
46); Wontons with Sweet-Sour Sauce (p. 8); Grilled
Chicken Salad (p. 34); Bruschetta Chicken (p. 81).

Best of
Taste of Home
The First 10 Years

PICTURED ON FRONT COVER. From top: Strawberry Meringue Pie (p. 152), Rosemary Pork Roast (p. 284) and Asparagus Nut Stir-Fry (p. 66).

PICTURED ON BACK COVER. Clockwise from top left: Berry Shortbread Dreams (p. 132), Banana Split Supreme (p. 180), Cranberry Cherry Pie (p. 158), Lemon Trifle (p. 174) and Sour Cream Chocolate Cake (p. 142).

FOR ADDITIONAL COPIES of this book, write *Taste of Home* Books, P.O. Box 908, Greendale WI 53129.

To order by credit card, call toll-free 1-800/344-2560 or visit our Web site at www.reimanpub.com.

Mouth-Watering Recipe Collection Showcases a Decade of Good Eating

Food editors faced a challenge selecting Taste of Home's best.

FOR THE PAST 10 years, *Taste of Home* magazine has been featuring delicious recipes from great cooks all across the country, including those shared by a unique staff of 1,000 field editors.

What started as an interesting idea quickly grew to be the largest-circulated food magazine in North America. One reason for this popularity is the focus on family-favorite recipes that have common, readily available ingredients.

This beautiful book, *Best of Taste of Home—The First 10 Years*, captures 570 of the most loved recipes from that remarkable first decade.

This treasury is destined to become the cookbook you turn to again and again when it comes to satisfying the taste buds and appetites of your family and guests. Almost every recipe is pictured in color, so don't be surprised if you can't decide which one to try first.

For some tasty suggestions, consider how our food editors selected recipes for this book from the thousands of wonderful ones that have appeared on the pages of *Taste of Home*.

Prize-Winners Galore

First, the food editors gathered recipe contest winners like Rye Party Puffs (p. 11). Start off any meal or party right with these creamy savory bites. They were the Grand Prize winner of our "Party Appetizer" contest in the October/November 1997 issue.

Deluxe German Potato Salad (p. 31) is a standout side dish at any meal. It was the Grand Prize winner of our "Pass the Potatoes" contest in the February/March 1994 issue.

If you crave something sweet, you can't pass up a batch of Three-Chip English Toffee (p. 177). For the June/July 2001 issue, our panel of judges gave this scrumptious melt-in-your-mouth toffee Grand Prize honors in the "Chock-Full of Chips" contest.

Or spread smiles by serving up a platter of Chocolate Malted Cookies (p. 122). They took the top spot in October/November 1995 in the "Cookie Collection" contest.

Readers' Favorite Recipes

Next, the food editors looked at which recipes prompted the most fan mail from readers. Over the years, readers have thanked us many times for recipes that make up complete meals.

This book spotlights seven Meals on a Budget, 10 Meals in Minutes, eight "My Mom's Best Meals" and eight Editors' Meals. That's an inspiring lineup for every season and situation.

Clever and do-able meals in "Getting in the Theme of Things", like the seven we've included here, always generate considerable excitement and reader praise. Two in particular sparked letters from folks who successfully re-created aspects of the themes themselves.

One is the "Make the Grade with Class Party" (p. 334) that a mom put together for the birthday of her 5-year-old daughter who was about to start kindergarten. It originally appeared in the August/September 1998 issue. Readers adored the School Bus Cake.

The other is the "Host a Hibernation Celebration" meal (p. 328). The "beary" cute Teddy Bear Rolls brought in loads of compliments after they appeared in the February/March 1996 issue.

Editors' Picks

Finally, the food editors included recipes that have brought raves from members of our Test Kitchen and editorial staffs, who have made and served them in their own homes.

Some of our personal favorites include Lemon Herbed Salmon (p. 89) from the April/May 1993 issue, Slow-Cooked Pepper Steak (p. 104) from the April/May 1994 issue and Tomato-Onion Phyllo Pizza (p. 13), which was the second place-winner in the "Tempting Tomatoes" contest in the August/September 2001 issue.

More, Much More

Whether you need a great side dish like Ultimate Scalloped Potatoes (p. 66), a scrumptious bread like Herbed Oatmeal Pan Bread (p. 120), a potluck dish to pass such as Rainbow Pasta Salad (p. 191) or a small-quantity entree like Pot Roast for Two (p. 216), this volume has it all.

There's no better way to celebrate a milestone anniversary than with delicious recipes your family will love. With this one-of-a-kind cookbook, you can dig into the best of the best. Enjoy!

FANTASTIC FOODS. Clockwise from upper left: Deluxe German Potato Salad (p. 31), Lemon Herbed Salmon (p. 89), School Bus Cake (p. 335), Teddy Bear Rolls (p. 329), Tomato-Onion Phyllo Pizza (p. 13) and Three-Chip English Toffee (p. 177).

Kayla

Snacks & Beverages

This extraordinary selection of sweet and savory spreads, dips, appetizers and beverages is sure to perk up a party, beat the late-night munchies or start a great meal off right.

BEST BEGINNINGS! Clockwise from upper left: Cheddar Pepper Crisps (p. 14), Wontons with Sweet-Sour Sauce (p. 8), Fruity Red Smoothies, Banana Pineapple Slush and Grape Punch (p. 23), Sesame Chicken Strips (p. 11) and Fruit on a Stick (p. 16).

Pronto Mini Pizzas
(Pictured above)

These quick pizzas on pita bread crusts are an excellent snack anytime. I also serve them as a light meal on busy days. —Debbi Smith, Crossett, Arkansas

    1 pound ground beef *or* turkey
    1 cup sliced fresh mushrooms
 1/2 cup chopped green pepper
 1/2 cup chopped onion
    2 garlic cloves, minced
    1 can (8 ounces) tomato sauce
    1 teaspoon fennel seed
 1/2 teaspoon salt
 1/2 teaspoon dried oregano
    4 pita breads
    1 cup (4 ounces) shredded mozzarella cheese

In a skillet, cook meat, mushrooms, green pepper, onion and garlic until meat is browned and vegetables are tender; drain. Stir in tomato sauce, fennel, salt and oregano. Simmer for 1-2 minutes. Meanwhile, warm pitas in the microwave. Top each with meat mixture; sprinkle with cheese. Microwave or broil until cheese is melted. Cut into quarters. **Yield:** 4 servings.

— 🍽 🍽 🍽 —

Wontons with Sweet-Sour Sauce
(Pictured at right and on page 6)

This simple finger food makes an awesome appetizer and is perfect for potlucks. I serve these crispy pork rolls with sweet-and-sour sauce, and they disappear in a hurry—folks can't seem to get enough of them.
—Korrin Grigg, Neenah, Wisconsin

    1 can (14 ounces) pineapple tidbits
 1/2 cup packed brown sugar
    1 tablespoon cornstarch
 1/3 cup cider vinegar
    1 tablespoon soy sauce
 1/2 cup chopped green pepper
 1/2 pound ground pork
    2 cups finely shredded cabbage
 3/4 cup finely chopped canned bean sprouts
    1 small onion, finely chopped
    2 eggs, lightly beaten
 1/2 teaspoon salt
 1/4 teaspoon pepper
    2 packages (12 ounces *each*) wonton wrappers*
Vegetable oil for frying

Drain pineapple, reserving juice. Set pineapple aside. In a saucepan, combine brown sugar and cornstarch; stir in pineapple juice, vinegar and soy sauce until smooth. Bring to a boil; cook and stir for 2 minutes or until thickened. Reduce heat; stir in green pepper and pineapple. Cover and simmer for 5 minutes; set aside and keep warm.

In a bowl, combine pork, cabbage, sprouts, onion, eggs, salt and pepper. Place about 1 tablespoonful in the center of each wrapper. Moisten edges with water; fold opposite corners together over filling and press to seal. In an electric skillet, heat 1 in. of oil to 375°. Fry wontons for 2-1/2 minutes or until golden brown, turning once. Drain on paper towels. Serve with sauce. **Yield:** about 8-1/2 dozen (2-1/2 cups sauce).

*Editor's Note: Fill wonton wrappers a few at a time, keeping others covered until ready to use.

Mozzarella Sticks

(Pictured above)

I'm particularly fond of these tasty snacks because they're baked, not fried. Cheese is one of my family's favorite foods. Being of Italian descent, I cook often with ricotta and mozzarella cheeses.
—Mary Merchant, Barre, Vermont

    2 eggs
    1 tablespoon water
    1 cup dry bread crumbs
2-1/2 teaspoons Italian seasoning
  1/2 teaspoon garlic powder
  1/8 teaspoon pepper
   12 sticks string cheese*
    3 tablespoons all-purpose flour
    1 tablespoon butter *or* margarine, melted
    1 cup marinara *or* spaghetti sauce, heated

In a small bowl, beat eggs and water. In a plastic bag, combine bread crumbs, Italian seasoning, garlic powder and pepper. Coat cheese sticks in flour, then dip in egg mixture and bread crumb mixture. Repeat egg and bread crumb coatings. Cover and chill for at least 4 hours or overnight.

Place on an ungreased baking sheet; drizzle with butter. Bake, uncovered, at 400° for 6-8 minutes or until heated through. Allow to stand for 3-5 minutes before serving. Use marinara or spaghetti sauce for dipping. **Yield:** 4-6 servings.

***Editor's Note:** Regular mozzarella cheese, cut into 4-in. x 1/2-in. sticks, can be substituted for the string cheese.*

— 🥄 🥄 🥄 —

Baked Potato Skins

I combined two separate recipes to come up with this delightfully seasoned baked snack, which my family requests often.
—Trish Perrin, Keizer, Oregon

    4 large baking potatoes, baked
    3 tablespoons vegetable oil

    1 tablespoon grated Parmesan cheese
  1/2 teaspoon salt
  1/4 teaspoon garlic powder
  1/4 teaspoon paprika
  1/8 teaspoon pepper
    8 bacon strips, cooked and crumbled
1-1/2 cups (6 ounces) shredded cheddar cheese
  1/2 cup sour cream
    4 green onions, sliced

Cut potatoes in half lengthwise; scoop out pulp, leaving a 1/4-in. shell (save pulp for another use). Place potato skins on a greased baking sheet. Combine the oil, Parmesan cheese, salt, garlic powder, paprika and pepper; brush over both sides of skins.

Bake at 475° for 7 minutes; turn. Bake until crisp, about 7 minutes. Sprinkle the bacon and cheddar cheese inside skins. Bake 2 minutes longer or until cheese is melted. Top with sour cream and onions. Serve immediately. **Yield:** 8 servings.

— 🥄 🥄 🥄 —

Cheesy Olive Snacks

(Pictured below)

Olive lovers will snap up these easy appetizers. The topping can be made ahead and they bake for only 7 minutes.
—Dorothy Anderson, Ottawa, Kansas

    1 cup (4 ounces) shredded mozzarella
      cheese
    1 cup (4 ounces) shredded cheddar cheese
    1 can (4-1/4 ounces) chopped ripe olives,
      drained
  1/2 cup mayonnaise
  1/3 cup chopped green onions
Triscuit crackers

In a bowl, combine the first five ingredients. Spread on crackers. Place on an ungreased baking sheet. Bake at 375° for 7 minutes. Serve immediately. **Yield:** about 4 dozen.

pepper, salt and cayenne; pour over beef mixture. Sprinkle with cheese. Bake at 375° for 20 minutes or until a knife inserted near the center comes out clean. **Yield:** 1-1/2 dozen.

Pepper Poppers

(Pictured below)

These creamy and zippy stuffed jalapenos are the most popular appetizer I make. My husband and co-workers are always hinting that I should prepare a batch.
—*Lisa Byington, Port Crane, New York*

> 1 package (8 ounces) cream cheese, softened
> 1 cup (4 ounces) shredded sharp cheddar cheese
> 1 cup (4 ounces) shredded Monterey Jack cheese
> 6 bacon strips, cooked and crumbled
> 1/4 teaspoon salt
> 1/4 teaspoon chili powder
> 1/4 teaspoon garlic powder
> 1 pound fresh jalapenos, halved lengthwise and seeded*
> 1/2 cup dry bread crumbs
> Sour cream, onion dip *or* ranch salad dressing

In a mixing bowl, combine cheeses, bacon and seasonings; mix well. Spoon about 2 tablespoonfuls into each pepper half. Roll in bread crumbs. Place in a greased 15-in. x 10-in. x 1-in. baking pan. Bake, uncovered, at 300° for 20 minutes for spicy flavor, 30 minutes for medium and 40 minutes for mild. Serve with sour cream, dip or dressing. **Yield:** about 2 dozen.

*Editor's Note:** When cutting or seeding hot peppers, use rubber or plastic gloves to protect your hands. Avoid touching your face.

Ground Beef Snack Quiches

(Pictured above)

My husband, Cory, farms, so supper can sometimes be quite late. A hearty appetizer like these meaty mini quiches is a perfect way to start the meal. They taste super made with ground beef, but I sometimes substitute bacon, ham, ground pork or sausage.
—*Stacey Atkinson, Rugby, North Dakota*

> 1/4 pound ground beef
> 1/8 to 1/4 teaspoon garlic powder
> 1/8 teaspoon pepper
> 1 cup biscuit/baking mix
> 1/4 cup cornmeal
> 1/4 cup cold butter *or* margarine
> 2 to 3 tablespoons boiling water
> 1 egg
> 1/2 cup half-and-half cream
> 1 tablespoon chopped green onion
> 1 tablespoon chopped sweet red pepper
> 1/8 to 1/4 teaspoon salt
> 1/8 to 1/4 teaspoon cayenne pepper
> 1/2 cup finely shredded cheddar cheese

In a saucepan over medium heat, cook beef, garlic powder and pepper until meat is no longer pink; drain and set aside. In a bowl, combine the biscuit mix and cornmeal; cut in butter. Add enough water to form a soft dough. Press onto the bottom and up the sides of greased miniature muffin cups. Place teaspoonfuls of beef mixture into each shell.

In a bowl, combine the egg, cream, onion, red

Remove to wire racks. Immediately cut a slit in each puff to allow steam to escape; cool. In a mixing bowl, combine the first eight filling ingredients; mix well. Stir in olives. Split puffs; add filling. Refrigerate until serving. **Yield:** 4-1/2 dozen.

— 🍴 🍴 🍴 —

Sesame Chicken Strips

(Pictured below and on page 6)

These tasty chicken strips dipped in the lightly sweet sauce are a wonderful finger food. They go over really well at outdoor summer gatherings. —Teri Rasey
Cadillac, Michigan

    1 cup mayonnaise
    2 teaspoons dried minced onion
    2 teaspoons ground mustard
    1 cup crushed butter-flavored crackers
      (about 25 crackers)
1/2 cup sesame seeds
    8 boneless skinless chicken breast halves
      (2 pounds)
SAUCE:
    1 cup mayonnaise
    2 tablespoons honey

In a bowl, combine mayonnaise, onion and mustard. In another bowl, combine the cracker crumbs and sesame seeds. Cut chicken lengthwise into 1/4-in. strips. Dip strips into mayonnaise mixture, then into the sesame seed mixture. Place in a single layer on a large greased baking sheet. Bake at 425° for 15-18 minutes or until juices run clear. Combine sauce ingredients and serve with chicken strips. **Yield:** 10-12 servings.

Rye Party Puffs

(Pictured above)

These puffs are pretty enough for a wedding reception yet hearty enough to snack on while watching a football game on television. —Kelly Thornberry
LaPorte, Indiana

    1 cup water
1/2 cup butter *or* margarine
1/2 cup all-purpose flour
1/2 cup rye flour
    2 teaspoons dried parsley flakes
1/2 teaspoon garlic powder
1/4 teaspoon salt
    4 eggs
Caraway seeds
CORNED BEEF FILLING:
    2 packages (8 ounces *each*) cream cheese,
      softened
    2 packages (2-1/2 ounces *each*) cooked
      corned beef, finely chopped
1/2 cup mayonnaise
1/4 cup sour cream
    2 tablespoons minced chives
    2 tablespoons finely chopped onion
    1 teaspoon spicy brown *or* horseradish
      mustard
1/8 teaspoon garlic powder
    10 small stuffed olives, chopped

In a saucepan over medium heat, bring water and butter to a boil. Add flours, parsley, garlic powder and salt all at once; stir until a smooth ball forms. Remove from the heat; let stand for 5 minutes. Beat in eggs, one at time. Beat until smooth. Drop the batter by rounded teaspoonfuls 2 in. apart onto greased baking sheets. Sprinkle with caraway seeds. Bake at 400° for 18-20 minutes or until golden.

Asparagus Ham Swirls

(Pictured below)

I came across the recipe for this hot appetizer years ago and have made it many times to share with friends and co-workers. Asparagus, ham and cheese combine into a fun finger food.
—*Nancy Ingersol*
Midlothian, Illinois

    16 fresh asparagus spears, trimmed
     3 tablespoons Dijon mustard
    16 thin slices fully cooked ham
    16 slices process Swiss cheese
     2 eggs, beaten
     1 cup dry bread crumbs
Vegetable oil for frying

In a skillet, cook asparagus in a small amount of water until crisp-tender, about 6-8 minutes; drain well. Spread about 1 teaspoon of mustard on each ham slice. Top with one slice of cheese. Place an asparagus spear at one end (trim to fit if needed). Roll up each ham slice tightly; secure with three toothpicks.

Dip ham rolls in egg, then roll in bread crumbs. In an electric skillet, heat 1 in. of oil to 350°. Fry rolls, a few at a time, until golden, about 3-4 minutes. Drain on paper towels; keep warm. Cut each roll between the toothpicks into three pieces. **Yield:** 4 dozen.

Toasted Zucchini Snacks

(Pictured above)

I added green pepper to this recipe I got years ago from a friend. I prepare this rich snack for company when zucchini is plentiful. Everyone seems to enjoy it.
—*Jane Bone, Cape Coral, Florida*

     2 cups shredded zucchini
     1 teaspoon salt
    1/2 cup mayonnaise *or* salad dressing
    1/2 cup plain yogurt
    1/4 cup grated Parmesan cheese
    1/4 cup finely chopped green pepper
     4 green onions, thinly sliced
     1 garlic clove, minced
     1 teaspoon Worcestershire sauce
    1/4 teaspoon hot pepper sauce
    36 slices snack rye bread

In a bowl, toss the zucchini and salt; let stand for 1 hour. Rinse and drain, pressing out excess liquid. Add the next eight ingredients; stir until combined. Spread a rounded teaspoonful on each slice of bread; place on a baking sheet. Bake at 375° for 10-12 minutes or until bubbly. Serve hot. **Yield:** 3 dozen.

blespoon Parmesan cheese. Repeat layers five times, folding edges for each layer. Top with remaining dough, folding edges to fit pan; brush with remaining butter.

Sprinkle with mozzarella cheese; arrange onion and tomatoes over the cheese. Sprinkle with the oregano, thyme, salt, pepper and remaining Parmesan. Bake at 375° for 20-25 minutes or until edges are golden brown. **Yield:** 28 slices.

—— ☕ ☕ ☕ ——

Reuben Roll-Ups

(Pictured below)

This recipe turns the popular Reuben sandwich into an interesting and hearty snack. We love these roll-ups at our house. —Patty Kile, Greentown, Pennsylvania

   1 tube (10 ounces) refrigerated pizza dough
   1 cup sauerkraut, well drained
   1 tablespoon Thousand Island salad dressing
   4 slices corned beef, halved
   4 slices Swiss cheese, halved

Roll dough into a 12-in. x 9-in. rectangle. Cut into eight 3-in. x 4-1/2-in. rectangles. Combine sauerkraut and salad dressing. Place a slice of beef on each rectangle. Top with about 2 tablespoons of the sauerkraut mixture and a slice of cheese. Roll up. Place with seam side down on a greased baking sheet. Bake at 425° for 12-14 minutes or until golden brown. **Yield:** 8 roll-ups.

Tomato-Onion Phyllo Pizza

(Pictured above)

With a delicate crust and lots of lovely tomatoes on top, this dish is a special one to serve to guests. I make it often when fresh garden tomatoes are in season. It freezes well unbaked, so I can keep one on hand to pop in the oven for a quick dinner. —Neta Cohen
Bedford, Virginia

   5 tablespoons butter *or* margarine, melted
   7 sheets phyllo dough (18 inches x 14 inches)
   7 tablespoons grated Parmesan cheese, *divided*
   1 cup (4 ounces) shredded mozzarella cheese
   1 cup thinly sliced onion
   7 to 9 plum tomatoes (about 1-1/4 pounds), sliced
1-1/2 teaspoons minced fresh oregano *or* 1/2 teaspoon dried oregano
   1 teaspoon minced fresh thyme *or* 1/4 teaspoon dried thyme
Salt and pepper to taste

Brush a 15-in. x 10-in. x 1-in. baking pan with some of the melted butter. Lay a sheet of phyllo in pan, folding edges in to fit (keep remaining dough covered with waxed paper to avoid drying out). Brush dough with butter and sprinkle with 1 ta-

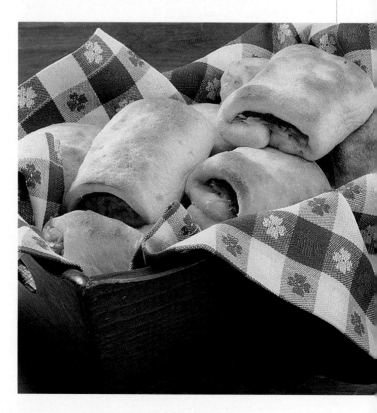

Cheddar Pepper Crisps

(Pictured below and on page 6)

I got the idea for these cheesy, peppery, crispy snacks at my bridal shower. They're popular for munching by themselves or with a dip. —Wendy Prevost
Cody, Wyoming

1-3/4 cups all-purpose flour
1/2 cup cornmeal
1/2 teaspoon baking soda
1/2 teaspoon sugar
1/2 teaspoon salt
1/2 cup cold butter *or* margarine
1-1/2 cups (6 ounces) shredded sharp cheddar cheese
1/2 cup cold water
2 tablespoons vinegar
Coarsely ground pepper

In a large bowl, combine the first five ingredients. Cut in butter until crumbly. Stir in cheese. Sprinkle with water and vinegar. Toss with a fork until a ball forms. Wrap tightly in plastic wrap; refrigerate for 1 hour or until dough is firm.

Divide dough into six portions. On a lightly floured surface, roll each portion into an 8-in. circle. Cut into eight wedges and place on greased baking sheets. Sprinkle with pepper; lightly press into dough. Bake at 375° for 10-14 minutes or until golden brown and crisp. Cool on wire racks. Store in an airtight container. **Yield:** 4 dozen.

Cajun Party Mix

(Pictured above)

This savory snack mix packs a little punch, thanks to the cayenne pepper and hot pepper sauce.
—Miriam Hershberger, Holmesville, Ohio

2-1/2 cups Corn Chex
2 cups Rice Chex
2 cups Crispix
1 cup mini pretzels
1 cup mixed nuts
1/2 cup butter *or* margarine, melted
1 tablespoon dried parsley flakes
1 teaspoon celery salt
1 teaspoon garlic powder
1/4 to 1/2 teaspoon cayenne pepper
1/4 teaspoon hot pepper sauce

Combine the cereals, pretzels and nuts. Pour into an ungreased 15-in. x 10-in. x 1-in. baking pan. Mix remaining ingredients; pour over the cereal mixture and stir to coat. Bake at 250° for 40-60 minutes, stirring every 15 minutes. Store in airtight containers. **Yield:** 8 cups.

Lemon Cloud Popcorn

(Pictured at right)

I love the unexpected lemony flavor of this light snack. I'm sure your family will, too! —Trudie Hagen
Roggen, Colorado

4-1/2 quarts popped popcorn
2 cups sugar
1/2 cup light corn syrup
1/2 cup water
1 tablespoon lemon extract

1/2 teaspoon baking soda
1-1/2 teaspoons grated lemon peel

Place popcorn in two greased 15-in. x 10-in. x 1-in. baking pans. Keep warm in a 225° oven. Meanwhile, in a heavy saucepan, combine sugar, corn syrup and water; bring to a boil over medium heat. Stir occasionally until mixture reaches 290° on a candy thermometer (soft-crack stage).

Remove from the heat; quickly stir in extract and baking soda. Pour over warm popcorn. Sprinkle with lemon peel; stir until well coated. Store in an airtight container. **Yield:** 5 quarts.

— 🥤 🥤 🥤 —

Ribbon-o-Fudge Popcorn Bars

(Pictured below)

Two sweet layers of butterscotch- and marshmallow-coated popcorn are held together with chocolate in these yummy bars. —Flo Burtnett, Gage, Oklahoma

2 cups (12 ounces) semisweet chocolate chips
2 tablespoons shortening
3 tablespoons butter *or* margarine
4 cups miniature marshmallows
1 cup butterscotch chips
3 quarts popped popcorn

In a microwave or heavy saucepan, melt chocolate chips and shortening. Chill for 15-20 minutes or until thickened. Meanwhile, line a 9-in. square baking pan with foil; grease the foil and set pan aside. In a heavy saucepan over low heat, melt butter. Stir in marshmallows and butterscotch chips until melted and smooth.

Place the popcorn in a large bowl; add marshmallow mixture and toss until coated. Firmly press half of the mixture into prepared pan. Spread chocolate mixture evenly over popcorn. Firmly press remaining popcorn mixture over chocolate. Chill for 30 minutes. Lift out of pan, using foil edges. Remove foil; cut into bars. **Yield:** 2 dozen.

KERNEL OF TRUTH. Snacks like Lemon Cloud Popcorn and Ribbon-o-Fudge Popcorn Bars (shown above, top to bottom) are made for munching.

In a large resealable plastic bag, combine sugar, cinnamon and nutmeg; set aside. Cut tortillas into 3-in. x 2-in. strips. Heat 1 in. of oil in a skillet or electric fry pan to 375°; fry 4-5 strips at a time for 30 seconds on each side or until golden brown. Drain on paper towels. While still warm, place strips in bag with sugar mixture; shake gently to coat. Serve immediately or store in an airtight container. **Yield:** 5 dozen.

— 🝳 🝳 🝳 —

Savory Party Bread

(Pictured below)

It's impossible to stop nibbling on warm pieces of this cheesy, oniony bread. The sliced loaf fans out for a fun presentation. —Kay Daly
Raleigh, North Carolina

> 1 unsliced round loaf (1 pound) sourdough bread
> 1 pound Monterey Jack cheese, sliced
> 1/2 cup butter *or* margarine, melted
> 1/2 cup chopped green onions
> 2 to 3 teaspoons poppy seeds

Cut the bread lengthwise and crosswise without cutting through the bottom crust. Insert cheese between cuts. Combine butter, onions and poppy seeds; drizzle over the bread. Wrap in foil; place on a baking sheet. Bake at 350° for 15 minutes. Unwrap; bake 10 minutes longer or until the cheese is melted. **Yield:** 6-8 servings.

Fruit on a Stick

(Pictured above and on page 6)

In the summer, my family likes to snack on an assortment of the season's freshest fruits. To make this nutritious snack a little more fun, I serve fruit "kabobs" with a sweet and creamy dip. —Faye Hintz
Springfield, Missouri

> 1 package (8 ounces) cream cheese, softened
> 1 jar (7 ounces) marshmallow creme
> 3 to 4 tablespoons milk
> Halved strawberries
> Melon and kiwifruit, cut into bite-size pieces

Mix cream cheese, marshmallow creme and milk until smooth. Thread fruit on wooden skewers. Serve with dip. **Yield:** 1-1/2 cups dip.

— 🝳 🝳 🝳 —

Fried Cinnamon Strips

I first made these crispy Mexican-style strips for a special family night at our church. Most of them were snapped up before dinner! —Nancy Johnson
Laverne, Oklahoma

> 1 cup sugar
> 1 teaspoon ground cinnamon
> 1/4 teaspoon ground nutmeg
> 10 flour tortillas (8 inches)
> Vegetable oil

Zesty Chicken Wings

(Pictured below)

These spicy barbecue wings are so easy to make. I fix a double batch since my family thinks they're great. You should see them disappear! —Joan Rose
Langley, British Columbia

1/2 cup corn syrup
1/2 cup ketchup
1/4 cup cider vinegar
1/4 cup Worcestershire sauce
1/4 cup Dijon mustard
1 small onion, chopped
3 garlic cloves, minced
1 tablespoon chili powder
16 whole chicken wings (about 3 pounds)

In a saucepan, combine the first eight ingredients. Bring to a boil. Reduce heat; simmer, uncovered, for 15-20 minutes or until thickened. Meanwhile, cut chicken wings into three sections; discard wing tips. Place wings in a well-greased 15-in. x 10-in. x 1-in. baking pan. Bake at 375° for 30 minutes, turning once.

   Brush wings with sauce. Bake 20-25 minutes longer, turning and basting once, or until chicken juices run clear. Serve with additional sauce if desired. **Yield:** 10-12 servings.

BLT Bites

(Pictured above)

These quick hors d'oeuvres may be mini, but their bacon and tomato flavor is full-size. I serve them at parties, brunches and picnics, and they're always a hit ...even my kids love them. —Kellie Remmen
Detroit Lakes, Minnesota

16 to 20 cherry tomatoes
1 pound bacon, cooked and crumbled
1/2 cup mayonnaise *or* salad dressing
1/3 cup chopped green onions
3 tablespoons grated Parmesan cheese
2 tablespoons snipped fresh parsley

Cut a thin slice off each tomato top. Scoop out and discard pulp. Invert the tomatoes on a paper towel to drain. In a small bowl, combine all remaining ingredients; mix well. Spoon into tomatoes. Refrigerate for several hours. **Yield:** 16-20 servings.

Cool the Heat

Blue cheese salad dressing and celery sticks pair well with spicy hot chicken wings. But experiment with other dressings (like ranch) and vegetables (like cucumber slices).

Southwestern Star Dip

(Pictured below)

I enjoyed this sensational dip at a holiday party and begged for the recipe. —Joan Hallford
North Richland Hills, Texas

    2 cups (8 ounces) shredded sharp cheddar
      cheese
    1 cup mayonnaise*
    1 can (4-1/4 ounces) chopped ripe olives,
      drained, *divided*
    1 can (4 ounces) chopped green chilies,
      undrained
  1/4 teaspoon garlic powder
  1/8 teaspoon hot pepper sauce
    1 medium tomato, chopped
  1/4 cup chopped green onions
Tortilla chips

In a bowl, combine cheese, mayonnaise, 1/3 cup olives, chilies, garlic powder and hot pepper sauce. Transfer to an ungreased 9-in. pie plate. Bake, uncovered, at 350° for 20 minutes or until hot and bubbly. Sprinkle tomato on top in the shape of a star; outline with remaining olives. Sprinkle onions around the star. **Yield:** 2-2/3 cups.

*Editor's Note: Light or fat-free mayonnaise may not be substituted for regular mayonnaise in this recipe.

Ruby-Red Pretzel Dip

(Pictured below left)

Plain pretzels get a pretty coating and tangy taste from this thick, festive blend. —Grace Yaskovic
Branchville, New Jersey

    1 can (16 ounces) jellied cranberry sauce
  3/4 cup sugar
  1/4 cup vinegar
    1 teaspoon ground ginger
    1 teaspoon ground mustard
  1/4 teaspoon ground cinnamon
  1/8 teaspoon pepper
    1 tablespoon all-purpose flour
    1 tablespoon cold water
Red food coloring, optional
Pretzels

In a saucepan, combine the first seven ingredients; whisk over medium heat until smooth. Combine flour and cold water until smooth; add to cranberry mixture. Bring to a boil; cook and stir for 2 minutes. Transfer to a bowl; stir in food coloring if desired. Cover and chill overnight. Serve with pretzels. **Yield:** 2 cups.

— 🏺 🏺 🏺 —

Christmas Cheese Ball

(Pictured at left)

This rich cheese spread is delicious and wonderfully attractive. —Esther Shank, Harrisonville, Virginia

    2 packages (8 ounces *each*) cream cheese,
      softened
    2 cups (8 ounces) shredded sharp cheddar
      cheese
    1 tablespoon finely chopped onion
    1 tablespoon diced pimientos
    1 tablespoon diced green pepper
    2 teaspoons Worcestershire sauce
    1 teaspoon lemon juice
Chopped pecans, toasted
Assorted crackers

In a mixing bowl, combine the first seven ingredients; mix well. Shape into two balls; roll in pecans. Cover and chill. Remove from the refrigerator 15 minutes before serving. Serve with crackers. **Yield:** 2 cheese balls (1-1/2 cups each).

— 🏺 🏺 🏺 —

Corn and Bacon Dip

(Pictured above right)

The recipe for this creamy appetizer or snack dip was given to me about 20 years ago by a friend. It becomes

FESTIVE finger foods really perk up a party. Try Ruby-Red Pretzel Dip, Southwestern Star Dip and Christmas Cheese Ball (shown above, clockwise from top right).

a favorite wherever I share it. People are constantly asking me for the recipe. Sometimes I simply serve it with corn chips. —*Carolyn Zaschak, Corning, New York*

> 1 package (8 ounces) cream cheese, softened
> 1 cup (8 ounces) sour cream
> 1/4 cup mayonnaise
> 2 garlic cloves, minced
> 1/4 teaspoon hot pepper sauce
> 1 can (15-1/4 ounces) whole kernel corn, drained
> 8 bacon strips, cooked and crumbled
> Assorted raw vegetables *and/or* crackers

In a mixing bowl, combine the first five ingredients. Stir in corn and bacon. Cover and refrigerate for several hours. Serve with vegetables and/or crackers. **Yield:** 3 cups.

Layered Vegetable Cheesecake

(Pictured at right)

A cake that's savory instead of sweet? Absolutely! Everyone who tastes this cheesy concoction, topped with a dilly of a cucumber sauce, will relish its richness and come back for more. It's a family favorite.
—*Donna Cline, Pensacola, Florida*

> 1-1/3 cups dry bread crumbs
> 1/3 cup butter *or* margarine, melted
> 2 packages (8 ounces *each*) cream cheese, softened
> 2 eggs
> 1 cup (8 ounces) sour cream
> 1/3 cup all-purpose flour
> 1/4 cup finely chopped onion

> 1/4 teaspoon salt
> 1/4 teaspoon white pepper
> 3/4 cup shredded carrots
> 3/4 cup diced green pepper
> 3/4 cup diced sweet red pepper
> Optional garnishes: carrots and sweet red pepper cut into flowers, green pepper cut into leaves, green onions, fresh savory and bay leaves
> CUCUMBER DILL SAUCE:
> 1 cup (8 ounces) plain yogurt
> 1/3 cup mayonnaise *or* salad dressing
> 1/2 cup finely chopped unpeeled cucumber
> 1/4 teaspoon salt
> 1/4 teaspoon dill weed

Combine bread crumbs and butter; press onto the bottom and 1 in. up the sides of an ungreased 9-in. springform pan. In a mixing bowl, beat cream cheese until fluffy. Add eggs, one at a time, beating well after each addition. Add sour cream, flour, onion, salt and pepper; mix well. Pour 1 cup into the crust; sprinkle with carrots. Continue layering with 1 cup cream cheese mixture, green pepper, another cup of cream cheese mixture, red pepper, then remaining cream cheese mixture.

Bake at 300° for 1 hour or until set. Turn oven off; cool cheesecake in oven for 1 hour with the door propped open. Carefully run a knife between crust and sides of pan. Cool completely at room temperature. Chill at least 8 hours. Just before serving, remove sides of pan. Garnish as desired with vegetables and herbs. Serve cool or warm.

To serve warm, remove from the refrigerator 1 hour before serving. Let cheesecake come to room temperature for 30 minutes, then reheat at 300° for 20-25 minutes or until warm. Combine sauce ingredients in a small bowl; chill. Serve with the cheesecake. **Yield:** 12-14 appetizer servings; 10-12 main-dish servings.

Editor's Note: Cheesecake may be baked a day ahead and refrigerated.

In a large bowl, combine the first five ingredients; set aside. In a microwave-safe bowl, heat chips and oil on medium-high for 2 minutes, stirring once. Microwave on high for 10 seconds; stir until smooth. Pour over cereal mixture and mix well. Spread onto three waxed paper-lined baking sheets. Cool; break apart. Store in an airtight container. **Yield:** 5 quarts.

Editor's Note: This recipe was tested using a 700-watt microwave.

— 🍷 🍷 🍷 —

Tangy Texas Salsa

(Pictured below)

I'm a "transplant" from Wisconsin. Even after some 20 years, I still can't get enough of our wonderful local citrus. The mix of tangy fruit, spicy jalapeno and distinctive cilantro is perfect with chips. We also serve it over meat, poultry or fish. —Lois Kildahl, McAllen, Texas

```
   1  medium grapefruit
   1  large navel orange
   1  each medium green, sweet red and yellow
      pepper, chopped
   1  medium tomato, seeded and chopped
   1  jalapeno pepper, seeded and chopped*
   3  tablespoons chopped red onion
   1  tablespoon minced fresh cilantro or
      parsley
1-1/2 teaspoons sugar
 1/2  teaspoon salt
```

Peel, section and dice the grapefruit and orange, removing all membrane. Place in a bowl; add remaining ingredients and mix well. Cover and refrigerate for at least 2 hours. **Yield:** about 5 cups.

*Editor's Note: When cutting or seeding hot peppers, use rubber or plastic gloves to protect your hands. Avoid touching your face.

Fudgy Fruit Dip

(Pictured above)

This rich chocolaty dip is especially nice at holiday gatherings or served with fresh strawberries.
—Wilma Knobloch, Steen, Minnesota

☑ Uses less fat, sugar or salt. Includes Nutritional Analysis and Diabetic Exchanges

```
 1/3  cup fat-free sugar-free hot fudge topping
 1/3  cup fat-free vanilla yogurt
1-1/2 teaspoons orange juice concentrate
Fresh strawberries
```

In a bowl, combine fudge topping, yogurt and orange juice concentrate. Cover and refrigerate for at least 30 minutes. Serve with strawberries. **Yield:** about 1/2 cup.

Nutritional Analysis: One serving (2 tablespoons of dip) equals 67 calories, trace fat (trace saturated fat), trace cholesterol, 32 mg sodium, 15 g carbohydrate, trace fiber, 1 g protein. **Diabetic Exchanges:** 1/2 starch, 1/2 fruit.

— 🍷 🍷 🍷 —

White Chocolate Party Mix

My family has stated that the holidays wouldn't be complete without bowls brimming with this satisfying snack. —Norene Wright, Manilla, Indiana

```
   1  package (10 ounces) mini pretzels
   5  cups Cheerios
   5  cups Corn Chex
   2  cups salted peanuts
   1  pound M&M's
   2  packages (12 ounces each) vanilla chips
   3  tablespoons vegetable oil
```

Dutch Hot Chocolate

When my grandchildren come over, they like to snack on cookies and mugs of this hot chocolate. It has a sweet chocolate flavor with a hint of cinnamon. The flavor of store-bought mixes just can't compare.
—Edna Hoffman, Hebron, Indiana

        3 quarts milk
        6 cups water
    1-1/2 cups sugar, *divided*
        3 squares (1 ounce *each*) semisweet
          chocolate
        1 cinnamon stick, broken
      1/2 cup packed brown sugar

In a saucepan, combine the milk, water, 1 cup sugar, chocolate and cinnamon stick. Bring to a boil. Reduce heat to low; cook and stir until chocolate is melted. Add brown sugar and remaining sugar; cook and stir until heated through. Discard cinnamon stick. **Yield:** 18 servings.

Holiday Wassail

Warm and fruity, this richly colored beverage is perfect for Christmas and very easy to prepare.
—Lucy Meyring, Walden, Colorado

      1 quart hot tea
      1 cup sugar
      1 bottle (32 ounces) cranberry juice
      1 bottle (32 ounces) apple juice
      2 cups orange juice
    3/4 cup lemon juice
      2 cinnamon sticks (3 inches *each*)
     24 whole cloves, *divided*
      1 orange, sliced

In a large kettle, combine tea and sugar. Add juices, cinnamon sticks and 12 of the cloves. Bring to a boil and boil for 2 minutes. Remove from the heat. Serve warm or cool. Garnish punch bowl with orange slices studded with remaining cloves. **Yield:** 12-16 servings (1 gallon).

Hot Apple Cider

Friends and I threw a bridal shower with a "You're the Apple of Our Eye" theme. This cider was one of the recipes. —Marlys Benning, Wellsburg, Iowa

    2/3 cup packed brown sugar
      1 teaspoon whole cloves
      1 teaspoon ground allspice
      3 cinnamon sticks (3 inches), broken
      1 gallon apple cider

Fill the filter-lined basket of a large automatic percolator with the brown sugar, cloves, allspice and cinnamon sticks. Prepare as you would coffee according to manufacturer's directions, but substitute cider for water. **Yield:** 16-20 servings.
    Editor's Note: Do not use a drip-style coffeemaker for this recipe.

Mocha Punch
(Pictured below)

I first tried this smooth, creamy punch at a friend's Christmas open house. It was so special and distinctive that I didn't leave until I had the recipe.
—Yvonne Hatfield, Norman, Oklahoma

    1-1/2 quarts water
      1/2 cup instant chocolate drink mix
      1/2 cup sugar
      1/4 cup instant coffee granules
      1/2 gallon vanilla ice cream
      1/2 gallon chocolate ice cream
        1 cup whipping cream, whipped
    Chocolate curls, optional

In a large saucepan, bring the water to a boil. Remove from the heat. Add drink mix, sugar and coffee; stir until dissolved. Cover and refrigerate for 4 hours or overnight. About 30 minutes before serving, pour into a punch bowl. Add ice cream by scoopfuls; stir until partially melted. Garnish with dollops of whipped cream and chocolate curls if desired. **Yield:** 20-25 servings (about 5 quarts).

Aunt Frances' Lemonade

(Pictured above)

My sister and I spent a week each summer with Aunt Frances, who always had this thirst-quenching lemonade in a stoneware crock in the refrigerator. It tastes so much like fresh citrus. —Debbie Blackburn
Camp Hill, Pennsylvania

    5 lemons
    5 limes
    5 oranges
    3 quarts water
1-1/2 to 2 cups sugar

Squeeze the juice from four of the lemons, limes and oranges; pour into a gallon container. Thinly slice the remaining fruit and set aside for garnish. Add water and sugar to juices; mix well. Store in the refrigerator. Serve on ice with fruit slices. **Yield:** 12-16 servings (about 1 gallon).

— 🥤 🥤 🥤 —

Chocolate Malts

I can whip up this decadent ice cream drink in just minutes. It's a favorite with kids after a day in the pool or for dessert after a barbecue. —Marion Lowery
Medford, Oregon

3/4 cup milk
1/2 cup caramel ice cream topping
    2 cups chocolate ice cream, softened
    3 tablespoons malted milk powder

2 tablespoons chopped pecans, optional
Grated chocolate, optional

In a blender, combine the first five ingredients; cover and process until blended. Pour into chilled glasses. Sprinkle with grated chocolate if desired. **Yield:** 2-1/2 cups.

— 🥤 🥤 🥤 —

Six-Vegetable Juice

(Pictured below)

Our family and friends enjoy my vegetable garden by the glassful. My husband likes spicy foods, and after one sip, he proclaimed this juice perfect. For more delicate palates, you can leave out the hot peppers.
—Deborah Moyer, Liberty, Pennsylvania

    5 pounds ripe tomatoes, peeled and
        chopped
1/2 cup water
1/4 cup chopped green pepper
1/4 cup chopped carrot
1/4 cup chopped celery
1/4 cup lemon juice
    2 tablespoons chopped onion
    1 tablespoon salt
    1 to 1-1/2 small serrano peppers*

In a large Dutch oven or soup kettle, combine the first eight ingredients. Remove stems and seeds if desired from peppers; add to tomato mixture. Bring to a boil; reduce heat. Cover and simmer for 30 minutes or until vegetables are tender. Cool. Press mixture through a food mill or fine sieve. Refrigerate or freeze. Shake or stir juice well before serving. **Yield:** 2 quarts.

  *Editor's Note: When cutting or seeding hot peppers, use rubber or plastic gloves to protect your hands. Avoid touching your face.

Banana Pineapple Slush

(Pictured below right and on page 6)

This sunny, tropical slush refreshes on summer days and is perfect for brunches and showers.
—*Beth Myers, Lewisburg, West Virginia*

☑ Uses less fat, sugar or salt. Includes Nutritional Analysis and Diabetic Exchanges.

  4 cups sugar
  2 cups water
  1 can (46 ounces) pineapple juice
  3 cups orange juice
  3/4 cup lemon juice
  1/2 cup orange juice concentrate
  8 medium ripe bananas, mashed
  2 bottles (2 liters *each*) cream soda
  3 cans (12 ounces *each*) lemon-lime soda

In a saucepan, bring sugar and water to a boil over medium heat; cool. Pour into a freezer container; add juices, orange juice concentrate and bananas. Cover and freeze. To serve, thaw mixture until slushy; stir in cream soda and lemon-lime soda. **Yield:** about 9-1/2 quarts.
  Nutritional Analysis: One 3/4-cup serving (prepared with sugar-free soda) equals 119 calories, 0 fat (0 saturated fat), 0 cholesterol, 23 mg sodium, 30 g carbohydrate, 1 g fiber, 0 protein. **Diabetic Exchange:** 2 fruit.

— 🍷 🍷 🍷 —

Grape Punch

(Pictured at right and on page 6)

With its beautiful purple color, fruity flavor and fun fizz, this punch always prompts requests for refills. It goes together in a snap with only three ingredients. I like to serve it with Mexican and Italian foods.
—*Gayle Lewis, Yucaipa, California*

  2 cups red grape juice, chilled
  2 cups white grape juice, chilled
  5 cups lemon-lime soda, chilled

In a large bowl or pitcher, combine both juices; mix well. Stir in the lemon-lime soda just before serving. **Yield:** 18 (1/2-cup) servings.

— 🍷 🍷 🍷 —

Fruity Red Smoothies

(Pictured at right and on page 6)

This thick, tangy drink combines the refreshing flavors of cranberries, raspberries and strawberries. Once you start sipping it, you can't stop!
—*Beverly Coyde, Gasport, New York*

  1 carton (8 ounces) strawberry yogurt
  1/2 to 3/4 cup cranberry juice
  1-1/2 cups frozen unsweetened strawberries, quartered
  1 cup frozen unsweetened raspberries
  1 to 1-1/2 teaspoons sugar

In a blender or food processor, combine yogurt and cranberry juice. Add strawberries, raspberries and sugar; cover and process until blended. Pour into glasses; serve immediately. **Yield:** 2 servings.

DAZZLING DRINKS. Add color and flavor to snacktime with Fruity Red Smoothies, Banana Pineapple Slush and Grape Punch (shown above, clockwise from top).

Salads & Dressings

*The first decade of Taste of Home has featured
many delicious salads for the first, second or main course.
Along with homemade dressings, these cool and crisp or
warm and wonderful salads make a memorable meal.*

——— 🍶 🍶 🍶 ———

SUPER SELECTIONS. Clockwise from upper left:
Grilled Chicken Salad (p. 34), Deluxe German
Potato Salad (p. 31), Honey Fruit Dressing (p. 39)
and Pineapple Gelatin Salad (p. 37).

Rosy Rhubarb Mold
(Pictured below)

Any meal benefits from this ruby-red salad. The combination of sweet, tangy and crunchy ingredients is irresistible. —Regina Albright
Southhaven, Mississippi

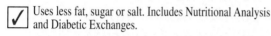
✓ Uses less fat, sugar or salt. Includes Nutritional Analysis and Diabetic Exchanges.

    4 cups chopped fresh *or* frozen rhubarb
    1 cup water
    2/3 cup sugar
    1/4 teaspoon salt
    1 package (6 ounces) strawberry gelatin
1-1/2 cups cold water
    1/4 cup lemon juice
    2 cans (11 ounces *each*) mandarin oranges, drained
    1 cup chopped celery
Optional garnishes: lettuce leaves, sliced strawberries, green grapes, sour cream and ground nutmeg

In a saucepan, combine rhubarb, water, sugar and salt; bring to a boil over medium heat. Boil for 1-2 minutes or until the rhubarb is tender; remove from the heat. Stir in gelatin until dissolved. Stir in cold water and lemon juice. Chill until partially set. Fold in oranges and celery. Pour into a 6-cup mold or an 8-in. square dish coated with nonstick cooking spray. Chill until set.

Unmold onto lettuce leaves or cut into squares. If desired, garnish with fruit and serve with sour cream sprinkled with nutmeg. **Yield:** 12 servings.

Nutritional Analysis: One 1/2-cup serving (prepared with sugar-free gelatin; calculated without garnishes) equals 79 calories, 98 mg sodium, 0 cholesterol, 19 g carbohydrate, 2 g protein, trace fat. **Diabetic Exchange:** 1 fruit.

Fruit Salad with Apricot Dressing
(Pictured below right)

When I serve this lovely, refreshing salad for picnics and holidays, the bowl always empties fast. There's something about the bright colors that makes you want to dig right in. —Carol Lambert
El Dorado, Arkansas

    1 cup sugar
    1 tablespoon cornstarch
    2 cans (5-1/2 ounces *each*) apricot nectar
    1 teaspoon vanilla extract
    6 large red apples, coarsely chopped
    8 medium firm bananas, sliced
    1 medium fresh pineapple, peeled, cored and cut into chunks (about 5 cups)
    1 quart fresh strawberries, quartered
    2 cups green grapes

In a microwave-safe bowl, stir sugar, cornstarch and apricot nectar until smooth. Microwave, uncovered, on high for 6-8 minutes or until slightly thickened, stirring every 2 minutes. Stir in the vanilla. Refrigerate. In a large bowl, combine the fruit. Drizzle with dressing; gently toss to coat. Cover and chill until serving. **Yield:** 26 (1-cup) servings.

Editor's Note: This recipe was tested in an 850-watt microwave.

———— 🍵 🍵 🍵 ————

Avocado Citrus Toss
(Pictured at right)

The light poppy seed dressing doesn't mask the goodness of sweet citrus sections, crisp lettuce, crunchy almonds and mellow avocados. —Marie Hattrup
The Dalles, Oregon

    6 cups torn salad greens
    2 medium grapefruit, peeled and sectioned
    3 navel oranges, peeled and sectioned
    1 ripe avocado, peeled and sliced
    1/4 cup slivered almonds, toasted
DRESSING:
    1/2 cup vegetable oil
    1/3 cup sugar
    3 tablespoons vinegar
    2 teaspoons poppy seeds
    1 teaspoon finely chopped onion
    1/2 teaspoon ground mustard
    1/2 teaspoon salt

In a large salad bowl, toss the greens, grapefruit, oranges, avocado and almonds. In a jar with tight-fitting lid, combine the dressing ingredients; shake well. Drizzle over the salad and toss to coat. **Yield:** 6 servings.

Chilly Melon Cups

(Pictured below)

This cool treat is stored in the freezer so it's always handy. It's a great way to use what's left from a fruit platter or melon boat. —Katie Koziolek
Hartland, Minnesota

　1　cup water
　1　cup sugar
1/2　cup lemonade concentrate
1/2　cup orange juice concentrate

　4　cups watermelon balls *or* cubes
　2　cups cantaloupe balls *or* cubes
　2　cups honeydew balls *or* cubes
　2　cups pineapple chunks
　2　cups fresh raspberries

In a large bowl, combine the water, sugar and concentrates; stir until the sugar is dissolved. Add fruit and stir gently to coat. Spoon into foil-lined muffin cups or 3-oz. plastic cups. Freeze for up to 3 months. Before serving, thaw overnight in the refrigerator or at room temperature for 30-45 minutes until mixture is slushy. **Yield:** 12-14 servings.

COOL DOWN and tempt taste buds with Fruit Salad with Apricot Dressing, Avocado Citrus Toss and Chilly Melon Cups (shown above, clockwise from top), which feature refreshing fruit.

Superstar Spinach Salad

(Pictured below)

Cantaloupe really "stars" in this delicious salad—especially if you cut pieces into that shape. But no matter how you present this dish, it's always festive, filling and wonderful. —Kathy Crow, Payson, Arizona

    1 cantaloupe half, seeded and peeled
    7 cups torn fresh spinach
1-1/2 cups cubed fully cooked ham
    1 cup thinly sliced red onion
1/2 cup halved green grapes
DRESSING:
    3 tablespoons sugar
    2 tablespoons orange juice
    2 tablespoons cider vinegar
    1 tablespoon chopped onion
1-1/2 teaspoons grated orange peel
Dash pepper
1/3 cup vegetable oil

MARVELOUS MELON shines in dishes like Watermelon Boat, Superstar Spinach Salad and Chicken Salad on Cantaloupe Rings (shown above, clockwise from top). Family and friends will dig into these special salads.

1 teaspoon poppy seeds
1/3 cup chopped pecans, toasted

Cut melon half into 1/2-in. rings. Cut rings with a 1-1/2-in. star-shaped cookie cutter or into 1-in. pieces; place in a bowl. Add the spinach, ham, onion and grapes. Chill for at least 2 hours.

Place the sugar, orange juice, vinegar, onion, orange peel and pepper in a blender; cover and blend until smooth. With the blender running, gradually add oil until slightly thickened. Stir in poppy seeds. Cover and chill. Just before serving, pour dressing over salad and toss. Top with pecans. **Yield:** 6 servings.

— 🍳 🍳 🍳 —

Watermelon Boat

(Pictured at left)

"Wow!" is what folks will say when they first see this lovely fruit salad piled high in an eye-catching watermelon boat. The light dressing really lets the fresh flavor of fruit shine through. —Ruth Seitz Columbus Junction, Iowa

1 cup lemon juice
1 cup sugar
2 teaspoons all-purpose flour
2 eggs, beaten
1 cup whipping cream, whipped
1 large watermelon
1 large honeydew, cut into cubes *or* balls
1 large cantaloupe, cut into cubes *or* balls
2 pints fresh strawberries, sliced
1/2 pound green grapes

Combine the lemon juice, sugar and flour in a saucepan; bring to a boil. Reduce heat to low. Stir 1/4 cup into eggs; return all to pan. Cook and stir for 15 minutes or until the mixture coats a spoon (do not boil). Cool. Fold in whipped cream; cover and chill until serving.

For watermelon boat, cut a thin slice from bottom of melon with a sharp knife to allow it to sit flat (see diagram above right). Mark a horizontal cutting line 2 in. above center of melon. With a long sharp knife, cut into melon along cutting line, making sure to cut all the way through. Gently pull off top section of rind. Remove fruit from both sections and cut into cubes or balls; set aside.

To cut decorative edge, place melon on its side. Position a 2-1/2-in. 8-point star cookie cutter against inside edge of melon, allowing only half of star to cut through rind (see diagram at top right). Use a mallet if necessary to help push cookie cutter through melon. Insert a toothpick into flat edge of removed piece. Attach piece onto melon edge where last cut ends. Repeat cutting and at-

taching pieces until the entire melon edge is completed. Combine honeydew, cantaloupe, strawberries, grapes and watermelon; spoon into boat. Serve dressing on the side. **Yield:** 32-36 servings (about 2 cups dressing).

Editor's Note: Any star or petal cutter with an even number of points may be used to make a decorative "boat". Or serve this salad in an 8-qt. bowl.

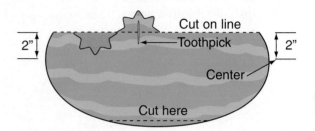

Chicken Salad on Cantaloupe Rings

(Pictured at far left)

A hearty chicken salad on a cantaloupe ring is a fun and flavorful way to perk up a summer luncheon. The creamy salad gets crunch from celery and almonds. —Sharon Bickett, Chester, South Carolina

2-1/2 cups cubed cooked chicken
1 cup thinly sliced celery
1 cup halved green grapes
2 tablespoons minced fresh parsley
1/2 cup mayonnaise
1 tablespoon lemon juice
1 tablespoon cider vinegar
1-1/2 teaspoons prepared mustard
1/2 teaspoon salt
1/2 teaspoon sugar
1/8 teaspoon pepper
4 cantaloupe rings
Toasted sliced almonds

In a large bowl, combine chicken, celery, grapes and parsley. Combine the next seven ingredients; mix well. Pour over chicken mixture and toss. Chill for at least 1 hour. To serve, place 1 cup of chicken salad on each cantaloupe ring; sprinkle with almonds. **Yield:** 4 servings.

Slick Gelatin Mold Tips

To get gelatin cleanly out of a mold, first run a thin, warm knife around the edge. Then wet a kitchen towel with warm water, squeeze almost dry and wrap around the mold for a few minutes. The gelatin will slide right out. Also, wet the serving dish before turning the gelatin out onto it. You'll be able to slide the gelatin to the center of the plate.

Cashew Pea Salad

(Pictured below)

My son-in-law frequently requests this crisp pea salad of mine. It has plenty of fresh ingredients and a tangy dressing. Peas are positively palate-pleasing paired with cashews in the cool side dish.
—Barbara Birk, American Fork, Utah

    3/4 cup vegetable oil
    1/4 cup cider vinegar *or* red wine vinegar
      1 garlic clove, minced
      2 to 3 teaspoons Dijon mustard
      1 teaspoon Worcestershire sauce
    1/2 to 3/4 teaspoon salt
    1/2 teaspoon lemon juice
    1/4 teaspoon pepper
    1/4 teaspoon sugar
      1 package (10 ounces) frozen peas, thawed
      2 celery ribs, thinly sliced
      2 green onions, thinly sliced
    1/2 cup sour cream
      4 bacon strips, cooked and crumbled
    3/4 cup chopped cashews
Lettuce leaves and tomato wedges, optional

For dressing, combine the first nine ingredients in a small bowl; mix well. Cover and refrigerate for 1 hour. In a large bowl, combine peas, celery and onions. Combine sour cream and 2 tablespoons of dressing (refrigerate remaining dressing); mix well. Fold into the pea mixture. Just before serving, stir in bacon and cashews. If desired, serve on lettuce with a tomato garnish. **Yield:** 6-8 servings.

    Editor's Note: Remaining dressing may be served on a tossed salad.

Colorful Corn Salad

(Pictured above)

This colorful, tasty corn salad is an excellent choice for a summer picnic. The seasonings add a bold, refreshing Southwestern flavor that brings people back for seconds. It's nice to have a different kind of salad to share. —*Helen Koedel, Hamilton, Ohio*

      2 packages (10 ounces *each*) frozen corn,
        thawed
      2 cups diced green pepper
      2 cups diced sweet red pepper
      2 cups diced celery
      1 cup minced fresh parsley
      1 cup chopped green onions
    1/2 cup shredded Parmesan cheese
      2 teaspoons ground cumin
  1-1/2 teaspoons salt
    3/4 teaspoon pepper
    1/2 teaspoon hot pepper sauce
    1/8 teaspoon cayenne pepper
      3 tablespoons olive *or* vegetable oil
      2 garlic cloves, minced
      6 tablespoons lime juice

In a large bowl, combine the first 12 ingredients. In a microwave-safe dish, combine oil and garlic. Microwave, uncovered, on high for 1 minute. Cool. Whisk in lime juice. Pour over the corn mixture and toss to coat. Cover and refrigerate until serving. **Yield:** 16-18 servings.

In a large bowl, combine potatoes, carrots and parsley; pour the warm dressing over and stir gently to coat. Season to taste with additional salt. Spoon into a serving dish; garnish with crumbled bacon. Serve warm. **Yield:** 14-16 servings.

— ☞ ☞ ☞ —

Tropical Slaw

(Pictured below)

This refreshing dish is an excellent accompaniment to any meal on a hot day. I also enjoy it during the cold months—the blend of crunchy cabbage, sweet fruit and chewy coconut seems to mentally transport me to a warm tropical island. It goes over well at potlucks.
—Anna Marie Nichols, Americus, Georgia

   1 can (20 ounces) pineapple tidbits
   1 tablespoon lemon juice
   1 medium firm banana, sliced
   3 cups shredded cabbage
   1 can (11 ounces) mandarin oranges, drained
   1 cup miniature marshmallows
   1 cup flaked coconut
   1 cup chopped walnuts
   1 cup raisins
1/2 teaspoon salt
   1 carton (8 ounces) pineapple yogurt

Drain pineapple, reserving 2 tablespoons juice; set pineapple aside. Stir lemon juice and banana into reserved pineapple juice. In a large salad bowl, combine the cabbage, oranges, marshmallows, coconut, walnuts, raisins, salt, pineapple and banana mixture. Add yogurt; toss to coat. Cover and refrigerate until serving. **Yield:** 10 servings.

Deluxe German Potato Salad

(Pictured above and on page 24)

I make this salad for all occasions—it goes well with any kind of meat. I often take this salad to potlucks, and there's never any left over. The celery, carrots and ground mustard are a special touch not usually found in traditional German potato salad. —*Betty Perkins Hot Springs, Arkansas*

1/2 pound sliced bacon
   1 cup thinly sliced celery
   1 cup chopped onion
   1 cup sugar
   2 tablespoons all-purpose flour
   1 cup cider vinegar
1/2 cup water
   1 teaspoon salt
3/4 teaspoon ground mustard
   5 pounds unpeeled red new potatoes, cooked and sliced
   2 carrots, shredded
   2 tablespoons chopped fresh parsley
Additional salt to taste

In a skillet, cook bacon until crisp. Drain, reserving 1/4 cup drippings. Crumble bacon and set aside. Saute the celery and onion in drippings until tender. Combine sugar and flour; add to skillet with vinegar, water, salt and mustard. Cook, stirring constantly, until mixture thickens and bubbles.

Summer Spaghetti Salad
(Pictured below)

This lovely, fresh-tasting salad features a bounty of garden vegetables and starts with a bottle of store-bought dressing. —Lucia Johnson, Massena, New York

✓ Uses less fat, sugar or salt. Includes Nutritional Analysis and Diabetic Exchanges.

    1 package (16 ounces) thin spaghetti, halved
    3 medium tomatoes, diced
    3 small zucchini, diced
    1 large cucumber, halved, seeded and diced
    1 medium green pepper, diced
    1 medium sweet red pepper, diced
    1 bottle (8 ounces) Italian salad dressing
    2 tablespoons grated Parmesan cheese
 1-1/2 teaspoons sesame seeds
 1-1/2 teaspoons poppy seeds
    1/2 teaspoon paprika
    1/4 teaspoon celery seed
    1/8 teaspoon garlic powder

Cook spaghetti according to package directions; drain and rinse in cold water. Place in a large bowl; add tomatoes, zucchini, cucumber and peppers. Combine remaining ingredients; pour over salad and toss to coat. Cover and refrigerate for at least 2 hours. **Yield:** 16 servings.

Nutritional Analysis: One 1-cup serving (prepared with fat-free salad dressing and nonfat Parmesan cheese topping) equals 137 calories, 150 mg sodium, trace cholesterol, 27 g carbohydrate, 5 g protein, 1 g fat. **Diabetic Exchanges:** 1-1/2 starch, 1 vegetable.

Parsley Tortellini Toss
(Pictured above)

Two ladies from our church brought this over after I had my first child. Every time I make it, I think of those two dear sisters who made my initial days as a mom easier. —Jacqueline Graves, Lawrenceville, Georgia

    1 package (16 ounces) frozen cheese tortellini
 1-1/2 cups cubed provolone cheese
 1-1/2 cups cubed mozzarella cheese
    1 cup cubed fully cooked ham
    1 cup cubed cooked turkey
    1 cup frozen peas, thawed
    2 medium carrots, shredded
    1/2 medium sweet red pepper, diced
    1/2 medium green pepper, diced
    1 cup minced fresh parsley
    1/2 cup olive *or* vegetable oil
    3 tablespoons cider vinegar *or* red wine vinegar
    2 tablespoons grated Parmesan cheese
    2 garlic cloves, minced

Cook tortellini according to package directions; drain and rinse in cold water. Place in a large bowl; add the next eight ingredients. In a jar with a tight-fitting lid, combine the remaining ingredients; shake well. Pour over salad and toss to coat. Cover and chill until serving. **Yield:** 12-15 servings.

Wild Rice Salad

(Pictured below)

Since I spend part of my summers in northern Minnesota near the wild rice fields, I have tried many recipes featuring this delicious, nutty-flavored grain in the past 40-plus years. This salad is often requested.
—*Florence Jacoby, Granite Falls, Minnesota*

☑ Uses less fat, sugar or salt. Includes Nutritional Analysis and Diabetic Exchanges.

    1 cup uncooked wild rice
Seasoned salt, optional
    2 cups diced cooked chicken
1-1/2 cups halved green grapes
    1 cup sliced water chestnuts, drained
  3/4 cup reduced-fat mayonnaise
    1 cup cashews, optional
Lettuce leaves

Cook rice according to package directions, omitting salt or substituting seasoned salt if desired. Drain well; cool to room temperature. Spoon into a large bowl; add chicken, grapes, water chestnuts and mayonnaise. Toss gently with a fork. Cover and chill. Just before serving, add cashews if desired. Serve on lettuce leaves or line a bowl with lettuce leaves and fill with salad. **Yield:** 6 servings.

   Nutritional Analysis: One serving (prepared without cashews or additional salt) equals 318 calories, 229 mg sodium, 38 mg cholesterol, 40 g carbohydrate, 19 g protein, 10 g fat. **Diabetic Exchanges:** 2 lean meat, 1 starch, 1 fruit, 1 vegetable, 1 fat.

Tuna-Stuffed Jumbo Shells

(Pictured above)

These light, fresh-tasting stuffed shells really star as part of a luncheon menu. I came up with this distinctive combination of ingredients by accident one day using leftovers from other recipes. It's a cool summer main dish. —*Phy Bresse, Lumberton, North Carolina*

   10 jumbo pasta shells
  1/2 cup mayonnaise
    2 tablespoons sugar
    1 can (12 ounces) tuna, drained and flaked
    1 cup diced celery
  1/2 cup diced green onions
  1/2 cup diced green pepper
  1/2 cup shredded carrot
    2 tablespoons minced fresh parsley
CREAMY CELERY DRESSING:
  1/4 cup sour cream
  1/4 cup sugar
  1/4 cup cider vinegar
    2 tablespoons mayonnaise
    1 teaspoon celery seed
    1 teaspoon onion powder
Lettuce leaves and red onion rings, optional

Cook pasta according to package directions; drain and rinse in cold water. In a bowl, combine mayonnaise and sugar. Stir in the tuna, celery, onions, green pepper, carrot and parsley. Spoon into pasta shells; cover and refrigerate.

   For the dressing, combine sour cream, sugar, vinegar, mayonnaise, celery seed and onion powder. Arrange lettuce, onion rings and stuffed shells on a serving platter; drizzle with dressing. **Yield:** 5 servings.

Citrus Shrimp Salad

(Pictured above)

I tasted this refreshing salad at a gathering I attended with my sister. I pestered her until she got me a copy of the recipe. —Nancy Rollag, Kewaskum, Wisconsin

✓ Uses less fat, sugar or salt. Includes Nutritional Analysis and Diabetic Exchanges.

> 2 tablespoons reduced-fat plain yogurt
> 4-1/2 teaspoons Dijon mustard
> 1 tablespoon honey
> 2 tablespoons orange juice
> 2 tablespoons white wine vinegar *or* cider vinegar
> 1/4 cup fat-free Italian salad dressing
> 1/8 teaspoon pepper
> 3 tablespoons finely chopped green onions
> 2 pounds cooked medium shrimp, peeled and deveined
> 8 cups torn romaine
> 2 cups pink grapefruit sections (about 2 large)
> 2 cups navel orange sections (3 to 4 large)

In a large bowl, whisk together the first eight ingredients in the order listed. Add shrimp; toss to coat. Let stand for 15-30 minutes. Drain, reserving the marinade. Arrange romaine on a serving platter or individual plates; top with shrimp, grapefruit and oranges. Drizzle with reserved marinade. **Yield:** 8 servings.
   Nutritional Analysis: One serving (1 cup) equals 136 calories, 1 g fat (0 saturated fat), 135 mg cholesterol, 341 mg sodium, 15 g carbohydrate, 3 g fiber, 17 g protein. **Diabetic Exchanges:** 2 very lean meat, 1 fruit.

Grilled Chicken Salad

(Pictured below and on page 24)

My husband and I enjoy going on picnics and dining on this satisfying salad. —Juli Stewart
Coppell, Texas

> 6 boneless skinless chicken breast halves
> 2 tablespoons fresh lemon juice
> 1 pound macaroni, ziti *or* corkscrew pasta, cooked and drained
> 1 medium sweet red pepper, chopped
> 2-1/2 cups sliced celery
> 1 medium red onion, chopped
> 1/4 cup minced fresh dill *or* 5 teaspoons dill weed
> 3 tablespoons white wine vinegar
> 2 tablespoons mayonnaise
> 2 tablespoons Dijon mustard
> 1/2 teaspoon salt
> 1/4 teaspoon pepper
> 2/3 cup olive *or* vegetable oil
> Leaf lettuce

Grill the chicken breasts over medium-hot heat for 15-18 minutes, turning once, or until tender and juices run clear. Remove from the grill and place in a single layer on a platter; sprinkle with lemon juice and set aside.
   In a large bowl, toss pasta, red pepper, celery, onion and dill. Remove chicken from platter; pour juices into a bowl. Slice chicken crosswise into thin strips; add to pasta mixture. To the juices, add vinegar, mayonnaise, mustard, salt and pepper; whisk well. Add oil very slowly in a stream until dressing is thickened. Pour over salad and toss. Serve in a lettuce-lined bowl or on individual lettuce-lined plates. **Yield:** 6 servings.

Spicy Beef Salad
(Pictured above)

This recipe was inspired by my love of spicy flavors and light, nutritious entrees. The pretty salad has an appealing variety of textures. —Peggy Allen
Pasadena, California

✓ Uses less fat, sugar or salt. Includes Nutritional Analysis and Diabetic Exchanges.

- 1/2 pound boneless sirloin steak
- 1/3 cup fresh lime juice
- 1 tablespoon brown sugar
- 1 tablespoon soy sauce
- 1 tablespoon minced fresh basil *or* 1 teaspoon dried basil
- 2 teaspoons minced fresh mint *or* 3/4 teaspoon dried mint
- 1 jalapeno pepper, minced
- 2 to 3 garlic cloves, minced
- 1 teaspoon grated fresh gingerroot *or* 1/4 to 1/2 teaspoon ground ginger
- 1 large sweet red pepper, julienned
- 1/2 medium cucumber, chopped
- 6 cups torn mixed salad greens

Partially freeze beef. Slice across the grain into thin strips; set aside. For dressing, combine lime juice, brown sugar, soy sauce, basil and mint; set aside. In a nonstick skillet coated with nonstick cooking spray, saute jalapeno, garlic and ginger for 30 seconds. Add beef; stir-fry until cooked as desired.

Remove beef from pan; gently toss with red pepper and cucumber. Place greens in a large bowl or divide among individual bowls or plates; top with beef mixture. Add dressing to pan and bring to a boil; remove from the heat and drizzle over salad. Serve immediately. **Yield:** 4 servings.

Nutritional Analysis: One serving (prepared with low-sodium soy sauce) equals 152 calories, 171 mg sodium, 45 mg cholesterol, 11 g carbohydrate, 17 g protein, 5 g fat. **Diabetic Exchanges:** 2 very lean meat, 2 vegetable.

Mexican Garden Salad
(Pictured below)

I'm always watching for delicious new recipes to try, and when I found this salad, I knew it would taste as good as it looks. Although similar to a traditional taco salad, this recipe adds tasty extras like broccoli and carrot. It's stunning on the table.
—Dianne Esposite, New Middletown, Ohio

- 1 pound ground beef
- 1 jar (16 ounces) thick and chunky salsa, *divided*
- 1/4 cup water
- 1 envelope taco seasoning mix
- 1-1/2 heads iceberg lettuce, torn
- 3 cups broccoli florets
- 1 small red onion, thinly sliced into rings
- 1 medium carrot, shredded
- 1 large tomato, chopped
- 1 can (4 ounces) chopped green chilies, drained
- 1/2 to 1 cup shredded cheddar cheese
- 1 cup (8 ounces) sour cream
Tortilla chips, optional

In a skillet, brown ground beef; drain. Add 1 cup salsa, water and taco seasoning; bring to a boil. Reduce heat and simmer for 20 minutes; cool.

In a 3- or 4-qt. glass bowl, layer vegetables in order given. Top with the chilies, beef mixture and cheese. Combine sour cream and remaining salsa; serve with salad and tortilla chips if desired. **Yield:** 6-8 servings.

Southwestern Bean Salad

(Pictured below)

I've served this zippy salad many times and received compliments. When it comes to bean salad, most people think of the sweet, three-bean variety, so this is a nice surprise. —Lila Jean Allen, Portland, Oregon

✓ Uses less fat, sugar or salt. Includes Nutritional Analysis and Diabetic Exchanges.

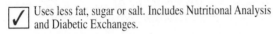

1 can (16 ounces) kidney beans, rinsed
  and drained
1 can (15 ounces) black beans, rinsed
  and drained
1 can (15 ounces) garbanzo beans, rinsed
  and drained
2 celery ribs, sliced
1 medium red onion, diced
1 medium tomato, diced
1 cup frozen corn, thawed

DRESSING:
3/4 cup thick and chunky salsa
1/4 cup vegetable oil
1/4 cup lime juice
1-1/2 teaspoons chili powder
1 teaspoon salt, optional
1/2 teaspoon ground cumin

In a bowl, combine beans, celery, onion, tomato and corn. In a small bowl, combine salsa, oil, lime juice, chili powder, salt if desired and cumin; mix well. Pour over bean mixture and toss to coat. Cover and chill at least 2 hours. **Yield:** 10 servings.

Nutritional Analysis: One 3/4-cup serving (prepared without added salt) equals 210 calories, 382 mg sodium, 0 cholesterol, 32 g carbohydrate, 8 g protein, 7 g fat. **Diabetic Exchanges:** 2 starch, 1 vegetable, 1 fat.

Pecan-Pear Tossed Salad

(Pictured above)

To save time, I prepare the ingredients and dressing the day before, then combine them just before serving. This salad has become a star at family gatherings. Once, when I forgot to bring it, dinner was postponed so I could go home and get it! —Marjean Claassen
Sedgwick, Kansas

2 tablespoons fresh raspberries
3/4 cup olive *or* vegetable oil
3 tablespoons cider vinegar
2 tablespoons plus 1 teaspoon sugar
1/4 to 1/2 teaspoon pepper

SALAD:
4 medium ripe pears, thinly sliced
2 teaspoons lemon juice
8 cups torn salad greens
2/3 cup pecan halves, toasted
1/2 cup fresh raspberries
1/3 cup (2 ounces) crumbled feta *or*
  blue cheese

Press raspberries through a sieve, reserving juice. Discard seeds. In a jar with a tight-fitting lid, combine oil, vinegar, sugar, pepper and reserved raspberry juice; shake well. Toss pear slices with lemon juice; drain. In a salad bowl, combine the salad greens, pears, pecans and raspberries. Sprinkle with cheese. Drizzle with dressing. **Yield:** 8 servings.

Marinated Mushroom Salad

(Pictured below)

Packed with mushrooms and loads of crunchy color-ful colorful ingredients, this salad is perfect at picnics and par-ties. It keeps well in the refrigerator, so you can easi-ly make it ahead of time. —Sandra Johnson
Tioga, Pennsylvania

2-1/2 quarts water
   3 tablespoons lemon juice
   3 pounds small fresh mushrooms
   2 carrots, sliced
   2 celery ribs, sliced
1/2 medium green pepper, chopped
   1 small onion, chopped
   1 tablespoon minced fresh parsley
1/2 cup sliced stuffed olives
   1 can (2-1/4 ounces) sliced ripe olives, drained
DRESSING:
1/2 cup prepared Italian salad dressing
1/2 cup red *or* white wine vinegar
   1 garlic clove, minced
1/2 teaspoon dried oregano
1/2 teaspoon salt

In a large saucepan, bring water and lemon juice to a boil. Add mushrooms and cook for 3 minutes, stirring occasionally. Drain; cool. Place mushrooms in a large bowl; add carrots, celery, green pepper, onion, parsley and olives. Combine all dressing in-gredients in a small bowl or a jar with tight-fitting lid; shake or mix well. Pour over salad. Cover and refrigerate overnight. **Yield:** 6-8 servings.

Pineapple Gelatin Salad

(Pictured above and on page 24)

My family enjoys this lovely layered salad in the sum-mer with grilled hamburgers. A good friend shared the recipe with me, and every time I make it, I think of her. —Susan Kirby, Tipton, Indiana

   1 can (20 ounces) crushed pineapple
   1 package (6 ounces) lemon gelatin
   3 cups boiling water
   1 package (8 ounces) cream cheese, softened
   1 carton (16 ounces) frozen whipped topping, thawed
3/4 cup sugar
   3 tablespoons lemon juice
   3 tablespoons water
   2 tablespoons all-purpose flour
   2 egg yolks, lightly beaten

Drain pineapple, reserving juice. Dissolve gelatin in water; add pineapple. Pour into a 13-in. x 9-in. x 2-in. dish; chill until almost set, about 45 min-utes. In a mixing bowl, beat cream cheese and whipped topping until smooth. Carefully spread over gelatin; chill for 30 minutes.

Meanwhile, in a saucepan over medium heat, combine sugar, lemon juice, water, flour, egg yolks and reserved pineapple juice; bring to a boil, stir-ring constantly. Cook for 1 minute or until thick-ened. Cool. Carefully spread over cream cheese layer. Chill for at least 1 hour. **Yield:** 12-16 servings.

Tomatoes with Thyme Dressing

When my garden harvest yields an abundance of tomatoes, I appreciate this easy-to-assemble side dish.
—Margaret Allen, Abingdon, Virginia

1 cup (8 ounces) sour cream
2 tablespoons cider vinegar *or*
  red wine vinegar
1-1/2 teaspoons minced fresh thyme
  or 1/2 teaspoon dried thyme
1 teaspoon sugar
1/2 teaspoon salt
1/4 teaspoon celery seed
Dash pepper
4 medium tomatoes, cut into wedges

In a small bowl, combine the sour cream, vinegar and seasonings; mix well. Cover and chill for 1 hour. Drizzle 1/3 to 1/2 cup over tomatoes. Refrigerate remaining dressing. **Yield:** 4-6 servings.

— 🏆 🏆 🏆 —

Asparagus Vinaigrette

(Pictured below)

I love to cook and especially enjoy trying new recipes. I took a cooking class and discovered this delightful salad. It's nice for a spring luncheon with the fresh taste of asparagus. *—Marcy Fechtig*
Burnt Prairie, Illinois

1-1/2 cups olive *or* vegetable oil
1/2 cup cider vinegar *or* white wine vinegar
2 teaspoons Dijon mustard
1/2 teaspoon salt
1/8 teaspoon pepper
3 to 4 radishes, sliced
1/4 cup chopped green pepper
3 tablespoons dill pickle relish
1 tablespoon chopped fresh parsley
1 tablespoon snipped fresh chives
2 pounds fresh asparagus spears, cooked
  and drained

Lettuce leaves
3 hard-cooked eggs, sliced
2 medium tomatoes, cut into wedges

In a bowl, whisk together the oil, vinegar, mustard, salt and pepper. Add radishes, green pepper, relish, parsley and chives. Place asparagus in a shallow glass dish; pour dressing over asparagus. Cover and chill at least 4 hours or overnight.

To serve, arrange the lettuce on a serving platter; remove asparagus from dressing with a slotted spoon and arrange over lettuce. Garnish with eggs and tomatoes. Drizzle with some of the dressing. **Yield:** 6-8 servings.

— 🏆 🏆 🏆 —

Hot Bacon Dressing

You get an explosion of flavor in this hot dressing that's perfect for strong-flavored greens like spinach.
—Connie Simon, Reed City, Michigan

3/4 pound sliced bacon, diced
1/2 cup chopped onion
1 cup cider vinegar
2 cups water
1-1/2 cups sugar
1 jar (2 ounces) diced pimientos, drained
2 tablespoons Dijon mustard
1 teaspoon salt
1/4 teaspoon pepper
3 tablespoons cornstarch
2 tablespoons cold water

In a large skillet, cook bacon until crisp; remove bacon and set aside. Drain, reserving 2 tablespoons drippings in the skillet. Add onion and saute until tender; remove from the heat. Add vinegar, water, sugar, pimientos, mustard, salt, pepper and bacon; mix well.

Combine cornstarch and cold water; stir into skillet. Cook and stir until mixture comes to a boil. Boil 2 minutes, stirring constantly. Serve warm over fresh spinach or mixed greens. Refrigerate leftovers; reheat before serving. **Yield:** about 4 cups.

— 🏆 🏆 🏆 —

Blue Cheese Dressing

(Pictured above right)

I tasted this tangy dressing for the first time at a friend's house. She gave me the recipe, and now I make it every week. I always keep some in my refrigerator. It tastes fresher than bottled blue cheese dressing and is a snap to make. *—Barbara Nowakowski*
North Tonawanda, New York

1-1/2 cups mayonnaise
1/2 cup sour cream
1/4 cup cider vinegar
  4 teaspoons sugar
1/2 teaspoon ground mustard
1/2 teaspoon garlic powder
1/2 teaspoon onion powder
  1 package (4 ounces) blue cheese, crumbled

In a bowl, combine the first seven ingredients. Stir in the blue cheese. Cover and chill at least 2 hours. Serve over salad greens. Store in the refrigerator. **Yield:** 2 cups.

— ♟ ♟ ♟ —

Basil Vinaigarette

A splash of this delicate dressing lets the goodness of fresh salad greens shine through. —Vivian Haen
Menomonee Falls, Wisconsin

1/4 cup olive *or* vegetable oil
4-1/2 teaspoons red wine vinegar *or*
        cider vinegar
1/4 teaspoon ground mustard
1/4 teaspoon dried basil
1/8 teaspoon garlic powder
Salt and pepper to taste

In a jar with a tight-fitting lid, combine all ingredients; shake well. Serve over salad greens. **Yield:** 1/4 cup.

— ♟ ♟ ♟ —

Poppy Seed Dressing

The best way to use up fruit all year long is with this tongue-tingling sweet and tangy topping. Why not treat your family with this tonight? —Patricia Staudt
Marble Rock, Iowa

3/4 cup sugar
1-1/2 teaspoons onion salt
  1 teaspoon ground mustard
1/3 cup cider vinegar
  1 cup vegetable oil
  1 tablespoon poppy seeds

In a mixing bowl, combine sugar, onion salt and mustard. Add vinegar; mix well. Gradually add oil while beating on medium speed; beat for 5 minutes or until very thick. Stir in poppy seeds. Serve over fruit or greens. Refrigerate leftovers. **Yield:** 1-2/3 cups.

— ♟ ♟ ♟ —

Honey Fruit Dressing

(Pictured below and on page 24)

Mix this dressing with a medley of melon, peaches, grapes, strawberries or whatever you have on hand.
—Dorothy Anderson, Ottawa, Kansas

2/3 cup sugar
  1 teaspoon ground mustard
  1 teaspoon paprika
  1 teaspoon celery seed
1/4 teaspoon salt
1/3 cup honey
1/3 cup cider vinegar
  1 tablespoon lemon juice
  1 teaspoon grated onion
  1 cup vegetable oil

In a mixing bowl, combine sugar, mustard, paprika, celery seed and salt. Add honey, vinegar, lemon juice and onion. Add oil very slowly, beating constantly. Serve with fresh fruit. Store in the refrigerator. **Yield:** 2 cups.

Soups & Sandwiches

These satisfying soups and sandwiches are sure to solicit smiles and compliments.

DELICIOUS DUOS. Clockwise from upper left: Grilled Beef Gyros (p. 54), Cheeseburger Soup (p. 48), Baked Southwest Sandwiches (p. 52) and Slow-Cooker Vegetable Soup (p. 46).

Classic Chicken Noodle Soup

(Pictured below)

After working all day, my husband, Todd, and I enjoy this hearty soup along with crusty rolls and a salad. It's real comfort food. —Nila Grahl
Des Plaines, Illinois

1 broiler/fryer chicken (3 to 4 pounds), cut up
10 cups water
1 large carrot, sliced
1 large onion, sliced
1 celery rib, sliced
1 garlic clove, minced
1 bay leaf
1 teaspoon dried thyme
1 teaspoon salt
1/4 teaspoon pepper

SOUP INGREDIENTS:
2 large carrots, sliced
2 celery ribs, sliced
1 medium onion, chopped
2 cups uncooked fine egg noodles
1 cup frozen peas
1/2 cup frozen cut green beans

In a large soup kettle or Dutch oven, combine the first 10 ingredients. Bring to a boil. Reduce heat; cover and simmer for 1-1/2 to 2 hours or until meat is tender.

Remove chicken; cool. Remove and discard skin and bones. Chop chicken; set aside. Strain broth, discarding vegetables and bay leaf. Return broth to pan; add carrots, celery and onion. Bring to a boil. Reduce heat; cover and simmer for 10 minutes or until vegetables are tender.

Add noodles and chicken. Bring to a boil. Reduce heat; cover and simmer for 6 minutes. Stir in peas and beans. Cook for 2-4 minutes or until the beans and noodles are tender. **Yield:** 6-8 servings.

——— 🍵 🍵 🍵 ———

Baked Potato Soup

(Pictured at left)

My husband and I enjoyed a delicious potato soup at a restaurant while on vacation, and I came home determined to duplicate it. It took me 5 years to get the taste right! —Joann Goetz, Genoa, Ohio

4 large baking potatoes (about 2-3/4 pounds)
2/3 cup butter *or* margarine
2/3 cup all-purpose flour
3/4 teaspoon salt
1/4 teaspoon white pepper
6 cups milk
1 cup (8 ounces) sour cream
1/4 cup thinly sliced green onions
10 bacon strips, cooked and crumbled
1 cup (4 ounces) shredded cheddar cheese

Bake potatoes at 350° for 65-75 minutes or until tender; cool completely. Peel and cube potatoes. In a large saucepan, melt butter; stir in flour, salt and pepper until smooth. Gradually add milk. Bring to a boil; cook and stir for 2 minutes or until thickened. Remove from the heat; whisk in sour cream. Add potatoes and green onions. Garnish with bacon and cheese. **Yield:** 10 servings.

NOTHING warms up a cool day in a more satisfying way than steaming soups like Classic Chicken Noodle Soup, Baked Potato Soup and French Onion Tomato Soup (shown above, top to bottom).

French Onion Tomato Soup

(Pictured at lower left)

Tomato juice gives extra flavor to this wonderful soup that's so quick and easy to prepare. I found the recipe years ago in a recipe book of my mother's and have shared it with many people. —Clara Honeyager
Mukwonago, Wisconsin

- 4 cups thinly sliced onions
- 1 garlic clove, minced
- 2 tablespoons butter *or* margarine
- 1 can (46 ounces) tomato juice
- 2 teaspoons beef bouillon granules
- 3 tablespoons lemon juice
- 2 teaspoons dried parsley flakes
- 2 teaspoons brown sugar
- 6 slices French bread, toasted
- 2 cups (8 ounces) shredded mozzarella cheese

In a large saucepan, saute onions and garlic in butter until tender. Add the tomato juice, bouillon, lemon juice, parsley and brown sugar. Bring to a boil. Reduce heat; simmer, uncovered, for 10 minutes, stirring occasionally.

Ladle soup into 10-oz. ovenproof soup bowls or ramekins. Top with French bread; sprinkle with cheese. Broil 4-6 in. from the heat for 2-3 minutes or until cheese is bubbly. **Yield:** 6 servings.

Vidalia Onion Soup

There's no question of the star in this traditional favorite soup. Rich Swiss cheese delightfully tops off a heaping bowlful of sweet, succulent Vidalia onions. —Ruby Jean Bland, Glennville, Georgia

- 4 to 5 large Vidalia *or* sweet onions, chopped
- 3 tablespoons butter *or* margarine
- 1/4 teaspoon pepper
- 1 tablespoon all-purpose flour
- 4 cups beef broth
- 1-1/2 cups water
- 1 bay leaf
- 8 slices French bread, toasted
- 1/2 cup shredded Swiss cheese

In a soup kettle or Dutch oven, saute the onions in butter until lightly browned. Sprinkle with pepper and flour. Cook and stir for 1 minute. Add the broth, water and bay leaf; simmer for 30-40 minutes, stirring occasionally. Discard bay leaf. Ladle into ovenproof soup bowls; top with bread and cheese. Bake at 400° for 10 minutes or until cheese is golden brown. **Yield:** 8 servings (2 quarts).

Summer Fruit Soup

(Pictured above)

I've served this delightful medley for about 40 years, and it has never failed to elicit raves from those eating it. —Gladys De Boer, Castleford, Idaho

- 1/2 cup sugar
- 3 tablespoons quick-cooking tapioca
- 2-1/2 cups water, *divided*
- 1 can (6 ounces) frozen orange juice concentrate
- 1 package (10 ounces) frozen sliced sweetened strawberries, thawed
- 2 cups fresh *or* frozen sliced peaches, thawed and cut into bite-size pieces
- 1 can (11 ounces) mandarin oranges, drained
- 2 medium ripe bananas, sliced
- 1 pint lime sherbet, optional

In a saucepan, combine sugar, tapioca and 1-1/2 cups water. Cook over medium heat for 5-6 minutes or until thickened and clear. Remove from the heat; stir in orange juice concentrate and remaining water until the concentrate is thawed. Stir in strawberries, peaches and oranges. Cover and refrigerate for 2 hours.

Just before serving, stir in the bananas. Top each serving with a scoop of sherbet if desired. **Yield:** 6 servings.

Turkey Wild Rice Soup

(Pictured below)

An area turkey grower shared this recipe with me. A rich and smooth soup, it makes great use of two Minnesota resources—turkey and wild rice. Be prepared to serve seconds!
                              —Terri Holmgren
                              Swanville, Minnesota

    1 medium onion, chopped
    2 celery ribs, diced
    2 carrots, diced
1/2 cup butter *or* margarine
1/2 cup all-purpose flour
    4 cups chicken *or* turkey broth
    2 cups cooked wild rice
    2 cups half-and-half cream
    2 cups diced cooked turkey
    1 teaspoon dried parsley flakes
1/2 teaspoon salt
1/4 teaspoon pepper

In a soup kettle or Dutch oven, saute onion, celery and carrots in butter until onion is transparent. Reduce heat. Blend in flour and cook until bubbly. Gradually add the broth, stirring constantly. Bring to a boil; boil for 1 minute. Reduce heat; add the wild rice, cream, turkey, parsley, salt and pepper; simmer for 20 minutes. **Yield:** 10-12 servings (about 3 quarts).

Hearty Hash Brown Soup

(Pictured above)

Once they take a spoonful of this soup, which is chock-full of potatoes and ham, folks will think you fussed. Since it uses frozen hash browns, it's simple and fast to make.   *—Frances Rector, Vinton, Iowa*

    2 pounds frozen hash brown potatoes
    4 cups water
    1 large onion, chopped
3/4 cup sliced celery
    4 chicken bouillon cubes
1/2 teaspoon celery seed
1/4 teaspoon pepper
    4 cans (10-3/4 ounces *each*) condensed
        cream of chicken soup, undiluted
    4 cups milk
    2 cups cubed fully cooked ham
    1 tablespoon dried parsley flakes
1-1/2 teaspoons garlic salt
    8 bacon strips, cooked and crumbled

In a soup kettle or Dutch oven, combine the first seven ingredients; bring to a boil. Reduce heat; cover and simmer for 20 minutes or until vegetables are tender. Mash vegetables with cooking liquid. Add soup and milk; stir until smooth. Add ham, parsley and garlic salt; simmer for 10 minutes or until heated through. Garnish with bacon. **Yield:** 12-16 servings (4 quarts).

Cream of Asparagus Soup

It's not difficult to fix a batch of this smooth, comforting soup. It has wonderful homemade goodness. A single steaming bowl really warms me up...but I usually can't resist going back for seconds. —Veva Hepler
Walla Walla, Washington

> 1/2 cup chopped onion
> 1 tablespoon vegetable oil
> 2 cans (14-1/2 ounces *each*) chicken broth
> 2-1/2 pounds fresh asparagus, trimmed and cut into 1-inch pieces
> 1/4 teaspoon dried tarragon
> 1/4 cup butter *or* margarine
> 1/4 cup all-purpose flour
> 1/2 teaspoon salt
> 1/4 teaspoon white pepper
> 3 cups half-and-half cream
> 1-1/2 teaspoons lemon juice
> Shredded Swiss cheese

In a large saucepan over medium heat, saute onion in oil until tender. Add broth, asparagus and tarragon; simmer until the asparagus is tender, about 8-10 minutes. In a blender or food processor, puree the asparagus in batches; set aside.

In a soup kettle or Dutch oven, melt the butter; stir in flour, salt and pepper. Cook and stir for 2 minutes or until golden. Gradually add cream. Add the pureed asparagus and lemon juice; heat through. Garnish with cheese if desired. **Yield:** 8 servings.

Microwave Clam Chowder

This tastes as good as the chowder served at many restaurants on Fisherman's Wharf in San Francisco. In my opinion, nothing beats homemade cooking.
—Mary Jane Cantrell, Turlock, California

> 4 bacon strips, cut into 1/2-inch pieces
> 2 cans (6-1/2 ounces *each*) chopped clams
> 1-1/2 cups diced peeled uncooked potatoes
> 1/3 cup chopped onion
> 2 tablespoons all-purpose flour
> 1-1/2 cups milk, *divided*
> 1/2 teaspoon salt
> Pinch pepper
> 1 teaspoon butter *or* margarine
> Minced fresh parsley

In a 2-qt. microwave-safe dish, cover and cook bacon on high for 4-5 minutes or until crisp. Remove with a slotted spoon; set aside. Drain clam juice into the bacon drippings. Stir in potatoes and onion. Cover and cook on high for 8-10 min-

utes or until potatoes are tender, stirring once or twice. Stir flour into 1/4 cup of milk; add to potato mixture. Stir in salt, pepper and remaining milk. Cover and microwave at 50% power for 6 minutes, stirring once or twice. Let stand for 3-5 minutes. Stir in clams and butter. Garnish with bacon and parsley. **Yield:** 4 servings (1 quart).

Editor's Note: This recipe was tested in a 700-watt microwave.

Broccoli Cheddar Soup
(Pictured below)

This cheesy blend proves that soup doesn't need to be made in big batches to be good. —Cheryl McRae
West Valley, Utah

> 1/4 cup chopped onion
> 1/4 cup butter *or* margarine
> 1/4 cup all-purpose flour
> 1/4 teaspoon salt
> 1/4 teaspoon pepper
> 3/4 cup chicken broth
> 1-1/2 cups milk
> 1 cup chopped cooked fresh *or* frozen broccoli
> 1/2 cup shredded cheddar cheese

In a saucepan, saute the onion in butter until tender. Stir in flour, salt and pepper; cook and stir until smooth and bubbly. Add broth and milk all at once; cook and stir until the mixture boils and thickens. Add broccoli. Simmer, stirring constantly, until heated through. Remove from the heat and stir in cheese until melted. **Yield:** 2 servings.

Curried Pumpkin Soup

(Pictured below)

I whipped up this satisfying soup one Thanksgiving for my family, and everyone was crazy about it! Even my brother, one of the pickiest eaters I know, passed his bowl for seconds. —Kimberly Knepper, Euless, Texas

- 1/2 pound fresh mushrooms, sliced
- 1/2 cup chopped onion
- 2 tablespoons butter *or* margarine
- 2 tablespoons all-purpose flour
- 1/2 to 1 teaspoon curry powder
- 3 cups vegetable broth
- 1 can (15 ounces) solid-pack pumpkin
- 1 can (12 ounces) evaporated milk
- 1 tablespoon honey
- 1/2 teaspoon salt
- 1/4 teaspoon pepper
- 1/4 teaspoon ground nutmeg

Sour cream and chives, optional

In a large saucepan, saute the mushrooms and onion in butter until tender. Stir in flour and curry powder until blended. Gradually add the broth. Bring to a boil; cook and stir for 2 minutes or until thickened. Add the pumpkin, milk, honey, salt, pepper and nutmeg; heat through. Garnish individual servings with sour cream and chives if desired. **Yield:** 7 servings.

Slow-Cooker Vegetable Soup

(Pictured above and on page 40)

What a treat to come home from work and have this savory soup ready to eat. I like to pair it with crusty rolls topped with melted mozzarella cheese.
—Heather Thurmeier, Pense, Saskatchewan

✓ Uses less fat, sugar or salt. Includes Nutritional Analysis and Diabetic Exchanges.

- 1 pound boneless round steak, cut into 1/2-inch cubes
- 1 can (14-1/2 ounces) diced tomatoes, undrained
- 3 cups water
- 2 medium potatoes, peeled and cubed
- 2 medium onions, diced
- 3 celery ribs, sliced
- 2 carrots, sliced
- 3 beef bouillon cubes
- 1/2 teaspoon dried basil
- 1/2 teaspoon dried oregano
- 1/2 teaspoon salt, optional
- 1/4 teaspoon pepper
- 1-1/2 cups frozen mixed vegetables

In a slow cooker, combine the first 12 ingredients. Cover and cook on high for 6 hours. Add mixed vegetables; cover and cook on high 2 hours longer or until the meat and vegetables are tender. **Yield:** 8-10 servings (about 2-1/2 quarts).

Nutritional Analysis: One 1-cup serving (prepared without salt) equals 143 calories, 464 mg sodium, 31 mg cholesterol, 15 g carbohydrate, 13 g protein, 3 g fat. **Diabetic Exchanges:** 1 starch, 1 lean meat, 1 vegetable.

Gazpacho
(Pictured below)

This dish comes in handy for luncheons in summer since it's so colorful and refreshing. —*Pat Waymire*
Yellow Springs, Ohio

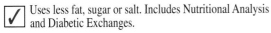 Uses less fat, sugar or salt. Includes Nutritional Analysis and Diabetic Exchanges.

- **4 cups tomato juice**
- **2 cups chopped seeded peeled tomatoes**
- **1 cup diced green pepper**
- **1 cup diced celery**
- **1 cup diced seeded cucumber**
- **2 garlic cloves, minced**
- **1/2 cup diced onion**
- **1/3 cup tarragon vinegar**
- **2 tablespoons minced fresh parsley**
- **1 tablespoon minced chives**
- **1 teaspoon Worcestershire sauce**
- **1 teaspoon salt, optional**
- **1/2 teaspoon pepper**
- **2 tablespoons vegetable oil**

In a large bowl, combine the first 13 ingredients. Cover and chill for at least 4 hours. Stir in oil before serving. Serve cold. **Yield:** 8 servings.

Nutritional Analysis: One 1-cup serving (prepared with low-sodium tomato juice and without salt) equals 96 calories, 56 mg sodium, 0 cholesterol, 13 g carbohydrate, 2 g protein, 4 g fat. **Diabetic Exchanges:** 2 vegetable, 1 fat.

Mushroom Barley Soup
(Pictured above)

With beef, barley and vegetables, this soup is hearty enough to be a meal. A big steaming bowl and a slice of crusty bread tastes great on a cold day.
—*Lynn Thomas, London, Ontario*

- **1-1/2 pounds boneless beef chuck, cut into 3/4-inch cubes**
- **1 tablespoon vegetable oil**
- **2 cups finely chopped onion**
- **1 cup diced carrots**
- **1/2 cup sliced celery**
- **1 pound fresh mushrooms, sliced**
- **2 garlic cloves, minced**
- **1/2 teaspoon dried thyme**
- **1 can (14-1/2 ounces) beef broth**
- **1 can (14-1/2 ounces) chicken broth**
- **2 cups water**
- **1/2 cup medium pearl barley**
- **1 teaspoon salt**
- **1/2 teaspoon pepper**
- **3 tablespoons chopped fresh parsley**

In a soup kettle or Dutch oven, brown meat in oil. Remove meat with a slotted spoon and set aside. Saute onion, carrots and celery in drippings over medium heat until tender, about 5 minutes. Add mushrooms, garlic and thyme; cook and stir for 3 minutes. Add broth, water, barley, salt and pepper. Return meat to pan; bring to a boil. Reduce heat; cover and simmer for 1-1/2 to 2 hours or until barley and meat are tender. Stir in parsley. **Yield:** about 10 servings (2-3/4 quarts).

Meanwhile, in small skillet, melt remaining butter. Add flour; cook and stir for 3-5 minutes or until bubbly. Add to soup; bring to a boil. Cook and stir for 2 minutes. Reduce heat to low. Add cheese, milk, salt and pepper; cook and stir until cheese is melted. Remove from the heat; stir in sour cream. **Yield:** 8 servings (2-1/4 quarts).

Chili in Bread Bowls

(Pictured below)

Some say you can have your cake and eat it, too...I say eat your chili and the bowl, too! I work the graveyard shift at a post office. During those hours, there is no place to buy meals, so I often bring in this chili to share. —Nancy Clancy, Standish, Maine

   1 **tablespoon all-purpose flour**
1/4 **teaspoon salt**
1/8 **teaspoon pepper**
1/2 **pound *each* lean beef stew meat, boneless skinless chicken breast and boneless pork, cut into cubes**
   1 **tablespoon vegetable oil**
   1 **medium onion, chopped**
   1 **medium green pepper, chopped**
   1 **jalapeno pepper, seeded and chopped***
   1 **can (28 ounces) diced tomatoes, drained**
   1 **can (16 ounces) kidney beans, rinsed and drained**

Cheeseburger Soup

(Pictured above and on page 40)

After a local restaurant wouldn't share their recipe for a similar soup with me, I developed my own, starting from a recipe for potato soup. I was really pleased at how good this "all American" soup turned out. —Joanie Shawhan, Madison, Wisconsin

1/2 **pound ground beef**
3/4 **cup chopped onion**
3/4 **cup shredded carrots**
3/4 **cup diced celery**
   1 **teaspoon dried basil**
   1 **teaspoon dried parsley flakes**
   4 **tablespoons butter *or* margarine, *divided***
   3 **cups chicken broth**
   4 **cups diced peeled potatoes (1-3/4 pounds)**
1/4 **cup all-purpose flour**
   8 **ounces process American cheese, cubed (2 cups)**
1-1/2 **cups milk**
3/4 **teaspoon salt**
1/4 **to 1/2 teaspoon pepper**
1/4 **cup sour cream**

In a 3-qt. saucepan, brown beef; drain and set aside. In the same saucepan, saute onion, carrots, celery, basil and parsley in 1 tablespoon butter until vegetables are tender, about 10 minutes. Add broth, potatoes and beef; bring to a boil. Reduce heat; cover and simmer 10-12 minutes or until potatoes are tender.

1 can (15-1/2 ounces) navy beans *or* great
   northern beans, rinsed and drained
1 can (8 ounces) tomato sauce
1 tablespoon chili powder
1 garlic clove, minced
1-1/2 teaspoons ground cumin
1/2 teaspoon dried basil
1/4 to 1/2 teaspoon cayenne pepper
9 large hard rolls
**Sour cream, chopped green onions and sweet
red pepper, optional**

In a large resealable plastic bag, combine the flour, salt and pepper. Add meat in batches; toss to coat. In a large skillet, brown meat in oil in batches. Transfer to a 5-qt. slow cooker with a slotted spoon. Stir in onion, peppers, tomatoes, beans, tomato sauce and seasonings. Cover and cook on low for 7-8 hours or until the meat is tender.

Cut tops off rolls; carefully hollow out bottom halves. Spoon about 1 cup of chili into each roll. Garnish with sour cream, onions and red pepper if desired. **Yield:** 9 servings.

*Editor's Note: When cutting or seeding hot peppers, use rubber or plastic gloves to protect your hands. Avoid touching your face.

— 🍷 🍷 🍷 —

Reuben Soup

This soup is often served in the staff cafeteria at the high school where I work. It's been a special favorite for years. —Mary Lindell, Sanford, Michigan

1/2 cup chopped onion
1/2 cup sliced celery
2 tablespoons butter *or* margarine
1 cup chicken broth
1 cup beef broth
1/2 teaspoon baking soda
2 tablespoons cornstarch
2 tablespoons water
3/4 cup sauerkraut, rinsed and drained
2 cups half-and-half cream
2 cups chopped cooked corned beef
1 cup (4 ounces) shredded Swiss cheese
Salt and pepper to taste
Rye croutons, optional

In a large saucepan, saute onion and celery in butter until tender. Add broth and baking soda. Combine cornstarch and water; add to pan. Bring to a boil; boil for 2 minutes, stirring occasionally. Reduce heat. Add sauerkraut, cream and corned beef; simmer and stir for 15 minutes. Add cheese; heat until melted. Add salt and pepper. Garnish with croutons if desired. **Yield:** about 6 servings.

White Chili

(Pictured above)

This recipe was given to me by a friend who got it from another friend. The day after I served it to company, someone called for the recipe, too! —Karen Gardiner
Eutaw, Alabama

✓ Uses less fat, sugar or salt. Includes Nutritional Analysis and Diabetic Exchanges.

2 pounds dried great northern beans
1-1/2 cups diced onion
1 tablespoon vegetable oil
1 tablespoon dried oregano
2 teaspoons ground cumin
1-1/2 teaspoons seasoned salt
1/2 teaspoon cayenne pepper
4-1/2 quarts chicken broth
2 garlic cloves, minced
2 pounds boneless skinless chicken breast
   halves, cubed
2 cans (4 ounces *each*) chopped green
   chilies

Place beans in a saucepan and cover with water. Bring to a boil; boil for 2 minutes. Remove from the heat. Soak for 1 hour; drain and rinse. In an 8-qt. Dutch oven, saute onion in oil until tender. Combine seasonings; add half to Dutch oven. Saute for 1 minute. Add beans, broth and garlic; bring to a boil. Reduce heat; simmer for 2 hours.

Coat chicken with remaining seasoning mixture; place in a 15-in. x 10-in. x 1-in. baking pan. Bake at 350° for 15 minutes or until juices run clear. Add chicken and chilies to bean mixture. Simmer for 1-1/2 to 2 hours. **Yield:** 20 servings.

Nutritional Analysis: One 1-cup serving (prepared with low-sodium broth) equals 169 calories, 365 mg sodium, 29 mg cholesterol, 17 g carbohydrate, 18 g protein, 3 g fat. **Diabetic Exchanges:** 2 lean meat, 1 starch.

Waldorf Turkey Sandwiches

(Pictured below)

Apples, celery and raisins give this special turkey salad a great flavor and tempting texture.
—Meghan Bodas, Rapid City, South Dakota

✓ Uses less fat, sugar or salt. Includes Nutritional Analysis and Diabetic Exchanges.

1-1/4 cups cubed cooked turkey breast
1 small apple, chopped
1/4 cup diced celery
3 tablespoons fat-free mayonnaise
2 tablespoons plain nonfat yogurt
2 tablespoons chopped walnuts
1 tablespoon raisins
1/8 teaspoon ground nutmeg
1/8 teaspoon ground cinnamon
8 slices raisin bread, toasted
4 lettuce leaves

In a bowl, combine the first nine ingredients. Cover and refrigerate for 1 hour. Spoon 3/4 cup onto four slices of bread; top with a lettuce leaf and remaining bread. **Yield:** 4 servings.
  Nutritional Analysis: One serving (calculated without bread) equals 127 calories, 114 mg sodium, 26 mg cholesterol, 9 g carbohydrate, 12 g protein, 5 g fat, 1 g fiber. **Diabetic Exchanges:** 1-1/2 lean meat, 1/2 fruit.

Meatball Sub Sandwiches

(Pictured above)

These hot, meaty sandwiches have a tangy barbecue-style sauce rather than the more traditional Italian tomato sauce. Onion and pepper slices make each bite twice as nice.
—Kim Marie Van Rheenen
Mendota, Illinois

9 submarine sandwich buns
1-1/2 pounds lean ground beef
1 egg
1/4 cup milk
1 tablespoon diced onion
1 teaspoon salt
1/4 teaspoon pepper
2 tablespoons vegetable oil, *divided*
2 medium green peppers, julienned
1 medium onion, sliced
1 tablespoon all-purpose flour
1 bottle (12 ounces) chili sauce
1 cup water
1 tablespoon brown sugar
1 teaspoon ground mustard

Cut a thin slice off the top of each roll; scoop out bread from inside. Crumble 1-1/4 cups of bread and place in a large bowl. Cover rolls and tops with plastic wrap; set aside. To the crumbled bread, add beef, egg, milk, diced onion, salt and pepper. Shape into 27 meatballs, about 1-1/2 in. each.
  In a large skillet, cook meatballs in 1 tablespoon of oil for 20-25 minutes or until no longer pink. Remove with a slotted spoon. Add remaining oil to skillet; saute green peppers and sliced onion until tender. Remove with a slotted spoon; set aside.

Stir flour into the skillet. Add chili sauce and water; bring to a boil. Cook and stir for 1-2 minutes. Stir in brown sugar and mustard. Add meatballs, peppers and onion; cover and simmer for 20 minutes. Meanwhile, warm rolls in a 325° oven for 8-10 minutes. Spoon three meatballs and sauce into each roll; replace tops. **Yield:** 9 servings.

Brisket for a Bunch

To get very thin slices of this tender beef, chill the brisket before slicing, then reheat the meat in the juices. —Dawn Fagerstrom, Warren, Minnesota

    1 beef brisket* (2-1/2 pounds), cut in half
    1 tablespoon vegetable oil
1/2 cup chopped celery
1/2 cup chopped onion
3/4 cup beef broth
1/2 cup tomato sauce
1/4 cup water
1/4 cup sugar
    2 tablespoons onion soup mix
    1 tablespoon cider vinegar
  12 hamburger buns, split

In a large skillet, brown the brisket on all sides in oil; transfer to a slow cooker. In the same skillet, saute celery and onion for 1 minute. Gradually add broth, tomato sauce and water; stir to loosen the browned bits from pan. Add sugar, soup mix and vinegar; bring to a boil. Pour over brisket.

Cover and cook on low for 7-8 hours or until meat is tender. Let stand for 5 minutes before slicing. Skim fat from cooking juices. Serve meat in buns with juices. **Yield:** 12 servings.

***Editor's Note:** This is a fresh beef brisket, not corned beef.

Sausage Sandwich Squares

(Pictured at right)

As Sunday school teachers, my husband and I often host youth groups, so I dreamed up this "handy" recipe to feed hungry teenagers. They loved this pizza-like sandwich and still request it when they visit. —Mary Merrill, Bloomingdale, Ohio

    3 to 3-1/2 cups all-purpose flour
    1 package (1/4 ounce) active dry yeast
1/2 teaspoon salt
1-1/3 cups warm water (120° to 130°)
    1 pound bulk Italian sausage
    1 medium sweet red pepper, diced
    1 medium green pepper, diced
    1 large onion, diced
    4 cups (16 ounces) shredded mozzarella cheese
    1 egg
    1 tablespoon water
    2 tablespoons grated Parmesan cheese
    2 tablespoons minced fresh parsley
1/2 teaspoon dried oregano
1/8 teaspoon garlic powder

In a bowl, combine 2 cups flour, yeast and salt. Add warm water; mix well. Add enough remaining flour to form a firm dough. Turn onto a floured surface; knead until smooth and elastic, about 6 minutes. Place in a greased bowl, turning once to grease top. Cover and let rise in a warm place until doubled, about 50 minutes.

In a skillet, cook sausage until no longer pink; remove with a slotted spoon and set aside. In the drippings, saute peppers and onion until tender; drain. Press half of the dough onto the bottom and 1/2 in. up the sides of a greased 15-in. x 10-in. x 1-in. baking pan. Spread sausage evenly over the crust. Top with peppers and onion. Sprinkle with mozzarella cheese.

Roll out remaining dough to fit pan; place over cheese and seal the edges. In a small bowl, beat egg and water. Add remaining ingredients; mix well. Brush over dough. Cut slits in top. Bake at 400° for 20-25 minutes or until golden brown. Cut into squares. **Yield:** 12-15 servings.

Nutty Tuna Sandwiches

Here's a fresh-tasting sandwich that'll spark up a lunch. Chopped salted peanuts and ranch dressing add an unexpected twist to traditional tuna salad.
—Cheryl Miller, Fort Collins, Colorado

  1 can (6-1/8 ounces) tuna, drained and flaked
  1 hard-cooked egg, chopped
  1 green onion, sliced
1/4 cup chopped salted peanuts
1/4 cup ranch salad dressing
  2 teaspoons lemon juice
  2 whole wheat pita breads, halved
  4 lettuce leaves

In a bowl, combine the tuna, egg, onion, peanuts, dressing and lemon juice. Line each pita half with a lettuce leaf; stuff with tuna mixture. **Yield:** 2-4 servings.

— 🍷 🍷 🍷 —

Baked Southwest Sandwiches

(Pictured above and on page 40)

I like to fix these tasty sandwiches whenever I have friends over for lunch. The combination of toppings is out of this world. I'm often asked for the recipe.
—Holly Sorensen, Reedley, California

  1 can (4-1/4 ounces) chopped ripe olives, drained
1/2 teaspoon chili powder
1/2 teaspoon ground cumin
1/4 teaspoon salt
1/2 cup mayonnaise
1/3 cup sour cream
1/3 cup chopped green onions
  8 slices Italian bread
3/4 to 1 pound thinly sliced cooked turkey
  2 medium tomatoes, thinly sliced
  2 ripe avocados, sliced
3/4 cup shredded cheddar cheese
3/4 cup shredded Monterey Jack cheese

In a bowl, combine olives, chili powder, cumin and salt; set aside 2 tablespoons. Add the mayonnaise, sour cream and onions to the remaining olive mixture. Place bread on an ungreased baking sheet; spread 1 tablespoon of mayonnaise mixture over each slice. Top with turkey and tomatoes. Spread with another tablespoon of mayonnaise mixture; top with avocados and cheeses. Sprinkle with reserved olive mixture. Bake at 350° for 15 minutes or until heated through. **Yield:** 8 servings.

Kielbasa Bundles

(Pictured below)

My family really enjoys these stuffed sausage sandwiches.
—Robin Touhey, San Angelo, Texas

1/2 pound fully cooked kielbasa *or* Polish sausage, chopped
  1 small onion, chopped
1/4 cup chopped green pepper
  1 garlic clove, minced
  1 tablespoon butter *or* margarine
1/3 cup barbecue sauce

2 tubes (8 ounces *each*) refrigerated
  crescent rolls
4 slices process American cheese, halved
1 egg white
1 tablespoon water
Sesame seeds

In a large skillet, cook sausage for 5-8 minutes;
drain. Add onion, green pepper, garlic and butter;
cook until vegetables are tender. Stir in barbecue
sauce; heat through. Unroll crescent roll dough and
separate into eight rectangles; seal perforations.

Place a cheese slice on half of each rectangle;
top with 2 tablespoons sausage mixture. Fold
dough over filling and pinch edges to seal; fold
seam under. Beat egg white and water; brush over
dough. Sprinkle with sesame seeds. Place seam
side down on greased baking sheets. Bake at 350°
for 15-18 minutes or until golden brown. **Yield:** 8
servings.

Spicy Sausage Sandwiches

*These hearty sandwiches are packed with flavor and
very versatile. They're terrific for breakfast, lunch or a
light supper. The pretty corn and pepper salsa is a garden-fresh topper for the browned sausage patties.*
—Eileen Sullivan, Lady Lake, Florida

SALSA:
   2 jalapeno peppers
   1 large fresh banana pepper
   1/2 cup diced sweet red pepper
   1/2 cup diced Vidalia *or* sweet onion
   1/2 cup fresh *or* frozen corn
   1 tablespoon chopped fresh cilantro *or*
     parsley
SANDWICH:
   1 pound bulk pork sausage
   6 English muffins, split and toasted
   6 slices Colby-Monterey Jack cheese

Remove seeds and membranes from jalapeno and
banana peppers if desired (for a less spicy salsa).
Dice peppers and place in a bowl; add remaining
salsa ingredients and mix well. Cover and refrigerate until ready to serve.

Form the sausage into six patties; cook in a skillet over medium heat until meat is no longer pink.
Place each on an English muffin half; top with 1 tablespoon salsa and a slice of cheese. Cover with
other muffin half. Serve remaining salsa on the side.
Yield: 6 servings.

***Editor's Note:** When cutting or seeding hot pep-
pers, use rubber or plastic gloves to protect your
hands. Avoid touching your face.

Super Sandwich
(Pictured above)

*This big sandwich is one I've made many times when
I knew I'd be feeding a hungry bunch. Everyone re-
marks on the tasty olive salad tucked between slices
of meat and cheese.* —Patrice Barker, Tampa, Florida

   1 medium cucumber, peeled, seeded and
     chopped
   1 medium tomato, seeded and chopped
   1 small onion, chopped
   1/2 cup pitted ripe olives, chopped
   1/2 cup stuffed olives, chopped
   1/4 cup Italian salad dressing
   1 unsliced round loaf (1-1/2 pounds)
     sourdough, white *or* whole wheat bread
   1/2 pound sliced fully cooked ham
   1/4 pound sliced salami
   1/4 pound sliced cooked pork
   1/2 pound sliced Swiss cheese
   1/2 pound sliced Muenster cheese

In a bowl, combine the cucumber, tomato, onion,
olives and salad dressing; set aside. Cut 1 in. off
top of loaf; set aside. Carefully hollow out top and
bottom, leaving a 1/2-in. shell (discard removed
bread or save for another use). Layer a fourth of
the ham, salami, pork and cheeses inside shell.

Top with a third of the vegetable mixture. Repeat
layers, ending with meat and cheeses, gently pressing down to flatten as needed. Replace bread top;
wrap tightly in plastic wrap. Refrigerate until serving. **Yield:** 8 servings.

Editor's Note: This sandwich may be made a day
ahead.

Grilled Beef Gyros

(Pictured above and on page 40)

A spicy marinade adds zip to these grilled beef slices tucked inside pita bread. Friends from Greece gave us their recipe for the cucumber sauce, which provides a cool contrast to the hot beef. —Lee Rademaker
Hayfork, California

    1 medium onion, cut into chunks
    2 garlic cloves
    2 tablespoons sugar
    1 tablespoon ground mustard
1/2 teaspoon ground ginger *or* 2 teaspoons
        minced fresh gingerroot
1-1/2 teaspoons pepper
1/2 teaspoon cayenne pepper
1/2 cup soy sauce
1/4 cup water
    1 boneless beef sirloin tip roast (2 to 3
        pounds), cut into 1/4-inch-thick slices
CUCUMBER SAUCE:
    1 medium cucumber, peeled, seeded and
        cut into chunks
    4 garlic cloves
1/2 teaspoon salt
1/3 cup cider vinegar
1/3 cup olive *or* vegetable oil
    2 cups (16 ounces) sour cream
    8 to 10 pita breads, warmed and halved
Thinly sliced onion
Chopped tomato

In a blender or food processor, place onion, garlic, sugar, mustard, ginger, pepper and cayenne; cover and process until onion is finely chopped. Add soy sauce and water; process until blended. Place beef in a large resealable plastic bag. Add marinade. Seal bag and turn to coat; refrigerate for 1-2 hours.

For sauce, combine the cucumber, garlic and salt in a blender or food processor; cover and process until cucumber is chopped. Add vinegar and oil; process until blended. Transfer to a bowl; stir in sour cream. Refrigerate until serving.

Drain and discard marinade. Grill beef, covered, over medium-hot heat until meat reaches desired doneness. Place beef in pita halves. Top with cucumber sauce, sliced onion and chopped tomato. **Yield:** 8-10 sandwiches.

Italian Grilled Cheese

These crumb-coated sandwiches are a tasty dressed-up version of the traditional favorite.
—*Vera Ambroselli, Lehigh Acres, Florida*

    4 slices Italian bread (1 inch thick)
    4 slices mozzarella *or* provolone cheese
    3 eggs
1/2 cup milk
3/4 teaspoon Italian seasoning
1/2 teaspoon garlic salt
2/3 cup Italian-seasoned bread crumbs

Cut a 3-in. pocket in each slice of bread; place a slice of cheese in each pocket. In a bowl, beat eggs, milk, Italian seasoning and garlic salt; soak bread for 2 minutes on each side. Coat with the bread crumbs. Cook on a greased hot griddle until golden brown on both sides. **Yield:** 4 servings.

Honey-Mustard Chicken Sandwiches

These chicken sandwiches are homemade "fast food" that's more delicious than the kind you go out to pick up. —*Christina Levrant, Bensalem, Pennsylvania*

✓ Uses less fat, sugar or salt. Includes Nutritional Analysis and Diabetic Exchanges.

1/4 cup Dijon mustard
    2 tablespoons honey
    1 teaspoon dried oregano
    1 teaspoon water
1/4 teaspoon garlic powder
1/8 to 1/4 teaspoon cayenne pepper
    4 boneless skinless chicken breast halves
        (1 pound)
    4 sandwich buns, split
    8 thin tomato slices
    1 cup shredded lettuce

In a bowl, combine the first six ingredients. Broil

chicken 4 in. from the heat for 3 minutes on each side. Brush with mustard sauce. Broil 4-6 minutes longer or until juices run clear, basting and turning several times. Serve on buns with tomato and lettuce. **Yield:** 4 servings.

Nutritional Analysis: One serving (calculated without bun) equals 185 calories, 438 mg sodium, 63 mg cholesterol, 13 g carbohydrate, 24 g protein, 4 g fat. **Diabetic Exchanges:** 3 very lean meat, 1 starch.

— 🥄 🥄 🥄 —

Teriyaki Chicken Sandwiches

(Pictured below)

After trying a similar dish in Hawaii, I was inspired to create these hearty sandwiches. —*Opal Reed Tyler, Texas*

      1/2 **cup vegetable oil**
      1/4 **cup soy sauce**
        3 **tablespoons honey**
        2 **tablespoons white wine vinegar**
        1 **teaspoon ground ginger**
      3/4 **teaspoon garlic powder**
        4 **boneless skinless chicken breast halves**
        4 **hard rolls *or* croissants, split**
        1 **cup finely shredded lettuce**
        8 **tomato slices**
        4 **green pepper rings**
      1/4 **cup mayonnaise, optional**

Combine the first six ingredients in a blender; process for 30 seconds. Reserve 1/4 cup. Pour remaining sauce into a large resealable plastic bag. Add chicken; seal and refrigerate overnight.

Drain, discarding marinade. Broil chicken 4 in. from the heat for 5 minutes on each side or until juices run clear. On the bottom half of each roll, layer lettuce, tomato, chicken and green pepper. Drizzle with reserved sauce; spread with mayonnaise if desired. Replace roll tops. **Yield:** 4 servings.

Editor's Note: Chicken may be grilled, covered, over low heat for 10-12 minutes or until juices run clear.

— 🥄 🥄 🥄 —

Pork Spiedis

(Pictured above)

Spiedis (pronounced "speed-eez") are a type of grilled meat sandwich considered a local specialty. This recipe is my own, but there are many variations in our area. —Beatrice Riddell, Chenango Bridge, New York

☑ Uses less fat, sugar or salt. Includes Nutritional Analysis and Diabetic Exchanges.

        4 **pounds pork tenderloin, cubed**
        2 **cups tomato juice**
        2 **large onions, finely chopped**
   4 to 5 **garlic cloves, minced**
        2 **tablespoons Worcestershire sauce**
        2 **teaspoons chopped fresh basil *or* 1 teaspoon dried basil**
Pepper to taste
       12 **slices Italian bread, optional**

In a large resealable plastic bag, combine the first seven ingredients. Seal and refrigerate overnight. Drain, discarding marinade. Thread pork on metal or soaked wooden skewers; grill or broil for 15-20 minutes, turning occasionally, until meat is no longer pink and pulls away easily from skewers. To serve, wrap a slice of bread around about five pork cubes and pull off skewer. **Yield:** 12 servings.

Nutritional Analysis: One serving (calculated without bread) equals 214 calories, 152 mg sodium, 77 mg cholesterol, 1 g carbohydrate, 24 g protein, 12 g fat. **Diabetic Exchange:** 4 lean meat.

Side Dishes & Condiments

Whether you're looking to round out a meal or top a favorite food, you and your family will savor this luscious lineup of recipes.

——— 🏺 🏺 🏺 ———

PERFECT PARTNERS. Clockwise from upper left: Twice-Baked Ranch Potatoes (p. 66), Campfire Potatoes (p. 64), Four-Berry Spread (p. 72), Fried Rice and Stir-Fried Vegetables (p. 60) and Four-Tomato Salsa (p. 69).

Hungarian Noodle Side Dish

(Pictured below)

I first served this creamy, rich casserole at our ladies meeting at church. Everyone liked it and many of the ladies wanted the recipe. The original recipe was from a friend, but I changed it a bit to suit our tastes.
— *Betty Sugg, Akron, New York*

- 3 chicken bouillon cubes
- 1/4 cup boiling water
- 1 can (10-3/4 ounces) condensed cream of mushroom soup, undiluted
- 1/2 cup chopped onion
- 2 tablespoons Worcestershire sauce
- 2 tablespoons poppy seeds
- 1/8 to 1/4 teaspoon garlic powder
- 1/8 to 1/4 teaspoon hot pepper sauce
- 2 cups (16 ounces) cottage cheese
- 2 cups (16 ounces) sour cream
- 1 package (16 ounces) medium noodles, cooked and drained
- 1/4 cup shredded Parmesan cheese
Paprika

In a large bowl, dissolve bouillon in water. Add the next six ingredients; mix well. Stir in the cottage cheese, sour cream and noodles; mix well. Pour into a greased 2-1/2-qt. baking dish. Sprinkle with the Parmesan cheese and paprika. Cover and bake at 350° for 45 minutes or until heated through. **Yield:** 8-10 servings.

Editor's Note: Casserole may be prepared ahead, covered and refrigerated overnight. Remove from the refrigerator 30 minutes before baking.

Garlic Pasta

This is one of many recipes I obtained while living in France. It makes an excellent side dish.
— *Sandi Pichon, Slidell, Louisiana*

- 1 whole garlic bulb
- 1/2 cup olive *or* vegetable oil
- 1/2 cup chopped fresh parsley
- 1/4 cup chopped fresh oregano *or* 4 teaspoons dried oregano
- 1 teaspoon salt
- 1/4 teaspoon pepper
- 1 pound pasta, cooked and drained

Separate garlic into cloves; remove papery skins. In a large skillet over low heat, saute garlic in oil for 20 minutes or until golden brown. Remove from the heat; add parsley, oregano, salt and pepper. Toss with pasta; serve immediately. **Yield:** 4 servings.

— 🍷 🍷 🍷 —

Herbed Macaroni 'n' Cheese

Herbs make this macaroni and cheese recipe different and delicious. — *Lois McAtee, Oceanside, California*

✓ Uses less fat, sugar or salt. Includes Nutritional Analysis and Diabetic Exchanges.

- 1 tablespoon margarine
- 3 tablespoons all-purpose flour
- 2 cups fat-free milk
- 3/4 to 1 teaspoon dried marjoram
- 1/2 teaspoon dried thyme
- 1/8 teaspoon ground nutmeg
- 1/8 teaspoon paprika
- 1 tablespoon Dijon mustard
- 1/2 cup grated Parmesan cheese, *divided*
- 1 package (7 ounces) elbow macaroni, cooked and drained
- 1 cup low-fat cottage cheese

In a large saucepan, melt margarine. Stir in flour until smooth. Gradually add milk, stirring constantly. Bring to a boil over medium heat; boil for 2 minutes or until thickened. Add the marjoram, thyme, nutmeg and paprika; stir until blended. Remove from the heat. Stir in mustard and 1/3 cup Parmesan cheese; mix well. Add macaroni and cottage cheese; stir until coated.

Pour into an 8-in. square baking dish coated with nonstick cooking spray. Sprinkle with remaining Parmesan. Bake, uncovered, at 350° for 30 minutes or until top is golden. **Yield:** 4 servings.

Nutritional Analysis: One serving equals 372 calories, 615 mg sodium, 20 mg cholesterol, 50 g carbohydrate, 23 g protein, 9 g fat. **Diabetic Exchanges:** 3 starch, 2 meat.

Fabulous Fettuccine

(Pictured below)

My mother-in-law is from Italy, so my husband, Bob, grew up eating pasta dishes. I've been preparing this fresh-tasting version for several years. Bob requests it often, and even his mom thinks it's very good.
—*Mary Kay Morris, Cokato, Minnesota*

1/2 **pound sliced bacon, diced**
3 **tablespoons olive *or* vegetable oil**
2 **large onions, chopped**
3 **pounds fresh tomatoes, peeled, seeded and chopped *or* 2 cans (14-1/2 ounces *each*) diced tomatoes, undrained**
3 **garlic cloves, minced**
2 **tablespoons minced fresh tarragon *or* 2 teaspoons dried tarragon**
1/2 **teaspoon salt**
1/4 **teaspoon pepper**
Pinch to 1/8 teaspoon cayenne pepper
1/4 **cup minced fresh parsley**
1 **pound fettuccine**
Shredded Parmesan cheese

In a skillet, cook bacon until crisp. Remove to paper towels. Drain, reserving 1 tablespoon drippings. Add oil and onions to drippings; saute until tender, about 5 minutes. Add tomatoes and garlic; simmer, uncovered, for 5 minutes. Stir in tarragon, salt, pepper and cayenne; cover and simmer for 20 minutes, stirring occasionally.

Meanwhile, cook fettuccine according to package directions. Add parsley to the tomato mixture; simmer 5 minutes longer. Stir in bacon. Drain fettuccine; top with tomato mixture. Sprinkle with Parmesan cheese. **Yield:** 4-6 servings.

Broccoli-Pasta Side Dish

(Pictured above)

I love to fix new recipes for my husband, Robert, and our children. With garlic and cheese, this is a tasty way to get kids to eat broccoli. It goes great with many main dishes. —*Judi Lacourse*
Mesa, Arizona

2-1/2 **pounds fresh broccoli**
2 **garlic cloves, minced**
1/3 **cup olive *or* vegetable oil**
1 **tablespoon butter *or* margarine**
1 **teaspoon salt**
1/4 **teaspoon pepper**
Pinch cayenne pepper
8 **ounces linguine *or* thin spaghetti**
Grated Romano *or* Parmesan cheese

Cut florets and tender parts of broccoli stems into bite-size pieces. In a large skillet, saute broccoli with garlic, oil, butter, salt, pepper and cayenne over medium heat for about 10 minutes or until just tender, stirring frequently. Menwhile, cook the pasta according to package directions. Drain and place in a serving dish; top with the broccoli mixture. Sprinkle with cheese. Serve immediately. **Yield:** 4-6 servings.

Stir-Fried Vegetables

(Pictured below and on page 56)

For a colorful nutritious blend of crisp-tender vegetables in a mildly seasoned sauce, try this recipe. There's no restriction on good taste! —Cindy Winter-Hartley
Cary, North Carolina

✓ Uses less fat, sugar or salt. Includes Nutritional Analysis and Diabetic Exchanges.

    2 medium green peppers, julienned
    2 medium sweet red peppers, julienned
    2 medium carrots, julienned
    2 cups broccoli florets
    3 tablespoons vegetable oil
    2 tablespoons light soy sauce
    1 teaspoon ground ginger
    6 green onions, thinly sliced
    2 tablespoons cornstarch
    1 cup reduced-sodium chicken broth
 1/4 cup cold water

In a large skillet or wok, saute the peppers, carrots and broccoli in oil until crisp-tender, about 3 minutes. Combine soy sauce and ginger; add to pan with onions. Cook and stir for 1 minute. Combine cornstarch, broth and water until smooth; gradually stir into vegetables. Bring to a boil; cook and stir for 2 minutes or until thickened. **Yield:** 4 servings.

Nutritional Analysis: One serving (1/2 cup) equals 183 calories, 308 mg sodium, 1 mg cholesterol, 20 g carbohydrate, 4 g protein, 1 g fat. **Diabetic Exchanges:** 2 vegetable, 2 fat, 1/2 starch.

Fried Rice

(Pictured below and on page 56)

Instead of reheating leftover cooked rice, turn it into this tasty new side dish. It's a snap to put together and tastes as good as any restaurant variety.
—Suzanne McKinley, Lyons, Georgia

✓ Uses less fat, sugar or salt. Includes Nutritional Analysis and Diabetic Exchanges.

 1/2 cup chopped green pepper
 Egg substitute equivalent to 2 eggs
    4 cups cooked rice
    2 tablespoons light soy sauce

In a skillet coated with nonstick cooking spray, saute green pepper until crisp-tender. Add egg substitute; cook and stir until egg is completely set. Chop egg into small pieces. Add rice and soy sauce; heat through. **Yield:** 9 servings.

Nutritional Analysis: One serving (1/2 cup) equals 105 calories, 226 mg sodium, trace cholesterol, 20 g carbohydrate, 4 g protein, 1 g fat. **Diabetic Exchanges:** 1 starch, 1 vegetable.

Continental Zucchini

(Pictured above)

Zucchini are big and plentiful here, and people often joke about using them up before they multiply! This easy recipe wins raves at church gatherings.
—Martha Fehl, Brookville, Indiana

✓ Uses less fat, sugar or salt. Includes Nutritional Analysis and Diabetic Exchanges.

- 1 tablespoon vegetable oil
- 1 pound zucchini (about 3 small), cubed
- 1 to 2 garlic cloves, minced
- 1 jar (2 ounces) chopped pimientos, drained
- 1 can (15-1/2 ounces) whole kernel corn, drained
- 1 teaspoon salt, optional
- 1/4 teaspoon lemon-pepper seasoning
- 1/2 cup shredded mozzarella cheese

Heat oil in a large skillet. Saute zucchini and garlic for 3-4 minutes. Add pimientos, corn, salt if desired and lemon-pepper; cook and stir for 2-3 minutes or until zucchini is tender. Sprinkle with cheese and heat until cheese is melted. **Yield:** 6 servings.
Nutritional Analysis: One serving (prepared with low-fat mozzarella cheese and without added salt) equals 131 calories, 107 mg sodium, 10 mg cholesterol, 15 g carbohydrate, 8 g protein, 6 g fat. **Diabetic Exchanges:** 1 vegetable, 1 meat, 1/2 starch.

Three-Rice Pilaf

My family's favorite rice dish is this tempting medley of white, brown and wild rice. I prepare it as a side dish or a stuffing. —Ricki Bingham, Ogden, Utah

- 1/2 cup uncooked brown rice
- 1/2 cup finely chopped carrots
- 1/2 cup chopped onion

- 1/2 cup sliced fresh mushrooms
- 2 tablespoons vegetable oil
- 1/2 cup uncooked wild rice
- 3 cups chicken broth
- 1/4 teaspoon dried thyme
- 1/4 teaspoon dried rosemary, crushed
- 1/2 cup uncooked long grain rice
- 1/3 cup chopped dried apricots
- 2 tablespoons minced green onions
- 1/4 teaspoon salt
- 1/8 teaspoon pepper
- 1/2 cup chopped pecans, toasted

In a large saucepan, saute brown rice, carrots, onion and mushrooms in oil for 10 minutes or until rice is golden. Add wild rice, broth, thyme and rosemary; bring to a boil. Reduce heat; cover and simmer for 25 minutes.
Stir in long grain rice; cover and simmer for 25 minutes or until liquid is absorbed and wild rice is tender. Remove from the heat; stir in apricots, green onions, salt and pepper. Cover and let stand for 5 minutes. Sprinkle with pecans just before serving. **Yield:** 8-10 servings.

Baked Onion Rings

Everyone loves the flavor of these homemade onion rings. The coating is delightfully seasoned.
—Peggy Burdick, Burlington, Michigan

✓ Uses less fat, sugar or salt. Includes Nutritional Analysis and Diabetic Exchanges.

- 1-1/2 cups crushed cornflakes
- 2 teaspoons sugar
- 1 teaspoon paprika
- 1/4 teaspoon seasoned salt
- 1/4 teaspoon garlic salt
- 2 large sweet onions

Egg substitute equivalent to 2 eggs

In a large bowl, combine the first five ingredients; set aside. Cut onions into 1/2-in.-thick slices. Separate into rings, reserving the small rings for another use. In a small mixing bowl, beat egg substitute until frothy. Dip onion rings into egg, then into crumb mixture, coating well.
Place in a single layer on baking sheets coated with nonstick cooking spray. Bake at 375° for 15-20 minutes or until onions are tender and coating is crispy. **Yield:** about 6 servings.
Nutritional Analysis: One serving (four onion rings) equals 143 calories, 442 mg sodium, trace cholesterol, 30 g carbohydrate, 5 g protein, 1 g fat. **Diabetic Exchange:** 2 starch.

Kathy's Herbed Corn

(Pictured below)

My husband and I agreed that the original recipe for this corn needed a little jazzing up, so I added the thyme and cayenne pepper. Now fresh summer corn makes a regular appearance on our grill.
—*Kathy vonKorff, North College Hill, Ohio*

- 1/2 cup butter *or* margarine, softened
- 2 tablespoons minced fresh parsley
- 2 tablespoons minced fresh chives
- 1 teaspoon dried thyme
- 1/2 teaspoon salt
- 1/4 teaspoon cayenne pepper
- 8 ears sweet corn, husked

In a small bowl, combine the first six ingredients. Spread 1 tablespoon over each ear of corn. Wrap corn individually in heavy-duty foil. Grill, covered, over medium heat for 10-15 minutes, turning frequently, or until corn is tender. **Yield:** 8 servings.

Marinated Brussels Sprouts

This unique and refreshing relish makes a lovely addition to any table. I especially like serving it at backyard barbecues. —*Marie Hattrup, The Dalles, Oregon*

 Uses less fat, sugar or salt. Includes Nutritional Analysis and Diabetic Exchanges.

- 1 package (10 ounces) frozen brussels sprouts
- 1 cup Italian salad dressing
- 1 tablespoon finely chopped onion

- 1 garlic clove, minced
- 1/2 teaspoon dill weed

Cook brussels sprouts according to package directions; drain. Combine remaining ingredients; pour over sprouts and toss to coat. Cover and refrigerate. **Yield:** 2-1/2 cups.
Nutritional Analysis: One 1/2-cup serving (prepared with fat-free salad dressing) equals 41 calories, 470 mg sodium, 0 cholesterol, 8 g carbohydrate, 2 g protein, trace fat. **Diabetic Exchange:** 1-1/2 vegetable.

— ☕ ☕ ☕ —

Grilled Mushrooms

(Pictured above)

Mushrooms cooked over hot coals always taste good, but this easy recipe makes the mushrooms taste fantastic. As the mother of two children, I love to cook entire meals on the grill. It's fun spending time outdoors with the kids.
—*Melanie Knoll*
Marshalltown, Iowa

- 1/2 pound whole fresh mushrooms (medium size work best)
- 1/4 cup butter *or* margarine, melted
- 1/2 teaspoon dill weed
- 1/2 teaspoon garlic salt

Thread mushrooms on skewers. Combine butter, dill and garlic salt; brush over mushrooms. Grill over hot heat for 10-15 minutes, basting and turning every 5 minutes. **Yield:** 4 servings.

— ☕ ☕ ☕ —

Zesty Buttered Peas

Whenever I share this recipe with someone, I include a small jar of my homegrown savory. This is my favorite recipe using that lively herb. —*Claire Talone*
Morrisville, Pennsylvania

✓ Uses less fat, sugar or salt. Includes Nutritional Analysis and Diabetic Exchanges.

- 2 tablespoons butter *or* margarine
- 1 package (10 ounces) frozen peas, thawed
- 1 cup sliced celery
- 1/2 cup chopped onion
- 1 tablespoon minced fresh savory *or* 1-1/2 teaspoons dried savory
- 1/2 teaspoon salt, optional
- 2 tablespoons diced pimientos

Melt butter in a heavy saucepan; add the next five ingredients. Cover and cook over medium heat for 6-8 minutes or until vegetables are tender. Stir in pimientos. **Yield:** 6 servings.

Nutritional Analysis: One serving (prepared with margarine and without salt) equals 74 calories, 93 mg sodium, 0 cholesterol, 8 g carbohydrate, 2 g protein, 4 g fat. **Diabetic Exchanges:** 1 fat, 1/2 starch.

— 🥄 🥄 🥄 —

Nutty Onion Green Beans

(Pictured below)

I never liked green beans until I tried this recipe. The beans, onion and chopped pecans are coated in a delicious orange-mustard sauce.   —Donna Buckley
Western Springs, Illinois

- 1/2 pound fresh green beans, cut in half
- 1 small red onion, sliced and separated into rings
- 1/3 cup chopped pecans
- 3 tablespoons butter *or* margarine
- 2 tablespoons brown sugar
- 2 tablespoons orange juice
- 1 tablespoon Dijon mustard
- 1/2 teaspoon salt

Place beans in a saucepan and cover with water; bring to a boil. Cook, uncovered, for 8-10 minutes or until crisp-tender; drain and set aside.

In a skillet, cook onion and pecans in butter until onion is tender. In a small bowl, combine the brown sugar, orange juice, mustard and salt; stir into the onion mixture. Cook 2-3 minutes longer or until sauce begins to thicken. Stir in beans; heat through. **Yield:** 3-4 servings.

Sesame Broccoli

(Pictured above)

With a tongue-tingling sauce and a topping of crunchy sesame seeds, broccoli makes a fancy but fuss-free side dish. This vegetable is so nutritious that it's great to have a special way to serve it.   —Doris Heath
Bryson City, North Carolina

✓ Uses less fat, sugar or salt. Includes Nutritional Analysis and Diabetic Exchanges.

- 1 package (10 ounces) frozen broccoli spears
- 1 tablespoon vegetable oil
- 1 tablespoon soy sauce
- 1 tablespoon sugar
- 2 teaspoons cider vinegar
- 2 teaspoons sesame seeds, toasted

Cook broccoli according to package directions. Meanwhile, in a small saucepan, combine oil, soy sauce, sugar and vinegar; heat on medium until sugar is dissolved. Drain broccoli; drizzle with soy sauce mixture and sprinkle with sesame seeds. **Yield:** 4 servings.

Nutritional Analysis: One serving (prepared with light soy sauce) equals 81 calories, 143 mg sodium, trace cholesterol, 9 g carbohydrate, 2 g protein, 3 g fat. **Diabetic Exchanges:** 2 vegetable, 1/2 fat.

Campfire Potatoes

(Pictured below and on page 56)

We like grilling because it's a no-fuss way to make a meal. This pleasing potato recipe is one we use often! The onion, cheddar cheese and Worcestershire sauce combine to make a super side dish for any grilled meat. Plus, cooking in the foil makes cleanup a breeze.
—JoAnn Dettbarn, Brainerd, Minnesota

    5 medium potatoes, peeled and thinly sliced
    1 medium onion, sliced
    6 tablespoons butter *or* margarine
1/3 cup shredded cheddar cheese
    2 tablespoons minced fresh parsley
    1 tablespoon Worcestershire sauce
Salt and pepper to taste
1/3 cup chicken broth

Place the potatoes and onion on a large piece of heavy-duty foil (about 20 in. x 20 in.); dot with butter. Combine the cheese, parsley, Worcestershire sauce, salt and pepper; sprinkle over potatoes. Fold foil up around potatoes and add broth. Seal the foil tightly. Grill, covered, over medium heat for 35-40 minutes or until the potatoes are tender. **Yield:** 4-6 servings.

Asparagus Mornay

(Pictured above)

When I was growing up on my parents' dairy farm, we always had a large asparagus patch. I still love asparagus, but my husband and two children weren't that eager to eat it until I found this recipe. Now even my toughest vegetable critic, our son Aaron, enjoys these savory spears. —Linda McKee
Big Prairie, Ohio

1-1/2 pounds fresh asparagus, trimmed
    1 tablespoon butter *or* margarine
    1 tablespoon all-purpose flour
    1 cup half-and-half cream
1/2 teaspoon chicken bouillon granules
1/8 teaspoon ground nutmeg
1/8 teaspoon salt
1/2 cup shredded Swiss cheese
    2 tablespoons crushed butter-flavored crackers

In a skillet, cook asparagus in a small amount of water until crisp-tender, about 6-8 minutes; drain. Arrange spears in the bottom of a greased 1-1/2-qt. baking dish; set aside and keep warm.
   In a small saucepan, melt butter over low heat. Add flour; cook and stir for 1 minute. Whisk in the cream, bouillon, nutmeg and salt; bring to a boil over medium heat. Cook and stir for 2 minutes. Remove from the heat; stir in cheese until melted. Pour over the asparagus. Sprinkle with cracker crumbs. Broil 6 in. from the heat for 3-5 minutes or until lightly browned. **Yield:** 4-6 servings.

1/4 teaspoon salt
1/8 teaspoon pepper
1/2 cup shredded Swiss cheese
1/2 cup grated Parmesan cheese

Slice the onions into 1/2-in.-thick rings; saute in butter until tender. Place in a greased 8-in. square baking dish. In a bowl, stir broth, cream, flour, salt and pepper until smooth; pour over onions. Sprinkle with cheeses. Bake, uncovered, at 350° for 25-30 minutes or until cheese is golden brown and mixture is bubbly. **Yield:** 8 servings.

—— 🏆 🏆 🏆 ——

Sweet 'n' Tangy Freezer Pickles

(Pictured above)

A batch of these puckery slices can keep in the freezer for up to 6 weeks—if they last that long. Mine never do.
—*Jean Vance, Charlotte, North Carolina*

10 to 12 medium pickling cucumbers
  (about 2 pounds), thinly sliced
3 medium onions, thinly sliced
1 large green pepper, chopped
3 tablespoons salt, *divided*
2 cups sugar
1 cup white vinegar
1 tablespoon celery seed

In a large container, combine cucumbers, onions, green pepper and 2 tablespoons salt. Cover with crushed ice; mix well. Refrigerate for 8 hours.

Drain; rinse and drain again. In a saucepan, combine the sugar, vinegar, celery seed and remaining salt. Bring to a boil; cook and stir for 1 minute. Spoon over cucumber mixture. Pour into jars or freezer containers. Cool. Top with lids. Cover and freeze for up to 6 weeks. Thaw at room temperature for 4 hours before serving. **Yield:** 4 pints.

—— 🏆 🏆 🏆 ——

Onions Au Gratin

Most everyone cooks with onions, but few think of serving them as a vegetable side dish. My family really loves this recipe. —*Christine Halandras*
Meeker, Colorado

6 medium yellow onions
1/4 cup butter *or* margarine
1/2 cup beef broth
1/2 cup whipping cream
2 tablespoons all-purpose flour

Carrots in Almond Sauce

(Pictured below)

Here's an easy way to add elegance and flavor to plain carrots. The touch of dill lends just the right "zip".
—*Carol Anderson, Salt Lake City, Utah*

1 pound carrots, julienned
1/2 cup thinly sliced green onions
1/4 cup butter *or* margarine
1 teaspoon cornstarch
1/2 cup water
1/2 teaspoon chicken bouillon granules
1/2 teaspoon dill weed
1/8 teaspoon pepper
1/4 cup sliced almonds, toasted

In a saucepan, cook carrots in a small amount of water until crisp-tender; drain. Transfer to a serving bowl and keep warm. In the same pan, saute onions in butter until tender. Combine cornstarch and water until smooth; stir into onions. Add bouillon, dill and pepper. Bring to a boil over medium heat; cook and stir for 1 minute or until thickened and bubbly. Stir in almonds. Pour over carrots; stir to coat. **Yield:** 6 servings.

Ultimate Scalloped Potatoes

(Pictured below)

My husband found this recipe when I called and informed him we were going to have guests for dinner. This tasty variation on traditional scalloped potatoes is dressed up with garlic, Swiss cheese and Parmesan cheese. —Glenda Malan, Lake Forest, California

1 teaspoon butter *or* margarine, softened
1 cup whipping cream
1/3 cup milk
1 teaspoon salt
1/2 teaspoon pepper
2 garlic cloves, crushed
6 medium potatoes
1 cup (4 ounces) shredded Swiss cheese
1/4 cup shredded Parmesan cheese

Grease a shallow 1-1/2-qt. baking dish with the butter; set aside. In a saucepan, combine cream, milk, salt, pepper and garlic. Cook just until bubbles begin to form around sides of pan. Remove from the heat; cool for 10 minutes.

Peel and thinly slice the potatoes; pat dry with paper towels. Layer half of the potatoes in prepared baking dish; top with half of the cream mixture and half of the cheeses. Repeat layers. Bake, uncovered, at 350° for 55-65 minutes or until potatoes are tender. Let stand for 5-10 minutes before serving. **Yield:** 6 servings.

Stuffed Baked Potatoes

(Pictured above and on page 56)

My mom gave me the recipe for these twice-baked potatoes, and I altered them by adding garlic, bacon and green onions. They're perfect for a potluck or even an elegant meal. My two boys absolutely love them! —Kristyn Drews, Omaha, Nebraska

5 medium baking potatoes
1/4 cup butter *or* margarine, softened
2 cups (8 ounces) shredded cheddar cheese, *divided*
3/4 cup sour cream
1 envelope ranch salad dressing mix
1 tablespoon snipped chives
1 garlic clove, minced
Crumbled cooked bacon and chopped green onions

Bake potatoes at 400° for 1 hour or until tender. Reduce heat to 375°. Cut each potato in half lengthwise; scoop out the pulp, leaving a thin shell. In a large mixing bowl, beat the pulp with butter. Stir in 1 cup of cheese, sour cream, salad dressing mix, chives and garlic. Spoon into potato shells. Sprinkle with remaining cheese.

Place on a baking sheet. Bake for 15-20 minutes or until heated through. Top with bacon and green onions. **Yield:** 10 servings.

Asparagus Nut Stir-Fry

(Pictured on front cover)

This pretty side dish is an excellent way to serve one of the first springtime vegetables from our garden. —Margaret Souders, Elizabethtown, Pennsylvania

1-1/2 pounds fresh asparagus spears, trimmed
   2 tablespoons vegetable oil
  1/4 cup thinly sliced sweet red pepper
  1/4 cup coarsely chopped walnuts
  1/4 teaspoon ground ginger *or* 1 teaspoon
      minced fresh gingerroot
   1 garlic clove, minced
  1/8 teaspoon crushed red pepper flakes
   2 tablespoons chicken broth
   2 tablespoons soy sauce
  1/2 teaspoon sugar
  1/2 teaspoon salt

In a skillet or wok, stir-fry asparagus in oil until crisp-tender, about 10 minutes. Remove and keep warm. In the same skillet, stir-fry red pepper, walnuts, ginger, garlic and pepper flakes for 2 minutes or until red pepper is crisp-tender. Stir in the broth, soy sauce, sugar and salt; heat through. Add asparagus; stir to coat. **Yield:** 6 servings.

— ☕ ☕ ☕ —

Chunky Rhubarb Applesauce

Our backyard was filled with rhubarb when I was growing up in Illinois, and Mom would always add some to her applesauce. —Cheryl Miller
Fort Collins, Colorado

  1 pound rhubarb, trimmed and cut into
     1/2-inch chunks
  2 pounds baking apples, peeled, cored and
     cut into 1/2-inch chunks
1/2 to 1 cup sugar
 1/4 teaspoon ground cinnamon
 1/8 teaspoon ground nutmeg

Place rhubarb, apples and sugar to taste in a large saucepan. Cover and simmer until fruit is soft, about 40-45 minutes. Stir in cinnamon and nutmeg. Serve warm or cold. **Yield:** 3-4 cups.

— ☕ ☕ ☕ —

Three-Bean Tomato Cups

(Pictured above right)

Cilantro and cumin give this delightful salad a Mexican flair. Served in hollowed-out tomatoes, the tasty bean blend makes a pretty addition to a ladies' luncheon or special-occasion meal.
—Audrey Green Ballon, Kentwood, Louisiana

3/4 pound fresh green beans, cut
    into 2-inch pieces
1/2 pound fresh wax beans, cut
    into 2-inch pieces

   1 can (15 ounces) black beans,
     rinsed and drained
   1 medium sweet red pepper, cut
     into 1-1/2-inch strips
   3 green onions, sliced
  1/4 cup minced fresh cilantro *or* parsley
  1/4 cup olive *or* vegetable oil
   3 tablespoons red wine vinegar
     or cider vinegar
   1 teaspoon ground cumin
   1 garlic clove, minced
  1/2 teaspoon salt
  1/4 teaspoon pepper
   6 large firm tomatoes

Place the green and wax beans in a saucepan and cover with water; bring to a boil. Cook, uncovered, for 8-10 minutes or until crisp-tender. Drain and place in a large bowl. Add the black beans, red pepper, onions and cilantro.

In a jar with a tight-fitting lid, combine the oil, vinegar, cumin, garlic, salt and pepper; shake well. Pour over bean mixture and toss to coat. Cover and refrigerate for 30 minutes.

To serve, cut a 1/4-in. slice off the top of each tomato; scoop out and discard the pulp. Using a slotted spoon, fill each tomato cup with bean mixture. **Yield:** 6 servings.

6 bacon strips
1/2 cup chopped onion
2 tablespoons all-purpose flour
2 garlic cloves, minced
1/2 teaspoon salt
1/2 teaspoon pepper
1 cup (8 ounces) sour cream
3-1/2 cups fresh *or* frozen whole kernel corn
1 tablespoon chopped fresh parsley
1 tablespoon chopped fresh chives

In a skillet, cook bacon until crisp. Drain, reserving 2 tablespoons drippings. Crumble bacon; set aside. Saute onion in drippings until tender. Add flour, garlic, salt and pepper. Cook and stir until bubbly; cook and stir 1 minute longer. Remove from the heat; stir in sour cream until smooth. Add corn, parsley and half of the bacon; mix well.

Transfer to a 1-qt. baking dish. Sprinkle with remaining bacon. Bake, uncovered, at 350° for 20-25 minutes or until heated through. Sprinkle with chives. **Yield:** 6-8 servings.

— 🏆 🏆 🏆 —

Stuffed Butternut Squash

(Pictured above)

I enjoy experimenting with new recipes and that's how I came up with this idea. Ham, mustard, apple and brown sugar go so well with butternut squash.
—*Bev Spain, Bellville, Ohio*

3 small butternut squash (about 1-1/2 pounds *each*)
2 cups cubed fully cooked ham
1 cup soft bread crumbs
1/2 cup shredded tart apple
1/4 cup packed brown sugar
2 tablespoons prepared mustard

Cut squash in half lengthwise; discard seeds. Place squash, cut side down, in a 15-in. x 10-in. x 1-in. baking pan. Fill pan with hot water to a depth of 1/2 in. Bake, uncovered, at 350° for 30 minutes.

Combine remaining ingredients. Turn squash cut side up; stuff with ham mixture. Cover stem end with foil. Bake at 350° for 30 minutes or until squash is tender. **Yield:** 6 servings.

— 🏆 🏆 🏆 —

Corn and Bacon Casserole

Corn is my three boys' favorite vegetable, so we eat a lot of it. This recipe has been a favorite for years. My husband, Bob, and the boys really enjoy it.
—*Marcia Hostetter, Canton, New York*

Italian Herb Blend

I dry the herbs from my garden for this Italian blend. I store it in airtight containers, then sprinkle it in soups and stews all winter. —*Frances Tiocano Morgan Hill, California*

6 tablespoons dried basil
2 tablespoons dried oregano
1 tablespoon dried marjoram
1 tablespoon dried thyme

Combine all ingredients. Use in stews, soups, meat loaf, spaghetti sauce and salad dressings.

— 🏆 🏆 🏆 —

Savory Steak Rub

Marjoram stars in this recipe. I use the rub on a variety of beef cuts...it locks in the natural juices of the meat for mouth-watering results. —*Donna Brockett Kingfisher, Oklahoma*

1 tablespoon dried marjoram
1 tablespoon dried basil
2 teaspoons garlic powder
2 teaspoons dried thyme
1 teaspoon dried rosemary, crushed
3/4 teaspoon dried oregano

Combine all ingredients; store in a covered container. Rub over steaks before grilling or broiling. Will season four to five steaks. **Yield:** 1/4 cup.

Mint Jelly

One whiff is all it takes to tell what we grow on our farm—peppermint! Harvesting 300 acres is hard work, but the invigorating scent keeps our taste buds tuned for minty treats. I use fresh mint or mint oil frequently in my cooking and baking. Try this aromatic jelly on lamb or oven-fresh biscuits. —Kandy Clarke
Columbia Falls, Montana

    1 cup packed peppermint leaves
    2 cups water
6-1/2 cups sugar
    1 cup white vinegar
  1/2 teaspoon butter *or* margarine
    1 package (6 ounces) liquid fruit pectin
    3 to 4 drops green food coloring

In a Dutch oven, bring mint and water to a boil. Boil for 1 minute. Remove from the heat and pour through a fine sieve, reserving mint liquid. Discard leaves. Return liquid to Dutch oven. Add sugar, vinegar and butter; bring to a boil, stirring constantly. Quickly add contents of both pouches of pectin; bring to a full boil.

Boil for 1 minute, stirring constantly. Remove from the heat; skim off any foam. Add food coloring. Immediately fill hot jars, leaving 1/4-in. headspace. Adjust caps. Refrigerate or process in a boiling-water bath for 5 minutes. **Yield:** about 6 half-pints.

— 🥄 🥄 🥄 —

Tangy Barbecue Sauce

(Pictured at right)

My mother-in-law created this recipe, and we just can't get enough of her delectable sauce! I always keep a little out of the basting dish prior to using it on the grill so we have some to serve at the table. It tastes terrific on any grilled meat. —Mary Kaye Rackowitz
Marysville, Washington

    1 cup ketchup
    2 tablespoons lemon juice
    2 tablespoons cider vinegar
  1/4 cup packed brown sugar
    2 teaspoons prepared mustard
    1 teaspoon salt
  1/2 to 1 teaspoon hot pepper sauce
    1 bay leaf
    1 garlic clove, minced
  1/2 cup water
    2 teaspoons Worcestershire sauce

Combine all of the ingredients in a small saucepan; bring to a boil, stirring occasionally. Reduce heat; cover and simmer for 30 minutes. Discard bay leaf.

Use as a basting sauce when grilling chicken, pork or beef. **Yield:** 1-1/2 cups.

— 🥄 🥄 🥄 —

Dill Mustard

I pick up small, decorative canning jars at rummage sales or in hardware stores to fill with the zesty mustard I make to give to friends. —Sue Braunschweig
Delafield, Wisconsin

    1 cup ground mustard
    1 cup cider vinegar
  3/4 cup sugar
  1/4 cup water
    2 teaspoons salt
1-1/2 teaspoons dill weed
    2 eggs, lightly beaten

In the top of a double boiler, combine mustard, vinegar, sugar, water, salt and dill. Cover and let stand at room temperature for 4 hours.

Bring water in bottom of double boiler to a boil. Add eggs to mustard mixture. Cook and stir until thickened and a thermometer reads 160°, about 10 minutes. Cool. Store in the refrigerator. **Yield:** about 2 cups.

Crisp Sweet Relish
(Pictured above)

Friends shared their garden bounty, so I needed a recipe to make good use of cucumbers. I adapted this recipe from one my mom used. This mouth-watering relish even won a blue ribbon at our county fair.
—*Joyce Hallisey, Mt. Gilead, North Carolina*

8 cups ground cucumbers (about 5 pounds)
4 cups ground onions
2 cups ground carrots
5 tablespoons salt
7 cups sugar
4 cups white vinegar
2 teaspoons celery seed
1 teaspoon ground turmeric
1 teaspoon ground nutmeg
1/2 teaspoon pepper

Combine the cucumbers, onions and carrots in a large bowl; sprinkle with the salt. Cover with ice cubes. Let stand for 6 hours. Drain; rinse and drain thoroughly. In a large kettle, combine sugar, vinegar, celery seed, turmeric, nutmeg and pepper. Add vegetables; bring to a boil over medium heat, stirring often. Reduce heat; simmer, uncovered, for 20 minutes, stirring occasionally.
Pack the hot mixture into hot jars, leaving 1/2-in. headspace. Adjust caps. Process for 10 minutes in a boiling-water bath. **Yield:** 8 pints.

Roasted Corn Salsa

This colorful salsa goes well with barbecued meats, but it's also tasty served with chips. It's one of those recipes that fits in just about anywhere, anytime.
—*Nancy Horsburgh, Everett, Ontario*

✓ Uses less fat, sugar or salt. Includes Nutritional Analysis and Diabetic Exchanges.

2 medium ears sweet corn in husks
2 medium tomatoes, chopped
1 small onion, chopped
2 tablespoons minced fresh cilantro *or* parsley
1 tablespoon lime juice
1 tablespoon finely chopped green pepper
1 tablespoon finely chopped sweet red pepper
1 teaspoon minced seeded jalapeno pepper
1/4 teaspoon salt
Dash pepper

Peel back husks of corn but don't remove; remove silk. Replace husks and tie with kitchen string. Place corn in a bowl and cover with water; soak for 20 minutes. Drain.
Grill corn, covered, over medium-high heat for 20-25 minutes or until husks are blackened and corn is tender, turning several times. Cool. Remove corn from cobs and place in a bowl. Add remaining ingredients. **Yield:** about 2-1/2 cups.
Nutritional Analysis: One serving (1/4 cup) equals 24 calories, 0 fat (0 saturated fat), 0 cholesterol, 64 mg sodium, 5 g carbohydrate, 1 g fiber, 1 g protein. **Diabetic Exchange:** 1 vegetable.

Basil Parsley Pesto

Pesto is an uncooked Italian sauce traditionally made from basil, olive oil, garlic, Parmesan cheese and sometimes pine nuts. This recipe is a favorite shared by Taste of Home's food editor, Janaan Cunningham.

1 cup tightly packed fresh basil *or* cilantro leaves
1 cup tightly packed fresh parsley leaves
1 to 2 garlic cloves
1/2 cup olive *or* vegetable oil
1/2 cup grated Parmesan cheese
1/4 teaspoon salt

Combine all ingredients in a food processor; cover and puree until smooth. Toss with hot cooked pasta or vegetables, spread on French bread or use in any recipe calling for pesto. Can be refrigerated for several weeks or frozen in a tightly covered container. **Yield:** 3/4 cup.

Four-Tomato Salsa

(Pictured below and on page 56)

A variety of tomatoes, onions and peppers makes this chunky salsa so good. It's super with tortilla chips or meat. —Connie Siese, Wayne, Michigan

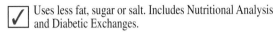
Uses less fat, sugar or salt. Includes Nutritional Analysis and Diabetic Exchanges.

    7 plum tomatoes, chopped
    7 medium tomatoes, chopped
    3 medium yellow tomatoes, chopped
    3 medium orange tomatoes, chopped
    1 teaspoon salt
    2 tablespoons lime juice
    2 tablespoons olive *or* vegetable oil
    1 medium white onion, chopped
  2/3 cup chopped red onion
    2 green onions, chopped
  1/2 cup *each* chopped sweet red, orange,
        yellow and green pepper
    3 pepperoncinis, chopped
    3 pickled sweet banana wax peppers, chopped
  1/2 cup minced fresh parsley
    2 tablespoons minced fresh cilantro *or*
        additional parsley
    1 tablespoon dried chervil

In a colander, combine the tomatoes and salt. Let drain for 10 minutes. Transfer to a large bowl. Stir in the lime juice, oil, onions, peppers, parsley, cilantro and chervil. Store in the refrigerator or freezer. **Yield:** 14 cups.

Nutritional Analysis: One serving (1/4 cup salsa) equals 16 calories, 1 g fat (0 saturated fat), 0 cholesterol, 63 mg sodium, 3 g carbohydrate, 1 g fiber, 1 g protein. **Diabetic Exchange:** Free food.

Editor's Note: Look for pepperoncinis (pickled peppers) and pickled banana peppers in the pickle and olive aisle of your grocery store.

Calico Chowchow

(Pictured above)

I make this special garden-fresh relish each fall. It goes well with both hot and cold meats. —Doris Haycroft Westbank, British Columbia

    7 cups shredded cabbage (about 1 small
        head)
    4 cups fresh corn (about 5 ears)
    4 cups cauliflowerets (about 1 small head)
    2 cups diced sweet red pepper
    1 cup diced green pepper
    1 cup chopped onion
  1/4 cup canning salt
    7 cups water, *divided*
3-1/2 cups packed brown sugar
  1/2 cup all-purpose flour
  1/4 cup ground mustard
    1 tablespoon celery seed
    2 teaspoons ground turmeric
1-1/2 teaspoons salt
    5 cups white vinegar

In a large bowl, combine the first six ingredients; sprinkle with canning salt. Add 6 cups water; cover and refrigerate for 4 hours. Drain and rinse well.

In a large heavy saucepan or Dutch oven, combine the brown sugar, flour, mustard, celery seed, turmeric and salt. Stir in vinegar and remaining water until smooth. Bring to a boil; cook and stir for 5 minutes or until thickened. Add vegetables; bring to a boil. Simmer, uncovered, for 8-10 minutes or until crisp-tender.

Pack the hot mixture into hot jars, leaving 1/4-in. headspace. Adjust caps. Process for 15 minutes in a boiling-water bath. **Yield:** 7 pints.

5-1/2 **pounds apples, peeled and finely chopped**
    4 **cups sugar**
    2 **to 3 teaspoons ground cinnamon**
1/4 **teaspoon ground cloves**
1/4 **teaspoon salt**

Place apples in a slow cooker. Combine sugar, cinnamon, cloves and salt; pour over apples and mix well. Cover and cook on high for 1 hour. Reduce heat to low; cover and cook for 9-11 hours or until thickened and dark brown, stirring occasionally (stir more frequently as it thickens to prevent sticking).

    Uncover and cook on low 1 hour longer. If desired, stir with a wire whisk until smooth. Spoon into freezer containers, leaving 1/2-in. headspace. Cover and refrigerate or freeze. **Yield:** 4 pints.

Holiday Cranberry Chutney
(Pictured below)

A chunky chutney like this one makes a lovely gift in a decorated jar. It's great served alongside a main dish or as an appetizer. —Cheryl Lottman
Stillwater, Minnesota

    1 **bag (12 ounces) fresh *or* frozen**
      cranberries
1-1/4 **cups sugar**
   3/4 **cup water**
    1 **large tart apple, chopped**
    2 **teaspoons ground cinnamon**
    1 **teaspoon ground ginger**
 1/4 **teaspoon ground cloves**

In a saucepan, combine all ingredients; bring to a boil, stirring constantly. Reduce heat; simmer for 15-20 minutes or until apple is tender and mixture thickens. Cool completely. Store in the refrigerator. Serve as a condiment with pork, ham or chicken or over cream cheese with crackers. **Yield:** 3 cups.

Four-Berry Spread
(Pictured above and on page 56)

For a big berry taste, you can't beat this tasty spread. With a flavorful foursome of blackberries, blueberries, raspberries and strawberries, this lovely jam brightens any breakfast. —Marie St. Thomas
Sterling, Massachusetts

    1 **cup fresh *or* frozen blackberries**
    1 **cup fresh *or* frozen blueberries**
1-1/2 **cups fresh *or* frozen strawberries**
1-1/2 **cups fresh *or* frozen raspberries**
    1 **box (1-3/4 ounces) powdered fruit pectin**
    7 **cups sugar**

Crush berries in a large kettle. Stir in pectin; bring to a full rolling boil over high heat, stirring constantly. Stir in sugar; return to a full rolling boil. Boil for 1 minute, stirring constantly. Remove from the heat; skim off any foam.

    Pour hot mixture into hot jars, leaving 1/4-in. headspace. Adjust caps. Process for 10 minutes in a boiling-water bath. **Yield:** about 7 half-pints.

All-Day Apple Butter

I make several batches of this simple and delicious apple butter to freeze in jars. Depending on the sweetness of the apples used, you can adjust the sugar to taste. —Betty Ruenholl, Syracuse, Nebraska

Summer Berry Salsa

(Pictured below)

Other fruits are often used in relishes and sauces, but I decided to make one with my favorites—strawberries and blueberries. I get rave reviews when I serve this fruity, distinctive salsa over meat. It's also delicious atop a spinach or lettuce salad. —Diane Hixon
Niceville, Florida

✓ Uses less fat, sugar or salt. Includes Nutritional Analysis and Diabetic Exchanges.

```
1 pint fresh blueberries
1 pint fresh strawberries, chopped
1/4 cup sugar
2 tablespoons finely chopped onion
1 tablespoon lemon juice
1/2 teaspoon pepper
2 drops hot pepper sauce
1/4 cup slivered or sliced almonds, toasted
```

In a bowl, combine the first seven ingredients. Cover and refrigerate for 1 hour. Just before serving, stir in almonds. Serve with chicken, pork or fish. **Yield:** 4 cups.

Nutritional Analysis: One serving (1/4 cup) equals 42 calories, 2 mg sodium, 0 cholesterol, 8 g carbohydrate, 1 g protein, 1 g fat, 1 g fiber. **Diabetic Exchange:** 1/2 fruit.

Pineapple Chutney

(Pictured above)

I love relish, so when I discovered the recipe for this tangy chutney, I knew I had to try it. I've made it many times since to serve with ham and pork or as an appetizer over cream cheese. Its sweet, spicy flavor adds zing to any dish. —Shirley Watanabe
Kula, Hawaii

```
2 cans (20 ounces each) pineapple tidbits,
    drained
4 cups diced onion
3 cups packed brown sugar
2 cups golden raisins
2 cups cider vinegar
2 teaspoons salt
2 teaspoons mustard seed
2 teaspoons ground turmeric
4 teaspoons grated orange peel
2 teaspoons grated lemon peel
2 medium yellow banana peppers, seeded
    and chopped, optional*
```

In a saucepan over medium heat, combine all ingredients; bring to a boil. Reduce heat; simmer, uncovered, for 1 to 1-1/2 hours or until chutney reaches desired thickness. Refrigerate. Serve with meat or over cream cheese as an appetizer spread. **Yield:** about 6 cups.

*Editors Note: When cutting or seeding hot peppers, use rubber or plastic gloves to protect your hands. Avoid touching your face.

Main Dishes

From beef and seafood to chicken and pork, these favorite down-home entrees will surely satisfy every hearty appetite.

THE MAIN EVENTS. Clockwise from upper left: Seafood Lasagna (p. 88), Roasted Pork Loin (p. 86), Steak with Citrus Salsa (p. 83), Lemon Herbed Salmon (p. 89) and Orange Walnut Chicken (p. 101).

Overnight Apple French Toast

(Pictured below)

My in-laws own and operate an orchard, so we have an abundance of fruit fresh from the trees. This dish includes fresh apples, apple jelly and applesauce all in one recipe. It's a warm, hearty breakfast for busy days.
—Debra Blazer, Hegins, Pennsylvania

- 1 cup packed brown sugar
- 1/2 cup butter *or* margarine
- 2 tablespoons light corn syrup
- 2 large tart apples, peeled and sliced 1/4 inch thick
- 3 eggs
- 1 cup milk
- 1 teaspoon vanilla extract
- 9 slices day-old French bread (3/4 inch thick)

SYRUP:
- 1 cup applesauce
- 1 jar (10 ounces) apple jelly
- 1/2 teaspoon ground cinnamon
- 1/8 teaspoon ground cloves

In a small saucepan, cook brown sugar, butter and corn syrup until thickened, about 5-7 minutes. Pour into an ungreased 13-in. x 9-in. x 2-in. baking dish; arrange apples on top. In a bowl, beat eggs, milk and vanilla. Dip bread slices into the egg mixture for 1 minute; place over apples. Cover and refrigerate overnight.

Remove from the refrigerator 30 minutes before baking. Bake, uncovered, at 350° for 35-40 minutes. Combine syrup ingredients in a saucepan; cook and stir until heated through. Serve with French toast. **Yield:** 9 servings.

Sheepherder's Breakfast

(Pictured above)

My sister-in-law always made this delicious morning entree when we were camping. Served with toast, juice and milk or coffee, it's a sure hit with the breakfast crowd! One-dish casseroles like this were a big help while I was raising my nine children...now I've passed this recipe on to them.
—Pauletta Bushnell, Albany, Oregon

- 1 pound sliced bacon, diced
- 1 medium onion, chopped
- 1 package (26 ounces) frozen shredded hash brown potatoes, thawed
- 7 eggs

Salt and pepper to taste
- 2 cups (8 ounces) shredded cheddar cheese, optional

Chopped fresh parsley

In a large skillet, cook bacon and onion until bacon is crisp. Drain all but 1/2 cup of the drippings. Add hash browns to skillet; mix well. Cook over medium heat for 10 minutes, turning when browned. Make seven "wells" evenly spaced in the hash browns. Place one egg in each well. Sprinkle with salt and pepper. Sprinkle with cheese if desired. Cover and cook over low heat for about 10 minutes or until eggs are set. Garnish with parsley; serve immediately. **Yield:** 7 servings.

— 🛒 🛒 🛒 —

Italian Omelet

Garden vegetables and herbs give a savory zing to this fresh-tasting omelet. This is a flavorful meal with a salad and bread. —Dixie Terry, Marion, Illinois

1 cup sliced fresh mushrooms
1 cup sliced zucchini
3 tablespoons butter *or* margarine, *divided*
4 eggs
3 tablespoons water
1/4 teaspoon salt
1/4 teaspoon pepper
1/2 cup shredded mozzarella cheese
SAUCE:
1 tablespoon butter *or* margarine
1 medium tomato, chopped
2 tablespoons minced fresh parsley
1 garlic clove, minced
1/2 teaspoon dried basil
1/8 teaspoon salt

In an 8-in. nonstick skillet, saute mushrooms and zucchini in 2 tablespoons butter until tender; remove and keep warm. In the same skillet, melt remaining butter. In a bowl, beat eggs, water, salt and pepper. Pour into the skillet; cook over medium heat. As eggs set, lift edges, letting uncooked portion flow underneath.

When eggs are nearly set, spoon vegetable mixture over half of the omelet; sprinkle with cheese. Fold omelet in half over filling. Cover and cook for 1-2 minutes or until cheese is melted. Meanwhile, for sauce, melt butter in a small saucepan over medium heat. Add remaining ingredients. Cook and stir for 5 minutes or until heated through. Serve over omelet. **Yield:** 1-2 servings.

— 🍷 🍷 🍷 —

BLT Egg Bake

BLTs are a favorite at my house, so I created this recipe to combine those flavors in a "dressier" dish. It was such a hit, I served it to my church ladies' group at a brunch I hosted. I received lots of compliments that day. —Priscilla Detrick, Catoosa, Oklahoma

1/4 cup mayonnaise
5 slices bread, toasted
4 slices process American cheese
12 bacon strips, cooked and crumbled
4 eggs
1 medium tomato, halved and sliced
2 tablespoons butter *or* margarine
2 tablespoons all-purpose flour
1/4 teaspoon salt
1/8 teaspoon pepper
1 cup milk
1/2 cup shredded cheddar cheese
2 green onions, thinly sliced
Shredded lettuce

Spread mayonnaise on one side of each slice of toast and cut into small pieces. Arrange toast, may-
onnaise side up, in a greased 8-in. square baking dish. Top with cheese slices and bacon. In a skillet, fry eggs over medium heat until completely set; place over bacon. Top with tomato slices; set aside.

In a saucepan, melt butter. Stir in flour, salt and pepper until smooth. Gradually add milk. Bring to a boil; cook and stir for 2 minutes or until thickened. Pour over tomato. Sprinkle with cheddar cheese and onions. Bake, uncovered, at 325° for 10 minutes. Cut into squares; serve with lettuce. **Yield:** 4 servings.

— 🍷 🍷 🍷 —

Breakfast Patties

(Pictured below)

This homemade sausage is terrific because it's so lean, holds together well and shrinks very little when cooked. It's incredibly easy to mix up a batch and make any breakfast special. —Jeannine Stallings
East Helena, Montana

1/4 cup water
2 teaspoons salt
2 teaspoons rubbed sage
1 teaspoon pepper
1/2 teaspoon ground nutmeg
1/4 teaspoon crushed red pepper flakes
1/8 teaspoon ground ginger
2 pounds ground pork

In a bowl, combine water and seasonings. Add pork and mix well. Shape into eight 4-in. patties. In a skillet over medium heat, cook patties for 5-6 minutes on each side or until no longer pink in the center. **Yield:** 8 patties.

Puff Pastry Chicken Bundles

(Pictured below)

Inside these golden puff pastry "packages" are chicken breasts rolled with spinach, herbed cream cheese and walnuts. I like to serve this elegant entree to guests. —Brad Moritz, Limerick, Pennsylvania

- 8 boneless skinless chicken breast halves (about 6 ounces *each*)
- 1 teaspoon salt
- 1/2 teaspoon pepper
- 40 large spinach leaves
- 2 cartons (8 ounces *each*) spreadable chive and onion cream cheese
- 1/2 cup chopped walnuts, toasted
- 2 sheets frozen puff pastry, thawed
- 1 egg
- 1/2 teaspoon cold water

Cut a lengthwise slit in each chicken breast to within 1/2 in. of the other side; open meat so it lies flat. Cover with plastic wrap; pound to flatten to 1/8-in. thickness. Remove plastic wrap. Sprinkle salt and pepper over chicken.

In a saucepan, bring 1 in. of water to a boil; add spinach. Cover and cook 1-2 minutes or until wilted; drain. Place five spinach leaves on each chicken breast. Spoon 2 tablespoons of cream cheese down the center of each chicken breast; sprinkle with walnuts. Roll up chicken and tuck in ends.

Unroll puff pastry; cut into eight portions. Roll each into an 8-in. x 7-in. rectangle. Combine egg and cold water; brush over edges of pastry. Place chicken at one short end; roll up tightly, tucking in ends. Place in a greased 15-in. x 10-in. x 1-in. baking pan. Bake at 350° for 25-30 minutes or until golden brown. **Yield:** 8 servings.

Chicken Cordon Bleu Calzones

These calzones are a dressy alternative to a traditional chicken pie. They combine the delicate flavor of chicken cordon bleu with the impressive look of beef Wellington. —Kathy Gounaud, Warwick, Rhode Island

- 4 boneless skinless chicken breast halves (1 pound)
- 1 cup sliced fresh mushrooms
- 1/2 medium onion, chopped
- 2 tablespoons butter *or* margarine
- 3 tablespoons cornstarch
- 1-1/4 cups milk
- 1 tablespoon minced fresh basil *or* 1 teaspoon dried basil
- 1 teaspoon salt
- 1/4 teaspoon pepper
- 1 package (17-1/4 ounces) frozen puff pastry, thawed
- 8 thin slices deli ham
- 4 slices provolone cheese

Additional milk, optional

Place chicken in a greased 2-qt. baking dish; cover with water. Cover and bake at 350° for 30 minutes or until juices run clear. Meanwhile, in a skillet, saute mushrooms and onion in butter until tender. Combine cornstarch and milk until smooth; stir into skillet. Add seasonings. Bring to a boil; cook and stir for 2 minutes or until thickened.

Drain chicken. Cut pastry sheets in half widthwise. On one side of each half, place a chicken breast, 1/4 cup mushroom mixture, two ham slices and one cheese slice. Fold pastry over filling; seal edges. Place on a greased baking sheet. Brush tops with milk if desired. Bake at 400° for 15-20 minutes or until puffed and golden. **Yield:** 4 servings.

———— 📯 📯 📯 ————

Chicken 'n' Biscuits

This comforting casserole has a colorful medley of vegetables and chunky chicken topped with golden from-scratch biscuits. We savor this easy version of an old-fashioned favorite. —Marilyn Minnick Hillsboro, Indiana

☑ Uses less fat, sugar or salt. Includes Nutritional Analysis and Diabetic Exchanges.

- 1 medium onion, chopped
- 2 teaspoons canola *or* vegetable oil
- 1/4 cup all-purpose flour
- 1/2 teaspoon dried basil
- 1/2 teaspoon dried thyme
- 1/4 teaspoon pepper
- 2-1/2 cups milk

- 1 tablespoon Worcestershire sauce
- 1 package (16 ounces) frozen mixed vegetables
- 2 cups cubed cooked chicken
- 2 tablespoons grated Parmesan cheese

BISCUITS:
- 1 cup all-purpose flour
- 1 tablespoon sugar
- 1-1/2 teaspoons baking powder
- 1/4 teaspoon salt
- 1/3 cup milk
- 3 tablespoons canola *or* vegetable oil
- 1 tablespoon minced fresh parsley

In a saucepan, saute the onion in oil until tender. Stir in the flour, basil, thyme and pepper until blended. Gradually stir in the milk and Worcestershire sauce until smooth. Bring to a boil; boil and stir for 2 minutes. Stir in the vegetables, chicken and Parmesan cheese; reduce heat to low.

Meanwhile, combine flour, sugar, baking powder and salt in a bowl. Combine milk, oil and parsley; stir into dry ingredients just until combined. Transfer hot chicken mixture to a greased 2-1/2-qt. baking dish. Drop biscuit batter by rounded tablespoonfuls onto chicken mixture. Bake, uncovered, at 375° for 30-40 minutes or until the biscuits are lightly browned. **Yield:** 8 servings.

Nutritional Analysis: One serving (prepared with fat-free milk) equals 246 calories, 284 mg sodium, 24 mg cholesterol, 31 g carbohydrate, 13 g protein, 8 g fat. **Diabetic Exchanges:** 2 starch, 1 meat, 1/2 fat.

Creamed Chicken in a Basket

(Pictured above right)

Chunks of tender chicken in a creamy sauce are spooned into puff pastry shells in this delicious dish, which has long been one of our family's favorites. I served it to my husband and our five children for years, and now it's a "must" for our Easter brunch.
—Sue Bolsinger, Anchorage, Alaska

- 6 bone-in chicken breast halves (about 4 pounds)
- 1 small onion, quartered
- 2 celery ribs with leaves, cut into chunks
- 2-1/2 cups water
- 2 teaspoons salt, *divided*
- 6 whole peppercorns
- 8 to 10 frozen puff pastry shells
- 1/2 cup butter *or* margarine
- 1/2 cup all-purpose flour
- 1/4 teaspoon ground nutmeg

- 1/8 teaspoon pepper
- 1/2 pound fresh mushrooms, sliced
- 1 can (5 ounces) sliced water chestnuts, drained
- 1 jar (2 ounces) diced pimientos, drained
- 1 tablespoon lemon juice
- 2 cups whipping cream

Place the chicken, onion, celery, water, 1 teaspoon salt and peppercorns in a large saucepan. Bring to a boil; skim foam. Reduce heat; cover and simmer for 35-40 minutes or until juices run clear. Remove chicken with a slotted spoon; set aside until cool enough to handle. Bake pastry shells according to package directions. Remove chicken from bones; cut into cubes and set aside. Discard skin and bones. Strain broth, discarding vegetables and peppercorns. Set aside 2 cups broth (refrigerate remaining broth for another use).

In a saucepan, melt the butter. Stir in flour until smooth. Gradually add reserved broth, nutmeg, pepper and remaining salt. Bring to a boil; cook and stir for 2 minutes. Remove from the heat; stir in the mushrooms, water chestnuts, pimientos, lemon juice and chicken. Return to the heat. Gradually stir in the cream and heat through (do not boil). Spoon into pastry shells. **Yield:** 8-10 servings.

Dilly Barbecued Turkey

(Pictured below)

This is my brother-in-law's recipe. The special marinade makes a tasty, tender turkey, and the tempting aroma prompts the family to gather around the grill.
—Sue Walker, Greentown, Indiana

✓ Uses less fat, sugar or salt. Includes Nutritional Analysis and Diabetic Exchanges.

    1 turkey breast half with bone (2-1/2 to
      3 pounds)
    1 cup plain yogurt
  1/4 cup lemon juice
    3 tablespoons canola *or* vegetable oil
  1/4 cup minced fresh parsley
  1/4 cup chopped green onions
    2 garlic cloves, minced
    2 tablespoons fresh minced dill *or* 2
      teaspoons dill weed
  1/2 teaspoon dried rosemary, crushed
  1/2 teaspoon salt, optional
  1/4 teaspoon pepper

Place the turkey in a shallow glass dish. Combine the remaining ingredients; spread over turkey. Cover and refrigerate for 6-8 hours or overnight. Remove turkey from dish. Grill, covered, over medium-hot heat for 1 to 1-1/4 hours or until juices run clear and a meat thermometer reads 170°. **Yield:** 6 servings.
   Nutritional Analysis: One serving (prepared with fat-free yogurt and without salt) equals 245 calories, 127 mg sodium, 40 mg cholesterol, 5 g carbohydrate, 28 g protein, 12 g fat. **Diabetic Exchanges:** 3 lean meat, 1 vegetable, 1 fat.

Slow-Cooked Lemon Chicken

(Pictured above)

Garlic, oregano and lemon juice give spark to this memorable main dish. It's easy to fix—just brown the chicken in a skillet, then let the slow cooker do the work.   —Walter Powell, Wilmington, Delaware

    6 bone-in chicken breast halves (about 3
      pounds), skin removed
    1 teaspoon dried oregano
  1/2 teaspoon seasoned salt
  1/4 teaspoon pepper
    2 tablespoons butter *or* margarine
  1/4 cup water
    3 tablespoons lemon juice
    2 garlic cloves, minced
    1 teaspoon chicken bouillon granules
    2 teaspoons minced fresh parsley
Hot cooked rice

Pat chicken dry with paper towels. Combine the oregano, seasoned salt and pepper; rub over chicken. In a large skillet over medium heat, brown the chicken in butter; transfer to a 5-qt. slow cooker. Add water, lemon juice, garlic and bouillon to the skillet; bring to a boil, stirring to loosen browned bits. Pour over chicken. Cover and cook on low for 3-4 hours.
   Baste the chicken. Add parsley. Cover and cook 15-30 minutes longer or until meat juices run clear. If desired, thicken cooking juices and serve over chicken and rice. **Yield:** 6 servings.

Bruschetta Chicken

(Pictured below)

My husband and I enjoy serving this tasty chicken to company as well as family. It looks like we fussed, but it's really fast and easy to fix.
—*Carolin Cattoi-Demkiw, Lethbridge, Alberta*

✓ Uses less fat, sugar or salt. Includes Nutritional Analysis and Diabetic Exchanges.

- 1/2 cup all-purpose flour
- 2 eggs, lightly beaten
- 4 boneless skinless chicken breast halves (1 pound)
- 1/4 cup grated Parmesan cheese
- 1/4 cup dry bread crumbs
- 1 tablespoon butter *or* margarine, melted
- 2 large tomatoes, seeded and chopped
- 3 tablespoons minced fresh basil
- 2 garlic cloves, minced
- 1 tablespoon olive *or* vegetable oil
- 1/2 teaspoon salt
- 1/4 teaspoon pepper

Place flour and eggs in separate shallow bowls. Dip chicken in flour, then in eggs; place in a greased 13-in. x 9-in. x 2-in. baking dish. Combine the Parmesan cheese, bread crumbs and butter; sprinkle over chicken. Loosely cover baking dish with foil. Bake at 375° for 20 minutes. Uncover; bake 5-10 minutes longer or until top is browned.

Meanwhile, in a bowl, combine the remaining ingredients. Spoon over the chicken. Return to the oven for 3-5 minutes or until tomato mixture is heated through. **Yield:** 4 servings.

Nutritional Analysis: One serving (prepared with 1/2 cup egg substitute) equals 358 calories, 13 g fat (5 g saturated fat), 86 mg cholesterol, 623 mg sodium, 22 g carbohydrate, 2 g fiber, 36 g protein. **Diabetic Exchanges:** 4-1/2 lean meat, 1 starch, 1 vegetable.

— 🛒 🛒 🛒 —

Herbed Chicken Quarters

I often grill chicken in the summer, and this herbed version is a big hit with my family. A salad and seasoned potatoes make scrumptious complements to the plump, juicy chicken. —*Erika Aylward, Clinton, Michigan*

- 4 medium lemons, cut into wedges
- 1/2 cup vegetable oil
- 8 garlic cloves, minced
- 4 teaspoons minced fresh basil
- 2 teaspoons minced fresh thyme
- 2 teaspoons salt
- 1/2 teaspoon cayenne pepper
- 1 broiler/fryer chicken (about 3 pounds), quartered

Gently squeeze juice from lemons into a large resealable plastic bag; leave lemon wedges in the bag. Add oil, garlic, basil, thyme, salt and cayenne. Add the chicken and turn to coat. Seal bag and refrigerate for 24 hours, turning frequently.

Drain and discard marinade. Grill chicken, covered, over medium heat, turning every 15 minutes, for 1 hour or until juices run clear. **Yield:** 4 servings.

— 🛒 🛒 🛒 —

Cilantro Chicken

Our family would eat Mexican food every day if we could, and this recipe is a favorite! Chicken breasts stay moist and tender topped with salsa, cilantro and cheese. —*Juline Goelzer, Arroyo Grande, California*

- 2 tablespoons lime juice
- 2 tablespoons vegetable oil
- 1 teaspoon honey
- 4 boneless skinless chicken breast halves (1 pound)
- 1 cup finely crushed tortilla chips
- 1 jar (16 ounces) salsa
- 2 tablespoons minced fresh cilantro
- 1/3 cup shredded Monterey Jack cheese

In a shallow bowl, combine lime juice, oil and honey. Dip chicken in lime juice mixture, then coat with tortilla chips. Place in an ungreased 11-in. x 7-in. x 2-in. baking dish. Bake, uncovered, at 350° for 25 minutes or until the juices run clear.

Combine salsa and cilantro; pour over chicken. Sprinkle with cheese. Bake 5-7 minutes longer or until cheese is melted. **Yield:** 4 servings.

Steak Diane

(Pictured below)

When I want to provide a memorable dinner but don't want to spend hours in the kitchen, this is the recipe I rely on. I've used it many times on holidays or other occasions for a quick, impressive main dish. We relish the savory sauce poured over the steaks.
—Phoebe Carre, Mullica Hill, New Jersey

4 beef rib eye steaks (1/2 inch thick)
1/4 teaspoon pepper
1/8 teaspoon salt
4 tablespoons butter *or* margarine, *divided*
2 tablespoons finely chopped green onions
1/2 teaspoon ground mustard
1 tablespoon lemon juice
1-1/2 teaspoons Worcestershire sauce
1 tablespoon minced fresh parsley
1 tablespoon minced fresh chives

Sprinkle steaks with pepper and salt. In a skillet, melt 2 tablespoons butter. Stir in onions and mustard; cook for 1 minute. Add steaks; cook for 2 minutes on each side or until the meat reaches desired doneness. Remove to a serving platter and keep warm. Add lemon juice, Worcestershire sauce and remaining butter to skillet; cook for 2 minutes. Add parsley and chives. Pour over steaks. **Yield:** 4 servings.

Marinated Rib Eyes

(Pictured above)

We have these tempting steaks weekly. Whenever I suggest a change in the recipe, my husband reminds me, "Don't fix it if it's not broken." Everyone enjoys the savory marinade.
—Rosalie Usry
Flaxton, North Dakota

1/3 cup hot water
3 tablespoons finely chopped onion
2 tablespoons cider vinegar *or* red wine vinegar
2 tablespoons olive *or* vegetable oil
2 tablespoons soy sauce
1 teaspoon beef bouillon granules
1 garlic clove, minced
1/2 teaspoon paprika
1/2 teaspoon coarsely ground pepper
2 beef rib eye steaks (about 1 inch thick and 12 ounces *each*)

In a bowl, combine the first nine ingredients. Remove 1/2 cup of marinade and refrigerate. Pierce steaks several times on both sides with a fork; place in an 11-in. x 7-in. x 2-in. glass dish. Pour remaining marinade over steaks; turn to coat. Cover and refrigerate overnight.

Remove steaks; discard marinade. Grill, uncovered, over medium-hot heat for 4-8 minutes on each side or until meat reaches desired doneness (for rare, a meat thermometer should read 140°; medium, 160°; well-done, 170°). Warm reserved marinade; serve with steaks. **Yield:** 2 servings.

Steak with Citrus Salsa

(Pictured below and on page 74)

A lime juice marinade really perks up these steaks. This snappy salsa is a super change from heavy steak sauce.
—Kathleen Smith, Pittsburgh, Pennsylvania

  1/2 cup soy sauce
  1/4 cup chopped green onions
    3 tablespoons lime juice
    2 tablespoons brown sugar
  1/8 teaspoon hot pepper sauce
    1 garlic clove, minced
1-1/2 pounds boneless sirloin steak (about 1 inch thick)
SALSA:
    2 navel oranges, peeled, sectioned and chopped
  1/4 cup chopped green onions
    2 tablespoons orange juice
    2 tablespoons cider vinegar *or* red wine vinegar
    2 tablespoons chopped lemon
    1 tablespoon chopped lime
    1 tablespoon sugar
    1 tablespoon minced fresh cilantro *or* parsley
    1 teaspoon minced jalapeno pepper*
  1/2 teaspoon grated lemon peel
  1/2 teaspoon grated lime peel
  1/8 teaspoon salt

In a large resealable plastic bag, combine the first six ingredients; add beef. Seal and refrigerate for 2 hours or overnight, turning occasionally.

Drain and discard marinade. Broil or grill steak, uncovered, over medium heat for 4-6 minutes on each side or until meat reaches desired doneness (for rare, a meat thermometer should read 140°; medium, 160°; well-done, 170°). Combine salsa ingredients in a bowl. Slice steak across the grain. Serve with salsa. **Yield:** 4-6 servings.

*Editor's Note: When cutting or seeding hot peppers, use rubber or plastic gloves to protect your hands. Avoid touching your face.

Peppered Beef Tenderloin

(Pictured above)

This peppery, tempting tenderloin is perfect for folks who really savor meat. It's important to let it rest for a few minutes before carving to allow the juices to work through the beef. —*Margaret Ninneman La Crosse, Wisconsin*

☑ Uses less fat, sugar or salt. Includes Nutritional Analysis and Diabetic Exchanges.

    1 teaspoon dried oregano
    1 teaspoon paprika
    1 teaspoon dried thyme
    1 teaspoon salt, optional
  1/2 teaspoon garlic powder
  1/2 teaspoon onion powder
  1/2 teaspoon pepper
  1/2 teaspoon white pepper
  1/8 to 1/4 teaspoon cayenne pepper
    1 beef tenderloin (3 pounds)

Combine the seasonings and rub over the entire tenderloin. Place on a rack in a roasting pan. Bake, uncovered, at 425° until the meat is cooked as desired. Allow approximately 45-50 minutes for rare or until a meat thermometer reads 140°, 55-60 minutes for medium-rare (150°), 62-65 minutes for medium (160°) and 67-70 minutes for well-done (170°). Let stand 10 minutes before carving. **Yield:** 8-10 servings.

Editor's Note: After seasoning, the uncooked tenderloin may be wrapped tightly and refrigerated overnight for a more intense flavor.

Nutritional Analysis: One 3-oz. serving (prepared without salt) equals 179 calories, 67 mg sodium, 61 mg cholesterol, 1 g carbohydrate, 28 g protein, 7 g fat. **Diabetic Exchanges:** 4 lean meat.

Mozzarella Meat Loaf

(Pictured above)

My children were not fond of meat loaf until I "dressed up" this recipe with pizza flavor. Now they're grown and have families of their own, and they make and serve this hearty, moist meat loaf. —Darlis Wilfer
Phelps, Wisconsin

    2 eggs, lightly beaten
    1 cup saltine cracker crumbs
    1 cup milk
    1/2 cup grated Parmesan cheese
    1/2 cup chopped onion
1-1/2 teaspoons salt
    1 teaspoon dried oregano
    2 pounds lean ground beef
    1 can (8 ounces) pizza sauce
    3 slices mozzarella cheese, halved
Green pepper rings and sliced mushrooms,
    optional
    2 tablespoons butter *or* margarine, optional
Fresh parsley sprigs, optional

In a bowl, combine eggs, crumbs, milk, Parmesan cheese, onion, salt and oregano. Add beef; mix well. Shape into a loaf and place in a greased 9-in. x 5-in. x 3-in. loaf pan. Bake at 350° for 1-1/4 hours or until meat is no longer pink and a meat thermometer reads 160°; drain.

Spoon pizza sauce over loaf; top with mozzarella cheese slices. Return to the oven for 10 minutes or until the cheese is melted. Meanwhile, if desired, saute green pepper and mushrooms in butter; arrange on top of meat loaf. Garnish with parsley if desired. **Yield:** 8-10 servings.

Roast Prime Rib

When I first prepared this roast for a family reunion, "scrumptious" was the word used most to describe it. This roast is an easy yet elegant entree that turns out moist and tender every time. —Wendell Obermeier
Charles City, Iowa

    1 tablespoon ground mustard
1-1/2 teaspoons salt
    1/2 teaspoon paprika
    1/4 teaspoon ground allspice
    1/4 teaspoon pepper
    1 prime rib roast (4 to 5 pounds), rolled and
      tied
    1 small onion, cut into thin slivers
    2 garlic cloves, cut into slivers
Fresh parsley sprigs

In a small bowl, combine mustard, salt, paprika, allspice and pepper; set aside. Using a sharp knife, cut long deep slits in the top of the roast, approximately 1 in. apart. Stuff each slit with onion, garlic, parsley and a small amount of the spice mixture. Rub remaining spice mixture on the outside of the roast.

Place on a rack in a deep roasting pan. Bake, uncovered, at 325° for 2 to 2-1/2 hours or until a meat thermometer reads 160°. **Yield:** 8-10 servings.

--- 🛒 🛒 🛒 ---

Zesty Grilled Ham

This is my children's first choice when it comes to ham dishes. The mix of sweet and tangy flavors is mouth-watering on grilled ham. Even the small ones eat big portions! —Mary Ann Lien, Tyler, Texas

    1 cup packed brown sugar
    1/3 cup prepared horseradish
    1/4 cup lemon juice
    1 fully cooked ham steak (1 to 1-1/2 pounds
      and 1 inch thick)

In a small saucepan, bring brown sugar, horseradish and lemon juice to a boil. Brush over both sides of ham. Grill over medium-hot heat, turning once, until heated through and well glazed, about 20-25 minutes. **Yield:** 4 servings.

Mighty Good Meat Loaf

To please picky eaters in your family who don't like chunks of onion or green pepper in their meat loaf, put those ingredients in the blender and blend before adding to the ground beef.

Barbecued Spareribs

(Pictured below)

My husband is a meat cutter at a supermarket and likes to find new ways to smoke or barbecue meat. Several years ago, he discovered this recipe for pork ribs covered in a rich tangy sauce. It was an instant success with our family and friends. —Bette Brotzel
Billings, Montana

 4 pounds pork spareribs, cut into
   serving-size pieces
 1 medium onion, quartered
 2 teaspoons salt
 1/4 teaspoon pepper
SAUCE:
 1/2 cup cider vinegar
 1/2 cup packed brown sugar
 1/2 cup ketchup
 1/4 cup chili sauce
 1/4 cup Worcestershire sauce
 2 tablespoons chopped onion
 1 tablespoon lemon juice
 1/2 teaspoon ground mustard
 1 garlic clove, minced
Dash cayenne pepper

Place ribs and onion in a Dutch oven; sprinkle with salt and pepper. Add enough water to cover ribs; bring to a boil. Reduce heat; cover and simmer for 1-1/2 hours or until tender; drain.

Combine all sauce ingredients in a saucepan. Simmer, uncovered, for 1 hour or until slightly thickened, stirring occasionally. Arrange ribs on a rack in a broiler pan. Brush with sauce. Broil 5 in. from the heat for 5 minutes on each side, brushing frequently with sauce. **Yield:** 4 servings.

Marinated Pork Kabobs

(Pictured above)

This recipe was originally for lamb, but I adapted it to pork and adjusted the spices. After tasting these flavorful kabobs, my husband became an instant fan of this recipe. It's often requested. —Bobbie Jo Devany
Fernly, Nevada

☑ Uses less fat, sugar or salt. Includes Nutritional Analysis and Diabetic Exchanges.

 2 cups plain yogurt
 2 tablespoons lemon juice
 4 garlic cloves, minced
 1/2 teaspoon ground cumin
 1/4 teaspoon ground coriander
 2 pounds pork tenderloin, cut into
   1-1/2-inch cubes
 8 small white onions, halved
 8 cherry tomatoes
 1 medium sweet red pepper, cut into
   1-1/2-inch pieces
 1 medium green pepper, cut into
   1-1/2-inch pieces

In a large resealable plastic bag, combine yogurt, lemon juice, garlic, cumin and coriander; mix well. Add pork; seal and refrigerate for 6 hours or overnight. Alternately thread pork, onions, tomatoes and peppers onto eight metal or soaked wooden skewers. Grill over medium heat for 30-35 minutes or until meat reaches desired doneness. **Yield:** 8 servings.

Nutritional Analysis: One serving (prepared with fat-free yogurt) equals 299 calories, 87 mg sodium, 94 mg cholesterol, 8 g carbohydrate, 31 g protein, 7 g fat. **Diabetic Exchanges:** 4 lean meat, 2 vegetable, 1/2 fat.

Roasted Pork Loin

(Pictured below and on page 74)

This roast is great holiday fare, with incredible seasoning. But it's too good to save just for special occasions. It makes a warm, satisfying supper.
—Grace Yaskovic, Branchville, New Jersey

1/2 cup finely chopped onion
1/2 cup finely chopped celery
1/2 cup finely chopped green pepper
  3 tablespoons butter *or* margarine
  6 garlic cloves, minced
  1 teaspoon salt
  1 teaspoon pepper
  1 teaspoon onion powder
  1 teaspoon dried thyme
  1 teaspoon paprika
  1 teaspoon ground mustard
1/2 teaspoon garlic powder
  1 boneless pork loin roast (4 to 5 pounds)

In a skillet, combine the first 12 ingredients; saute until the vegetables are tender. Untie roast and separate. Randomly cut 20 deep slits, 1 in. wide, on inside surface of roast. Fill slits with some of the vegetable mixture; retie roast. Place on a rack in a shallow baking pan. Spread remaining vegetable mixture over the roast. Bake, uncovered, at 325° for 2-3 hours or until a meat thermometer reads 160°-170°. Let stand for 10 minutes before slicing. **Yield:** 12-15 servings.

Old-World Stuffed Pork Chops

(Pictured above)

Years ago, a relative ran a restaurant in downtown Milwaukee, where several well-known German restaurants still operate. This is one of the recipes she developed. The savory stuffing and juicy pork chops are always a hit.
—Jeanne Schuyler
Wauwatosa, Wisconsin

  4 pork chops (1/2 inch thick)
  1 to 2 tablespoons vegetable oil
Salt and pepper to taste
  3 cups dry unseasoned bread cubes
  1 can (14-3/4 ounces) cream-style corn
  1 egg, lightly beaten
  1 teaspoon grated onion
1/2 teaspoon rubbed sage
1/2 teaspoon dried basil
1/2 teaspoon salt
1/4 teaspoon pepper

In a skillet, brown pork chops in oil on both sides; sprinkle with salt and pepper. Meanwhile, in a bowl, combine remaining ingredients and mix well. Alternate the pork chops and stuffing lengthwise in a greased 3-qt. or 11-in. x 7-in. x 2-in. baking dish. Bake, uncovered, at 350° for 1 hour or until juices run clear. **Yield:** 4 servings.

Savory Pork Chops

I love these tender pork chops smothered in a mouth-watering mustard sauce. They're not tricky to prepare and always impress my guests.
—*Debbie Terenzini Wilkerson, Lusby, Maryland*

2 tablespoons all-purpose flour
1 tablespoon ground mustard
1 teaspoon seasoned salt
1/8 teaspoon pepper
4 pork chops (3/4 inch thick)
2 tablespoons vegetable oil
MUSTARD SAUCE:
2 teaspoons ground mustard
1 cup water
1/2 cup chopped onion
2 tablespoons ketchup
2 tablespoons orange marmalade
1 tablespoon soy sauce
1 tablespoon Dijon mustard

In a bowl, combine the first four ingredients. Dredge pork chops in flour mixture. In a skillet over medium heat, brown chops in oil on both sides, about 8 minutes. Combine the sauce ingredients; pour over chops. Cover and simmer until meat is tender, about 20 minutes. Spoon sauce over chops when serving. **Yield:** 4 servings.

—— 🥄 🥄 🥄 ——

Spicy Pork Tenderloin

A friend shared this recipe for marvelously flavorful pork years ago. It really sparks up a barbecue and has been popular whenever I've served it.
—*Diana Steger, Prospect, Kentucky*

☑ Uses less fat, sugar or salt. Includes Nutritional Analysis and Diabetic Exchanges.

1 to 3 tablespoons chili powder
1 teaspoon salt
1/4 teaspoon ground ginger
1/4 teaspoon ground thyme
1/4 teaspoon pepper
2 pork tenderloins (about 1 pound *each*)

Combine the first five ingredients; rub over tenderloins. Cover and refrigerate for 2-4 hours. Grill over hot heat for 15 minutes on each side or until juices run clear and a meat thermometer reads 160°. **Yield:** 8 servings.
Nutritional Analysis: One serving equals 139 calories, 359 mg sodium, 73 mg cholesterol, 1 g carbohydrate, 24 g protein, 5 g fat. **Diabetic Exchange:** 3-1/2 lean meat.

Ham with Pineapple Sauce

(Pictured below)

This ham is served with a sweet pineapple sauce. A simple mixture of basic ingredients results in a mouth-watering main dish.
—*Debra Falkiner*
St. Charles, Missouri

1 boneless fully cooked ham (4 to 6 pounds)
3/4 cup water, *divided*
1 cup packed brown sugar
4-1/2 teaspoons soy sauce
4-1/2 teaspoons ketchup
1-1/2 teaspoons ground mustard
1-1/2 cups undrained crushed pineapple
2 tablespoons plus 1 teaspoon cornstarch

Place ham on a rack in a shallow roasting pan. Bake at 325° for 1-1/4 to 2 hours or until a meat thermometer reads 140° and the ham is heated through.
In a saucepan, combine 1/4 cup water, brown sugar, soy sauce, ketchup, mustard and pineapple. Bring to a boil. Reduce heat; cover and simmer for 10 minutes. Combine cornstarch and remaining water until smooth; stir into the pineapple mixture. Bring to a boil; cook and stir for 2 minutes or until thickened. Serve with the ham. **Yield:** 16-24 servings (3 cups sauce).

shrimp turn pink and scallops are firm and opaque, stirring gently. Drain, reserving cooking liquid; set seafood mixture aside.

In a saucepan, melt the remaining butter; stir in flour until smooth. Combine milk and reserved cooking liquid; gradually add to the saucepan. Add salt and remaining pepper. Bring to a boil; cook and stir for 2 minutes or until thickened. Remove from the heat; stir in cream and 1/4 cup Parmesan cheese. Stir 3/4 cup white sauce into the seafood mixture.

Spread 1/2 cup white sauce in a greased 13-in. x 9-in. x 2-in. baking dish. Top with three noodles; spread with half of the seafood mixture and 1-1/4 cups sauce. Repeat layers. Top with remaining noodles, sauce and Parmesan. Bake, uncovered, at 350° for 35-40 minutes or until golden brown. Let stand for 15 minutes before cutting. **Yield:** 12 servings.

—— 🍷 🍷 🍷 ——

Seafood Lasagna

(Pictured above and on page 74)

This rich satisfying dish, adapted from a recipe given to me by a friend, is my husband's favorite. I usually serve it on his birthday. It's loaded with scallops, shrimp and crab in a creamy sauce. I consider this the "crown jewel" in my repertoire of recipes.
—Elena Hansen, Ruidoso, New Mexico

- 1 **green onion, finely chopped**
- 2 **tablespoons vegetable oil**
- 2 **tablespoons plus 1/2 cup butter *or* margarine, *divided***
- 1/2 **cup chicken broth**
- 1 **bottle (8 ounces) clam juice**
- 1 **pound bay scallops**
- 1 **pound uncooked small shrimp, peeled and deveined**
- 1 **package (8 ounces) imitation crabmeat, chopped**
- 1/4 **teaspoon white pepper, *divided***
- 1/2 **cup all-purpose flour**
- 1-1/2 **cups milk**
- 1/2 **teaspoon salt**
- 1 **cup whipping cream**
- 1/2 **cup shredded Parmesan cheese, *divided***
- 9 **lasagna noodles, cooked and drained**

In a large skillet, saute onion in oil and 2 tablespoons butter until tender. Stir in broth and clam juice; bring to a boil. Add the scallops, shrimp, crab and 1/8 teaspoon pepper; return to a boil. Reduce heat; simmer, uncovered, for 4-5 minutes or until

Honey-Fried Walleye

(Pictured below)

We go fishing on most summer weekends, so we have lots of fresh fillets. It's a pleasure to serve this crisp, golden walleye since everyone who tries it loves it.
—Sharon Collis, Colona, Illinois

- 1 **egg**
- 1 **teaspoon honey**
- 1 **cup coarsely crushed saltines (about 22 crackers)**
- 1/3 **cup all-purpose flour**

1/4 teaspoon salt
1/4 teaspoon pepper
   4 to 6 walleye fillets (about 1-1/2 pounds),
      skin removed
Vegetable oil
Additional honey
Lemon *or* lime slices, optional

In a shallow bowl, beat egg and honey. In another bowl, combine the cracker crumbs, flour, salt and pepper. Dip fillets into egg mixture, then coat with crumb mixture. In a large skillet, heat 1/4 in. of oil; fry the fillets over medium-high heat for 3-4 minutes on each side or until fish flakes easily with a fork. Drizzle with honey; garnish with lemon or lime if desired. **Yield:** 4-6 servings.

— 🥄 🥄 🥄 —

Grilled Salmon Steaks

This is a terrific way to fix salmon...and it's so easy. The marinade mellows the fish flavor, and the dill sauce is a nice complement.
                    —Deb Essen
                    Victor, Montana

   2 tablespoons white wine vinegar *or*
      cider vinegar
   2 tablespoons sugar
   1 tablespoon dill weed
3/4 teaspoon salt
1/8 to 1/4 teaspoon pepper, optional
   4 salmon steaks (1 inch thick)
MUSTARD DILL SAUCE:
   3 tablespoons mayonnaise
   3 tablespoons Dijon mustard
   3 tablespoons dill weed
   1 tablespoon sugar
   4 teaspoons white wine vinegar *or*
      cider vinegar
1/4 teaspoon pepper, optional

In a large resealable plastic bag, combine the first five ingredients. Add salmon; seal bag and turn to coat. Refrigerate for 1 hour, turning occasionally. In a small bowl, combine the sauce ingredients; cover and refrigerate.

   Drain salmon, discarding marinade. Grill the salmon, covered, over medium-hot heat for 5 minutes. Turn; grill 7-9 minutes longer or until fish flakes easily with a fork. Serve with the mustard dill sauce. **Yield:** 4 servings.

Frozen Fish Fact

Store well-wrapped frozen fish in the freezer for up to 6 months.

Lemon Herbed Salmon

(Pictured above and on page 74)

The tasty topping can be used on other fish, too. Fresh thyme really sparks the flavor.
       —Perlene Hoekema, Lynden, Washington

2-1/2 cups soft bread crumbs
   4 garlic cloves, minced
1/2 cup chopped fresh parsley
   6 tablespoons grated Parmesan cheese
1/4 cup chopped fresh thyme *or* 1 tablespoon
      dried thyme
   2 teaspoons grated lemon peel
1/2 teaspoon salt
   6 tablespoons butter *or* margarine, melted,
      divided
   1 salmon fillet (3 to 4 pounds)

In a bowl, combine bread crumbs, garlic, parsley, Parmesan cheese, thyme, lemon peel and salt; mix well. Add 4 tablespoons butter and toss lightly to coat; set aside. Pat salmon dry. Place skin side down in a greased baking dish. Brush with remaining butter; cover with crumb mixture. Bake at 350° for 20-25 minutes or until salmon flakes easily with a fork. **Yield:** 8 servings.

Cheesy Crab Enchiladas

(Pictured below)

I created these rich delectable crab enchiladas with ranch dressing mix as my secret ingredient.
—Kelly Mockler, Madison, Wisconsin

    2 packages (8 ounces *each*) cream cheese, softened
    1 envelope ranch salad dressing mix
    3 tablespoons plus 1/4 cup milk, *divided*
    1 small red onion, diced
    2 garlic cloves, minced
    2 tablespoons butter *or* margarine
    1 pound fresh, frozen *or* canned crabmeat, flaked and cartilage removed
    2 cans (2-1/4 ounces *each*) sliced ripe olives, drained
    1 can (4 ounces) chopped green chilies
  1/2 teaspoon pepper
  1/4 teaspoon salt
    2 cups (8 ounces) shredded Monterey Jack cheese, *divided*
    8 flour tortillas (8 inches)
  1/2 cup shredded Colby cheese
Chopped green onions and tomatoes, shredded lettuce and sliced ripe olives, optional

In a mixing bowl, combine cream cheese, dressing mix and 3 tablespoons milk until smooth. Set aside 3/4 cup for topping. In a skillet, saute onion and garlic in butter until tender. Stir in crab, olives, chilies, pepper and salt. Fold crab mixture and 1-1/2 cups Monterey Jack into remaining cream cheese mixture.

Spoon about 2/3 cup down the center of each tortilla. Roll up and place seam side down in a greased 13-in. x 9-in. x 2-in. baking dish. Combine the remaining milk and reserved cream cheese mixture until blended; pour over tortillas. Sprinkle with Colby and remaining Monterey Jack. Cover and bake at 350° for 25 minutes. Uncover; bake 5-10 minutes longer or until heated through. Serve with green onions, tomatoes, lettuce and olives if desired. **Yield:** 8 enchiladas.

Spicy Island Shrimp

(Pictured above)

My husband got this recipe while he was living on St. Croix Island. I'm amazed at how even those who claim not to care for shrimp come out of their shells and devour them when they're prepared this way!
—Teresa Methe, Minden, Nebraska

    1 large green pepper, chopped
    1 large onion, chopped
  1/2 cup butter *or* margarine
2-1/4 pounds uncooked large shrimp, peeled and deveined
    2 cans (8 ounces *each*) tomato sauce
    3 tablespoons chopped green onions
    1 tablespoon minced fresh parsley
    1 teaspoon salt
    1 teaspoon pepper
    1 teaspoon paprika
  1/2 teaspoon garlic powder
  1/2 teaspoon dried oregano
  1/2 teaspoon dried thyme
  1/4 to 1/2 teaspoon white pepper
  1/4 to 1/2 teaspoon cayenne pepper
Hot cooked rice

In a large skillet, saute the green pepper and onion in butter until tender. Reduce heat; add shrimp. Cook for 5 minutes. Stir in the tomato sauce, green onions, parsley and seasonings. Bring to a boil. Reduce heat; simmer, uncovered, for 20 minutes or until slightly thickened. Serve with rice. **Yield:** 6 servings.

Pepperoni Pan Pizza

I've spent years trying to come up with the perfect pizza crust and sauce, and they're paired up in this recipe. I fix this crispy, savory pizza for my family often...it really satisfies my husband and three sons.
—Susan Lindahl, Alford, Florida

2-3/4 to 3 cups all-purpose flour
 1 package (1/4 ounce) active dry yeast
 1/4 teaspoon salt
 1 cup warm water (120° to 130°)
 1 tablespoon vegetable oil
SAUCE:
 1 can (14-1/2 ounces) diced tomatoes, undrained
 1 can (6 ounces) tomato paste
 1 tablespoon vegetable oil
 1 teaspoon salt
 1/2 teaspoon *each* dried basil, oregano, marjoram and thyme
 1/4 teaspoon garlic powder
 1/4 teaspoon pepper
 1 package (3-1/2 ounces) sliced pepperoni
 5 cups (20 ounces) shredded mozzarella cheese
 1/4 cup grated Parmesan cheese
 1/4 cup grated Romano cheese

In a mixing bowl, combine 2 cups flour, yeast and salt. Add water and oil; beat until smooth. Add enough remaining flour to form a soft dough. Turn onto a floured surface; knead until smooth and elastic, about 5-7 minutes. Cover and let stand for 10 minutes. Meanwhile, in a bowl, combine tomatoes, tomato paste, oil and seasonings.

Divide dough in half; press each portion into a 15-in. x 10-in. x 1-in. baking pan coated with non-stick cooking spray. Prick the dough generously with a fork. Bake at 425° for 12-16 minutes or until crust is lightly browned. Spread sauce over each crust; top with pepperoni and cheeses. Bake 8-10 minutes longer or until cheese is melted. Cut into squares. **Yield:** 2 pizzas (9 slices each).

— 🍵 🍵 🍵 —

Roasted Veggie Pizza

(Pictured at right)

A bold, flavorful garlic and basil pesto sauce is an awesome change of pace from traditional tomato-based pizza sauce. Roasted vegetables are a fantastic topping. Whenever I serve it alongside a standard meat pizza, this one's always the first to go!
—Cindy Elsbernd, Des Moines, Iowa

 8 to 10 medium fresh mushrooms, sliced
 1 small onion, sliced
 1/2 cup sliced green pepper
 1/2 cup sliced sweet red pepper
 2 teaspoons olive *or* vegetable oil
 2 garlic cloves, minced
 1/4 teaspoon *each* dried rosemary, oregano and thyme
PESTO SAUCE:
 1/2 cup coarsely chopped fresh basil
 1/4 cup olive *or* vegetable oil
 1/4 cup grated Parmesan cheese
 4 garlic cloves, minced
 1 prebaked Italian bread shell crust (1 pound)
 1 large tomato, thinly sliced
 2 cups (8 ounces) shredded mozzarella cheese

Place mushrooms, onion and peppers in a roasting pan or baking pan lined with heavy-duty foil. Combine oil, garlic, rosemary, oregano and thyme; drizzle over vegetables and toss to coat. Cover and bake at 400° for 20 minutes. Meanwhile, for pesto, combine basil, oil, Parmesan cheese and garlic in a food processor or blender; cover and process until smooth, scraping sides often. Set aside.

Place the crust on an ungreased 12-in. pizza pan. Spread with pesto; top with the tomato slices. Sprinkle with mozzarella cheese. Top with roasted vegetables. Bake for 15 minutes or until cheese is melted and bubbly. **Yield:** 8 slices.

Asparagus Swiss Quiche

(Pictured above)

Fresh asparagus stars along with bacon, onion and Swiss cheese in this hearty quiche.
—*Mary Ann Taylor, Rockwell, Iowa*

- **10 bacon strips, diced**
- **1/2 cup chopped onion**
- **1 pound fresh asparagus, trimmed**
- **1 cup (4 ounces) shredded Swiss cheese**
- **1 tablespoon all-purpose flour**
- **1/4 teaspoon salt**
- **1/8 teaspoon pepper**
- **1 unbaked pastry shell (9 inches)**
- **3 eggs**
- **1/2 cup half-and-half cream**

In a skillet, cook bacon over medium heat until crisp. Remove with a slotted spoon to paper towels; drain, reserving 1 tablespoon drippings. In the drippings, saute onion until browned; drain. Cut eight asparagus spears into 4-in.-long spears for garnish. Cut remaining asparagus into 1-in. pieces. In a saucepan, cook all of the asparagus in a small amount of boiling water until crisp-tender; drain.

In a bowl, toss the bacon, onion, asparagus pieces, cheese, flour, salt and pepper. Pour into pastry shell. In a bowl, beat eggs and cream; pour over bacon mixture. Top with asparagus spears. Bake at 400° for 30-35 minutes or until a knife inserted near the center comes out clean and crust is golden brown. Let stand for 10 minutes before cutting. **Yield:** 6-8 servings.

— 🛒 🛒 🛒 —

Farmhouse Pork and Apple Pie

(Pictured at right)

I've always loved pork and apples together, and this recipe combines them nicely to create a comforting main dish. *It calls for a bit of preparation, but my family and I agree that its wonderful flavor makes it well worth the extra effort.* —*Suzanne Strocsher Bothell, Washington*

- **1 pound sliced bacon, cut into 2-inch pieces**
- **3 medium onions, chopped**
- **3 pounds boneless pork, cubed**
- **3/4 cup all-purpose flour**
- **Vegetable oil, optional**
- **3 medium tart apples, peeled and chopped**
- **1 teaspoon rubbed sage**
- **1/2 teaspoon ground nutmeg**
- **1 teaspoon salt**
- **1/4 teaspoon pepper**
- **1 cup apple cider**
- **1/2 cup water**
- **4 medium potatoes, peeled and cubed**
- **1/2 cup milk**
- **5 tablespoons butter *or* margarine, *divided***
- **Additional salt and pepper**
- **Snipped fresh parsley, optional**

Cook bacon in an ovenproof 12-in. skillet until crisp. Remove with a slotted spoon to paper towels. In drippings, saute onions until tender; remove with a slotted spoon and set aside. Dust pork lightly with flour. Brown a third at a time in drippings, adding oil if needed. Remove from the heat; drain. To pork, add bacon, onions, apples, sage, nutmeg, salt and pepper. Stir in cider and water. Cover and bake at 325° for 2 hours or until pork is tender.

In a saucepan, cook potatoes in boiling water until tender. Drain and mash with milk and 3 tablespoons butter. Add salt and pepper to taste. Remove skillet from the oven and spread potatoes over pork mixture. Melt remaining butter; brush over potatoes. Broil 6 in. from the heat for 5 minutes or until topping is browned. Sprinkle with parsley if desired. **Yield:** 10 servings.

Beef Stew Pie

(Pictured above)

My daughter and I often serve this pie to our families, and it's always a hit. It's especially good made the day before, so the flavors can blend. —Karol Sprague
Gobles, Michigan

  6 tablespoons all-purpose flour, *divided*
1-1/2 teaspoons salt
  1/2 teaspoon pepper
    1 pound boneless beef round steak, cut into
      1-inch pieces
    2 tablespoons vegetable oil
  1/2 cup chopped onion
    2 garlic cloves, minced
2-1/4 cups water, *divided*
    1 tablespoon tomato paste
  1/2 teaspoon Italian seasoning
  1/2 teaspoon dried basil
    1 bay leaf
    2 cups cubed cooked potatoes
1-1/2 cups sliced cooked carrots
    2 tablespoons minced fresh parsley
Pastry for single-crust pie (9 inches)

In a large resealable plastic bag, combine 3 table-spoons flour, salt and pepper. Add beef in batches and shake to coat. In a large skillet, saute beef in oil until browned. Add onion and garlic; cook and stir until onion is tender. Add 1/4 cup water, stirring to scrape browned bits from skillet.

Combine 1-1/2 cups water, tomato paste, Italian seasoning and basil; gradually stir into skillet. Add bay leaf. Bring to a boil. Reduce heat; cover and simmer for 1-1/4 to 1-1/2 hours or until meat is tender. Combine the remaining flour and water until smooth; gradually stir into skillet. Bring to a boil; cook and stir for 2 minutes or until thickened and bubbly. Discard bay leaf. Stir in potatoes, carrots and parsley. Transfer to a greased 2-qt. baking dish.

On a floured surface, roll out pastry to fit dish. Place over filling; flute edges and cut slits in top. Bake at 425° for 25-30 minutes or until crust is golden brown. Let stand for 10 minutes before serving. **Yield:** 4-6 servings.

Farmer's Market Sausage Pie

(Pictured below)

Our son, Lukas, named this savory pie for the Saturday-morning market held near our state capitol. Most of the fresh ingredients called for in the recipe can be found there. —Teri Schuman, Oregon, Wisconsin

    4 Italian sausage links, casings removed,
      halved and cut into 1/2-inch pieces
    1 medium tomato, cut into chunks
    1 small yellow tomato, cut into chunks
    1 cup thinly sliced zucchini
    1 cup thinly sliced yellow summer squash
  1/2 cup julienned green pepper
  1/2 cup julienned sweet red pepper
    1 tablespoon Italian salad dressing mix
  1/2 teaspoon garlic powder
  1/4 to 1/2 teaspoon fennel seed, crushed
Pastry for double-crust pie (9 inches)
    1 cup (4 ounces) shredded cheddar cheese
    1 cup (4 ounces) shredded mozzarella
      cheese

In a large skillet, cook sausage over medium heat until no longer pink; drain. Stir in tomato, squash, peppers, salad dressing mix, garlic powder and fennel seed. Cook and stir for 10 minutes; drain. Cool for 10 minutes. Line a 9-in. pie plate with bottom pastry; trim even with edge. Fill with sausage mixture. Sprinkle with cheeses. Roll out remaining pastry to fit top of pie; place over filling. Trim, seal and flute edges. Cut slits in top.

Bake at 375° for 35-40 minutes or until filling is bubbly and crust is golden brown. Let stand for 10 minutes before cutting. **Yield:** 8 servings.

Chicken Parmesan

I rely often on this recipe with the convenience of bone-less skinless chicken breasts. Oregano gives the coat-ing a distinct, tasty flavor. —Sharon Kelley
Modesto, California

1/2 cup grated Parmesan cheese
1/4 cup dry bread crumbs
  1 teaspoon dried oregano
  1 teaspoon dried parsley flakes
1/4 teaspoon paprika
1/4 teaspoon salt
1/4 teaspoon pepper
  6 boneless skinless chicken breast halves
1/4 cup butter *or* margarine, melted

In a large bowl, combine the first seven ingredients. Dip chicken in butter and then into crumb mixture. Place in a greased 15-in. x 10-in. x 1-in. baking pan. Bake, uncovered, at 400° for 20-25 minutes or until chicken is tender and juices run clear. **Yield:** 6 servings.

— 🍴 🍴 🍴 —

Spaghetti and Meatballs

(Pictured at right)

When you have time, simmer some of this hearty sauce with home-style meatballs. It makes a memorable main course you'll make again and again for years to come.
—Dawnetta McGhee, Lewiston, Idaho

  1 large onion, finely chopped
  2 garlic cloves, minced
  2 tablespoons vegetable *or* olive oil
  3 cans (10-3/4 ounces *each*) tomato puree
  1 can (12 ounces) tomato paste
1-1/2 cups water
1/4 cup grated Parmesan cheese
  1 tablespoon dried oregano
  1 tablespoon salt
  1 tablespoon sugar
MEATBALLS:
  4 eggs, beaten
  2 garlic cloves, minced
  3 tablespoons grated Parmesan cheese
  1 teaspoon dried oregano
  1 pound ground beef
1/4 pound ground pork
3/4 cup finely crushed saltines
Hot cooked spaghetti

In a Dutch oven, saute onion and garlic in oil un-til tender. Add the next seven ingredients; mix well. Simmer, uncovered, for 1-1/2 hours. Meanwhile, combine the eggs, garlic, Parmesan cheese and oregano in a large bowl. Add beef, pork and crack-er crumbs; mix well. Shape into 1-1/2-in. balls; brown in a skillet, turning once. Add to sauce; sim-mer, uncovered, 1-1/2 hours longer. Serve over spaghetti. **Yield:** 6-8 servings.

— 🍴 🍴 🍴 —

Stuffed Zucchini

(Pictured at right)

An abundance of squash from my garden inspired me to make up this recipe. It's now a family favorite.
—Marjorie Roberts, West Chazy, New York

1-1/2 pounds lean ground beef
  1 large onion, chopped
  1 large green pepper, chopped
  1 jalapeno pepper, minced*
1-1/4 cups soft bread crumbs
  1 egg, beaten
  1 tablespoon dried parsley flakes
  1 teaspoon dried basil
  1 teaspoon Italian seasoning
  1 teaspoon salt
1/8 teaspoon pepper
  2 cans (8 ounces *each*) tomato sauce, *divided*
  2 medium tomatoes, coarsely chopped
  4 to 5 medium zucchini
  2 cups (8 ounces) shredded mozzarella cheese

In a large bowl, combine the first 11 ingredients and one can of tomato sauce; mix well. Stir in tomatoes. Halve zucchini lengthwise; scoop out seeds. Fill with meat mixture; place in two 13-in. x 9-in. x 2-in. baking dishes. Spoon remaining tomato sauce over each. Bake, uncovered, at 375° for 45 minutes or until the zucchini is ten-der. Sprinkle with cheese during the last few min-utes of baking. **Yield:** 8-10 servings.

***Editor's Note:** When cutting or seeding hot pep-pers, use rubber or plastic gloves to protect your hands. Avoid touching your face.

— 🍴 🍴 🍴 —

Calico Burgers

(Pictured at right)

These unique burgers featuring rice and special sea-sonings are always a hit at summer cookouts. Instead of ketchup, top the burgers with the savory home-made barbecue sauce. —Maryann Bondonese
Nazareth, Pennsylvania

1/2 cup cooked rice
1/4 cup chopped onion

1/4 cup chopped green pepper
1 tablespoon dried parsley flakes
1 teaspoon salt
1/4 teaspoon garlic powder
Dash pepper
1-1/2 pounds ground beef
BARBECUE SAUCE:
  2/3 cup water
  1/4 cup ketchup
  3 tablespoons chili sauce

1 teaspoon Worcestershire sauce
1/4 teaspoon dried basil

In bowl, combine the first seven ingredients. Add beef; mix well. Shape into four to six oval patties. Grill, uncovered, over medium-hot heat until the meat is no longer pink, about 15-20 minutes. Combine all sauce ingredients in a saucepan; simmer for 15 minutes. Serve with burgers. **Yield:** 4-6 servings.

GRAB THE GROUND BEEF. Hearty helpings of Spaghetti and Meatballs, Calico Burgers and Stuffed Zucchini (shown above, clockwise from upper left) are sure cures for "the hungries".

pour over meat mixture. Spoon into a greased 13-in. x 9-in. x 2-in. baking dish.

Toss bread crumbs, butter and dill; stir in cheese and walnuts. Sprinkle over the casserole. Bake, uncovered, at 350° for 30 minutes or until heated through. **Yield:** 8-10 servings.

Oregano Turkey Casserole

This comforting casserole is a great way to use up leftover turkey—the oregano really enhances its flavor.
—Edie DeSpain, Logan, Utah

    4 ounces uncooked spaghetti
    2 cups sliced fresh mushrooms
1/2 cup julienned green pepper
1/4 cup butter *or* margarine
    2 tablespoons all-purpose flour
    2 tablespoons minced fresh oregano *or* 2
       teaspoons dried oregano
1/2 teaspoon salt
1/4 teaspoon pepper
    1 teaspoon chicken bouillon granules
1/4 cup boiling water
1-1/3 cups evaporated milk
2-1/2 cups cubed cooked turkey
    2 tablespoons chopped pimientos
    2 tablespoons grated Parmesan cheese

Cook spaghetti according to package directions. Meanwhile, in a skillet, saute mushrooms and green pepper in butter until tender. Stir in flour, oregano, salt and pepper. Dissolve bouillon in water; gradually add to skillet. Stir in milk. Bring to a boil; cook and stir for 2 minutes or until thickened. Add turkey and pimientos.

Drain spaghetti; toss with turkey mixture. Pour into a greased 11-in. x 7-in. x 2-in. baking dish. Sprinkle with Parmesan cheese. Bake, uncovered, at 350° for 18-22 minutes or until heated through. **Yield:** 6-8 servings.

Tuna Mushroom Casserole

(Pictured at right)

I love to serve this dressed-up version of a tuna casserole. The green beans add nice texture, color and flavor. The first time I made this dish, my uncle asked for seconds, even though tuna casseroles are not usually his favorite. —Jone Furlong, Santa Rosa, California

1/2 cup water
    1 teaspoon chicken bouillon granules
    1 package (10 ounces) frozen green beans
    1 cup chopped onion

Cordon Bleu Casserole

(Pictured above)

Whenever I'm invited to attend a potluck, people usually ask me to bring this tempting casserole. The turkey, ham and cheese are delectable combined with the crunchy topping. —Joyce Paul
Moose Jaw, Saskatchewan

    4 cups cubed cooked turkey
    3 cups cubed fully cooked ham
    1 cup (4 ounces) shredded cheddar cheese
    1 cup chopped onion
1/4 cup butter *or* margarine
1/3 cup all-purpose flour
    2 cups half-and-half cream
    1 teaspoon dill weed
1/8 teaspoon ground mustard
1/8 teaspoon ground nutmeg
TOPPING:
    1 cup dry bread crumbs
    2 tablespoons butter *or* margarine, melted
1/4 teaspoon dill weed
1/4 cup shredded cheddar cheese
1/4 cup chopped walnuts

In a large bowl, combine turkey, ham and cheese; set aside. In a saucepan, saute onion in butter until tender. Add flour; stir to form a paste. Gradually add cream, stirring constantly. Bring to a boil; boil 1 minute or until thick. Add dill, mustard and nutmeg; mix well. Remove from the heat and

1 cup sliced fresh mushrooms
1/4 cup chopped celery
1 garlic clove, minced
1/2 teaspoon dill weed
1/2 teaspoon salt
1/8 teaspoon pepper
4 teaspoons cornstarch
1-1/2 cups milk
1/2 cup shredded Swiss cheese
1/4 cup mayonnaise
2-1/2 cups medium noodles, cooked and
   drained
1 can (12-1/4 ounces) tuna, drained and
   flaked
1/3 cup dry bread crumbs
1 tablespoon butter *or* margarine

In a large saucepan, bring water and bouillon to a boil, stirring to dissolve. Add the next eight ingredients; bring to a boil. Reduce heat; cover and simmer 5 minutes or until vegetables are tender. Dissolve cornstarch in milk; add to vegetable mixture, stirring constantly. Bring to a boil; boil for 2 minutes or until thickened.

Remove from the heat; stir in cheese and mayonnaise until cheese is melted. Fold in noodles and tuna. Pour into a greased 2-1/2-qt. baking dish. Brown bread crumbs in butter; sprinkle on top of casserole. Bake, uncovered, at 350° for 25-30 minutes or until heated through. **Yield:** 4-6 servings.

Mexican Turkey Roll-Ups

(Pictured above)

This is the perfect recipe when you're hungry for a dish with Mexican flavor and want to use turkey. These roll-ups are fun and so tasty, even kids like them. It comes in handy to use up leftover turkey after Thanksgiving.
—Marlene Muckenhirn, Delano, Minnesota

2-1/2 cups cubed cooked turkey
1-1/2 cups (12 ounces) sour cream, *divided*
3 teaspoons taco seasoning, *divided*
1 can (10-3/4 ounces) condensed cream of
   mushroom soup, undiluted, *divided*
1-1/2 cups (6 ounces) shredded cheddar cheese,
   divided
1 small onion, chopped
1/2 cup salsa
1/4 cup sliced ripe olives
10 flour tortillas (7 inches)
Shredded lettuce, chopped tomatoes and
   additional salsa and olives, optional

In a bowl, combine turkey, 1/2 cup sour cream, 1-1/2 teaspoons taco seasoning, half of the soup, 1 cup of cheese, onion, salsa and olives. Place 1/3 cup filling on each tortilla. Roll up and place seam side down in a greased 13-in. x 9-in. x 2-in. baking dish. Combine remaining sour cream, taco seasoning and soup; pour over roll-ups.

Cover and bake at 350° for 30 minutes or until heated through. Sprinkle with the remaining cheese. Top with lettuce, tomatoes, salsa and olives if desired. **Yield:** 10 roll-ups.

Ham and Vegetable Linguine

(Pictured below)

I've been pleasing dinner guests with this delicious pasta dish for years. The delicate cream sauce blends well with the colorful and hearty mix of vegetables. I chop the vegetables ahead of time and later prepare this dish in a snap. —Kerry Kerr McAvoy Rockford, Michigan

- 1 package (8 ounces) linguine
- 1/2 pound fresh asparagus, cut into 1-inch pieces
- 1/2 pound fresh mushrooms, sliced
- 1 medium carrot, thinly sliced
- 1 medium zucchini, diced
- 2 cups julienned fully cooked ham
- 1/4 cup butter *or* margarine
- 1 cup whipping cream
- 1/2 cup frozen peas
- 3 green onions, sliced
- 1/4 cup grated Parmesan cheese
- 1 teaspoon dried basil
- 3/4 teaspoon salt

Dash *each* pepper and ground nutmeg
Additional Parmesan cheese, optional

Cook linguine according to package directions. Meanwhile, in a large skillet, saute asparagus, mushrooms, carrot, zucchini and ham in butter until the vegetables are tender. Add cream, peas, onions, Parmesan, basil, salt, pepper and nutmeg; bring to a boil. Reduce heat; simmer for 3 minutes, stirring frequently. Drain linguine; add to vegetable mixture and toss to coat. Sprinkle with Parmesan cheese if desired. **Yield:** 4 servings.

Homemade Manicotti

(Pictured above)

These tender manicotti are much easier to stuff than the purchased variety. People are amazed when I say I made my own noodles. When my son fixed this recipe for friends, they were impressed with his cooking skills. —SueAnn Bunt, Painted Post, New York

CREPE NOODLES:
- 1-1/2 cups all-purpose flour
- 1 cup milk
- 3 eggs
- 1/2 teaspoon salt

FILLING:
- 1-1/2 pounds ricotta cheese
- 1/4 cup grated Romano cheese
- 1 egg
- 1 tablespoon minced fresh parsley *or* 1 teaspoon dried parsley flakes
- 1 jar (28 ounces) spaghetti sauce

Shredded Romano cheese, optional

Place flour in a bowl; whisk in milk, eggs and salt until smooth. Pour about 2 tablespoons onto a hot greased 8-in. skillet; spread to a 5-in. circle. Cook over medium heat until set; do not brown or turn. Repeat with remaining batter, making 18 crepes. Stack crepes between waxed paper; set aside.

For filling, combine cheeses, egg and parsley. Spoon 3-4 tablespoons down the center of each crepe; roll up. Pour half of the spaghetti sauce into an ungreased 13-in. x 9-in. x 2-in. baking dish. Place crepes seam side down over the sauce; pour remaining sauce over top. Cover and bake at 350° for 20 minutes. Uncover and bake 20 minutes longer or until heated through. Sprinkle with Romano cheese if desired. **Yield:** 6 servings.

Dijon Sirloin Tips

(Pictured below)

I received this recipe years ago. This beef and mush-room dish is such a hit with our family that it's become a tradition for birthdays and Christmas.
—Janelle Lee, Lake Charles, Louisiana

1-1/4 pounds sirloin tips, cubed
   2 tablespoons butter *or* margarine
   1 tablespoon vegetable oil
   3 cups sliced fresh mushrooms
   1 garlic clove, minced
 1/2 cup beef broth
 1/4 cup white wine vinegar *or* cider vinegar
1-1/2 teaspoons soy sauce
   2 teaspoons Dijon mustard
   2 teaspoons cornstarch
 1/2 cup whipping cream
Hot cooked noodles
Chopped fresh parsley, optional

In a skillet, brown the meat in butter and oil; transfer to an ungreased 2-qt. baking dish. In the same skillet, saute mushrooms and garlic until mushrooms are tender, about 3 minutes. Pour mushrooms, garlic and drippings over meat. Cover and bake at 325° for 1-3/4 to 2 hours or until meat is tender.

In a skillet, combine the broth, vinegar and soy sauce; bring to a boil. Boil for 2 minutes; set aside. Combine mustard, cornstarch and cream; stir into broth mixture. Bring to a boil; boil for 2 minutes, stirring constantly. Drain juices from baking dish into broth mixture. Cook over medium heat, stirring constantly, until thickened and bubbly. Add beef mixture. Serve over noodles. Garnish with parsley if desired. **Yield:** 4 servings.

Chicken Cheese Lasagna

(Pictured above)

This creamy casserole gives an old favorite a new twist! Three cheeses and chicken combined with the fresh taste of spinach make it a real crowd-pleaser.
—Mary Ann Kosmas, Minneapolis, Minnesota

   1 medium onion, chopped
   1 garlic clove, minced
 1/2 cup butter *or* margarine
 1/2 cup all-purpose flour
   1 teaspoon salt
   2 cups chicken broth
1-1/2 cups milk
   4 cups (16 ounces) shredded mozzarella cheese, *divided*
   1 cup grated Parmesan cheese, *divided*
   1 teaspoon dried basil
   1 teaspoon dried oregano
 1/2 teaspoon white pepper
   1 carton (15 ounces) ricotta cheese
   1 tablespoon minced fresh parsley
   9 lasagna noodles cooked and drained
   2 packages (10 ounces *each*) frozen spinach, thawed and well drained
   2 cups cubed cooked chicken

In a saucepan, saute onion and garlic in butter until tender. Stir in flour and salt; cook until bubbly. Gradually stir in broth and milk. Bring to a boil, stirring constantly; boil for 1 minute. Stir in 2 cups of mozzarella, 1/2 cup of Parmesan cheese, basil, oregano and pepper; set aside. In a bowl, combine ricotta cheese, parsley and remaining mozzarella; set aside. Spread a quarter of the cheese sauce into a greased 13-in. x 9-in. x 2-in. baking dish; cover with three noodles.

Top with half of the ricotta mixture, half of the spinach and half of the chicken. Cover with a quarter of cheese sauce and three noodles. Repeat layers of ricotta mixture, spinach, chicken and cheese sauce. Cover with remaining noodles and cheese sauce. Sprinkle remaining Parmesan over all. Bake, uncovered, at 350° for 35-40 minutes. Let stand 15 minutes before cutting. **Yield:** 12 servings.

Chicken Stir-Fry

(Pictured below)

This is a tasty, healthy meal that everyone in my family enjoys! The broccoli and carrots add great color.
—*Lori Schlecht, Wimbledon, North Dakota*

✓ Uses less fat, sugar or salt. Includes Nutritional Analysis and Diabetic Exchanges.

- 1 **pound boneless skinless chicken breasts, cut into 1/2-inch strips**
- 3 **tablespoons cornstarch**
- 2 **tablespoons soy sauce**
- 1/2 **teaspoon ground ginger**
- 1/4 **teaspoon garlic powder**
- 3 **tablespoons vegetable oil,** *divided*
- 2 **cups broccoli florets**
- 1 **cup sliced celery (1/2-inch pieces)**
- 1 **cup thinly sliced carrots**
- 1 **small onion, cut into wedges**
- 1 **cup water**
- 1 **teaspoon chicken bouillon granules**

Place chicken strips in a resealable plastic bag; add cornstarch and toss to coat. Combine soy sauce, ginger and garlic powder; add to bag and shake well. Refrigerate for 30 minutes.

In a large skillet or wok, heat 2 tablespoons of oil; stir-fry chicken until no longer pink, about 3-5 minutes. Remove and keep warm. Add remaining oil; stir-fry broccoli, celery, carrots and onion for 4-5 minutes or until crisp-tender. Add water and bouillon. Return chicken to the pan. Cook and stir until thickened and bubbly. **Yield:** 4 servings.

Nutritional Analysis: One serving (prepared with light soy sauce and low-sodium bouillon) equals 306 calories, 239 mg sodium, 73 mg cholesterol, 18 g carbohydrate, 30 g protein, 14 g fat. **Diabetic Exchanges:** 3 lean meat, 2 vegetable, 1 fat, 1/2 starch.

Turkey Asparagus Stir-Fry

(Pictured above)

Mild turkey picks up delightful flavor in this colorful stir-fry. My husband, who never cared for asparagus, enjoys it in this entree.
—*Darlene Kennedy*
Plymouth, Ohio

✓ Uses less fat, sugar or salt. Includes Nutritional Analysis and Diabetic Exchanges.

- 1 **pound uncooked boneless turkey breast, cut into strips**
- 1 **pound fresh asparagus, cut into 1-inch pieces**
- 2 **medium carrots, quartered lengthwise and cut into 1-inch pieces**
- 4 **green onions, cut into 1-inch pieces**
- 4 **ounces fresh mushrooms, sliced**
- 2 **garlic cloves, minced**
- 1/2 **teaspoon ground ginger**
- 2/3 **cup water**
- 2 **tablespoons soy sauce**
- 1 **tablespoon plus 1 teaspoon cornstarch**
- 1 **can (8 ounces) sliced water chestnuts, drained**

Hot cooked white *or* **brown rice**
- 1 **medium tomato, cut into eight wedges**

Lightly coat a large skillet or wok with nonstick cooking spray. Add turkey; stir-fry over medium-high heat until no longer pink, about 5 minutes. Remove and keep warm. Stir-fry asparagus, carrots, onions, mushrooms, garlic and ginger until vegetables are crisp-tender, about 5 minutes.

Combine water, soy sauce and cornstarch; add to skillet with water chestnuts. Cook and stir until thickened and bubbly. Return turkey to the skillet and heat through. Serve over rice; garnish with tomato. **Yield:** 5 servings.

Nutritional Analysis: One 1-cup serving (prepared with light soy sauce; calculated without rice) equals 148 calories, 355 mg sodium, 55 mg cholesterol, 13 g carbohydrate, 22 g protein, 1 g fat. **Diabetic Exchanges:** 3 vegetable, 2 very lean meat.

Orange Walnut Chicken

(Pictured on page 74)

For an impressive main dish that's not tricky to prepare, try this mouth-watering chicken. With orange juice concentrate, lemon juice and orange marmalade, the pretty sauce has a zesty taste. —*TerryAnn Moore Haddon Township, New Jersey*

- 3 tablespoons orange juice concentrate
- 3 tablespoons vegetable oil, *divided*
- 1 tablespoon soy sauce
- 1 garlic clove, minced
- 4 boneless skinless chicken breast halves
- 1/2 cup coarsely chopped walnuts
- 1 tablespoon butter *or* margarine
- 4 green onions, thinly sliced, *divided*
- 1/2 cup orange marmalade
- 1/2 cup orange juice
- 1/4 cup lemon juice
- 2 tablespoons honey
- 1 to 2 tablespoons grated orange peel
- 2 to 3 teaspoons grated lemon peel
- 1/2 teaspoon salt
- 1/8 teaspoon pepper

Hot cooked rice

In a large resealable plastic bag, combine orange juice concentrate, 2 tablespoons oil, soy sauce and garlic. Add chicken; seal bag and turn to coat. Refrigerate for 2-3 hours.

Remove chicken; reserve marinade. In a skillet, cook chicken in remaining oil until juices run clear. Meanwhile, in a saucepan, saute walnuts in butter until lightly browned; remove and set aside. Set aside 1/4 cup green onions for garnish. Add remaining onions to saucepan; saute until tender.

Add reserved marinade and the next eight ingredients. Bring to a rolling boil; boil for 2 minutes. Reduce heat; simmer, uncovered, for 5-10 minutes or until sauce reaches desired consistency. Serve chicken over rice; top with sauce and reserved walnuts and onions. **Yield:** 4 servings.

🍲 🍲 🍲

Pork and Pear Stir-Fry

(Pictured at right)

I've served this full-flavored stir-fry for years, always to rave reviews. Tender pork and ripe pears make a sweet combination, and a spicy sauce adds plenty of zip. This dish is a must for help-yourself luncheons or fellowship dinners. —*Betty Phillips French Creek, West Virginia*

✓ Uses less fat, sugar or salt. Includes Nutritional Analysis and Diabetic Exchanges.

- 1/2 cup plum preserves
- 3 tablespoons soy sauce
- 2 tablespoons lemon juice
- 1 tablespoon prepared horseradish
- 2 teaspoons cornstarch
- 1/4 teaspoon crushed red pepper flakes
- 1 medium sweet yellow *or* green pepper, julienned
- 1/8 to 1/4 teaspoon ground ginger *or* 1/2 to 1 teaspoon minced fresh gingerroot
- 1 tablespoon vegetable oil
- 3 medium ripe pears, peeled and sliced
- 1 pound pork tenderloin, cut into 1/4-inch strips
- 1 can (8 ounces) sliced water chestnuts, drained
- 1-1/2 cups fresh *or* frozen snow peas
- 1 tablespoon sliced almonds, toasted

Hot cooked rice

In a bowl, combine the first six ingredients; set aside. In a skillet or wok, stir-fry yellow pepper and ginger in oil for 2 minutes. Add the pears; stir-fry for 1 minute or until pepper is crisp-tender. Remove and keep warm. Stir-fry half of the pork at a time for 1-2 minutes or until meat is no longer pink.

Return the pear mixture and all of the pork to pan. Add water chestnuts and reserved sauce. Bring to a boil; cook and stir for 2 minutes. Add the peas and heat through. Sprinkle with almonds. Serve over rice. **Yield:** 4 servings.

Nutritional Analysis: One serving (prepared with light soy sauce and reduced-sugar apricot fruit spread instead of plum preserves; calculated without rice) equals 368 calories, 563 mg sodium, 67 mg cholesterol, 45 g carbohydrate, 28 g protein, 9 g fat, 8 g fiber. **Diabetic Exchanges:** 3 lean meat, 1-1/2 fruit, 1 starch, 1 vegetable.

Chicken Fajitas

(Pictured above)

Fresh flavor with a flair describes this quick and easy recipe. Fajitas are great for hot summer evenings when you want to serve something fun and tasty, yet keep cooking to a minimum. Top them with sour cream, guacamole or both.
—Lindsay St. John
Plainfield, Indiana

✓ Uses less fat, sugar or salt. Includes Nutritional Analysis and Diabetic Exchanges.

- 1/4 cup lime juice
- 1 garlic clove, minced
- 1 teaspoon chili powder
- 1/2 teaspoon ground cumin
- 2 whole boneless skinless chicken breasts, cut into strips
- 1 medium onion, cut into thin wedges
- 1/2 medium sweet red pepper, cut into strips
- 1/2 medium yellow pepper, cut into strips
- 1/2 medium green pepper, cut into strips
- 1/2 cup salsa
- 12 flour tortillas (8 inches), warmed
- 1-1/2 cups (6 ounces) shredded cheddar *or* Monterey Jack cheese

In a bowl, combine lime juice, garlic, chili powder and cumin. Add chicken; stir. Refrigerate for 15 minutes. In a nonstick skillet, saute onion and chicken with marinade for 3 minutes or until chicken is no longer pink. Add peppers; saute for 3-5 minutes or until crisp-tender. Stir in salsa. Divide mixture among tortillas; top with cheese. Roll up; serve immediately. **Yield:** 6 servings.

Nutritional Analysis: One serving (prepared with cheddar cheese) equals 228 calories, 353 mg sodium, 39 mg cholesterol, 19 g carbohydrate, 17 g protein, 12 g fat. **Diabetic Exchanges:** 2 meat, 1 vegetable, 1 starch.

Hearty New England Dinner

(Pictured below)

This favorite slow-cooker recipe came from a friend. At first, my husband was a bit skeptical about a roast that wasn't fixed in the oven, but he loves the old-fashioned goodness of this version with zesty gravy.
—Claire McCombs, San Diego, California

- 2 medium carrots, sliced
- 1 medium onion, sliced
- 1 celery rib, sliced
- 1 boneless chuck roast (about 3 pounds)
- 1 teaspoon salt, *divided*
- 1/4 teaspoon pepper
- 1 envelope onion soup mix
- 2 cups water
- 1 tablespoon cider vinegar
- 1 bay leaf
- 1/2 small head cabbage, cut into wedges
- 3 tablespoons butter *or* margarine
- 2 tablespoons all-purpose flour
- 1 tablespoon dried minced onion
- 2 tablespoons prepared horseradish

Place carrots, onion and celery in a 5-qt. slow cooker. Place the roast on top; sprinkle with 1/2 teaspoon salt and pepper. Add soup mix, water, vinegar and bay leaf. Cover and cook on low for 7-9 hours or until beef is almost tender; discard bay leaf. Increase heat to high. Add cabbage. Cover and cook for 30-40 minutes or until cabbage is tender.

Meanwhile, melt butter in a saucepan; stir in flour and minced onion. Add 1-1/2 cups cooking liquid from the slow cooker. Stir in horseradish and remaining salt; bring to a boil. Cook and stir over low heat until thick and smooth, about 2 minutes. Serve with roast and vegetables. **Yield:** 6-8 servings.

Chicken and Barley Boiled Dinner

(Pictured below)

I like this recipe because it's nutritious and adequately feeds my two teenage sons and husband. I'm a busy teacher, and time is of the essence. —Susan Greeley Morrill, Maine

- 2 broiler/fryer chickens (about 3 pounds *each*), cut up and skin removed
- 3 tablespoons vegetable oil
- 2 quarts chicken broth
- 1 cup uncooked brown rice
- 1/2 cup medium pearl barley
- 1 medium onion, chopped
- 2 bay leaves
- 1/2 teaspoon dried basil
- 2 teaspoons salt
- 1/4 teaspoon pepper
- 8 carrots, cut into 1-inch pieces
- 2-1/2 cups frozen cut green beans
- 2 celery ribs, cut into 1-inch pieces

In an 8-qt. kettle or Dutch oven, brown chicken in oil. Remove chicken and set aside. Drain. In the same kettle, combine the broth, rice, barley, onion, bay leaves, basil, salt and pepper; bring to a boil. Reduce heat. Return chicken to pan; cover and simmer for 45 minutes.

Stir in the carrots, beans and celery. Cook over medium heat for 30 minutes or until the chicken, rice and barley are tender. Remove bay leaves before serving. **Yield:** 6-8 servings.

Catfish Jambalaya

(Pictured above)

My family owns a catfish-processing plant. This colorful, zippy main dish is a great favorite of ours.
—Mrs. Bill Saul, Macon, Mississippi

☑ Uses less fat, sugar or salt. Includes Nutritional Analysis and Diabetic Exchanges.

- 2 cups chopped onion
- 1/2 cup chopped celery
- 1/2 cup chopped green pepper
- 2 garlic cloves, minced
- 1/4 cup butter *or* margarine, optional
- 1 can (10 ounces) diced tomatoes and green chilies, undrained
- 1 cup sliced fresh mushrooms
- 1/4 teaspoon cayenne pepper
- 1/2 teaspoon salt, optional
- 1 pound catfish fillets, cubed
- Hot cooked rice, optional
- Sliced green onions, optional

In a saucepan over medium-high heat, saute onion, celery, green pepper and garlic in butter until tender, about 10 minutes. Add tomatoes, mushrooms, cayenne and salt if desired; bring to a boil. Add catfish. Reduce heat; cover and simmer until the fish flakes easily with a fork, about 10 minutes. If desired, serve with rice and top with green onions. **Yield:** 4 servings.

Nutritional Analysis: One serving prepared with nonstick cooking spray instead of butter and without salt; calculated without rice) equals 161 calories, 395 mg sodium, 66 mg cholesterol, 12 g carbohydrate, 21 g protein, 4 g fat. **Diabetic Exchanges:** 3 very lean meat, 2 vegetable.

Slow-Cooked Pepper Steak

(Pictured below)

After a long day in our greenhouse raising bedding plants for sale, I appreciate coming in to this hearty beef dish for supper. —Sue Gronholz
Beaver Dam, Wisconsin

1-1/2 to 2 pounds beef round steak
2 tablespoons vegetable oil
1/4 cup soy sauce
1 cup chopped onion
1 garlic clove, minced
1 teaspoon sugar
1/2 teaspoon salt
1/4 teaspoon pepper
1/4 teaspoon ground ginger
4 tomatoes, cut into eighths *or* 1 can (14-1/2 ounces) diced tomatoes, undrained
2 large green peppers, cut into strips
1 tablespoon cornstarch
1/2 cup cold water
Hot cooked noodles *or* rice

Cut beef into 3-in. x 1-in. strips; brown in oil in a skillet. Transfer to a slow cooker. Combine the next seven ingredients; pour over beef. Cover and cook on low for 5-6 hours or until meat is tender.

Add tomatoes and green peppers; cook on low 1 hour longer. Combine the cornstarch and cold water until smooth; stir into liquid in slow cooker. Cook on high until thickened. Serve over noodles or rice. **Yield:** 6-8 servings.

Sauerkraut 'n' Sausage

I've fixed this satisfying stovetop supper for dozens of group gatherings, and everyone enjoys the wonderful blend of flavors. Sweet and tart ingredients balance nicely, complemented with bacon and spices. —Edna Hoffman, Hebron, Indiana

1 small onion, chopped
1 tablespoon butter *or* margarine
1 jar (32 ounces) sauerkraut, rinsed and drained
1 pound fully cooked Polish sausage, cut into 1/2-inch chunks
3-1/2 cups diced cooked peeled potatoes
1 cup apple juice
1 medium unpeeled apple, diced
2 tablespoons brown sugar
2 tablespoons all-purpose flour
1 tablespoon caraway seeds
3 bacon strips, cooked and crumbled

In a large saucepan, saute onion in butter until tender. Add sauerkraut, sausage, potatoes, apple juice and apple. In a small bowl, combine the brown sugar, flour and caraway; stir into saucepan. Simmer for 35 minutes, stirring occasionally. Garnish with bacon. **Yield:** 10-12 servings.

— 🛒 🛒 🛒 —

Turkey Stew with Dumplings

(Pictured above right)

My husband and I love dumplings. This mild-tasting, homey dish has flavorful dumplings atop a tasty turkey and vegetable stew. It really hits the spot on chilly fall and winter days. —Rita Taylor
St. Cloud, Minnesota

8 medium carrots, cut into 1-inch chunks
4 celery ribs, cut into 1-inch chunks
1 cup chopped onion
1/2 cup butter *or* margarine
2 cans (10-1/2 ounces *each*) beef consomme
4-2/3 cups water, *divided*
2 teaspoons salt
1/4 teaspoon pepper
3 cups cubed cooked turkey
2 cups frozen cut green beans
1/2 cup all-purpose flour
2 teaspoons Worcestershire sauce
DUMPLINGS:
1-1/2 cups all-purpose flour
2 teaspoons baking powder
1 teaspoon salt
2 tablespoons minced fresh parsley

1/8 teaspoon poultry seasoning
3/4 cup milk
1 egg

In a Dutch oven or soup kettle, saute carrots, celery and onion in butter for 10 minutes. Add consomme, 4 cups water, salt and pepper. Cover and cook over low heat 15 minutes or until vegetables are tender. Add turkey and beans; cook for 5 minutes. In a bowl, combine flour, Worcestershire sauce and remaining water until smooth. Stir into turkey mixture; bring to a boil. Reduce heat; cover and simmer 5 minutes, stirring occasionally.

For dumplings, combine flour, baking powder and salt in a bowl. Stir in parsley and poultry seasoning. Combine milk and egg; stir into flour mixture just until moistened. Drop by tablespoons onto simmering stew. Cover and simmer for 10 minutes; uncover and simmer 10 minutes longer. **Yield:** 10-12 servings.

— 🍵 🍵 🍵 —

Herbed Beef Stew

(Pictured at right)

This stew looks as terrific as it tastes! Flavored with a variety of herbs and chock-full of vegetables, this recipe lists salt as an option, making it ideal for family members and friends who must restrict sodium.
—*Marlene Severson, Everson, Washington*

2 pounds beef stew meat, cut into 1-inch cubes

2 tablespoons vegetable oil
3 cups water
1 large onion, chopped
2 teaspoons pepper
1 to 2 teaspoons salt, optional
1-1/2 teaspoons garlic powder
1 teaspoon dried rosemary, crushed
1 teaspoon dried oregano
1 teaspoon dried basil
1 teaspoon ground marjoram
2 bay leaves
1 can (6 ounces) tomato paste
2 cups cubed peeled potatoes
2 cups sliced carrots
1 large green pepper, chopped
1 package (10 ounces) frozen green beans
1 package (10 ounces) frozen peas
1 package (10 ounces) frozen kernel corn
1/4 pound mushrooms, sliced
3 medium tomatoes, chopped

In a Dutch oven, brown meat in oil. Add water, onion, seasonings and tomato paste. Cover and simmer for 1-1/2 hours or until meat is tender.

Stir in potatoes, carrots and green pepper; simmer for 30 minutes. Add additional water if necessary. Stir in remaining ingredients; cover and simmer for 20 minutes. Remove bay leaves. **Yield:** 10-12 servings.

Breads, Rolls & Muffins

Tempting oven-fresh breads, rolls and muffins make an irresistible snack or accompaniment to any meal.

HOME-BAKED GOODIES. Clockwise from upper left: Cappuccino Muffins (p. 113), Italian Cheese Twists (p. 121), Sesame Wheat Bread (p. 117), Mini Blue Cheese Rolls (p. 120) and Lemon Cheese Braid (p. 111).

Idaho Spudnuts

(Pictured below)

Raising eight children on a potato farm in Idaho, Mother was creative at using an abundant crop. We especially liked her light, fluffy potato doughnuts. We encouraged Mother to let us help make them often. Now I prepare them to share with friends and neighbors.
—Sandi Jones, Windsor, California

> 1 **pound russet potatoes, peeled and quartered**
> 2 **packages (1/4 ounce *each*) active dry yeast**
> 1-1/2 **cups warm milk (110° to 115°)**
> 1/2 **cup vegetable oil**
> 1/2 **cup sugar**
> 2 **eggs**
> 1 **teaspoon salt**
> 7-1/2 **cups all-purpose flour**
> **Oil for deep-fat frying**
> 4 **cups confectioners' sugar**
> 1/3 **cup water**
> 1 **teaspoon vanilla extract**

Place potatoes in a saucepan and cover with water. Bring to a boil; cook until tender. Drain, reserving 1/2 cup of cooking liquid; cool to 110°-115°. Discard remaining cooking liquid. Mash potatoes without milk or butter. In a large mixing bowl, dissolve yeast in reserved cooking liquid. Add mashed potatoes, milk, oil, sugar, eggs and salt. Add enough flour to form a soft dough.

Place in a greased bowl, turning once to grease top. Cover and let rise in a warm place until doubled, about 1 hour. Punch dough down; let rise again until doubled, about 20 minutes. Roll out on a floured surface to 1/2-in. thickness. Cut with a floured 3-in. doughnut cutter. In an electric skillet or deep-fat fryer, heat oil to 375°. Fry doughnuts, a few at a time, until golden brown. Combine glaze ingredients; dip warm doughnuts in glaze. Cool on wire racks. **Yield:** 4 dozen.

Buttermilk Pecan Waffles

(Pictured above)

I like cooking with buttermilk. These nutty, golden waffles are my husband's favorite breakfast, so we enjoy them often. They're as easy to prepare as regular waffles, but their unique taste makes them exceptional.
—Edna Hoffman, Hebron, Indiana

> 2 **cups all-purpose flour**
> 1 **tablespoon baking powder**
> 1 **teaspoon baking soda**
> 1/2 **teaspoon salt**
> 4 **eggs**
> 2 **cups buttermilk**
> 1/2 **cup butter *or* margarine, melted**
> 3 **tablespoons chopped pecans**

Combine the flour, baking powder, baking soda and salt; set aside. In a mixing bowl, beat eggs until light. Add buttermilk; mix well. Add dry ingredients and beat until batter is smooth. Stir in butter. Pour about 3/4 cup batter onto a lightly greased preheated waffle iron. Sprinkle with a few pecans. Bake according to manufacturer's directions until golden brown. Repeat with remaining batter and pecans. **Yield:** 7 waffles (about 8 inches each).

Mini Elephant Ears

Our kids love to help stretch the pieces of convenient frozen dough to make these ears. After I fry them, the kids brush them with butter and sprinkle on the cinnamon-sugar. Then we all dig in! *—Malea Kruse*
Huntertown, Indiana

Frozen white dinner roll dough (10 rolls)
Oil for deep-fat frying
> 1/2 **cup sugar**

1 tablespoon ground cinnamon
3 tablespoons butter *or* margarine, melted

Cover the dough with plastic wrap and thaw at room temperature for about 2 hours. Heat oil in an electric skillet or deep-fat fryer to 375°. Combine the sugar and cinnamon; set aside. Stretch each piece of dough into a flat ear shape. Fry, a few at a time, for 1-1/2 minutes per side or until browned. Drain on paper towels. Brush with butter and sprinkle with cinnamon-sugar. **Yield:** 10 servings.

French Toast Fingers

(Pictured below)

Bite-size French toast "fingers" are great for a buffet...and kids of all ages love them. The strawberry center is tasty. —Mavis Diment, Marcus, Iowa

✓ Uses less fat, sugar or salt. Includes Nutritional Analysis and Diabetic Exchanges.

  2 eggs
1/4 cup milk
1/4 teaspoon salt
1/2 cup strawberry preserves
  8 slices day-old white bread
Confectioners' sugar, optional

In a small bowl, beat eggs, milk and salt; set aside. Spread preserves on four slices of bread; top with remaining bread. Trim crusts; cut each sandwich into three strips. Dip both sides in egg mixture. Cook on a lightly greased hot griddle for 2 minutes on each side or until golden brown. Dust with confectioners' sugar if desired. **Yield:** 4 servings.
   Nutritional Analysis: One serving of three strips (prepared with egg substitute, fat-free milk and sugar-free preserves and without confectioners' sugar) equals 235 calories, 500 mg sodium, 2 mg cholesterol, 42 g carbohydrate, 10 g protein, 4 g fat. **Diabetic Exchanges:** 2 starch, 1 meat, 1/2 fruit.

Orange-Glazed Crullers

(Pictured above)

The dough is made ahead, so this recipe is great for a morning gathering. —Muriel Lerdal, Humboldt, Iowa

  1 package (1/4 ounce) active dry yeast
1/4 cup warm water (110° to 115°)
3/4 cup warm milk (110° to 115°)
1/2 cup butter *or* margarine, softened
1/4 cup sugar
  1 teaspoon salt
  2 eggs, beaten
  4 cups all-purpose flour
Oil for deep-fat frying
GLAZE:
  2 cups confectioners' sugar
  3 tablespoons orange juice
  1 teaspoon grated orange peel

In a mixing bowl, dissolve yeast in water. Add milk, butter, sugar, salt and eggs; mix well. Beat in 2 cups flour until smooth. Add remaining flour. Place in a greased bowl, turning once to grease top. Cover and refrigerate overnight. Punch dough down; divide in half. Return one portion to the refrigerator. On a floured surface, roll out second portion into an 18-in. x 9-in. rectangle; cut widthwise into 3/4-in. strips. Fold each strip in half lengthwise and twist several times. Pinch ends to seal.
   Place on greased baking sheets. Repeat with the remaining dough. Cover and let rise until almost doubled, about 35-45 minutes. In an electric skillet or deep-fat fryer, heat oil to 375°. Fry crullers, a few at a time, until golden, about 1 minute on each side, turning with a slotted spoon. Drain on paper towels. Combine glaze ingredients; brush over warm crullers. **Yield:** about 3 dozen.

and place on an ungreased baking sheet. Brush with milk; sprinkle with remaining sugar.

Bake at 400° for 12-15 minutes or until lightly browned. Combine glaze ingredients if desired; drizzle over scones. Combine orange butter ingredients; serve with warm scones. **Yield:** 10 scones.

Cinnamon Rolls in a Snap

(Pictured below)

A friend called one morning to see if I wanted company for coffee. I was going to make biscuits for breakfast but wanted something fancier to share. So I quickly turned those biscuits into hot cinnamon rolls. Was my friend impressed when she arrived to the sweet aroma! —Laura McDermott, Big Lake, Minnesota

4-1/2 cups biscuit/baking mix
1-1/3 cups milk
FILLING:
   2 tablespoons butter *or* margarine, softened
   1/4 cup sugar
   1 teaspoon ground cinnamon
   1/3 cup raisins, optional
ICING:
   2 cups confectioners' sugar
   2 tablespoons milk
   2 tablespoons butter *or* margarine, melted
   1 teaspoon vanilla extract

In a bowl, combine biscuit mix and milk. Turn onto a floured surface; knead 8-10 times. Roll into a 12-in. x 10-in. rectangle. Spread with butter. Combine sugar, cinnamon and raisins if desired; sprinkle over butter. Roll up from a long side; pinch seam to seal. Cut into 12 slices; place with cut side down on a greased baking sheet.

Bake at 450° for 10-12 minutes or until golden brown. Meanwhile, combine the icing ingredients; spread over rolls. Serve warm. **Yield:** 1 dozen.

Cranberry Orange Scones

(Pictured above)

Moist and scrumptious, these scones come out perfect every time. I savor the chewy dried cranberries and sweet orange glaze. There's nothing better than serving these remarkable scones warm with delicate orange butter. —Karen McBride
Indianapolis, Indiana

   2 cups all-purpose flour
   10 teaspoons sugar, *divided*
   1 tablespoon grated orange peel
   2 teaspoons baking powder
   1/2 teaspoon salt
   1/4 teaspoon baking soda
   1/3 cup cold butter *or* margarine
   1 cup dried cranberries
   1/4 cup orange juice
   1/4 cup half-and-half cream
   1 egg
   1 tablespoon milk
GLAZE (optional):
   1/2 cup confectioners' sugar
   1 tablespoon orange juice
ORANGE BUTTER:
   1/2 cup butter, softened
   2 to 3 tablespoons orange marmalade

In a bowl, combine flour, 7 teaspoons sugar, orange peel, baking powder, salt and baking soda. Cut in butter until the mixture resembles coarse crumbs; set aside. In a small bowl, combine cranberries, orange juice, cream and egg. Add to flour mixture and stir until a soft dough forms. Turn onto a floured surface; gently knead 6-8 times. Pat dough into an 8-in. circle. Cut into 10 wedges. Separate wedges

Quick Cherry Turnovers

(Pictured above)

These fruit-filled pastries are my family's favorite at breakfast. You can substitute other fillings for cherry.
—Elleen Oberrueter, Danbury, Iowa

- 1 tube (8 ounces) refrigerated crescent rolls
- 1 cup cherry pie filling
- 1/2 cup confectioners' sugar
- 1 to 2 tablespoons milk

Unroll dough and separate into eight triangles; make four squares by pressing the seams of two triangles together and rolling into shape. Place on an ungreased baking sheet. Spoon 1/4 cup pie filling in one corner of each square. Fold to make triangles; pinch to seal.

Bake at 375° for 10-12 minutes or until golden. Combine sugar and enough milk to reach drizzling consistency; drizzle over turnovers. Serve warm. **Yield:** 4 servings.

— 🥄 🥄 🥄 —

Lemon Cheese Braid

(Pictured at right and on page 106)

This recipe came from my mom, who is an excellent cook. It always gets rave reviews. Although it's fairly simple to make, you'll feel a sense of accomplishment because it tastes delicious and looks so impressive.
—Grace Dickey, Vernonia, Oregon

- 1 package (1/4 ounce) active dry yeast
- 3 tablespoons warm water (110° to 115°)
- 1/4 cup sugar
- 1/3 cup milk
- 1/4 cup butter *or* margarine, melted
- 2 eggs
- 1/2 teaspoon salt
- 3 to 3-1/2 cups all-purpose flour

FILLING:
- 2 packages (one 8 ounces, one 3 ounces) cream cheese, softened
- 1/2 cup sugar
- 1 egg
- 1 teaspoon grated lemon peel

ICING:
- 1/2 cup confectioners' sugar
- 2 to 3 teaspoons milk
- 1/4 teaspoon vanilla extract

In a mixing bowl, dissolve yeast in warm water; let stand for 5 minutes. Add sugar, milk, butter, eggs, salt and 2 cups flour; beat on low speed for 3 minutes. Stir in enough of the remaining flour to form a soft dough. Turn out onto a floured surface; knead until smooth and elastic, about 6-8 minutes. Place in a greased bowl, turning once to grease top. Cover and let rise in a warm place until doubled, about 1 hour.

Meanwhile, beat filling ingredients in a mixing bowl until fluffy; set aside. Punch dough down. On a floured surface, roll into a 14-in. x 12-in. rectangle. Place on a greased baking sheet. Spread filling down center third of rectangle.

On each long side, cut 1-in.-wide strips, 3 in. into center. Starting at one end, fold alternating strips at an angle across filling. Seal end. Cover and let rise for 30 minutes. Bake at 375° for 25-30 minutes or until golden brown. Cool. Combine icing ingredients; drizzle over bread. **Yield:** 12-14 servings.

Fill greased jumbo muffin cups half full with batter. Divide cream cheese filling and preserves evenly between muffin cups; swirl gently. Cover with remaining batter. Sprinkle with topping. Bake at 350° for 30-35 minutes or until muffins test done. Cool for 5 minutes before removing from pans to wire racks. **Yield:** 7 jumbo muffins or 14 regular muffins.

Editor's Note: If using regular-size muffin cups, bake for 20-25 minutes.

Cherry Almond Muffins
(Pictured above)

As a kid, I loved doughnuts filled with custard or jelly. So I decided to experiment with fillings in muffins. The result was this recipe. They're almost like a pastry.
—John Montgomery, Fortuna, California

1-3/4 cups all-purpose flour
1/2 cup plus 1 tablespoon sugar
1/2 teaspoon baking powder
1/2 teaspoon baking soda
1/4 teaspoon salt
1/2 cup cold butter *or* margarine
1 egg
3/4 cup sour cream
1 teaspoon almond extract
FILLING:
1 package (8 ounces) cream cheese, softened
1 egg
1/4 cup sugar
1/2 teaspoon vanilla extract
3/4 cup cherry preserves
TOPPING:
1/3 cup all-purpose flour
2 tablespoons sugar
2 tablespoons cold butter *or* margarine
1/3 cup chopped sliced almonds

In a bowl, combine flour, sugar, baking powder, baking soda and salt. Cut in butter until mixture resembles coarse crumbs. In another bowl, beat the egg, sour cream and almond extract until smooth. Stir into dry ingredients just until moistened (batter will be thick). In a mixing bowl, beat cream cheese, egg, sugar and vanilla until smooth. In a saucepan over low heat, warm the preserves.

For topping, combine flour and sugar in a small bowl; cut in butter until crumbly. Stir in almonds.

Nutty Apple Muffins
(Pictured below)

I teach quick-bread making for 4-H, and I'm always on the lookout for good new recipes. My sister-in-law shared this recipe with me for a slightly different kind of muffin. With apples and coconut, they are moist, chewy and tasty. —Gloria Kaufmann, Orrville, Ohio

1-1/2 cups all-purpose flour
1-1/2 teaspoons baking powder
3/4 teaspoon salt
1/2 teaspoon ground nutmeg
1/4 teaspoon baking soda
2 eggs
3/4 cup sugar
1/3 cup vegetable oil
3 tablespoons milk
1-1/2 cups diced peeled apples
1 cup chopped walnuts
3/4 cup flaked coconut

In a large bowl, combine the flour, baking powder, salt, nutmeg and baking soda. In another bowl, beat eggs, sugar, oil and milk. Stir in apples, nuts and coconut. Stir into dry ingredients just until moistened. Fill 18 greased muffin cups three-fourths full. Bake at 350° for 20-25 minutes or until a toothpick comes out clean. Cool for 10 minutes before removing from pans to wire racks. **Yield:** 1 dozen.

Cappuccino Muffins

(Pictured below and on page 106)

These are my favorite muffins to serve with a cup of coffee or a tall glass of cold milk. Not only are they great for breakfast, they make a tasty midnight snack or dessert. I get lots of recipe requests when I serve these. —Janice Bassing, Racine, Wisconsin

ESPRESSO SPREAD:
4 ounces cream cheese, cubed
1 tablespoon sugar
1/2 teaspoon instant coffee granules
1/2 teaspoon vanilla extract
1/4 cup miniature semisweet chocolate chips
MUFFINS:
2 cups all-purpose flour
3/4 cup sugar
2-1/2 teaspoons baking powder
1 teaspoon ground cinnamon
1/2 teaspoon salt
1 cup milk
2 tablespoons instant coffee granules
1/2 cup butter *or* margarine, melted
1 egg
1 teaspoon vanilla extract
3/4 cup miniature semisweet chocolate chips

In a food processor or blender, combine spread ingredients; cover and process until well blended. Cover and refrigerate until serving. In a bowl, combine flour, sugar, baking powder, cinnamon and salt. In another bowl, stir milk and coffee granules until the coffee is dissolved. Add butter, egg and vanilla; mix well. Stir into dry ingredients just until moistened. Fold in chocolate chips.

Fill greased or paper-lined muffin cups two-thirds full. Bake at 375° for 17-20 minutes or until muffins test done. Cool for 5 minutes before removing from pans to wire racks. Serve with espresso spread. **Yield:** about 14 muffins (1 cup spread).

Chocolate Cookie Muffins

(Pictured above)

I'm always happy to discover new ways to make muffins. This fun version includes crushed cream-filled chocolate cookies in the batter. They're a double treat. —Jan Blue, Cuyahoga Falls, Ohio

1-3/4 cups all-purpose flour
1/4 cup sugar
3 teaspoons baking powder
1/3 cup cold butter *or* margarine
1 egg
1 cup milk
16 cream-filled chocolate sandwich cookies, coarsely chopped
TOPPING:
3 tablespoons all-purpose flour
3 tablespoons sugar
5 cream-filled chocolate sandwich cookies, finely crushed
2 tablespoons cold butter *or* margarine
1 cup vanilla *or* white chips
1 tablespoon shortening

In a large bowl, combine flour, sugar and baking powder. Cut in butter until the mixture resembles coarse crumbs. Beat egg and milk; stir into dry ingredients just until moistened. Fold in chopped cookies. Fill greased muffin cups two-thirds full.

For topping, combine flour, sugar and crushed cookies; cut in butter until crumbly. Sprinkle about 1 tablespoon over each muffin. Bake at 400° for 16-18 minutes or until muffins test done. Cool for 5 minutes before removing from pan to a wire rack. In a heavy saucepan over low heat, melt chips and shortening until smooth. Drizzle over cooled muffins. **Yield:** 1 dozen.

Potato Pan Rolls

(Pictured above)

Beautiful color and light-as-a-feather texture make these rolls our family's favorite for holiday meals. I won the Reserve Champion award at a 4-H yeast bread competition with this recipe. —LeAnne Hofferichter
Floresville, Texas

        2 medium potatoes, peeled and quartered
1-1/2 cups water
        2 packages (1/4 ounce *each*) active dry
            yeast
        1 teaspoon sugar
    1/2 cup butter *or* margarine, melted
    1/2 cup honey
    1/4 cup vegetable oil
        2 eggs
        2 teaspoons salt
        6 to 7 cups all-purpose flour

In a saucepan, bring potatoes and water to a boil. Reduce heat; cover and simmer for 15-20 minutes or until tender. Drain, reserving 1 cup cooking liquid; cool liquid to 110°-115°. Mash potatoes; set aside 1 cup to cool to 110°-115° (save remaining potatoes for another use).

    In a mixing bowl, dissolve yeast and sugar in reserved potato liquid; let stand for 5 minutes. Add butter, honey, oil, eggs, salt, 1-1/2 cups flour and reserved mashed potatoes; beat until smooth. Stir in enough remaining flour to form a soft dough. Turn onto a floured surface; knead until smooth and elastic, about 6-8 minutes. Place in a greased bowl, turning once to grease top. Cover and let rise in a warm place until doubled, about 1 hour.

    Punch dough down and turn onto a floured surface; divide into 30 pieces. Shape each piece into a ball. Place 10 balls each in three greased 9-in. round baking pans. Cover and let rise until doubled, about 30 minutes. Bake at 400° for 20-25 minutes or until golden brown. Remove from pans to wire racks to cool. **Yield:** 2-1/2 dozen.

— 🥄 🥄 🥄 —

Angel Biscuits

I first received a sample of these light, wonderful biscuits, along with the recipe, from an elderly gentleman friend. I now bake them often as a Saturday-morning treat. They're perfect with sausage gravy, too.
—Faye Hintz, Springfield, Missouri

        2 packages (1/4 ounce *each*) active dry
            yeast
    1/4 cup warm water (110° to 115°)
        2 cups warm buttermilk (110° to 115°)
        5 cups all-purpose flour
    1/3 cup sugar
        2 teaspoons baking powder
        1 teaspoon baking soda
        2 teaspoons salt
        1 cup shortening
Melted butter *or* margarine

Dissolve yeast in warm water. Let stand for 5 minutes. Stir in the buttermilk; set aside. In a large mixing bowl, combine flour, sugar, baking powder, baking soda and salt. Cut in shortening with a pastry blender until crumbly. Stir in yeast mixture; mix well. Turn out onto a lightly floured surface; knead lightly 3-4 times.

    Roll out to 1/2-in. thickness. Cut with a 2-1/2-in. biscuit cutter. Place on lightly greased baking sheets. Cover and let rise in a warm place for about 1-1/2 hours.

    Bake at 450° for 8-10 minutes. Brush tops with melted butter. Remove from pans to wire racks. **Yield:** about 2-1/2 dozen.

🥄 Flour Facts

Flour should be stored in a cool dry place. All-purpose and whole wheat flour will keep for 1 year stored at 70° and 2 years at 40°. Flour can be frozen in airtight containers, but let it come to room temperature before using.

Sour Cream 'n' Chive Biscuits

I grow chives in my front yard and like to use them in as many recipes as I can. These moist, tender biscuits are delectable as well as attractive. —Lucille Proctor
Panguitch, Utah

    2 cups all-purpose flour
    1 tablespoon baking powder
  1/2 teaspoon salt
  1/4 teaspoon baking soda
  1/3 cup shortening
  3/4 cup sour cream
  1/4 cup milk
  1/4 cup snipped fresh chives

In a bowl, combine dry ingredients. Cut in shortening until mixture resembles coarse crumbs. With a fork, stir in sour cream, milk and chives until the mixture forms a ball. On a lightly floured surface, knead 5-6 times. Roll out to 3/4-in. thickness; cut with a 2-in. biscuit cutter. Place on an ungreased baking sheet. Bake at 350° for 12-15 minutes or until golden brown. **Yield:** 12-15 biscuits.

Sky-High Biscuits

My recipe for high and flaky biscuits never fails to win a ribbon. —Ruth Burrus, Zionsville, Indiana

    2 cups all-purpose flour
    1 cup whole wheat flour
    2 tablespoons sugar
4-1/2 teaspoons baking powder
  3/4 teaspoon cream of tartar
  1/2 teaspoon salt
  3/4 cup cold butter *or* margarine
    1 egg
    1 cup milk

In a bowl, combine the first six ingredients. Cut in butter until crumbly. Combine egg and milk; stir into crumb mixture just until moistened. Turn onto a floured surface; knead 10-15 times. Roll out to 1-in. thickness; cut with a 2-1/2-in. biscuit cutter. Place on a greased baking sheet. Bake at 450° for 10-15 minutes or until golden brown. **Yield:** 1 dozen.

Cheddar English Muffins

(Pictured at right)

These chewy English muffins have a scrumptious mild cheese flavor that intensifies when they're split and toasted. My family enjoys them at breakfast or brunch. —Marge Goral, Ridgefield, Connecticut

✓ Uses less fat, sugar or salt. Includes Nutritional Analysis and Diabetic Exchanges.

    3 to 3-1/4 cups bread flour
    1 tablespoon sugar
    1 package (1/4 ounce) active dry yeast
    1 teaspoon salt
  3/4 cup water (120° to 130°)
    2 tablespoons canola oil
    1 egg
    1 tablespoon cider vinegar
  1/2 cup shredded cheddar cheese
    4 tablespoons cornmeal, divided

In a mixing bowl, combine 2 cups flour, sugar, yeast and salt. Add water and oil; beat on medium speed for 2 minutes. Add egg and vinegar; beat on high for 2 minutes. Stir in cheese and enough remaining flour to form a stiff dough. Turn onto a floured surface; knead until dough is smooth and no longer sticky, about 2 minutes.

Roll dough to about 1/2-in. thickness. Cut with a 3-in. round cutter. Roll scraps if desired. Coat baking sheets with nonstick cooking spray and sprinkle with 2 tablespoons cornmeal. Place muffins 2 in. apart on prepared pans. Sprinkle tops with remaining cornmeal. Cover and let rise until doubled, about 1 hour.

Heat an ungreased griddle or electric skillet to 325°. Cook muffins for 20-25 minutes or until golden brown, turning every 5 minutes. Remove to wire racks to cool. Split with a fork and toast if desired. **Yield:** about 16 muffins.

Nutritional Analysis: One muffin equals 128 calories, 3 g fat (1 g saturated fat), 17 mg cholesterol, 173 mg sodium, 21 g carbohydrate, 1 g fiber, 5 g protein. **Diabetic Exchanges:** 1-1/2 starch, 1/2 fat.

Pineapple Sweet Rolls

(Pictured below right)

A pan of these marvelous rolls makes any breakfast a holiday! Folks expect typical cinnamon rolls and are pleasantly surprised by these unusual treats.
—Pat Walter, Pine Island, Minnesota

- 2 packages (1/4 ounce *each*) active dry yeast
- 1/2 cup warm water (110° to 115°)
- 1-1/2 cups warm milk (110° to 115°)
- 6 tablespoons butter *or* margarine, melted
- 1 cup sugar
- 1 teaspoon salt
- 2 eggs, beaten
- 6 to 6-1/2 cups all-purpose flour

FILLING:
- 1 tablespoon butter *or* margarine
- 1 tablespoon all-purpose flour
- 1/2 cup orange juice
- 2 tablespoons grated orange peel
- 1 can (8 ounces) crushed pineapple, drained
- 1/3 cup sugar
- 1/8 teaspoon salt

GLAZE:
- 1/2 cup confectioners' sugar
- 1 tablespoon orange juice

Dissolve yeast in water. Add milk, butter, sugar, salt, eggs and 1-1/3 cups flour; beat until smooth. Stir in enough remaining flour to form a soft dough. Turn onto a floured surface; knead until smooth and elastic, about 6-8 minutes. Place in a greased bowl, turning once to grease top. Cover and let rise in a warm place until doubled, about 1 hour.

Meanwhile, melt butter in a saucepan. Add remaining filling ingredients; bring to a boil, stirring constantly. Reduce heat; simmer 3-4 minutes or until thickened. Remove from the heat; cool. Punch

YEAST BREAD BONUS. If you "knead" ideas for special loaves and raised-dough treats, why not try Peppery Cheese Bread, Pineapple Sweet Rolls or Homemade Egg Bread (shown above, clockwise from upper left)?

dough down; divide in half. Roll each half into a 15-in. x 12-in. rectangle; spread with filling. Roll up jelly-roll style starting with long side. Slice into 1-in. rolls. Place with cut side down in two greased 13-in. x 9-in. x 2-in. baking pans. Cover and let rise until doubled, about 1 hour. Bake at 350° for 20-25 minutes. Cool. Combine glaze ingredients; drizzle over rolls. **Yield:** 2-1/2 dozen.

— ☕ ☕ ☕ —

Peppery Cheese Bread

(Pictured below left)

Savory slices of this batter bread will complement any meal. Or use it to liven up sandwiches.
—Sue Braunschweig, Delafield, Wisconsin

> 1 package (1/4 ounce) active dry yeast
> 1/4 cup warm water (110° to 115°)
> 1 cup (8 ounces) sour cream
> 1 egg, beaten
> 2 tablespoons sugar
> 1 teaspoon salt
> 2-1/3 to 2-1/2 cups all-purpose flour
> 1 cup (4 ounces) shredded cheddar cheese
> 1/2 teaspoon pepper

In a mixing bowl, dissolve yeast in water. Add the sour cream, egg, sugar, salt and 2/3 cup flour; beat until smooth. Stir in enough remaining flour to form a soft dough. Fold in cheese and pepper (dough will be sticky). Do not knead. Place in a greased 8-in. x 4-in. x 2-in. loaf pan. Cover and let rise in a warm place until doubled, about 1 hour. Bake at 350° for 35-40 minutes. Remove from pan to a wire rack to cool. **Yield:** 1 loaf.

— ☕ ☕ ☕ —

Homemade Egg Bread

(Pictured at far left)

People rave about this tender, delicate bread every time I serve it. The recipe makes two loaves...one to enjoy and one to share.   —June Mullins, Livonia, Missouri

> 2 packages (1/4 ounce *each*) active dry yeast
> 1/2 cup warm water (110° to 115°)
> 1-1/2 cups warm milk (110° to 115°)
> 1/4 cup sugar
> 1 tablespoon salt
> 3 eggs, beaten
> 1/4 cup butter *or* margarine, softened
> 7 to 7-1/2 cups all-purpose flour
> 1 egg yolk
> 2 tablespoons water
Sesame seeds

Dissolve the yeast in warm water. Add the milk, sugar, salt, eggs, butter and 3-1/2 cups flour; mix well. Stir in enough remaining flour to form a soft dough. Turn onto a floured surface; knead until smooth and elastic, about 6-8 minutes. Place in a greased bowl, turning once to grease top. Cover and let rise in a warm place until doubled, 1-1/2 to 2 hours.

Punch dough down. Cover and let rise until almost doubled, about 30 minutes. Divide into six portions. On a floured surface, shape each into a 14-in.-long rope. For each loaf, braid three ropes together on a greased baking sheet; pinch ends to seal. Cover and let rise until doubled, 50-60 minutes. Beat egg yolk and water; brush over loaves. Sprinkle with sesame seeds. Bake at 375° for 30-35 minutes. Remove from pans to wire racks to cool. **Yield:** 2 loaves.

— ☕ ☕ ☕ —

Sesame Wheat Bread

(Pictured on page 106)

Unlike many whole wheat breads that are dense and heavy, this recipe makes a light tender loaf.
—Rene Ralph, Broken Arrow, Oklahoma

> 2 packages (1/4 ounce *each*) active dry yeast
> 1 cup warm water (110° to 115°)
> 1 cup warm milk (110° to 115°)
> 1/2 cup honey
> 3 tablespoons shortening
> 1 tablespoon salt
> 1 egg
> 1/4 cup sesame seeds, toasted
> 2-1/2 cups whole wheat flour
> 3 to 3-1/2 cups all-purpose flour
> 2 tablespoons butter *or* margarine, melted
Additional sesame seeds, optional

In a mixing bowl, dissolve yeast in water. Add milk, honey, shortening, salt, egg, sesame seeds, whole wheat flour and 1-1/2 cups all-purpose flour. Beat until smooth. Stir in enough remaining all-purpose flour to form a stiff dough. Turn onto a floured surface; knead until smooth and elastic, about 6-8 minutes. Place in a greased bowl, turning once to grease top. Cover and let rise in a warm place until doubled, about 1 hour.

Punch dough down. Turn onto a lightly floured surface; divide in half. Shape into loaves. Place in two greased 9-in. x 5-in. x 3-in. loaf pans. Brush with butter; sprinkle with sesame seeds if desired. Cover; let rise until doubled, about 45 minutes. Bake at 350° for 35-40 minutes or until golden. Remove from pans to wire racks to cool. **Yield:** 2 loaves.

Rosemary Garlic Braid

(Pictured above)

*This moist savory bread pairs nicely with a variety of main dishes. It's great with soup...and makes a wonderful grilled ham and cheese sandwich. I came up with the recipe a few years ago when I wanted to use up the fresh rosemary in my garden.   —Cori Oakley
Traverse City, Michigan*

    5 whole garlic bulbs
    2 teaspoons olive oil
1/4 cup minced fresh rosemary *or* 4 teaspoons
      dried rosemary, crushed
    1 tablespoon chicken broth
    9 to 9-1/2 cups bread flour
1/2 cup sugar
    3 packages (1/4 ounce *each*) quick-rise
      yeast
    3 teaspoons salt
1-1/2 cups milk
    1 cup water
3/4 cup butter, *divided*
    1 egg
1-1/2 teaspoons garlic salt

Remove papery outer skin from garlic (do not peel or separate cloves). Cut top off garlic heads, leaving root end intact. Place cut side up in a small baking dish. Brush with oil; sprinkle with rosemary. Cover and bake at 425° for 30-35 minutes or until softened. Cool for 10 minutes; squeeze softened garlic into a bowl. Add broth; lightly mash.
    In a large mixing bowl, combine 3 cups flour, sugar, yeast and salt. In a saucepan, heat milk,

water and 1/2 cup butter to 120°-130°. Add to dry ingredients; beat just until moistened. Beat in egg and garlic paste until smooth. Stir in enough remaining flour to form a soft dough (dough will be sticky). Turn onto a floured surface; knead until smooth and elastic, about 6-8 minutes. Cover and let rest for 10 minutes.
    Turn dough onto a lightly floured surface; divide into thirds. Divide each portion into three pieces; shape each into an 18-in. rope. Place three ropes on a greased baking sheet and braid; pinch ends to seal and tuck under. Repeat with remaining dough. Cover and let rise in a warm place until doubled, about 30 minutes.
    Bake at 350° for 15 minutes. Melt remaining butter; add garlic salt. Brush over bread. Bake 10-15 minutes longer or until golden brown. Remove from pans to wire racks to cool. **Yield:** 3 loaves.

Sunflower Oat Bread

*This golden bread incorporates grains that my sons, Tim and Jon, wouldn't normally touch.   —Kay Krause
Sioux Falls, South Dakota*

    3 to 4 cups all-purpose flour
    1 cup old-fashioned oats, *divided*
1/4 cup sugar
    3 tablespoons chopped walnuts
    2 tablespoons sunflower kernels
    2 teaspoons active dry yeast
3/4 teaspoon salt
3/4 cup water
1/3 cup vegetable oil
1/4 cup buttermilk
1/4 cup honey
    2 eggs
3/4 cup whole wheat flour
    1 tablespoon cold water

In a mixing bowl, combine 2 cups all-purpose flour, 3/4 cup oats, sugar, walnuts, sunflower kernels, yeast and salt. In a saucepan, heat the water, oil, buttermilk and honey to 120°-130°. Add to dry ingredients; beat until well blended. Beat in 1 egg until smooth. Stir in whole wheat flour and enough remaining all-purpose flour to form a soft dough. Turn onto a floured surface; knead until smooth and elastic, about 6-8 minutes. Place in a greased bowl, turning once to grease top. Cover and let rise in a warm place until doubled, about 1 hour.
    Punch dough down; turn onto a lightly floured surface. Divide in half; shape into round loaves. Sprinkle 2 tablespoons oats on a greased baking sheet; place loaves over oats. Cover and let rise until doubled, about 45 minutes. Beat remaining

egg and cold water; brush over loaves. Sprinkle with remaining oats. Bake at 350° for 20-25 minutes or until golden brown. Cool on wire racks. **Yield:** 2 loaves.

Onion Dill Bread

(Pictured above)

Moist and flavorful, this bread owes its richness to cottage cheese and sour cream. —Ruth Andrewson
Leavenworth, Washington

    2 teaspoons active dry yeast
3-1/2 cups bread flour
    1 teaspoon salt
    1 egg
  3/4 cup cream-style cottage cheese
  3/4 cup sour cream
    3 tablespoons sugar
    3 tablespoons dried minced onion
    2 tablespoons dill seed
1-1/2 tablespoons butter *or* margarine

In bread machine pan, place first four ingredients in order suggested by manufacturer. In a saucepan, combine remaining ingredients and heat just until warm (do not boil). Pour into bread pan. Select the basic bread setting. Choose crust color and loaf size if available. Bake according to bread machine directions. **Yield:** 1 loaf (1-1/2 pounds).

    Editor's Note: If your bread machine has a time-delay feature, we recommend you do not use it for this recipe.

Delicious Pumpkin Bread

(Pictured below)

An enticing aroma wafts through my house when this tender cake-like bread is in the oven. I bake extra loaves to give as holiday gifts. My friends wait eagerly for it every year. —Linda Burnett, Stanton, California

    5 eggs
1-1/4 cups vegetable oil
    1 can (15 ounces) solid-pack pumpkin
    2 cups all-purpose flour
    2 cups sugar
    2 packages (3 ounces *each*) cook-and-serve
      vanilla pudding mix
    1 teaspoon baking soda
    1 teaspoon ground cinnamon
  1/2 teaspoon salt

In a mixing bowl, beat the eggs. Add oil and pumpkin; beat until smooth. Combine remaining ingredients; gradually beat into pumpkin mixture. Pour batter into five greased 5-in. x 2-1/2-in. x 2-in. loaf pans. Bake at 325° for 50-55 minutes or until a toothpick inserted near the center comes out clean. Cool for 10 minutes; remove from pans to wire racks to cool completely. **Yield:** 5 miniature loaves.

    Editor's Note: Bread may also be baked in two greased 8-in. x 4-in. x 2-in. loaf pans for 75-80 minutes.

Perfect Biscuits

Flat heavy biscuits can be the result of over-kneaded biscuit dough. Limit your kneading to 10 to 12 strokes. Gently pat or roll dough before cutting biscuits.

Herbed Oatmeal Pan Bread

(Pictured below)

This beautiful, golden pan bread is especially good with a steaming bowl of homemade soup. The oats give it a distinctive flavor, and we really like the herb and Parmesan cheese topping. —Karen Bourne
Magrath, Alberta

1-1/2 cups boiling water
  1 cup old-fashioned oats
  2 packages (1/4 ounce *each*) active dry yeast
1/2 cup warm water (110° to 115°)
1/4 cup sugar
  3 tablespoons butter *or* margarine, softened
  2 teaspoons salt
  1 egg, lightly beaten
  4 to 4-3/4 cups all-purpose flour
TOPPING:
1/4 cup butter *or* margarine, melted, *divided*
  2 tablespoons grated Parmesan cheese
  1 teaspoon dried basil
1/2 teaspoon dried oregano
1/2 teaspoon garlic powder

In a small bowl, combine boiling water and oats; cool to 110°-115°. In a mixing bowl, dissolve yeast in warm water. Add sugar, butter, salt, egg, oat mixture and 2 cups of flour; beat until smooth. Add enough remaining flour to form a soft dough. Turn onto a floured surface; knead until smooth and elastic, about 6-8 minutes. Place in a greased bowl, turning once to grease top. Cover and let rise in a warm place until doubled, about 30 minutes.

Punch dough down and press evenly into a greased 13-in. x 9-in. x 2-in. baking pan. With a very sharp knife, cut diagonal lines 1-1/2 in. apart completely through dough. Repeat in opposite direction, creating a diamond pattern. Cover and let rise in a warm place until doubled, about 1 hour. Redefine pattern by gently poking along cut lines with knife tip. Brush with 2 tablespoons melted butter. Bake at 375° for 15 minutes.

Meanwhile, combine Parmesan cheese, basil, oregano and garlic powder. Brush bread with remaining butter; sprinkle with cheese mixture. Bake for 5 minutes. Loosely cover with foil and bake 5 minutes longer. Serve warm. **Yield:** 8-10 servings.

———— 🛒 🛒 🛒 ————

Swiss-Onion Bread Ring

With the ease of prepared bread dough, this tempting cheesy bread has delicious down-home goodness. Its pleasant onion flavor goes great with any entree. You'll find it crisp and golden on the outside, rich and buttery on the inside. —Judi Messina, Coeur d'Alene, Idaho

2-1/2 teaspoons poppy seeds, *divided*
  1 tube (17.4 ounces) refrigerated white bread dough
  1 cup (4 ounces) shredded Swiss cheese
3/4 cup sliced green onions
1/4 cup butter *or* margarine, melted

Sprinkle 1/2 teaspoon poppy seeds in a greased 10-in. fluted tube pan. Cut the dough into twenty 1-in. pieces; place half in prepared pan. Sprinkle with half of the cheese and onions. Top with 1 teaspoon poppy seeds; drizzle with half of the butter. Repeat layers. Bake at 375° for 25 minutes or until golden brown. Immediately invert onto a wire rack. Serve warm. **Yield:** 1 loaf.

———— 🛒 🛒 🛒 ————

Mini Blue Cheese Rolls

(Pictured on page 106)

It's easy to keep the ingredients on hand for these tasty rolls to round out meals on busy nights. I've used this recipe more than 30 years and find they're also quick appetizers. —Myrtle Albrecht
Cameron Park, California

1/4 cup butter *or* margarine
1/2 cup (4 ounces) blue cheese
  1 tube (11 ounces) refrigerated breadsticks

In a saucepan, melt the butter and blue cheese over low heat. Unroll dough and cut each breadstick into six pieces; place in a foil-lined 11-in. x 7-in. x 2-in. baking pan. Pour cheese mixture over dough. Bake at 400° for 20 minutes or until butter is absorbed and rolls are lightly browned. Carefully lift foil out of pan. Serve hot. **Yield:** 4-6 servings.

Italian Cheese Twists

(Pictured below and on page 106)

My family loves breadsticks, and this recipe was an immediate success. The breadsticks look delicate and fancy, but they aren't tricky to make using prepared bread dough. —Marna Heitz, Farley, Iowa

- 1 loaf (1 pound) frozen white bread dough, thawed
- 1/4 cup butter *or* margarine, softened
- 1/4 teaspoon garlic powder
- 1/4 teaspoon *each* dried basil, oregano and marjoram
- 3/4 cup shredded mozzarella cheese
- 1 egg
- 1 tablespoon water
- 2 tablespoons sesame seeds *and/or* grated Parmesan cheese

On a lightly floured surface, roll dough into a 12-in. square. Combine butter and seasonings; spread over dough. Sprinkle with mozzarella cheese. Fold dough into thirds. Cut crosswise into 24 strips, 1/2 in. each. Twist each strip twice; pinch ends to seal. Place 2 in. apart on a greased baking sheet. Cover and let rise in a warm place until almost doubled, about 30 minutes.

In a small bowl, beat egg and water; brush over the twists. Sprinkle with sesame seeds and/or Parmesan cheese. Bake at 375° for 10-12 minutes or until light golden brown. Serve warm. **Yield:** 2 dozen.

Sweet Onion Muffins

(Pictured above)

These savory muffins are wonderful alongside any main dish and also make a great snack warm or cold. This recipe from my niece is one of my favorites. —Mildred Spinn, Cameron, Texas

- 1-1/2 cups all-purpose flour
- 1/2 cup sugar
- 1-1/2 teaspoons baking powder
- 1/2 teaspoon salt
- 2 eggs
- 1 cup finely chopped onion
- 1/2 cup butter *or* margarine, melted
- 1-1/2 cups chopped walnuts

In a bowl, combine the flour, sugar, baking powder and salt. In another bowl, beat eggs, onion and butter until blended; stir into dry ingredients just until moistened. Fold in walnuts. Fill greased or paper-lined miniature muffin cups three-fourths full. Bake at 400° for 10-12 minutes or until muffins test done. Cool for 5 minutes before removing from pans to wire racks. **Yield:** 3 dozen mini muffins or 1 dozen regular muffins.

Editor's Note: If using regular-size muffin cups, bake for 20-25 minutes.

Time-Saving Trick

To grease plastic wrap for covering yeast dough as it rises, simply press the wrap into the prepared loaf pan or empty greased bowl, then peel off and place greased side down over the dough.

Cookies & Bars

With these favorite recipes, you'll soon have a platter stacked with mouth-watering treats.

PIECES OF PLEASURE. Clockwise from upper left: Butter Fudge Fingers (p. 134), Chocolate Marshmallow Cookies (p. 126), Peanut Butter Sandwich Cookies (p. 127), Chocolate Dipped Brownies (p. 138), Apricot Meringue Bars (p. 137) and Chocolate Malted Cookies (p. 128).

Deluxe Sugar Cookies

Christmas cutouts signal the season for our family. Usually I "paint" these with colorful icing—or if time is short, I sprinkle them with colored sugar.
—Dawn Fagerstrom, Warren, Michigan

> 1 cup butter (no substitutes), softened
> 1-1/2 cups confectioners' sugar
> 1 egg
> 1 teaspoon vanilla extract
> 1/2 teaspoon almond extract
> 2-1/2 cups all-purpose flour
> 1 teaspoon baking soda
> 1 teaspoon cream of tartar

In a mixing bowl, cream butter and sugar. Beat in egg and extracts. Combine flour, baking soda and cream of tartar; gradually add to the creamed mixture and mix well. Chill for at least 1 hour.

On a surface lightly sprinkled with confectioners' sugar, roll out a quarter of the dough to 1/8-in. thickness. Cut into desired shapes with 2-in. cookie cutters. Place on ungreased baking sheets. Repeat with the remaining dough. Bake at 350° for 7-8 minutes or until the edges begin to brown. Remove to wire racks to cool. **Yield:** 5 dozen.

Editor's Note: Cookies may be sprinkled with colored sugar before baking or frosted after being baked and cooled.

— 🏺 🏺 🏺 —

Butterfinger Cookies

These candy-like cookies don't last long around our house—when I want to serve company, I make a double batch! No one can resist their chocolaty flavor.
—Carol Kitchens, Ridgeland, Mississippi

> 1/2 cup butter (no substitutes), softened
> 3/4 cup sugar
> 2/3 cup packed brown sugar
> 2 egg whites
> 1-1/4 cups chunky peanut butter
> 1-1/2 teaspoons vanilla extract
> 1 cup all-purpose flour
> 1/2 teaspoon baking soda
> 1/4 teaspoon salt
> 5 Butterfinger candy bars (2.1 ounces *each*), coarsely chopped

In a mixing bowl, cream butter and sugars. Add egg whites; beat well. Blend in peanut butter and vanilla. Combine flour, baking soda and salt; add to creamed mixture and mix well. Stir in candy bars. Shape into 1-1/2-in. balls; place on greased baking sheets. Bake at 350° for 10-12 minutes or until golden brown. Cool on wire racks. **Yield:** 4 dozen.

Sour Cream Cutouts

(Pictured above)

These soft buttery cookies make a comforting afternoon or evening snack. They have a delicious, delicate flavor and cake-like texture that pairs well with the sweet frosting.
—Marlene Jackson
Kingsburg, California

> 1 cup butter (no substitutes), softened
> 1-1/2 cups sugar
> 3 eggs
> 1 cup (8 ounces) sour cream
> 2 teaspoons vanilla extract
> 3-1/2 cups all-purpose flour
> 2 teaspoons baking powder
> 1 teaspoon baking soda
> FROSTING:
> 1/3 cup butter *or* margarine, softened
> 2 cups confectioners' sugar
> 2 to 3 tablespoons milk
> 1-1/2 teaspoons vanilla extract
> 1/4 teaspoon salt

In a mixing bowl, cream butter and sugar. Beat in eggs. Add sour cream and vanilla; mix well. Combine flour, baking powder and baking soda; add to the creamed mixture and mix well. Chill dough at least 2 hours or overnight.

Roll on a heavily floured board to 1/4-in. thickness. Cut with a 3-in. cutter. Place on lightly greased baking sheets. Bake at 350° for 10-12 minutes or until cookie springs back when lightly touched. Remove to wire racks to cool. In a mixing bowl, beat frosting ingredients until smooth; spread over cookies. **Yield:** about 3-1/2 dozen.

Chocolate Pinwheels

(Pictured below)

I prepare these eye-catching sweets every Christmas. My husband's 95-year-old grandfather was intrigued with how the swirls got in these cookies!
—*Patricia Kile, Greentown, Pennsylvania*

  1/2 cup butter (no substitutes), softened
    1 cup sugar
  1/4 cup packed brown sugar
    1 egg
1-1/2 teaspoons vanilla extract
    2 cups all-purpose flour
    1 teaspoon baking powder
Pinch salt
FILLING:
    2 cups (12 ounces) semisweet chocolate
      chips
    2 tablespoons butter *or* margarine
  1/4 teaspoon vanilla extract
Pinch salt

In a mixing bowl, cream butter and sugars. Add egg and vanilla; beat until light and fluffy. Combine dry ingredients; beat into creamed mixture. Divide dough in half; place each half between two sheets of waxed paper. Roll into 12-in. x 10-in. rectangles. Chill until almost firm, about 30 minutes.

In a saucepan over low heat, melt chips and butter. Add vanilla and salt; mix well. Spread over dough. Carefully roll up each rectangle into a tight jelly roll; wrap in waxed paper. Chill for 2 hours or until firm. Cut into 1/8-in. slices with a sharp knife; place on greased or parchment-lined baking sheets. Bake at 350° for 7-10 minutes or until lightly browned. Cool on wire racks. **Yield:** about 9 dozen.

Almond Icebox Cookies

(Pictured above)

I frequently have a roll of this cookie dough on hand so I can serve freshly baked cookies in a snap.
—*Elizabeth Montgomery, Taylorville, Illinois*

1-1/2 cups butter (no substitutes), softened
    1 cup sugar
    1 cup packed brown sugar
    3 eggs
    4 cups all-purpose flour
    1 tablespoon ground cinnamon
    1 teaspoon baking soda
  1/2 cup finely chopped almonds
    2 packages (2-1/4 ounces *each*) whole
      unblanched almonds

In a mixing bowl, cream butter and sugars. Add eggs, one at a time, beating well after each addition. Combine flour, cinnamon and baking soda; gradually add to the creamed mixture. Fold in chopped almonds. Shape into two 15-in. rolls; wrap each in plastic wrap. Refrigerate for 2 hours or overnight.

Unwrap and cut into 1/4-in. slices. Place 2 in. apart on ungreased baking sheets; top each with a whole almond. Bake at 375° for 8-10 minutes or until edges begin to brown. Cool on wire racks. **Yield:** 10 dozen.

Cookie Jar Gingersnaps

(Pictured above)

My grandma kept two cookie jars in her pantry. One of the jars, which I now have, always had these crisp and chewy gingersnaps in it. They're still my favorite. My daughter used this recipe for a 4-H fair and won a blue ribbon. —Deb Handy, Pomona, Kansas

       3/4 cup shortening
         1 cup sugar
         1 egg
       1/4 cup molasses
         2 cups all-purpose flour
         2 teaspoons baking soda
    1-1/2 teaspoons ground ginger
         1 teaspoon ground cinnamon
       1/2 teaspoon salt
    Additional sugar

In a large mixing bowl, cream the shortening and sugar. Beat in the egg and molasses. Combine flour, baking soda, ginger, cinnamon and salt; gradually add to the creamed mixture. Roll teaspoonfuls of dough into balls. Dip one side of each ball into sugar; place with sugar side up on greased baking sheets. Bake at 350° for 12-15 minutes or until lightly browned and crinkly. Remove to wire racks to cool. **Yield:** 3-4 dozen.

— 🍵 🍵 🍵 —

Chocolate Marshmallow Cookies

(Pictured at right and on page 122)

What fun—these double-chocolaty delights have a surprise inside! Atop the chocolate cookie base, marsh-mallow peeks out under chocolate icing. Kids love them. —June Formanek, Belle Plaine, Iowa

       1/2 cup butter (no substitutes), softened
         1 cup sugar
         1 egg
       1/4 cup milk
         1 teaspoon vanilla extract
    1-3/4 cups all-purpose flour
       1/3 cup baking cocoa
       1/2 teaspoon baking soda
       1/2 teaspoon salt
    16 to 18 large marshmallows
    ICING:
         6 tablespoons butter *or* margarine
         2 tablespoons baking cocoa
       1/4 cup milk
    1-3/4 cups confectioners' sugar
       1/2 teaspoon vanilla extract
    Pecan halves

In a mixing bowl, cream butter and sugar. Add egg, milk and vanilla; mix well. Combine flour, cocoa, baking soda and salt; beat into creamed mixture. Drop by rounded teaspoonfuls onto ungreased baking sheets. Bake at 350° for 8 minutes. Meanwhile, cut marshmallows in half. Press a marshmallow half, cut side down, onto each cookie. Return to the oven for 2 minutes. Remove to wire racks to cool.

For icing, combine butter, cocoa and milk in a saucepan. Bring to a boil; boil for 1 minute, stirring constantly. Cool slightly; transfer to a small mixing bowl. Add confectioners' sugar and vanilla; beat well. Spread over the cooled cookies. Top each with a pecan half. **Yield:** about 3 dozen.

utes or until golden. Remove to wire racks to cool.

In a mixing bowl, beat peanut butter, confectioners' sugar, vanilla and enough milk to achieve desired frosting consistency. Spread on half of the cookies and top each with another cookie. **Yield:** about 4 dozen.

———— 🥤 🥤 🥤 ————

Rolled Oat Cookies

(Pictured below)

I like to keep some of this dough in the freezer at all times since it's so handy to slice, bake and serve at a moment's notice. These wholesome cookies are super with a cup of coffee—in fact, we occasionally grab a few for breakfast when we're in a hurry.
—*Kathi Peters, Chilliwack, British Columbia*

   1 cup butter (no substitutes), softened
   1 cup packed brown sugar
1/4 cup water
   1 teaspoon vanilla extract
   3 cups quick-cooking oats
1-1/4 cups all-purpose flour
   1 teaspoon salt
1/4 teaspoon baking soda

In a mixing bowl, cream butter and brown sugar. Add water and vanilla; mix well. Combine dry ingredients; add to creamed mixture and mix well. Chill for 30 minutes. Shape into two 1-1/2-in. rolls; wrap tightly in waxed paper. Chill for 2 hours or until firm.

Unwrap and cut into 1/2-in. slices. Place 2 in. apart on greased baking sheets. Bake at 375° for 12 minutes or until lightly browned. Remove to wire racks to cool. **Yield:** about 3-1/2 dozen.

Peanut Butter Sandwich Cookies

(Pictured above and on page 123)

I'm a busy mother of two children. I work in our school office and help my husband on our hog and cattle farm. When I find time to bake a treat, I like it to be special. The creamy filling gives traditional peanut butter cookies a new twist. —*Debbie Kokes*
Tabor, South Dakota

   1 cup butter-flavored shortening
   1 cup creamy peanut butter
   1 cup sugar
   1 cup packed brown sugar
   1 teaspoon vanilla extract
   3 eggs
   3 cups all-purpose flour
   2 teaspoons baking soda
1/4 teaspoon salt
FILLING:
1/2 cup creamy peanut butter
   3 cups confectioners' sugar
   1 teaspoon vanilla extract
   5 to 6 tablespoons milk

In a mixing bowl, cream the shortening, peanut butter and sugars. Add vanilla and eggs, one at a time, beating well after each addition. Combine flour, baking soda and salt; gradually add to the creamed mixture. Shape into 1-in. balls; place 2 in. apart on ungreased baking sheets. Flatten to 3/8-in. thickness with a fork. Bake at 375° for 7-8 min-

Chocolaty Double Crunchers

(Pictured above)

I first tried these crispy cookies at a family picnic when I was a child. Packed with oats, cornflakes and coconut, they quickly became a "regular" at our house. Years later, I still make them for my own family.
—Cheryl Johnson, Upper Marlboro, Maryland

> 1/2 cup butter (no substitutes), softened
> 1/2 cup sugar
> 1/2 cup packed brown sugar
> 1 egg
> 1/2 teaspoon vanilla extract
> 1 cup all-purpose flour
> 1/2 teaspoon baking soda
> 1/4 teaspoon salt
> 1 cup quick-cooking oats
> 1 cup crushed cornflakes
> 1/2 cup flaked coconut
> FILLING:
>   2 packages (3 ounces *each*) cream cheese, softened
> 1-1/2 cups confectioners' sugar
>   2 cups (12 ounces) semisweet chocolate chips, melted

In a mixing bowl, cream butter and sugars. Add egg and vanilla; mix well. Combine flour, baking soda and salt; add to creamed mixture and mix well. Add oats, cornflakes and coconut. Shape into 1-in. balls and place 2 in. apart on greased baking sheets. Flatten with a glass dipped lightly in flour. Bake at 350° for 8-10 minutes or until lightly browned. Remove to wire racks to cool.

For filling, in a mixing bowl, beat cream cheese and sugar until smooth. Add the chocolate; mix well. Spread about 1 tablespoon on half of the cookies and top each with another cookie. Store in the refrigerator. **Yield:** about 2 dozen.

Chocolate Malted Cookies

(Pictured below and on page 122)

These cookies are the next best thing to a good old-fashioned malted milk. With malted milk powder, chocolate syrup plus chocolate chips and chunks, these are the best cookies I've ever tasted...and with six kids, I've made a lot of cookies over the years.
—Teri Rasey-Bolf, Cadillac, Michigan

> 1 cup butter-flavored shortening
> 1-1/4 cups packed brown sugar
> 1/2 cup malted milk powder
> 2 tablespoons chocolate syrup
> 1 tablespoon vanilla extract
> 1 egg
> 2 cups all-purpose flour
> 1 teaspoon baking soda
> 1/2 teaspoon salt
> 1-1/2 cups semisweet chocolate chunks
> 1 cup (6 ounces) milk chocolate chips

In a mixing bowl, combine shortening, brown sugar, malted milk powder, chocolate syrup and vanilla; beat for 2 minutes. Add egg. Combine flour, baking soda and salt; gradually add to creamed mixture. Stir in chocolate chunks and chips.

Shape into 2-in. balls; place 3 in. apart on ungreased baking sheets. Bake at 375° for 12-14 minutes or until golden brown. Cool for 2 minutes before removing from pans to wire racks to cool completely. **Yield:** about 1-1/2 dozen.

Mountain Cookies

(Pictured above)

Wherever I take these cookies, people ask for the recipe. You'll be hard-pressed to eat just one!
—Jeanne Adams, Richmond, Vermont

1 cup butter (no substitutes), softened
1 cup confectioners' sugar
2 teaspoons vanilla extract
2 cups all-purpose flour
1/2 teaspoon salt
FILLING:
1 package (3 ounces) cream cheese, softened
1 cup confectioners' sugar
2 tablespoons all-purpose flour
1 teaspoon vanilla extract
1/2 cup finely chopped pecans
1/2 cup flaked coconut
TOPPING:
1/2 cup semisweet chocolate chips
2 tablespoons butter *or* margarine
2 tablespoons water
1/2 cup confectioners' sugar

In a mixing bowl, cream the butter, sugar and vanilla. Combine flour and salt; gradually add to the creamed mixture and mix well. Shape into 1-in. balls; place 2 in. apart on ungreased baking sheets. Make a deep indentation in the center of each cookie. Bake at 350° for 10-12 minutes or until the edges just start to brown. Remove to wire racks to cool completely.

For the filling, beat cream cheese, sugar, flour and vanilla in a mixing bowl. Add pecans and coconut; mix well. Spoon 1/2 teaspoon into each cookie. For topping, heat chocolate chips, butter and water in a small saucepan until melted. Stir in sugar. Drizzle over cookies. **Yield:** 4 dozen.

Toffee Almond Sandies

(Pictured below)

Crisp and loaded with goodies, these are my husband's favorite cookies. I used to bake them in large batches when our four sons still lived at home. Now I whip them up for our grandchildren.
—Alice Kahnk
Kennard, Nebraska

1 cup butter (no substitutes), softened
1 cup sugar
1 cup confectioners' sugar
1 cup vegetable oil
2 eggs
1 teaspoon almond extract
3-1/2 cups all-purpose flour
1 cup whole wheat flour
1 teaspoon baking soda
1 teaspoon cream of tartar
1 teaspoon salt
2 cups chopped almonds
1 cup English toffee bits *or* almond brickle chips
Additional sugar

In a mixing bowl, cream butter and sugars. Add oil, eggs and extract; mix well. Combine flours, baking soda, cream of tartar and salt; gradually add to the creamed mixture. Stir in almonds and toffee bits.

Shape into 1-in. balls; roll in sugar. Place on ungreased baking sheets; flatten with a fork. Bake at 350° for 12-14 minutes or until lightly browned. Remove to wire racks to cool. **Yield:** about 12 dozen.

Chocolate Pretzel Cookies

(Pictured below)

These pretzel-shaped buttery chocolate cookies are covered in a rich mocha glaze and drizzled with white chocolate. My family goes wild over their chocolaty crunch.   —Priscilla Anderson, Salt Lake City, Utah

  1/2 cup butter (no substitutes), softened
  2/3 cup sugar
   1 egg
   2 squares (1 ounce *each*) unsweetened chocolate, melted and cooled
   2 teaspoons vanilla extract
1-3/4 cups all-purpose flour
  1/2 teaspoon salt
MOCHA GLAZE:
   1 cup (6 ounces) semisweet chocolate chips
   1 teaspoon light corn syrup
   1 teaspoon shortening
   1 cup confectioners' sugar
   4 to 5 tablespoons hot coffee
   2 squares (1 ounce *each*) white baking chocolate, melted

In a mixing bowl, cream butter and sugar. Add the egg, chocolate and vanilla; mix well. Combine flour and salt; gradually add to creamed mixture and mix well. Cover and chill for 1 hour or until firm. Divide dough into fourths; form each portion into a 6-in. log. Divide each log into 12 pieces and roll each piece into a 9-in. rope. Place ropes on greased baking sheets; form into pretzel shapes and space 2 in. apart. Bake at 400° for 5-7 minutes or until firm. Cool 1 minute before removing to wire racks.

  For glaze, heat the chocolate chips, corn syrup and shortening in a small saucepan over low heat until melted. Stir in sugar and enough coffee to make a smooth glaze. Dip pretzels; place on waxed paper or wire racks to harden. Drizzle with white chocolate; let stand until chocolate is completely set. Store in an airtight container. **Yield:** 4 dozen.

Caramel Heavenlies

(Pictured above)

My mom made these dressy, sweet cookies for cookie exchanges when I was a little girl, letting me sprinkle on the almonds and coconut.   —Dawn Burns Troy, Ohio

  12 graham crackers (4-3/4 x 2-1/2 inches)
   2 cups miniature marshmallows
  3/4 cup butter *or* margarine
  3/4 cup packed brown sugar
   1 teaspoon ground cinnamon
   1 teaspoon vanilla extract
   1 cup sliced almonds
   1 cup flaked coconut

Line a 15-in. x 10-in. x 1-in. baking pan with foil. Place graham crackers in pan; cover with marshmallows. In a saucepan over medium heat, cook and stir butter, brown sugar and cinnamon until the butter is melted and the sugar is dissolved.

  Remove from the heat; stir in vanilla. Spoon over the marshmallows. Sprinkle with almonds and coconut. Bake at 350° for 14-16 minutes or until browned. Cool completely. Cut into 2-in. squares, then cut each square in half to form triangles. **Yield:** about 6 dozen.

—— 🏺 🏺 🏺 ——

Chocolate Meringue Stars

(Pictured above right)

These light chewy cookies sure make for merry munching. Their big chocolate flavor makes it difficult to keep the kids away from them long enough to get any on the cookie tray.   —Edna Lee, Greeley, Colorado

   3 egg whites
  3/4 teaspoon vanilla extract
  3/4 cup sugar
  1/4 cup baking cocoa

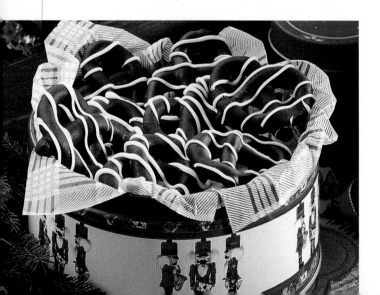

GLAZE:
    **3 squares (1 ounce *each*) semisweet
      chocolate**
    1 tablespoon shortening

In a mixing bowl, beat egg whites and vanilla until soft peaks form. Gradually add sugar, about 2 tablespoons at a time, beating until stiff peaks form. Gently fold in cocoa. Place in a pastry bag with a large open star tip (#8b). Line baking sheets with ungreased parchment paper. Pipe stars, about 1-1/4-in. diameter, onto parchment paper, or drop by rounded teaspoonfuls. Bake at 300° for 30-35 minutes or until lightly browned. Remove from parchment paper; cool on wire racks.

In a microwave or double boiler, melt chocolate and shortening; stir until smooth. Dip the cookies halfway into glaze; place on waxed paper to harden. **Yield:** about 4 dozen.

Pecan Meltaways

These sugared, nut-filled balls are a Christmas tradition. They make an attractive addition to a plate of cookies. —*Alberta McKay, Bartlesville, Oklahoma*

    1 cup butter (no substitutes), softened
    1/2 cup confectioners' sugar
    1 teaspoon vanilla extract
    2-1/4 cups all-purpose flour
    1/4 teaspoon salt
    3/4 cup finely chopped pecans
Additional confectioners' sugar

In a mixing bowl, cream the butter, sugar and vanilla; mix well. Combine the flour and salt; add to creamed mixture. Stir in pecans. Chill. Roll dough into 1-in. balls and place on ungreased baking

sheets. Bake at 350° for 10-12 minutes. Roll in confectioners' sugar while warm. Cool on wire racks; roll in sugar again. **Yield:** about 4 dozen.

Rosettes
(Pictured below)

Dipping the edges of these traditional favorites in icing beautifully defines their lacy pattern. People are always impressed to see a plate of these crisp cookies presented on the table at Christmas. —*Iola Egle
Bella Vista, Arkansas*

    2 eggs
    2 teaspoons sugar
    1 cup milk
    1 tablespoon vanilla extract
    1 cup all-purpose flour
    1/4 teaspoon salt
Cooking oil for deep-fat frying
ICING:
    2 cups confectioners' sugar
    1 teaspoon vanilla extract
    1 to 3 tablespoons water

In a mixing bowl, beat eggs and sugar; stir in milk and vanilla. Combine flour and salt; add to batter and beat until smooth. Heat 2-1/2 in. of oil to 365° in a deep-fat fryer or electric skillet. Place rosette iron in hot oil, then dip in batter, three-fourths up on sides of iron (do not let batter run over top of iron). Immediately place into hot oil; loosen rosette with fork and remove iron. Fry 1-2 minutes per side or until golden. Remove to a wire rack covered with paper towel. Repeat with remaining batter.

For icing, combine the confectioners' sugar, vanilla and enough water to make a dipping consistency. Dip edges of rosettes into icing; dry on wire racks. **Yield:** 4-5 dozen.

1 teaspoon salt
1/2 teaspoon baking soda
1/2 teaspoon ground cinnamon
1/4 teaspoon ground nutmeg
3/4 cup butter (no substitutes), softened
1 egg
1 cup mashed ripe bananas (about 2)
1-3/4 cups quick-cooking oats
1 cup (6 ounces) semisweet chocolate chips
1/2 cup chopped walnuts

In a mixing bowl, combine dry ingredients; beat in butter until mixture resembles coarse crumbs. Add egg, bananas and oats; mix well. Stir in chocolate chips and nuts. Drop by tablespoonfuls onto greased baking sheets. Bake at 375° for 13-15 minutes or until golden brown. Cool on wire racks. **Yield:** 4 dozen.

Berry Shortbread Dreams

(Pictured above)

Raspberry jam adds fruity sweetness to these rich-tasting cookies. They will absolutely melt in your mouth!
—Mildred Sherrer, Bay City, Texas

1 cup butter (no substitutes), softened
2/3 cup sugar
1/2 teaspoon almond extract
2 cups all-purpose flour
1/3 to 1/2 cup seedless raspberry jam
GLAZE:
1 cup confectioners' sugar
2 to 3 teaspoons water
1/2 teaspoon almond extract

In a mixing bowl, cream butter and sugar. Beat in extract; gradually add flour until dough forms a ball. Cover and refrigerate for 1 hour or until easy to handle. Roll into 1-in. balls. Place 1 in. apart on ungreased baking sheets. Using the end of a wooden spoon handle, make an indentation in the center of each ball. Fill with jam.

Bake at 350° for 14-18 minutes or until edges are lightly browned. Remove to wire racks to cool. Spoon additional jam into cookies if desired. Combine glaze ingredients; drizzle over cookies. **Yield:** about 3-1/2 dozen.

Banana Oatmeal Cookies

My mom made these cookies when I was young. Now my seven children like them as much as I did.
—Jacqueline Wilson, Armstrong Creek, Wisconsin

1-1/2 cups all-purpose flour
1 cup sugar

White Velvet Cutouts

We make these cutouts every Christmas and give lots of them as gifts.
—Kim Hinkle, Wauseon, Ohio

2 cups butter (no substitutes), softened
1 package (8 ounces) cream cheese, softened
2 cups sugar
2 egg yolks
1 teaspoon vanilla extract
4-1/2 cups all-purpose flour
BUTTER CREAM FROSTING:
3-1/2 cups confectioners' sugar, *divided*
3 tablespoons butter, softened
1 tablespoon shortening
1/2 teaspoon vanilla extract
3 to 4 tablespoons milk, divided
Red *and/or* green food coloring,* optional

In a mixing bowl, cream butter and cream cheese until light and fluffy. Add sugar, egg yolks and vanilla; mix well. Gradually add flour. Cover and chill for 2 hours or until firm. Roll out on a floured surface to 1/4-in. thickness. Cut into 3-in. shapes; place 1 in. apart on greased baking sheets. Bake at 350° for 10-12 minutes or until set (not browned). Cool for 5 minutes; remove to wire racks to cool.

For frosting, combine 1-1/2 cups sugar, butter, shortening, vanilla and 3 tablespoons milk in a mixing bowl; beat until smooth. Gradually add remaining sugar; beat until light and fluffy, about 3 minutes. Add enough remaining milk and food coloring until frosting reaches desired consistency. Frost cookies. **Yield:** about 7 dozen.

*Editor's Note: For a deeper color of frosting, tint with food coloring paste available at kitchen and cake decorating supply stores.

Rhubarb Custard Bars

(Pictured above)

Once I tried these rich gooey bars, I just had to have the recipe so I could make them for my family and friends. The shortbread-like crust and rhubarb and custard layers inspire folks to fix a batch for themselves. —*Shari Roach, South Milwaukee, Wisconsin*

    2 cups all-purpose flour
1/4 cup sugar
    1 cup cold butter *or* margarine
FILLING:
    2 cups sugar
    7 tablespoons all-purpose flour
    1 cup whipping cream
    3 eggs, beaten
    5 cups finely chopped fresh *or* frozen
        rhubarb, thawed and drained
TOPPING:
    2 packages (3 ounces *each*) cream cheese,
        softened
1/2 cup sugar
1/2 teaspoon vanilla extract
    1 cup whipping cream, whipped

In a bowl, combine flour and sugar; cut in butter until the mixture resembles coarse crumbs. Press into a greased 13-in. x 9-in. x 2-in. baking pan. Bake at 350° for 10 minutes. Meanwhile, for filling, combine sugar and flour in a bowl. Whisk in cream and eggs. Stir in the rhubarb. Pour over crust. Bake for 40-45 minutes or until custard is set. Cool.

For topping, in a mixing bowl, beat cream cheese, sugar and vanilla until smooth; fold in whipped cream. Spread over top. Cover and chill. Cut into bars. Store in the refrigerator. **Yield:** 3 dozen.

Cranberry Date Bars

(Pictured below)

I first discovered this recipe at Christmas a couple years ago, but it's a great way to use frozen cranberries throughout the year. It seems I'm always baking a batch of these moist bars for some event.
                    —*Bonnie Nieter, Warsaw, Indiana*

    1 package (12 ounces) fresh *or* frozen
        cranberries
    1 package (8 ounces) chopped dates
    2 tablespoons water
    1 teaspoon vanilla extract
    2 cups all-purpose flour
    2 cups old-fashioned oats
1-1/2 cups packed brown sugar
1/2 teaspoon baking soda
1/2 teaspoon salt
    1 cup butter *or* margarine, melted
GLAZE:
    2 cups confectioners' sugar
1/2 teaspoon vanilla extract
    2 to 3 tablespoons orange juice

In a covered saucepan over low heat, simmer cranberries, dates and water for 15 minutes, stirring occasionally until the cranberries have popped. Remove from the heat; stir in vanilla and set aside. In a large bowl, combine the flour, oats, brown sugar, baking soda and salt. Stir in butter until well blended. Pat half into an ungreased 13-in. x 9-in. x 2-in. baking pan. Bake at 350° for 8 minutes.

Spoon cranberry mixture over crust. Sprinkle with the remaining oat mixture. Pat gently. Bake at 350° for 25-30 minutes or until browned. Cool on a wire rack. Combine confectioners' sugar, vanilla and enough orange juice to achieve desired glaze consistency. Drizzle over bars. **Yield:** 3 dozen.

M&M Oat Bars

(Pictured below)

These irresistible bars made with seasonally colored M&M's can sweeten any holiday. They're fun to make and eat! —*Renee Schwebach, Dumont, Minnesota*

        1/2 cup butter *or* margarine, softened
          1 cup packed brown sugar
          1 egg
          1 teaspoon vanilla extract
    1-1/4 cups all-purpose flour
        1/2 teaspoon baking soda
        1/2 teaspoon salt
          2 cups quick-cooking oats
          1 package (14 ounces) caramels
          3 tablespoons water
          1 cup miniature semisweet chocolate chips
          1 cup chopped walnuts
          1 cup plain M&M's
          3 ounces white chocolate candy coating

In a mixing bowl, cream butter and brown sugar. Beat in egg and vanilla. Combine flour, baking soda and salt; add to the creamed mixture. Stir in oats. Press into a greased 15-in. x 10-in. x 1-in. baking pan. Bake at 350° for 10-15 minutes or until golden brown. Cool on a wire rack.

In a microwave-safe bowl, melt the caramels and water. Spread over crust. Sprinkle with chips, nuts and M&M's. Gently press into the caramel mixture. Melt candy coating; drizzle over the top. Cut into bars. **Yield:** 6 dozen.

Candy Coating Clue

Candy coating, sometimes called "almond bark" or "confectionary coating", is found in the baking section of most grocery stores. It is often sold in bulk packages of 1 to 1-1/2 pounds.

Butter Fudge Fingers

(Pictured above and on page 122)

These scrumptious brownies get dressed up with a delicious browned butter frosting. The combination is delightfully different and assures that they vanish fast. —*Peggy Mangus, Worland, Wyoming*

        2/3 cup butter (no substitutes)
          4 squares (1 ounce *each*) unsweetened chocolate
          4 eggs
          1 teaspoon salt
          2 cups sugar
    1-1/2 cups all-purpose flour
          1 teaspoon baking powder
          1 cup chopped pecans
BROWNED BUTTER FROSTING:
        1/2 cup butter
        1/3 cup whipping cream
          2 teaspoons vanilla extract
          4 cups confectioners' sugar
GLAZE:
          1 square (1 ounce) unsweetened chocolate
          1 tablespoon butter

In a microwave or double boiler, melt butter and chocolate; cool for 10 minutes. In a mixing bowl, beat eggs and salt until foamy. Gradually add sugar; mix well. Stir in chocolate mixture. Combine flour and baking powder; gradually add to chocolate mixture. Stir in pecans. Pour into a greased 15-in. x 10-in. x 1-in. baking pan. Bake at 350° for 20-25 minutes or until a toothpick inserted near the center comes out clean. Cool on a wire rack.

For frosting, heat butter in a saucepan over medium heat until golden brown, about 7 minutes. Remove from the heat; add cream and vanilla. Beat in sugar until smooth and thick. Frost bars. For glaze, melt the chocolate and butter in a microwave or double boiler; cool slightly. Drizzle over bars. **Yield:** about 5 dozen.

———— 🥄 🥄 🥄 ————

Homemade Candy Bars

I enter these treats, which are similar to Kit Kat bars, at the fair each year and win a blue ribbon. I've even had a judge ask how to make them! —Karen Grant
Tulare, California

    8 ounces Waverly crackers, *divided*
    1 cup butter *or* margarine
1/2 cup milk
    2 cups graham cracker crumbs
    1 cup packed brown sugar
1/3 cup sugar
2/3 cup creamy peanut butter
1/2 cup milk chocolate chips
1/2 cup butterscotch chips

Place a third of the crackers (about 25) in the bottom of an ungreased 13-in. x 9-in. x 2-in. pan. In a saucepan over medium-high heat, melt the butter. Add milk, graham cracker crumbs and sugars; bring to a boil. Boil, stirring constantly, for 5 minutes. Pour half of the mixture over crackers, carefully spreading to cover. Place half of remaining crackers (about 25) on top. Spread with remaining sugar mixture. Top with remaining crackers.

In a saucepan over low heat, stir the peanut butter and chips until melted and smooth. Spread over crackers. Chill until firm, about 1 hour. Cut into small squares. **Yield:** 3-4 dozen.

———— 🥄 🥄 🥄 ————

Chocolate Peanut Bars

This homemade version of the popular Baby Ruth candy bar is unbeatable and appeals to kids of all ages. A pan of these rich, chocolaty bars goes a long way.
—Carol Johnson, West Covina, California

1-1/2 cups light corn syrup
    1 cup sugar
    1 cup packed brown sugar
    1 cup peanut butter
    7 cups cornflakes
    1 can (12 ounces) salted peanuts
TOPPING:
    2 cups (12 ounces) semisweet chocolate
       chips
    3 tablespoons peanut butter
    2 tablespoons shortening

In a 3-qt. saucepan, combine corn syrup and sugars. Bring to a boil over medium heat; boil and stir for 1 minute. Remove from the heat; add peanut butter and mix well. Stir in the cornflakes and peanuts. Press into a greased 15-in. x 10-in. x 1-in. baking pan. In a microwave or double boiler, melt chocolate chips, peanut butter and shortening; pour over bars and quickly spread evenly. Refrigerate for 2-3 hours or until set before cutting. **Yield:** 3 dozen.

———— 🥄 🥄 🥄 ————

Brownie Kiss Cupcakes

(Pictured below)

It's fun to prepare individual brownie "cupcakes" with a chocolaty "surprise" inside. My goddaughter, Cara, asks me to make them for her birthday to share with her class at school. —Pamela Lute
Mercersburg, Pennsylvania

1/3 cup butter *or* margarine, softened
    1 cup sugar
    2 eggs
    1 teaspoon vanilla extract
3/4 cup all-purpose flour
1/2 cup baking cocoa
1/4 teaspoon baking powder
1/4 teaspoon salt
    9 milk chocolate kisses

In a mixing bowl, cream butter and sugar. Add eggs and vanilla; mix well. Combine flour, cocoa, baking powder and salt; add to the creamed mixture and mix well. Fill paper- or foil-lined muffin cups two-thirds full. Place a chocolate kiss, tip end down, in the center of each. Bake at 350° for 20-25 minutes or until top springs back when lightly touched. Cool on a wire rack. **Yield:** 9 cupcakes.

Pear Custard Bars

(Pictured below)

When I take this crowd-pleasing treat to a potluck, I come home with an empty pan every time. Cooking and baking come naturally for me—as a farm girl, I helped my mother feed my 10 siblings. —Jeannette Nord
San Juan Capistrano, California

    1/2 cup butter *or* margarine, softened
    1/3 cup sugar
    3/4 cup all-purpose flour
    1/4 teaspoon vanilla extract
    2/3 cup chopped macadamia nuts
FILLING/TOPPING:
      1 package (8 ounces) cream cheese,
        softened
    1/2 cup sugar
      1 egg
    1/2 teaspoon vanilla extract
      1 can (15-1/4 ounces) pear halves, drained
    1/2 teaspoon sugar
    1/2 teaspoon ground cinnamon

In a mixing bowl, cream butter and sugar. Beat in flour and vanilla until combined. Stir in the nuts. Press into a greased 8-in. square baking pan. Bake at 350° for 20 minutes or until lightly browned. Cool on a wire rack. Increase heat to 375°.

In a mixing bowl, beat the cream cheese until smooth. Add sugar, egg and vanilla; mix until combined. Pour over crust. Cut pears into 1/8-in. slices; arrange in a single layer over the filling. Combine sugar and cinnamon; sprinkle over pears.

Bake at 375° for 28-30 minutes (center will be soft set and will become firmer upon cooling). Cool on a wire rack for 45 minutes. Cover and refrigerate for at least 2 hours before cutting. Store in the refrigerator. **Yield:** 16 bars.

Chocolate Raspberry Bars

(Pictured above)

My family loves these rich, sweet bars. The chocolate and raspberry jam go together so well. I make a lot of cookies and bars, but these special treats are my favorite. They're so pretty served on a platter.
—Kathy Smedstad, Silverton, Oregon

      1 cup all-purpose flour
    1/4 cup confectioners' sugar
    1/2 cup cold butter *or* margarine
FILLING:
    1/2 cup seedless raspberry jam
      4 ounces cream cheese, softened
      2 tablespoons milk
      1 cup vanilla *or* white chips, melted
GLAZE:
    3/4 cup semisweet chocolate chips
      2 tablespoons shortening

In a bowl, combine flour and confectioners' sugar; cut in butter until crumbly. Press into an ungreased 9-in. square baking pan. Bake at 375° for 15-18 minutes or until browned. Spread jam over warm crust. In a small mixing bowl, beat cream cheese and milk until smooth. Add vanilla chips; beat until smooth. Spread carefully over jam layer. Cool completely. Chill until set, about 1 hour.

For glaze, melt chocolate chips and shortening; spread over filling. Chill for 10 minutes. Cut into bars; chill another hour before serving. Store leftovers in the refrigerator. **Yield:** 3 dozen.

Shortbread Lemon Bars

(Pictured below)

I've put together two family cookbooks over the years, and this recipe ranks among my favorites. These special lemon bars have a yummy shortbread crust and a refreshing flavor. I'm never afraid to make this dessert for guests since I know it will be a hit.
—Margaret Peterson, Forest City, Iowa

1-1/2 cups all-purpose flour
1/2 cup confectioners' sugar
1 teaspoon grated lemon peel
1 teaspoon grated orange peel
3/4 cup cold butter *or* margarine
FILLING:
4 eggs
2 cups sugar
1/3 cup lemon juice
1/4 cup all-purpose flour
2 teaspoons grated lemon peel
2 teaspoons grated orange peel
1 teaspoon baking powder
TOPPING:
2 cups (16 ounces) sour cream
1/3 cup sugar
1/2 teaspoon vanilla extract

In a food processor, combine flour, confectioners' sugar, and lemon and orange peel. Cut in butter until crumbly; process until mixture forms a ball. Pat into a greased 13-in. x 9-in. x 2-in. baking pan. Bake at 350° for 12-14 minutes or until set and the edges are lightly browned.

Meanwhile, in a mixing bowl, combine the filling ingredients; mix well. Pour over hot crust. Bake for 14-16 minutes or until set and lightly browned.

Combine topping ingredients; spread over filling. Bake 7-9 minutes longer or until topping is set. Cool on a wire rack. Refrigerate overnight. Cut into bars just before serving. **Yield:** 3 dozen.

Apricot Meringue Bars

(Pictured above and on page 122)

Each year for our family picnic, I'm expected to bring these wonderful treats. Their sweet apricot filling and delicate meringue topping make them everyone's favorite. I wouldn't dream of hosting a get-together without serving these bars.
—Krissy Fossmeyer, Huntley, Illinois

3 cups all-purpose flour
1 cup sugar, *divided*
1 cup cold butter (no substitutes)
4 eggs, *separated*
1 teaspoon vanilla extract
2 cans (12 ounces *each*) apricot filling
1/2 cup chopped pecans

In a bowl, combine the flour and 1/2 cup sugar; cut in butter until crumbly. Add the egg yolks and vanilla; mix well. Press into a greased 15-in. x 10-in. x 1-in. baking pan. Bake at 350° for 12-15 minutes or until lightly browned. Spread apricot filling over crust.

In a small mixing bowl, beat the egg whites until soft peaks form. Gradually add the remaining sugar, beating until stiff peaks form. Spread over apricot layer; sprinkle with pecans. Bake for 25-30 minutes or until lightly browned. Cool on a wire rack. Cut into bars. Store in the refrigerator. **Yield:** 32 bars.

Rich Chocolate Brownies
(Pictured below)

I'm one of those people who need chocolate on a regular basis. I looked high and low for a rich brownie recipe that called for cocoa instead of chocolate squares...and this is it. My family loves these brownies—they never last more than a day at our house.
—Karen Trapp, North Weymouth, Massachusetts

    1 cup sugar
    2 eggs
1/2 teaspoon vanilla extract
1/2 cup butter *or* margarine, melted
1/2 cup all-purpose flour
1/3 cup baking cocoa
1/4 teaspoon baking powder
1/4 teaspoon salt
FROSTING:
    3 tablespoons butter *or* margarine, melted
    3 tablespoons baking cocoa
    2 tablespoons warm water
    1 teaspoon instant coffee granules
1-1/2 cups confectioners' sugar

In a mixing bowl, beat sugar, eggs and vanilla. Add butter; mix well. Combine dry ingredients; add to batter and mix well. Pour into a greased 8-in. square baking pan. Bake at 350° for 25-30 minutes or until a toothpick inserted near the center comes out clean. Cool on a wire rack.

For frosting, combine butter, cocoa, water and coffee; mix well. Gradually stir in sugar until smooth, adding additional warm water if necessary to achieve a spreading consistency. Frost the brownies. **Yield:** 12-16 servings.

Chocolate Dipped Brownies
(Pictured above and on page 123)

My family calls these delicious bars "the world's chocolatiest brownies" and is more than happy to gobble up a batch whenever I make them.
—Jackie Archer, Clinton, Iowa

3/4 cup sugar
1/3 cup butter *or* margarine
    2 tablespoons water
    4 cups (24 ounces) semisweet chocolate chips, *divided*
    1 teaspoon vanilla extract
    2 eggs
3/4 cup all-purpose flour
1/2 teaspoon salt
1/4 teaspoon baking soda
    2 tablespoons shortening
1/2 cup chopped pecans, toasted

In a saucepan over medium heat, bring the sugar, butter and water to a boil; remove from the heat. Stir in 1 cup of chocolate chips and vanilla; stir until smooth. Cool for 5 minutes. Beat in eggs, one at a time, until well mixed. Combine flour, salt and baking soda; stir into the chocolate mixture. Stir in another cup of chips. Pour into a greased 9-in. square baking pan. Bake at 325° for 35 minutes. Cool completely. Place in the freezer for 30-40 minutes (do not freeze completely). Cut into bars.

In a microwave or double boiler, melt remaining chips with shortening; stir until smooth. Using a small fork, dip brownies to completely coat; shake off excess. Place on waxed paper-lined baking sheets; immediately sprinkle with pecans. Allow to harden. Store in an airtight container in a cool dry place. **Yield:** 3 dozen.

Peanut Butter Swirl Brownies

(Pictured below)

Peanut butter and chocolate are always a delicious duo, but they're extra special paired in this tempting treat. Even with a sizable collection of brownie recipes, I reach for this one quite often. The marbled look prompts curious tasters—the flavor brings them back for seconds.
—*Linda Craig*
Hay River, Northwest Territories

1/2 cup butter *or* margarine, softened
2/3 cup sugar
1/2 cup packed brown sugar
  2 eggs
  2 tablespoons milk
3/4 cup all-purpose flour
1/2 teaspoon baking powder
1/4 teaspoon salt
1/4 cup creamy peanut butter
1/3 cup peanut butter chips
1/3 cup baking cocoa
1/2 cup semisweet chocolate chips

In a mixing bowl, cream the butter and sugars. Add eggs and milk; mix well. Combine flour, baking powder and salt; add to creamed mixture and mix well. Divide the batter in half. To one portion, add peanut butter and peanut butter chips; mix well. To the other portion, add cocoa and chocolate chips; mix well.

In a greased 9-in. square baking pan, spoon the chocolate batter in eight mounds in a checkerboard pattern. Spoon seven mounds of peanut butter batter between the chocolate batter. Cut through batters with a knife to swirl. Bake at 350° for 25-30 minutes or until a toothpick inserted near the center comes out clean. Cool on a wire rack. **Yield:** 3 dozen.

Chunky Blond Brownies

(Pictured above)

Every bite of these chewy blond brownies is packed with chunks of white and semisweet chocolate and macadamia nuts. We have lots of excellent cooks in this rural community, so it's a challenge coming up with a potluck offering that stands out. These usually do, and they're snapped up fast. —*Rosemary Dreiske*
Keldron, South Dakota

1/2 cup butter *or* margarine, softened
3/4 cup sugar
3/4 cup packed brown sugar
  2 eggs
  2 teaspoons vanilla extract
1-1/2 cups all-purpose flour
  1 teaspoon baking powder
1/2 teaspoon salt
  1 cup vanilla *or* white chips
  1 cup semisweet chocolate chunks
  1 jar (3-1/2 ounces) macadamia nuts, chopped, *divided*

In a mixing bowl, cream butter and sugars. Add eggs and vanilla; mix well. Combine flour, baking powder and salt; add to creamed mixture and mix well. Stir in vanilla chips, chocolate chunks and 1/2 cup nuts. Spread into a greased 13-in. x 9-in. x 2-in. baking pan. Sprinkle with the remaining nuts. Bake at 350° for 25-30 minutes or until golden brown. Cool on a wire rack. **Yield:** 2 dozen.

Cakes & Pies

Any way you slice it, these scrumptious cakes and palate-pleasing pies make a flavorful finale for everyday suppers and special-occasion dinners.

TRIED-AND-TRUE TREATS. Clockwise from upper left: Black Forest Pie (p. 154), Chocolate Angel Cake (p. 143), Peanut Butter Cheesecake (p. 148), Pumpkin Pound Cake (p. 145) and Triple Fruit Pie (p. 156).

Sour Cream Chocolate Cake

(Pictured below and on back cover)

This luscious layer cake gets wonderful moistness from sour cream. —*Patsy Foster, Marion, Arkansas*

- 4 squares (1 ounce *each*) unsweetened chocolate, melted and cooled
- 1 cup water
- 3/4 cup sour cream
- 1/4 cup shortening
- 1 teaspoon vanilla extract
- 2 eggs, beaten
- 2 cups all-purpose flour
- 2 cups sugar
- 1-1/4 teaspoons baking soda
- 1 teaspoon salt
- 1/2 teaspoon baking powder

FROSTING:
- 1/2 cup butter (no substitutes), softened
- 6 squares (1 ounce *each*) unsweetened chocolate, melted and cooled
- 6 cups confectioners' sugar
- 1/2 cup sour cream
- 6 tablespoons milk
- 2 teaspoons vanilla extract
- 1/8 teaspoon salt

In a mixing bowl, combine the first six ingredients; mix well. Combine the dry ingredients; gradually add to chocolate mixture. Beat on low speed just until moistened. Beat on high for 3 minutes. Pour into two greased and floured 9-in. round baking pans. Bake at 350° for 30 minutes or until a toothpick inserted near the center comes out clean. Cool for 10 minutes before removing from pans to wire racks to cool completely.

In a mixing bowl, combine frosting ingredients. Beat until smooth and creamy. Spread over cake. Store in the refrigerator. **Yield:** 12-16 servings.

Sweetheart Walnut Torte

(Pictured above)

I always donate one of these lightly sweet tortes for our church bake sale. But the ladies in charge quickly put it aside for one of them to buy! —*Gladys Jenik, Orland Park, Illinois*

- 1/2 cup butter *or* margarine, softened
- 1/2 cup sugar
- 4 egg yolks
- 1/3 cup milk
- 1/2 teaspoon vanilla extract
- 1 cup all-purpose flour
- 2 teaspoons baking powder
- 1/8 teaspoon salt

MERINGUE:
- 4 egg whites
- 1/8 teaspoon cream of tartar
- 3/4 cup sugar
- 1 cup chopped walnuts

Walnut halves

FILLING:
- 1 cup cold milk
- 1 package (3.9 ounces) instant chocolate pudding
- 1 cup whipping cream, whipped

Grease two 9-in. heart-shaped pans. Line with waxed paper and grease the paper; set aside. In a mixing bowl, cream butter and sugar. Add egg yolks, milk and vanilla; mix well. Combine flour, baking powder and salt; gradually add to creamed mixture. Pour into prepared pans.

In a mixing bowl, beat egg whites and cream of tartar until soft peaks form. Gradually add sugar, beating until stiff and glossy. Fold in chopped nuts. Spread evenly over batter, sealing edges to sides of pan. Arrange walnut halves over meringue in one pan. Bake at 300° for 55 minutes or until golden brown. Cool for 10 minutes; remove to wire racks. Invert so meringue side is up; cool completely.

In a mixing bowl, beat the milk and pudding mix

until thickened. Fold in the whipped cream. Place the plain cake, meringue side up, on a serving plate. Spread with half of the filling; top with remaining cake. Frost the sides with remaining filling. **Yield:** 12-16 servings.

— ☕ ☕ ☕ —

Toffee-Mocha Cream Torte

(Pictured below)

When you really want to impress someone, this scrumptious torte is just the thing to make! Instant coffee granules give the moist chocolate cake a mild mocha flavor. The fluffy cream layers are deliciously rich.
—Lynn Rogers, Richfield, North Carolina

1 cup butter *or* margarine, softened
2 cups sugar
2 eggs
1-1/2 teaspoons vanilla extract
2-2/3 cups all-purpose flour
3/4 cup baking cocoa
2 teaspoons baking soda
1/4 teaspoon salt
1 cup buttermilk
2 teaspoons instant coffee granules
1 cup boiling water
TOPPING:
1/2 teaspoon instant coffee granules
1 teaspoon hot water
2 cups whipping cream
3 tablespoons light brown sugar
6 Heath candy bars (1.4 ounces *each*), crushed, *divided*

In a mixing bowl, cream butter and sugar. Beat in eggs and vanilla. Combine flour, cocoa, baking soda and salt; add to creamed mixture alternately with

buttermilk. Dissolve coffee in water; add to batter. Beat for 2 minutes. Pour into three greased and floured 9-in. round baking pans. Bake at 350° for 16-20 minutes or until a toothpick inserted near center comes out clean. Cool for 10 minutes before removing from pans to wire racks to cool completely.

For topping, dissolve coffee in water in a mixing bowl; cool. Add cream and brown sugar. Beat until stiff peaks form. Place bottom cake layer on a serving plate; top with 1-1/3 cups of topping. Sprinkle with 1/2 cup of crushed candy bars. Repeat layers twice. Store in the refrigerator. **Yield:** 12-14 servings

— ☕ ☕ ☕ —

Chocolate Angel Cake

(Pictured on page 140)

When I married in 1944, I could barely boil water. My dear mother-in-law taught me to make the lightest angel food cakes ever, like this yummy chocolate one.
—Joyce Shiffler, Manitou Springs, Colorado

1-1/2 cups confectioners' sugar
1 cup cake flour
1/4 cup baking cocoa
1-1/2 cups egg whites (about 10 eggs)
1-1/2 teaspoons cream of tartar
1/2 teaspoon salt
1 cup sugar
FROSTING:
1-1/2 cups whipping cream
1/2 cup sugar
1/4 cup baking cocoa
1/2 teaspoon salt
1/2 teaspoon vanilla extract
Chocolate leaves, optional

Sift together confectioners' sugar, flour and cocoa three times; set aside. In a mixing bowl, beat egg whites, cream of tartar and salt until soft peaks form. Add sugar, 2 tablespoons at a time, beating until stiff peaks form. Gradually fold in cocoa mixture, about a fourth at a time. Spoon into an ungreased 10-in. tube pan. Carefully run a metal spatula or knife through batter to remove air pockets. Bake on lowest oven rack at 375° for 35-40 minutes or until the top springs back when lightly touched and cracks feel dry.

Immediately invert pan; cool completely. Run a knife around edges and center tube to loosen; remove cake. In a mixing bowl, combine the first five frosting ingredients; cover and chill for 1 hour. Beat until stiff peaks form. Spread over top and sides of cake. Store in the refrigerator. Garnish with chocolate leaves if desired. **Yield:** 12-16 servings.

Caramel Apple Cake

(Pictured above)

When I go to potlucks or on fishing trips with my husband and son, this cake is a favorite dessert to bring. The flavorful cake stays moist as long as it lasts, which isn't long! —Marilyn Paradis, Woodburn, Oregon

1-1/2 cups vegetable oil
1-1/2 cups sugar
  1/2 cup packed brown sugar
    3 eggs
    3 cups all-purpose flour
    2 teaspoons ground cinnamon
  1/2 teaspoon ground nutmeg
    1 teaspoon baking soda
  1/2 teaspoon salt
3-1/2 cups diced peeled apples
    1 cup chopped walnuts
    2 teaspoons vanilla extract
CARAMEL ICING:
  1/2 cup packed brown sugar
  1/3 cup half-and-half cream
  1/4 cup butter *or* margarine
Dash salt
    1 cup confectioners' sugar
Chopped walnuts, optional

In a mixing bowl, combine oil and sugars. Add eggs, one at a time, beating well after each addition. Combine dry ingredients; add to batter and stir well. Fold in apples, walnuts and vanilla. Pour into a greased and floured 10-in. tube pan. Bake at 325° for 1-1/2 hours or until cake tests done. Cool in pan 10 minutes; remove to a wire rack to cool completely.

In the top of a double boiler over simmering water, heat brown sugar, cream, butter and salt until the sugar is dissolved. Cool to room temperature. Beat in confectioners' sugar until smooth; drizzle over cake. Sprinkle with nuts if desired. **Yield:** 12-16 servings.

———— 🍴 🍴 🍴 ————

Cinnamon Coffee Cake

(Pictured below)

I love the texture of this old-fashioned, streusel-topped coffee cake. Always a crowd pleaser, its sweet vanilla flavor enriched by sour cream may remind you of breakfast at Grandma's! —Eleanor Harris
Cape Coral, Florida

    1 cup butter *or* margarine, softened
2-3/4 cups sugar, *divided*
    2 teaspoons vanilla extract
    4 eggs
    3 cups all-purpose flour
    2 teaspoons baking powder
    1 teaspoon baking soda
    1 teaspoon salt
    2 cups (16 ounces) sour cream
    2 tablespoons ground cinnamon
  1/2 cup chopped walnuts

In a mixing bowl, cream butter and 2 cups sugar until fluffy. Add the vanilla. Add eggs, one at a time, beating well after each addition. Combine flour, baking powder, baking soda and salt; add alternately with sour cream, beating just enough after each addition to keep batter smooth. Spoon one-third of the batter into a greased 10-in. tube pan.

Combine the cinnamon, nuts and remaining sugar; sprinkle one-third over batter in pan. Repeat layers two more times. Bake at 350° for 70 minutes or until cake tests done. Cool for 10 minutes. Remove from pan to a wire rack to cool completely. **Yield:** 16-20 servings.

Marble Chiffon Cake

(Pictured above)

This confection's a proven winner—it earned a blue ribbon and was named Division Champion at the county fair some years back! —LuAnn Heikkila
Floodwood, Minnesota

      2 squares (1 ounce *each*) unsweetened
        chocolate
1-3/4 cups sugar, *divided*
  1/4 cup hot water
  1/4 teaspoon baking soda
      2 cups all-purpose flour
      1 tablespoon baking powder
      1 teaspoon salt
      7 eggs, *separated*
  3/4 cup water
  1/2 cup vegetable oil
      2 teaspoons vanilla extract
  1/2 teaspoon cream of tartar
FROSTING:
      4 squares (1 ounce *each*) semisweet
        chocolate
      1 tablespoon butter *or* margarine
      7 tablespoons whipping cream
      1 teaspoon vanilla extract
1-1/2 cups confectioners' sugar

In a small saucepan, melt unsweetened chocolate over low heat. Add 1/4 cup sugar, hot water and baking soda; mix well and set aside. In a mixing bowl, combine flour, baking powder, salt and remaining sugar. Form a well in the center; add yolks, water, oil and vanilla; blend until moistened. Beat for 3 minutes on medium speed; set aside.

In another mixing bowl, beat egg whites and cream of tartar on high until stiff peaks form. Gradually fold into batter. Divide in half; gradually fold

chocolate mixture into one portion. Alternately spoon the plain and chocolate batters into an ungreased 10-in. tube pan. Swirl with a knife. Bake at 325° for 55 minutes. Increase temperature to 350°; bake 10-15 minutes longer or until top springs back when lightly touched. Immediately invert cake; cool completely.

For frosting, melt semisweet chocolate and butter in a small saucepan over low heat. Stir in cream and vanilla. Remove from the heat; whisk in confectioners' sugar until smooth. Immediately spoon over cake. Cool. **Yield:** 12-16 servings.

———— 🍴 🍴 🍴 ————

Pumpkin Pound Cake

(Pictured on page 140)

This recipe for nicely spiced pound cake is one I rely on. It's impossible to resist a slice topped with the sweet walnut sauce. —Jean Volk
Jacksonville, Florida

1-1/2 cups butter *or* margarine, softened
2-3/4 cups sugar
      6 eggs
      1 teaspoon vanilla extract
      3 cups all-purpose flour
  3/4 teaspoon ground cinnamon
  1/2 teaspoon baking powder
  1/2 teaspoon salt
  1/2 teaspoon ground ginger
  1/4 teaspoon ground cloves
      1 cup cooked *or* canned pumpkin
WALNUT SAUCE:
      1 cup packed brown sugar
  1/2 cup whipping cream
  1/4 cup corn syrup
      2 tablespoons butter *or* margarine
  1/2 cup chopped walnuts
  1/2 teaspoon vanilla extract

In a mixing bowl, cream butter and sugar. Add eggs, one at a time, beating well after each addition. Stir in vanilla. Combine the dry ingredients; add to creamed mixture alternately with pumpkin, beating just until combined. Pour into two greased and floured 9-in. x 5-in. x 3-in. loaf pans.

Bake at 350° for 65-70 minutes or until a toothpick inserted near the center comes out clean. Cool for 10 minutes before removing from pans to wire racks to cool completely.

For sauce, combine brown sugar, cream, corn syrup and butter in a saucepan. Bring to a boil over medium heat, stirring constantly. Reduce heat; cook and stir 5 minutes longer. Remove from the heat; stir in walnuts and vanilla. Serve warm over the cake. **Yield:** 16 servings (1-2/3 cups sauce).

cake into two layers. Place bottom layer on serving plate; spread with about 1/2 cup frosting. Top with second cake layer; spread with half of the raspberry preserves. Repeat layers. Frost sides of cake with frosting.

Cut a small hole in the corner of a pastry or plastic bag; insert ribbon tip No. 47. Fill bag with remaining frosting; pipe a lattice design on top of cake. Using star tip No. 32, pipe stars around top and bottom edges of cake. Store in the refrigerator. **Yield:** 16 servings.

Raspberry Walnut Torte

(Pictured above)

I often serve this impressive cake for dinner parties or whenever a special dessert is called for. It's delicious and so pretty. —Bonnie Malloy, Norwood, Pennsylvania

1-1/2 cups whipping cream
  3 eggs
1-1/2 cups sugar
  3 teaspoons vanilla extract
1-3/4 cups all-purpose flour
  1 cup ground walnuts, toasted
  2 teaspoons baking powder
1/2 teaspoon salt
FROSTING:
1-1/2 cups whipping cream
  1 package (8 ounces) cream cheese, softened
  1 cup sugar
1/8 teaspoon salt
  1 teaspoon vanilla extract
  1 jar (12 ounces) raspberry preserves

In a small mixing bowl, beat cream until stiff peaks form; set aside. In a large mixing bowl, beat eggs, sugar and vanilla until thick and lemon-colored. Combine flour, walnuts, baking powder and salt; fold into egg mixture alternately with whipped cream. Pour into two greased and floured 9-in. round baking pans. Bake at 350° for 25-30 minutes or until a toothpick comes out clean. Cool for 10 minutes before removing from pans to wire racks to cool completely.

In a small mixing bowl, beat cream until stiff peaks form; set aside. In a large mixing bowl, beat cream cheese, sugar and salt until fluffy. Add vanilla; mix well. Fold in whipped cream. Split each

Special Rhubarb Cake

(Pictured below)

The women at church made this for my 84th birthday. A rich vanilla sauce is served over the cake. —Biena Schlabach, Millersburg, Ohio

  2 tablespoons butter (no substitutes), softened
  1 cup sugar
  1 egg
  2 cups all-purpose flour
  1 teaspoon baking powder
1/2 teaspoon baking soda
1/2 teaspoon salt
  1 cup buttermilk
  2 cups chopped rhubarb, thawed
STREUSEL TOPPING:
1/4 cup all-purpose flour
1/4 cup sugar
  2 tablespoons butter, melted
VANILLA SAUCE:
1/2 cup butter
3/4 cup sugar
1/2 cup evaporated milk
  1 teaspoon vanilla extract

In a mixing bowl, cream butter and sugar. Beat in egg. Combine flour, baking powder, baking soda and salt; add to creamed mixture alternately with buttermilk, beating just until moistened. Fold in the rhubarb. Pour into a greased 9-in. square baking dish. Combine topping ingredients; sprinkle over batter. Bake at 350° for 40-45 minutes or until a toothpick comes out clean. Cool on a wire rack.

For sauce, melt butter in a saucepan. Add sugar and milk. Bring to a boil; cook and stir for 2-3 minutes or until thickened. Remove from the heat; stir in vanilla. Serve with the cake. **Yield:** 9 servings (1-1/4 cups sauce).

— 🍥 🍥 🍥 —

Cranberry Cake

This traditional pudding-like dessert is my mother's recipe. It's always welcomed on holidays. The moist, colorful cake is served with a buttery cream sauce.
—Marion Lowery, Medford, Oregon

  3 tablespoons butter (no substitutes), softened
  1 cup sugar
  1 egg
  2 cups all-purpose flour
  2 teaspoons baking powder
  1 teaspoon ground nutmeg
  1 cup milk
  2 cups fresh *or* frozen cranberries, thawed
  2 tablespoons grated orange *or* lemon peel
CREAM SAUCE:
1-1/3 cups sugar
  1 cup whipping cream
  2/3 cup butter

In a mixing bowl, cream butter and sugar. Beat in egg. Combine the flour, baking powder and nutmeg; add to the creamed mixture alternately with milk. Stir in cranberries and orange peel. Pour into a greased 11-in. x 7-in. x 2-in. baking dish. Bake at 350° for 35-40 minutes or until a toothpick inserted near the center comes out clean.

In a saucepan, combine sauce ingredients. Cook and stir over medium heat until heated through. Cut warm cake into squares; serve with cream sauce. **Yield:** 8-10 servings.

— 🍥 🍥 🍥 —

Lemon Meringue Torte

(Pictured above right)

I copied this recipe from a notebook that my grandmother compiled as a teenager. Its old-fashioned goodness has stood the test of time. *—Sue Gronholz*
Beaver Dam, Wisconsin

  1/2 cup shortening
  1/2 cup sugar
  4 egg yolks
  6 tablespoons milk
  1 cup all-purpose flour
  1 teaspoon baking powder
FILLING:
  1 cup sugar
  3 tablespoons cornstarch
  1 cup cold water
  2 egg yolks, beaten
  1 tablespoon butter *or* margarine
  3 tablespoons lemon juice
  1 tablespoon grated lemon peel
TOPPING:
  6 egg whites
  3/4 cup sugar
  2 teaspoons ground cinnamon
  1 cup slivered almonds

In a mixing bowl, cream shortening and sugar. Beat in egg yolks and milk. Combine flour and baking powder; add to the creamed mixture and mix well. Spread into a greased 13-in. x 9-in. x 2-in. baking pan. Bake at 350° for 15 minutes or until a toothpick inserted near the center comes out clean.

In a saucepan, combine sugar and cornstarch; stir in water until smooth. Bring to a boil over medium heat; cook and stir for 1 minute. Remove from the heat. Stir a small amount into egg yolks; return all to pan. Cook over medium heat for 2 minutes. Remove from the heat. Add butter, lemon juice and peel; set aside.

In a small mixing bowl, beat the egg whites until soft peaks form. Gradually add sugar, beating until stiff peaks form. Beat in cinnamon. Fold in almonds. Spread hot filling over the crust. Spread topping over filling. Bake at 350° for 15 minutes or until lightly browned. Cool on a wire rack. Store in the refrigerator. **Yield:** 16 servings.

Chocolate Truffle Cheesecake

(Pictured below)

If you delight in the taste of chocolate, then this is the cheesecake for you. Every creamy bite melts in your mouth. It's so impressive yet not difficult to prepare.
—Mary Jones, Cumberland, Maine

1-1/2 cups chocolate wafer crumbs
    2 tablespoons sugar
    1/4 cup butter *or* margarine, melted
FILLING:
    1/4 cup semisweet chocolate chips
    1/4 cup whipping cream
    3 packages (8 ounces *each*) cream cheese, softened
    1 cup sugar
    1/3 cup baking cocoa
    3 eggs
    1 teaspoon vanilla extract
TOPPING:
1-1/2 cups semisweet chocolate chips
    1/4 cup whipping cream
    1 teaspoon vanilla extract
Whipped cream and miniature chocolate kisses, optional

In a small bowl, combine cookie crumbs and sugar; stir in butter. Press onto the bottom and 1-1/2 in. up the sides of a greased 9-in. springform pan. Bake at 350° for 10 minutes. Cool on a wire rack. Reduce heat to 325°. In a saucepan over low heat, melt chocolate chips; stir until smooth. Remove from the heat; add cream and mix well. Set aside

In a mixing bowl, beat cream cheese and sugar until smooth. Add cocoa; beat well. Add eggs; beat on low just until combined. Stir in vanilla and reserved chocolate mixture just until blended. Pour over crust. Place pan on a baking sheet. Bake for 45-50 minutes or until center is almost set.

For topping, melt chocolate chips in a saucepan over low heat, stirring until smooth. Remove from the heat. Stir in cream and vanilla; mix well. Spread over filling. Refrigerate overnight.

Carefully run a knife around edge of pan to loosen. Remove sides of pan. Just before serving, garnish with whipped cream and miniature chocolate kisses if desired. **Yield:** 12 servings.

———— 🍷 🍷 🍷 ————

Peanut Butter Cheesecake

(Pictured on page 140)

The first time I served this cheesecake, my friends all went wild over it. They were surprised when I told them the crust is made of pretzels.
—Lois Brooks
Newark, Delaware

1-1/2 cups crushed pretzels
    1/3 cup butter *or* margarine, melted
FILLING:
    5 packages (8 ounces *each*) cream cheese, softened
1-1/2 cups sugar
    3/4 cup creamy peanut butter
    2 teaspoons vanilla extract
    3 eggs
    1 cup peanut butter chips
    1 cup semisweet chocolate chips
TOPPING:
    1 cup (8 ounces) sour cream
    3 tablespoons creamy peanut butter
    1/2 cup sugar
    1/2 cup finely chopped unsalted peanuts

In a small bowl, combine pretzels and butter. Press onto the bottom and 1 in. up the sides of a greased 10-in. springform pan. Bake at 350° for 5 minutes. Cool on a wire rack. In a mixing bowl, beat cream cheese and sugar until smooth. Add peanut butter and vanilla; mix well. Add eggs; beat on low just until combined. Stir in the chips. Pour over the crust. Place pan on a baking sheet. Bake at 350° for 50-55 minutes or until the center is almost set. Cool on a wire rack for 15 minutes (leave the oven on).

Meanwhile, in a mixing bowl, combine sour cream, peanut butter and sugar; spread over filling. Sprinkle with nuts. Return to the oven for 5 minutes. Cool on a wire rack for 10 minutes. Carefully run a knife around the edge of the pan to loosen; cool 1 hour longer. Refrigerate overnight. Remove sides of pan. **Yield:** 12-14 servings.

Family-Favorite Cheesecake

This fluffy, delicate cheesecake has been a family favorite for almost 20 years. I've shared it at many gatherings over the years and have even started baking it for our friends instead of Christmas cookies.
—Esther Wappner, Mansfield, Ohio

2-1/2 cups graham cracker crumbs
     (about 40 squares)
  1/3 cup sugar
  1/2 teaspoon ground cinnamon
  1/2 cup butter *or* margarine, melted
FILLING:
    3 packages (8 ounces *each*) cream cheese,
     softened
1-1/2 cups sugar
    1 teaspoon vanilla extract
    4 eggs, *separated*
TOPPING:
  1/2 cup sour cream
    2 tablespoons sugar
  1/2 teaspoon vanilla extract
  1/2 cup whipping cream, whipped

In a small bowl, combine the cracker crumbs, sugar and cinnamon; stir in butter. Press onto the bottom and 2 in. up the sides of a greased 9-in. springform pan. Bake at 350° for 5 minutes. Cool on a wire rack. Reduce heat to 325°.

In a mixing bowl, beat cream cheese, sugar and vanilla until smooth. Add egg yolks; beat on low just until combined. In a small mixing bowl, beat egg whites until soft peaks form; fold into cream cheese mixture. Pour over crust. Place pan on a baking sheet. Bake for 1 hour or until center is almost set. Cool on a wire rack for 10 minutes. Carefully run a knife around edge of pan to loosen; cool 1 hour longer. Refrigerate until completely cooled.

Combine the sour cream, sugar and vanilla; fold in whipped cream. Spread over the cheesecake. Refrigerate overnight. Remove sides of pan. **Yield:** 12 servings.

Chocolate Chip Cookie Dough Cheesecake

(Pictured above right)

I created this recipe to combine two of my all-time favorites—cheesecake and chocolate chip cookie dough. Sour cream offsets the sweetness and adds a nice tang.
—Julie Craig, Jackson, Wisconsin

1-3/4 cups crushed chocolate chip cookies *or*
     chocolate wafer crumbs

  1/4 cup sugar
  1/3 cup butter *or* margarine, melted
FILLING:
    3 packages (8 ounces *each*) cream cheese,
     softened
    1 cup sugar
    3 eggs
    1 cup (8 ounces) sour cream
  1/2 teaspoon vanilla extract
COOKIE DOUGH:
  1/4 cup butter *or* margarine, softened
  1/4 cup sugar
  1/4 cup packed brown sugar
    1 tablespoon water
    1 teaspoon vanilla extract
  1/2 cup all-purpose flour
1-1/2 cups miniature semisweet chocolate
     chips, *divided*

In a small bowl, combine cookie crumbs and sugar; stir in butter. Press onto the bottom and 1 in. up the sides of a greased 9-in. springform pan; set aside. In a mixing bowl, beat cream cheese and sugar until smooth. Add eggs; beat on low just until combined. Add sour cream and vanilla; beat just until blended. Pour over crust; set aside.

In another mixing bowl, cream butter and sugars on medium speed for 3 minutes. Add water and vanilla. Gradually add flour. Stir in 1 cup chocolate chips. Drop dough by teaspoonfuls over filling, gently pushing dough below surface (dough should be completely covered by filling).

Place pan on a baking sheet. Bake at 350° for 45-55 minutes or until center is almost set. Cool on a wire rack for 10 minutes. Carefully run a knife around edge of pan to loosen; cool 1 hour longer. Refrigerate overnight; remove sides of pan. Sprinkle with remaining chips. **Yield:** 12-14 servings.

Strawberry Nut Roll

(Pictured below)

The oldest of seven children, I did a lot of cooking and baking while I was growing up. Desserts like this refreshing rolled shortcake are my favorite.
—Judy Hayes, Peosta, Iowa

    6 eggs, *separated*
  3/4 cup sugar, *divided*
    1 cup ground walnuts, toasted
  1/4 cup dry bread crumbs
  1/4 cup all-purpose flour
  1/8 teaspoon salt
Confectioners' sugar
FILLING:
    1 pint fresh strawberries
    1 cup whipping cream
    2 tablespoons sugar
    1 teaspoon vanilla extract
Confectioners' sugar

In a mixing bowl, beat egg whites until soft peaks form. Gradually add 1/4 cup sugar, beating until stiff peaks form. Set aside. In another mixing bowl, beat egg yolks and remaining sugar until thick and lemon-colored. Combine walnuts, bread crumbs, flour and salt; add to yolk mixture. Mix well. Fold in egg white mixture.

Line a greased 15-in. x 10-in. x 1-in. baking pan with waxed paper; grease the paper. Spread batter evenly into pan. Bake at 375° for 15 minutes or until cake springs back when lightly touched. Cool for 5 minutes. Invert cake onto a kitchen towel dusted with confectioners' sugar. Gently peel off waxed paper. Roll up cake in the towel jelly-roll style, starting with a short side. Cool on a wire rack.

Slice six large strawberries in half; set aside for garnish. Thinly slice remaining berries; set aside. In a mixing bowl, beat cream until soft peaks form. Gradually add sugar and vanilla, beating until stiff peaks form. Unroll cake; spread with filling to within 1/2 in. of edges. Top with sliced berries. Roll up again. Place seam side down on serving platter. Chill until serving. Dust with confectioners' sugar. Garnish with reserved strawberries. Refrigerate leftovers. **Yield:** 12 servings.

———— 🍷 🍷 🍷 ————

Ice Cream Sundae Cake

If you're looking for a cool, make-ahead dessert that will delight a crowd, this is it! —*Luanna Martin*
Denver, Pennsylvania

      6 eggs, *separated*
      2 cups sugar, *divided*
  1-1/3 cups all-purpose flour
    1/2 cup baking cocoa
  1-1/2 teaspoons baking powder
    2/3 cup water
      1 teaspoon vanilla extract
      1 gallon vanilla ice cream, softened
      2 jars (11-3/4 ounces *each*) hot fudge topping, warmed
  1-1/2 cups chopped salted peanuts
      2 cartons (8 ounces *each*) frozen whipped topping, thawed
      2 cups crushed cream-filled sandwich cookies

In a mixing bowl, beat egg whites until foamy. Gradually beat in 1 cup sugar until stiff peaks form; set aside. In another mixing bowl, beat egg yolks until thick and lemon-colored, about 2 minutes. Gradually beat in remaining sugar; beat 2 minutes longer. Combine flour, cocoa and baking powder; add to egg yolk mixture alternately with water. Beat in vanilla. Gently fold in egg whites. Transfer to two greased 13-in. x 9-in. x 2-in. baking pans.

Bake at 350° for 16-20 minutes or until a toothpick comes out clean. Cool on a wire rack. Spread each cake with ice cream. Drizzle with fudge topping; sprinkle with peanuts. Spread with whipped topping; sprinkle with cookies. Cover and freeze until firm. Remove from the freezer 15 minutes before serving. **Yield:** 2 desserts (15 servings each).

We've Got You Covered

The more airtight a cake storage container, the longer the cake will stay fresh and moist. To ensure that your cake stays moist, cut an apple in half and put it in the storage container with the cake.

Cookies-and-Cream Cake

(Pictured above)

I won first prize in a baking contest when I prepared this moist, fun-to-eat cake. —*Pat Habiger*
Spearville, Kansas

    1 package (18-1/4 ounces) white cake mix
1-1/4 cups water
  1/3 cup vegetable oil
    3 egg whites
    1 cup coarsely crushed cream-filled
      chocolate sandwich cookies (about 8)
FROSTING:
    4 to 4-1/2 cups confectioners' sugar
  1/2 cup shortening
  1/4 cup milk
    1 teaspoon vanilla extract
**Additional cream-filled chocolate sandwich
  cookies, halved *and/or* crushed, optional**

In a large mixing bowl, combine cake mix, water, oil and egg whites. Beat on low speed until moistened; beat on high for 2 minutes. Gently fold in the crushed cookies. Pour into two greased and floured 8-in. round cake pans. Bake at 350° for 30 minutes or until a toothpick inserted near the center comes out clean. Cool for 10 minutes; remove from pans to wire racks to cool completely.

In a mixing bowl, beat sugar, shortening, milk and vanilla until smooth. Frost between layers and over top and sides of cake. If desired, decorate the top with cookie halves and the sides with crushed cookies. **Yield:** 12 servings.

Peanutty Ice Cream Pie

(Pictured below)

A friend gave me this delicious recipe almost 20 years ago. The unique crust made of chopped peanuts makes these cool slices extra peanutty and perfect for a party. I keep the recipe handy since it's great for any occasion. I always get compliments when I serve it.
—*Donna Cline, Pensacola, Florida*

1-1/3 cups finely chopped peanuts
    3 tablespoons butter *or* margarine, melted
    2 tablespoons sugar
FILLING:
  1/4 cup peanut butter
  1/4 cup light corn syrup
  1/4 cup flaked coconut
    3 tablespoons chopped peanuts
    1 quart vanilla ice cream, softened
Miniature M&M's *or* semisweet chocolate chips

Combine the peanuts, butter and sugar; press onto the bottom and up the sides of a greased 9-in. pie plate. Cover and refrigerate for 15 minutes. In a large bowl, combine peanut butter and corn syrup. Add coconut and peanuts. Stir in ice cream just until combined. Spoon into crust. Cover and freeze overnight or until firm. Just before serving, sprinkle with M&M's or chocolate chips. **Yield:** 6-8 servings.

Cookie Ice Cream Pie

(Pictured below)

Searching for a summer dessert that's fast, easy and doesn't require baking? Just "chill out" and enjoy this chocolate-topped ice cream pie courtesy of the United Dairy Industry Association and the Wisconsin Milk Marketing Board.

- 10 **cream-filled chocolate sandwich cookies, finely crushed**
- 3 **tablespoons butter *or* margarine, melted**
- 14 **whole cream-filled chocolate sandwich cookies**

FILLING:
- 1/2 **gallon raspberry ripple ice cream, softened, *divided***
- 1/2 **cup prepared fudge topping, *divided***

Fresh raspberries, optional

Combine crushed cookies and butter; mix well. Press onto the bottom of a 9-in. pie plate. Stand whole cookies up around edges, pressing lightly into crust. Freeze for 1 hour.

Spread half of the ice cream into crust. Drizzle with 1/4 cup of fudge topping. Freeze for 1 hour. Spread remaining ice cream on top. Drizzle with remaining topping. Freeze for several hours or overnight. Garnish with raspberries if desired. Let pie stand at room temperature about 15 minutes before cutting. **Yield:** 8 servings.

Strawberry Meringue Pie

(Pictured above and on front cover)

This dessert is simple, so don't be put off by the long directions. It's impressive-looking and perfect for any occasion. —Kathleen Mercier, Orrington, Maine

- 1/3 **cup finely crushed saltines (about 12 crackers), *divided***
- 3 **egg whites**
- 1/4 **teaspoon cream of tartar**
- 1/8 **teaspoon salt**
- 1 **cup sugar**
- 1 **teaspoon vanilla extract**
- 1/2 **cup chopped pecans, toasted**
- 1 **package (4 ounces) German sweet chocolate**
- 2 **tablespoons butter *or* margarine**
- 4 **cups fresh strawberries, halved**
- 1 **cup whipping cream**
- 2 **tablespoons confectioners' sugar**

Sprinkle 2 tablespoons of cracker crumbs into a greased 9-in. pie plate. In a mixing bowl, beat egg whites, cream of tartar and salt until soft peaks form. Gradually add sugar and continue beating until stiff peaks form. Fold in vanilla, pecans and remaining cracker crumbs. Spread meringue onto the bottom and up the sides of the prepared pan. Bake at 300° for 45 minutes. Turn off oven and do not open door; let cool in oven overnight.

In a saucepan over low heat, melt chocolate and butter, stirring constantly. Drizzle over meringue. Let stand 15 minutes or until set. Top with berries. Whip cream and confectioners' sugar until soft peaks form; spoon over berries. **Yield:** 6-8 servings.

Apple Turnovers with Custard
(Pictured below)

When I was working on the apple section of my own cookbook, I knew I had to include this recipe. It outshines every other apple recipe I make!
—*Leora Muellerleile, Turtle Lake, Wisconsin*

CUSTARD:
- 1/3 cup sugar
- 2 tablespoons cornstarch
- 2 cups milk *or* half-and-half cream
- 3 egg yolks, lightly beaten
- 1 tablespoon vanilla extract

TURNOVERS:
- 4 medium baking apples, peeled and cut into 1/4-inch slices
- 1 tablespoon lemon juice
- 2 tablespoons butter *or* margarine, cubed
- 1/3 cup sugar
- 3/4 teaspoon ground cinnamon
- 1 tablespoon cornstarch

Pastry for double-crust pie
Milk

Combine sugar and cornstarch in a saucepan. Stir in milk until smooth. Cook and stir over medium-high heat until thickened and bubbly. Reduce heat; cook and stir for 2 minutes. Remove from the heat; stir 1 cup into yolks. Return all to pan. Bring to a gentle boil; cook and stir for 2 minutes. Remove from the heat; stir in vanilla. Cool slightly. Cover surface of custard with waxed paper; chill.

Place apples in a bowl; sprinkle with lemon juice. Add butter. Combine sugar, cinnamon and cornstarch; mix with apples and set aside. Divide pastry into eight portions; roll each into a 5-in. square. Spoon filling off-center on each. Brush edges with milk. Fold over to form a triangle; seal. Crimp with the tines of a fork. Cut slits in top. Place on greased baking sheets. Chill for 15 minutes. Brush with milk. Bake at 400° for 35 minutes. Serve warm with custard. **Yield:** 8 servings.

Lemon Supreme Pie
(Pictured above)

The combination of cream cheese and tart lemon in this pie I created is wonderful. —*Jana Beckman, Wamego, Kansas*

- 1 unbaked deep-dish pastry shell (9 inches)

LEMON FILLING:
- 1-1/4 cups sugar, *divided*
- 6 tablespoons cornstarch
- 1/2 teaspoon salt
- 1-1/4 cups water
- 2 tablespoons butter *or* margarine
- 2 teaspoons grated lemon peel
- 4 to 5 drops yellow food coloring, optional
- 1/2 cup fresh lemon juice

CREAM CHEESE FILLING:
- 2 packages (one 8 ounces, one 3 ounces) cream cheese, softened
- 3/4 cup confectioners' sugar
- 1-1/2 cups whipped topping
- 1 tablespoon fresh lemon juice

Line unpricked pastry shell with a double thickness of heavy-duty foil. Bake at 450° for 8 minutes. Remove foil; bake 5 minutes longer. Cool on a wire rack. In a saucepan, combine 3/4 cup sugar, cornstarch and salt. Stir in water; bring to a boil over medium-high heat. Reduce heat; add the remaining sugar. Cook and stir for 2 minutes or until thickened and bubbly. Remove from the heat; stir in butter, lemon peel and food coloring if desired. Gently stir in lemon juice (do not overmix). Cool to room temperature, about 1 hour.

In a mixing bowl, beat the cream cheese and sugar until smooth. Fold in whipped topping and lemon juice. Refrigerate 1/2 cup for garnish. Spread remaining cream cheese mixture into pastry shell; top with lemon filling. Chill overnight. Place reserved cream cheese mixture in a pastry bag with a #21 star tip; pipe stars onto pie. Store in the refrigerator. **Yield:** 6-8 servings.

Black Forest Pie

(Pictured above and on page 140)

With three active children, I don't usually fuss with fancy desserts. This one is simple but impressive—it's the one I make to show how much I care. The tempting combination of chocolate and tangy red cherries is guaranteed to make someone feel special.
—Trudy Black, Dedham, Massachusetts

3/4 cup sugar
1/3 cup baking cocoa
  2 tablespoons all-purpose flour
1/3 cup milk
1/4 cup butter *or* margarine
  2 eggs, lightly beaten
  1 can (21 ounces) cherry pie filling, *divided*
  1 unbaked pastry shell (9 inches)
Whipped topping, optional

In a saucepan, combine sugar, cocoa, flour and milk until smooth. Add butter. Bring to a boil; cook and stir for 2 minutes or until thickened. Remove from the heat. Stir a small amount of hot mixture into eggs. Return all to the pan. Fold in half of the pie filling. Pour into pastry shell. Bake at 350° for 35-40 minutes or until filling is almost set. Cool completely on a wire rack. Just before serving, top with remaining pie filling and whipped topping if desired. **Yield:** 6-8 servings.

Blueberry Cream Pie

(Pictured below)

Whenever I ask my family which pie they'd like me to make, everyone gives the same answer—Blueberry Cream Pie! This refreshing dessert has an enticing cream layer topped with lots of plump blueberries.
—Kim Erickson, Sturgis, Michigan

1-1/3 cups vanilla wafer crumbs
    2 tablespoons sugar
    5 tablespoons butter *or* margarine, melted
  1/2 teaspoon vanilla extract
FILLING:
  1/4 cup sugar
    3 tablespoons all-purpose flour
Pinch salt
    1 cup half-and-half cream
    3 egg yolks, beaten
    3 tablespoons butter *or* margarine
    1 teaspoon vanilla extract
    1 tablespoon confectioners' sugar
TOPPING:
    5 cups fresh blueberries, *divided*
  2/3 cup sugar
    1 tablespoon cornstarch

Combine the first four ingredients; press onto the bottom and sides of an ungreased 9-in. pie plate. Bake at 350° for 8-10 minutes or until crust just begins to brown. Cool. In a saucepan, combine sugar, flour and salt. Gradually whisk in cream; cook and stir over medium heat until thickened and bubbly. Cook and stir 2 minutes longer.

Gradually whisk half into egg yolks; return all to pan. Bring to a gentle boil; cook and stir for 2 minutes. Remove from the heat; stir in butter and vanilla until butter is melted. Cool for 5 minutes, stirring occasionally. Pour into the crust; sprinkle with confectioners' sugar. Chill for 30 minutes or until set.

Meanwhile, crush 2 cups of blueberries in a

medium saucepan; bring to a boil. Boil for 2 minutes, stirring constantly. Press berries through sieve; set aside 1 cup juice (add water if necessary). Discard pulp. In a saucepan, combine sugar and cornstarch. Gradually stir in blueberry juice; bring to a boil. Boil for 2 minutes, stirring constantly. Remove from the heat; cool for 15 minutes. Gently stir in remaining berries; carefully spoon over filling. Chill for 3 hours or until set. Store in the refrigerator. **Yield:** 6-8 servings.

Fresh Raspberry Pie

(Pictured above)

Mouth-watering fresh raspberries star in this luscious pie. There's nothing to distract from the tangy berry flavor and gorgeous ruby color. A big slice is an excellent way to enjoy the taste of summer.
—Patricia Staudt, Marble Rock, Iowa

  1/4 **cup sugar**
    1 **tablespoon cornstarch**
    1 **cup water**
    1 **package (3 ounces) raspberry gelatin**
    4 **cups fresh raspberries**
    1 **graham cracker crust (9 inches)**
Whipped cream, optional

In a saucepan, combine sugar and cornstarch. Add the water and bring to a boil, stirring constantly. Cook and stir for 2 minutes. Remove from the heat; stir in gelatin until dissolved. Cool for 15 minutes. Place raspberries in the crust; slowly pour gelatin mixture over berries. Chill until set, about 3 hours. Garnish with whipped cream if desired. **Yield:** 6-8 servings.

Creamy Banana Pie

(Pictured below)

Everyone who tastes this pie enjoys its delicious old-fashioned flavor. —Rita Pribyl, Indianapolis, Indiana

    1 **envelope unflavored gelatin**
  1/4 **cup cold water**
  3/4 **cup sugar**
  1/4 **cup cornstarch**
  1/2 **teaspoon salt**
2-3/4 **cups milk**
    4 **egg yolks, beaten**
    2 **tablespoons butter *or* margarine**
    1 **tablespoon vanilla extract**
    4 **medium firm bananas**
    1 **cup whipping cream, whipped**
    1 **pastry shell (10 inches), baked**
Juice and grated peel of 1 lemon
  1/2 **cup apple jelly**

In a small bowl, soften gelatin in cold water; set aside. In a saucepan, combine sugar, cornstarch and salt. Blend in milk and egg yolks; cook and stir over low heat until thickened and bubbly, about 20-25 minutes. Remove from the heat; stir in softened gelatin until dissolved. Stir in butter and vanilla. Cover surface of custard with plastic wrap and chill until no longer warm.

Slice 3 bananas; fold into custard with whipped cream. Spoon into pie shell. Chill until set, about 4-5 hours. Shortly before serving time, place lemon juice in a small bowl and slice the remaining banana into it. Melt jelly in a saucepan over low heat. Drain banana; pat dry and arrange on top of pie. Brush with jelly. Sprinkle with grated lemon peel. Serve immediately. **Yield:** 8 servings.

Editor's Note: The filling is very light in color. It is not topped with additional whipped cream.

Caramel Pear Pie
(Pictured below)

A dear friend shared the recipe for this attractive pie. The caramel drizzle and streusel topping make it almost too pretty to eat. Knowing this dessert is waiting is great motivation for our children to eat all their vegetables. —Mary Kaehler, Lodi, California

        6 cups sliced peeled ripe pears (about 6 medium)
        1 tablespoon lemon juice
    1/2 cup plus 3 tablespoons sugar, *divided*
        2 tablespoons quick-cooking tapioca
    3/4 teaspoon ground cinnamon
    1/4 teaspoon salt
    1/4 teaspoon ground nutmeg
        1 unbaked pastry shell (9 inches)
    3/4 cup old-fashioned oats
        1 tablespoon all-purpose flour
    1/4 cup cold butter *or* margarine
     18 caramels
        5 tablespoons milk
    1/4 cup chopped pecans

In a large bowl, combine pears and lemon juice. In another bowl, combine 1/2 cup sugar, tapioca, cinnamon, salt and nutmeg. Add to pears; stir gently. Let stand for 15 minutes. Pour into pastry shell. In a bowl, combine the oats, flour and remaining sugar. Cut in butter until crumbly. Sprinkle over pears. Bake at 400° for 45 minutes.

Meanwhile, in a saucepan over low heat, melt caramels with milk. Stir until smooth; add pecans. Drizzle over pie. Bake 8-10 minutes longer or until crust is golden brown and filling is bubbly. Cool on a wire rack. **Yield:** 6-8 servings.

Triple Fruit Pie
(Pictured above and on page 140)

My goal is to create pies as good as my mother's. I came up with this recipe to use up fruit in my freezer. The first time I made it, my family begged for seconds. If I continue making pies this good, maybe someday our two daughters will be striving to imitate mine! —Jeanne Freybler, Grand Rapids, Michigan

1-1/4 cups *each* fresh blueberries, raspberries and chopped rhubarb*
    1/2 teaspoon almond extract
1-1/4 cups sugar
    1/4 cup quick-cooking tapioca
    1/4 teaspoon ground nutmeg
    1/4 teaspoon salt
        1 tablespoon lemon juice
Pastry for double-crust pie (9 inches)

In a large bowl, combine fruits and extract; toss to coat. In another bowl, combine sugar, tapioca, nutmeg and salt. Add to fruit; stir gently. Let stand for 15 minutes. Line a 9-in. pie plate with bottom pastry; trim even with edge. Stir lemon juice into fruit mixture; spoon into the crust.

Roll out the remaining pastry and make a lattice crust. Seal and flute edges. Bake at 400° for 20 minutes. Reduce heat to 350°; bake 30 minutes longer or until the crust is golden brown and the filling is bubbly. **Yield:** 6-8 servings.

Editor's Note: Frozen berries and rhubarb may be substituted for fresh; thaw and drain before using.

Traditional Pumpkin Pie

(Pictured below)

Usually I prepare two different desserts for our holiday dinner, but one must be this pumpkin pie!
—Gloria Warczak, Cedarburg, Wisconsin

2 cups all-purpose flour
3/4 teaspoon salt
2/3 cup shortening
4 to 6 tablespoons cold water
FILLING:
6 eggs
1 can (29 ounces) solid-pack pumpkin
2 cups packed brown sugar
2 teaspoons ground cinnamon
1 teaspoon salt
1/2 teaspoon *each* ground cloves, nutmeg and ginger
2 cups evaporated milk

In a bowl, combine flour and salt; cut in shortening until crumbly. Sprinkle with water, 1 tablespoon at a time, tossing with a fork until dough forms a ball. Divide dough in half. On a floured surface, roll out each portion to fit a 9-in. pie plate. Place pastry in plates; trim pastry (set scraps aside if leaf cutouts are desired) and flute edges. Set shells aside.

For filling, beat eggs in a mixing bowl. Add the pumpkin, brown sugar, cinnamon, salt, cloves, nutmeg and ginger; beat just until smooth. Gradually stir in milk. Pour into pastry shells. Bake at 450° for 10 minutes. Reduce heat to 350°; bake 40-45 minutes longer or until a knife inserted near the center comes out clean. Cool on wire racks.

If desired, cut pastry scraps with a 1-in. leaf-shaped cookie cutter; place on an ungreased baking sheet. Bake at 350° for 10-15 minutes or until lightly browned. Place on baked pies. **Yield:** 2 pies (6-8 servings each).

Washington State Apple Pie

(Pictured above)

This pie won Grand Champion in the Apple Pie category at the 1992 Okanogan County Fair. The pie looks traditional, but making your own filling gives it a different flair and great taste. *—Dolores Scholz Tonasket, Washington*

6 cups sliced peeled tart apples (5 to 6 medium)
2 tablespoons water
1 tablespoon lemon juice
1/2 cup sugar
1/2 cup packed brown sugar
3 tablespoons all-purpose flour
1 teaspoon ground cinnamon
1/4 teaspoon ground nutmeg
1/8 teaspoon ground ginger
1/8 teaspoon salt
Pastry for double-crust pie (9 inches)

In a saucepan, combine apples, water and lemon juice; cook over medium-low heat just until the apples are tender. Remove from the heat and cool (do not drain). In a large bowl, combine sugars, flour, cinnamon, nutmeg, ginger and salt; add apples and toss to coat.

Line a 9-in. pie plate with bottom pastry; trim even with edge. Add filling. Roll out remaining pastry to fit top of pie; place over filling. Seal and flute edges. Cut slits in top. Bake at 450° for 10 minutes. Reduce heat to 350°; bake 35-45 minutes longer or until golden brown. **Yield:** 6-8 servings.

1 can (14 ounces) sweetened condensed
  milk
6 ounces limeade concentrate
4 drops green food coloring, optional
1 carton (8 ounces) frozen whipped
  topping, thawed, *divided*
1 graham cracker crust (9 inches)
1 kiwifruit, peeled and sliced
Mandarin oranges and chopped pistachios,
  optional

In a mixing bowl, beat cream cheese and milk until smooth. Add limeade and food coloring if desired. Fold in half of the whipped topping. Pour into crust. Cover and refrigerate for 2 hours. Garnish with kiwi, remaining whipped topping, and oranges and pistachios if desired. **Yield:** 6-8 servings.

Peachy Rhubarb Pie

(Pictured below)

My husband especially loves the combination of peaches and homegrown rhubarb in this pie.
—*Phyllis Galloway, Roswell, Georgia*

1 can (8-1/2 ounces) sliced peaches
2 cups chopped fresh *or* frozen rhubarb,
  thawed and drained
1 cup sugar
1/4 cup flaked coconut
3 tablespoons quick-cooking tapioca
1 teaspoon vanilla extract
Pastry for double-crust pie (9 inches)
1 tablespoon butter *or* margarine

Cranberry Cherry Pie

(Pictured above and on back cover)

Guests won't believe how quickly you made this sweet-tart pie. It starts with convenient canned pie filling.
—*Marilyn Williams, Matthews, North Carolina*

3/4 cup sugar
2 tablespoons cornstarch
1 can (21 ounces) cherry pie filling
2 cups cranberries
Pastry for double-crust pie (9 inches)
Milk and additional sugar

In a bowl, combine sugar and cornstarch. Stir in pie filling and cranberries. Line a 9-in. pie plate with bottom pastry; trim to 1 in. beyond edge of plate. Pour filling into crust. Roll out remaining pastry to fit top of pie. Cut slits in pastry or cut out stars with a star-shaped cookie cutter. Place pastry over filling; trim, seal and flute edges. Arrange star cutouts on pastry.

Brush with milk; sprinkle with sugar. Cover edges loosely with foil. Bake at 375° for 55-60 minutes or until crust is golden brown and filling is bubbly. Cool on a wire rack. **Yield:** 6-8 servings.

Cool Lime Pie

This sweet-tart dessert is so pretty to set on the table and easy to make. —*Waydella Hart, Parsons, Kansas*

1 package (8 ounces) cream cheese,
  softened

Drain peaches, reserving syrup; chop the peaches. Place peaches and syrup in a bowl; add rhubarb, sugar, coconut, tapioca and vanilla. Line a 9-in. pie plate with the bottom pastry. Add filling; dot with butter. Top with remaining pastry or a lattice crust; flute edges. If using a full top crust, cut slits in it. Bake at 350° for 1 hour or until crust is golden brown and filling is bubbly. **Yield:** 6-8 servings.

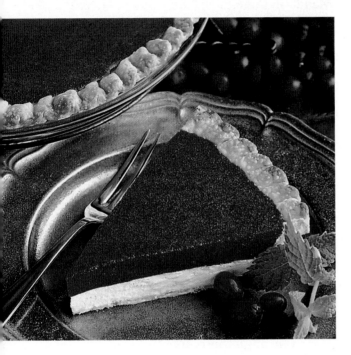

Fluffy Cranberry Cheese Pie

(Pictured above)

This pie has a light texture and zippy flavor that matches its vibrant color. It's festive for the holidays or anytime, and easy because you make it ahead. Folks tell me it's like getting two desserts at once—cheesecake and fruit pie! —Mary Parkonen
West Wareham, Massachusetts

CRANBERRY TOPPING:
      1 package (3 ounces) raspberry gelatin
    1/3 cup sugar
  1-1/4 cups cranberry juice
      1 can (8 ounces) jellied cranberry sauce
FILLING:
      1 package (3 ounces) cream cheese, softened
    1/4 cup sugar
      1 tablespoon milk
      1 teaspoon vanilla extract
    1/2 cup whipped topping
      1 pastry shell (9 inches), baked

In a mixing bowl, combine gelatin and sugar; set aside. In a saucepan, bring cranberry juice to a boil. Remove from the heat and pour over gelatin mixture, stirring to dissolve. Stir in the cranberry sauce. Chill until slightly thickened. Meanwhile, in another mixing bowl, beat cream cheese, sugar, milk and vanilla until fluffy. Fold in the whipped topping. Spread evenly into pie shell. Beat cranberry topping until frothy; pour over filling. Chill overnight. **Yield:** 6-8 servings.

— ☕ ☕ ☕ —

Poppy Seed Strawberry Pie

(Pictured below)

The combination of flavors in this pretty dessert won me over the first time I tasted it. —Kris Sackett
Eau Claire, Wisconsin

  1-1/3 cups all-purpose flour
      1 tablespoon poppy seeds
    1/4 teaspoon salt
    1/2 cup shortening
      3 tablespoons cold water
FILLING:
      2 pints strawberries, *divided*
      2 cups whipped topping
      2 tablespoons honey
    1/4 cup slivered almonds, toasted, optional

In a bowl, combine flour, poppy seeds and salt; cut in shortening until crumbly. Gradually add water, tossing with a fork until dough forms a ball. Roll out pastry to fit a 9-in. pie plate. Transfer pastry to plate; flute edges. Line unpricked pastry with a double thickness of heavy-duty foil. Bake at 450° for 8 minutes. Remove foil; bake 5 minutes longer. Cool on a wire rack.

Slice 1 pint of strawberries; fold into whipped topping. Spoon into pie shell. Cut remaining berries in half; arrange over top. Drizzle with honey. Sprinkle with almonds if desired. Refrigerate for at least 1 hour. **Yield:** 6-8 servings.

Chocolate Raspberry Pie

(Pictured below)

After tasting this pie at my sister-in-law's house, I had to have the recipe. I love the chocolate and raspberry layers separated by a dreamy cream layer.
—Ruth Bartel, Morris, Manitoba

- 1 unbaked pastry shell (9 inches)
- 3 tablespoons sugar
- 1 tablespoon cornstarch
- 2 cups unsweetened raspberries

FILLING:
- 1 package (8 ounces) cream cheese, softened
- 1/3 cup sugar
- 1/2 teaspoon vanilla extract
- 1/2 cup whipping cream, whipped

TOPPING:
- 2 squares (1 ounce *each*) semisweet chocolate
- 3 tablespoons butter *or* margarine

Line unpricked pastry shell with a double thickness of heavy-duty foil. Bake at 450° for 8 minutes. Remove foil; bake 5 minutes longer. Cool on a wire rack. In a saucepan, combine sugar and cornstarch. Stir in raspberries; bring to a boil over medium heat. Boil and stir for 2 minutes. Remove from the heat; cool for 15 minutes. Spread into pastry shell; refrigerate.

In a mixing bowl, beat cream cheese, sugar and vanilla until fluffy. Fold in the whipped cream. Carefully spread over the raspberry layer. Cover and refrigerate for at least 1 hour. For topping, melt chocolate and butter; cool for 4-5 minutes. Pour over filling. Cover and chill for at least 2 hours. Store in the refrigerator. **Yield:** 6-8 servings.

Mint Brownie Pie

(Pictured above)

When I served this treat to my family on St. Patrick's Day, it was an instant success. The cool creamy filling goes well with the rich chocolate crust.
—Karen Hayes, Conneaut Lake, Pennsylvania

- 6 tablespoons butter (no substitutes)
- 2 squares (1 ounce *each*) unsweetened chocolate
- 1 cup sugar
- 2 eggs, beaten
- 1/2 teaspoon vanilla extract
- 1/2 cup all-purpose flour

FILLING:
- 1 package (8 ounces) cream cheese, softened
- 3/4 cup sugar
- 1/2 teaspoon peppermint extract

Green food coloring, optional
- 1 carton (8 ounces) frozen whipped topping, thawed
- 1/4 cup semisweet chocolate chips, melted

Additional whipped topping and chocolate chips, optional

In a saucepan, melt butter and chocolate. Stir in sugar until well blended. Add eggs and vanilla; mix well. Stir in flour until well blended. Pour into a greased 9-in. springform pan. Place pan on a baking sheet. Bake at 350° for 18-20 minutes or until a toothpick inserted near the center comes out clean. Cool on a wire rack.

In a mixing bowl, beat cream cheese and sugar until smooth. Add extract and food coloring if desired; mix well. Fold in whipped topping. Spread evenly over brownie layer. Cover and refrigerate for at least 1 hour. Remove sides of pan just before serving. Melt chocolate chips; drizzle over the top. Garnish with whipped topping and chocolate chips if desired. **Yield:** 8 servings.

Tin Roof Fudge Pie

(Pictured below)

This delectable pie makes a great hostess gift for a holiday get-together or a wonderful ending to a meal for company. —Cynthia Kolberg, Syracuse, Indiana

- 2 squares (1 ounce *each*) semisweet baking chocolate
- 1 tablespoon butter (no substitutes)
- 1 pastry shell (9 inches), baked

PEANUT LAYER:
- 20 caramels
- 1/3 cup whipping cream
- 1-1/2 cups salted peanuts

CHOCOLATE LAYER:
- 8 squares (1 ounce *each*) semisweet baking chocolate
- 2 tablespoons butter
- 1 cup whipping cream
- 2 teaspoons vanilla extract

Whipped cream and salted peanuts, optional
TOPPING:
- 3 caramels
- 5 teaspoons whipping cream
- 1 tablespoon butter

In a microwave or double boiler, melt chocolate and butter. Spread onto bottom and up sides of crust; refrigerate until chocolate is set. In a saucepan over low heat, melt caramels and cream, stirring frequently until smooth. Remove from the heat; stir in peanuts. Spoon into pie shell; refrigerate. In a saucepan over low heat, melt chocolate and butter. Remove from the heat; let stand for 15 minutes.

Meanwhile, in a mixing bowl, beat cream and vanilla until soft peaks form. Carefully fold a third of the whipped cream into the chocolate mixture; fold in the remaining whipped cream. Spread over peanut layer; refrigerate until set. Garnish with whipped cream and peanuts if desired. In a small saucepan over low heat, melt caramels, cream and butter. Drizzle over pie. Refrigerate until serving. **Yield:** 8-10 servings.

———— 🍴 🍴 🍴 ————

Fudgy Pecan Pie

This started out as just a plain chocolate pie that I "dressed up" for company. Now when I serve it, guests often tell me, "Your pie looks too good to eat—but I won't let that stop me!" —Ellen Arndt Cologne, Minnesota

- 1 unbaked pastry shell (9 inches)
- 1 package (4 ounces) German sweet chocolate
- 1/4 cup butter *or* margarine
- 1 can (14 ounces) sweetened condensed milk
- 1/2 cup water
- 2 eggs, beaten
- 1 teaspoon vanilla extract
- 1/4 teaspoon salt
- 1/2 cup chopped pecans

FILLING:
- 1 cup cold milk
- 1 package (3.9 ounces) instant chocolate pudding mix
- 1 cup whipped topping

TOPPING:
- 1 cup whipping cream
- 1 tablespoon confectioners' sugar
- 1 teaspoon vanilla extract

Line unpricked pastry shell with a double thickness of heavy-duty foil. Bake at 450° for 5 minutes. Remove foil and set shell aside. Reduce heat to 375°.

In a heavy saucepan, melt chocolate and butter. Remove from the heat; stir in milk and water. Add a small amount of hot chocolate mixture to eggs; return all to the pan. Stir in vanilla and salt. Pour into shell; sprinkle with nuts. Cover edges with foil. Bake for 35 minutes or until a knife inserted near the center comes out clean. Remove to a wire rack to cool completely.

In a mixing bowl, beat the milk and pudding mix until smooth. Fold in whipped topping. Spread over nut layer; cover and refrigerate. In a mixing bowl, beat cream until soft peaks form. Add sugar and vanilla, beating until stiff peaks form. Spread over pudding layer. Refrigerate until set, about 4 hours. **Yield:** 6-8 servings.

ar is dissolved. Pour hot filling into crust. Spread meringue evenly over filling, sealing edges to crust.

Bake at 325° for 25-30 minutes or until golden brown. Cool on a wire rack for 1 hour. Chill for at least 3 hours before serving. Refrigerate leftovers. **Yield:** 6-8 servings.

— 🍴 🍴 🍴 —

Cheddar Pear Pie

(Pictured below)

I take this pie to lots of different gatherings, and I make sure to have copies of the recipe with me since people always ask for it. It's amusing to see some folks puzzling over what's in the filling—they expect apples but love the subtle sweetness of the pears.
—Cynthia LaBree, Elmer, New Jersey

    4 large ripe pears, peeled and thinly sliced
  1/3 cup sugar
    1 tablespoon cornstarch
  1/8 teaspoon salt
    1 unbaked pastry shell (9 inches)
TOPPING:
  1/2 cup shredded cheddar cheese
  1/2 cup all-purpose flour
  1/4 cup butter *or* margarine, melted
  1/4 cup sugar
  1/4 teaspoon salt

In a bowl, combine pears, sugar, cornstarch and salt. Pour into pastry shell. Combine topping ingredients until crumbly; sprinkle over filling. Bake at 425° for 25-35 minutes or until crust is golden and cheese is melted. Cool on a wire rack for 15-20 minutes. Serve warm. Store in the refrigerator. **Yield:** 6-8 servings.

Apricot Meringue Pie

(Pictured above)

My sister-in-law wanted to create an apricot pie recipe, so we experimented until we came up a combination of ingredients we liked. The meringue sits nice and high, while the sweet apricots retain a little of their chewy texture. It's yummy!   —Olive Rumage
                                                   Jacksboro, Texas

   12 ounces dried apricots, chopped
1-1/2 cups water
2-1/2 cups sugar, *divided*
    3 tablespoons cornstarch
  1/4 teaspoon salt
    4 eggs, *separated*
    2 tablespoons butter *or* margarine
  1/4 teaspoon cream of tartar
    1 pastry shell (9 inches), baked

In a saucepan, bring apricots and water to a boil. Reduce heat; simmer, uncovered, for 10 minutes or until apricots are softened. In a bowl, combine 2 cups sugar, cornstarch and salt; stir into apricot mixture. Bring to a boil. Reduce heat; cook and stir for 1 minute or until thickened. Remove from the heat; stir a small amount of hot filling into yolks. Return all to pan, stirring constantly. Bring to a gentle boil; cook and stir 1 minute longer or until glossy and clear. Remove from the heat; stir in butter. Keep warm.

In a mixing bowl, beat egg whites and cream of tartar on medium speed until soft peaks form. Gradually beat in remaining sugar, 1 tablespoon at a time, on high until stiff glossy peaks form and sug-

Candy Apple Pie

(Pictured below)

This is the only apple pie my husband will eat, but that's all right since he makes it as often as I do. Like a combination of apple and pecan pie, it's a sweet treat that usually tops off our holiday meals year-round.
—Cindy Kleweno, Burlington, Colorado

    6 cups thinly sliced peeled baking apples
    2 tablespoons lime juice
  3/4 cup sugar
  1/4 cup all-purpose flour
  1/2 teaspoon ground cinnamon *or* nutmeg
  1/4 teaspoon salt
Pastry for double-crust pie (9 inches)
    2 tablespoons butter *or* margarine
TOPPING:
  1/4 cup butter *or* margarine
  1/2 cup packed brown sugar
    2 tablespoons whipping cream
  1/2 cup chopped pecans

In a large bowl, toss apples with lime juice. Combine dry ingredients; add to the apples and toss lightly. Line a 9-in. pie plate with bottom pastry; add filling. Dot with butter. Cover with top crust. Flute edges high; cut steam vents. Bake at 400° for 40-45 minutes or until golden brown and apples are tender.

Meanwhile, for topping, melt butter in a small saucepan. Stir in brown sugar and cream; bring to a boil, stirring constantly. Remove from the heat and stir in pecans. Pour over top crust. Return to the oven for 3-4 minutes or until bubbly. Serve warm. **Yield:** 8 servings.

County Fair Pie

(Pictured above)

I'm glad my family loves this pie, because it's so quick and easy to make that I never have to say no to requests. At potlucks, someone always asks for the recipe. —Judy Acuff, Lathrop, Missouri

  1/2 cup butter *or* margarine, melted
    1 cup sugar
  1/2 cup all-purpose flour
    2 eggs
    1 teaspoon vanilla extract
    1 cup coarsely chopped walnuts
    1 cup (6 ounces) semisweet chocolate chips
  1/2 cup butterscotch chips
    1 unbaked pastry shell (9 inches)

In a mixing bowl, beat the butter, sugar, flour, eggs and vanilla until well blended. Stir in nuts and chips. Pour into pie shell. Bake at 325° for 1 hour or until golden brown. Cool on a wire rack. **Yield:** 6-8 servings.

Homemade Crumb Crusts

Combine 1-1/2 cups graham cracker crumbs (24 squares), 1/4 cup sugar and 1/3 cup melted butter or margarine. Press onto the bottom and up the sides of an ungreased 9-in. pie plate. Chill 30 minutes before filling or bake at 375° until lightly browned, about 8-10 minutes.

Just Desserts

For some folks, dessert is the best part of the meal! With these favorite recipes for crisps, cobblers, candies, puddings, ice cream and more, no sweet tooth will ever have to do without.

—— 🥄 🥄 🥄 ——

HAPPY ENDINGS. Clockwise from upper left: Mint Chip Ice Cream (p. 181), Peach Shortcake (p. 167), Melon Ambrosia (p. 168), Chocolate Peanut Sweeties (p. 178), Valentine Berries and Cream (p. 171) and Chocolate Eclairs (p. 173).

Easy Apple Crisp

This is a delicious dessert perfect for young cooks to prepare. It's easy to make since there's no crust—just a crumbly topping. Plus, with apples and oats, it's a wholesome treat.
—Sheri Hatten
Devil's Lake, North Dakota

10 to 11 cups sliced peeled baking apples
1/2 cup sugar
1 teaspoon ground cinnamon, *divided*
1 cup all-purpose flour
1 cup packed brown sugar
1/2 cup quick-cooking oats
1 teaspoon baking powder
1/4 teaspoon ground nutmeg
1/2 cup cold butter *or* margarine

Place apples in a greased 13-in. x 9-in. x 2-in. baking dish. Combine sugar and 1/2 teaspoon cinnamon; sprinkle over apples. Combine flour, brown sugar, oats, baking powder, nutmeg and remaining cinnamon; cut in butter until mixture resembles coarse crumbs. Sprinkle over the apples. Bake at 375° for 50-60 minutes or until apples are tender. **Yield:** 12-16 servings.

Blackberry Cobbler

(Pictured below)

It's fun to pick blackberries, especially when we know this dessert will be the result.
—Tina Hankins
Laconia, New Hampshire

1/4 cup butter *or* margarine, softened
1/2 cup sugar
1 cup all-purpose flour
2 teaspoons baking powder
1/2 cup milk
2 cups fresh *or* frozen blackberries

3/4 cup raspberry *or* apple juice
Ice cream *or* whipped cream, optional

In a mixing bowl, cream butter and sugar. Combine flour and baking powder; add to creamed mixture alternately with milk. Stir just until moistened. Pour into a greased 1-1/2-qt. baking dish. Sprinkle with blackberries. Pour juice over all. Bake at 350° for 45-50 minutes or until golden brown. Serve warm; top with ice cream or whipped cream if desired. **Yield:** 6-8 servings.

Rhubarb Raspberry Crisp

(Pictured above)

Every time I've entered our Boone County baking contest, I've won a blue ribbon. One summer, when the category was rhubarb, this recipe was the grand champion! See if your family thinks it's a winner, too. The orange juice and peel give it zest.
—Mabeth Shaw
Lebanon, Indiana

4 cups chopped fresh rhubarb (1-inch pieces)
2/3 cup sugar
Juice and grated peel of 1 orange
1 cup all-purpose flour
1/2 cup packed brown sugar
1/2 teaspoon ground cinnamon
1/2 cup cold butter *or* margarine, cubed
1/2 cup rolled oats
1/4 cup chopped pecans
1/2 pint fresh raspberries

In a large bowl, combine rhubarb, sugar, orange juice and peel. In another bowl, combine flour, brown sugar and cinnamon. Cut in butter until crumbly. Add oats and pecans; mix well. Transfer rhubarb mixture to an 8-in. square baking dish. Sprinkle evenly with raspberries and cover with crumb topping. Bake at 350° for 45 minutes or until topping is browned. **Yield:** 9 servings.

— 🍴 🍴 🍴 —

Peach Shortcake

(Pictured below and on page 164)

When fresh peaches are in plentiful supply, this appealing layered dessert can't be beat. Brown sugar and ginger give the shortcake its mellow, sweet-spicy flavor. —Karen Owen, Rising Sun, Indiana

      2 cups all-purpose flour
      2 tablespoons brown sugar
      1 tablespoon baking powder
  1/2 teaspoon salt
  1/2 teaspoon ground ginger
  1/2 cup cold butter *or* margarine
  2/3 cup milk
FILLING:
1-1/2 pounds ripe fresh peaches *or* nectarines,
      peeled and thinly sliced
      6 tablespoons brown sugar, *divided*
  1/4 teaspoon ground ginger
      1 cup whipping cream
  1/4 cup chopped pecans, toasted

Combine the first five ingredients in a bowl; cut in butter until mixture resembles coarse crumbs. Add milk, stirring only until moistened. Turn onto a lightly floured surface; knead 10 times. Pat evenly into a greased 8-in. round baking pan. Bake at 425° for 20-25 minutes or until golden brown. Remove from the pan to cool on a wire rack.

Just before serving, combine peaches, 4 tablespoons brown sugar and ginger. Whip cream with remaining brown sugar until stiff. Split shortcake into two layers; place bottom layer on a serving platter. Spoon half of the peach mixture over cake; top with half of the cream. Cover with second cake layer and remaining peach mixture. Garnish with remaining cream; sprinkle with pecans. **Yield:** 8-10 servings.

Upside-Down Cranberry Crunch

(Pictured above)

For special occasions, I often serve this sweet-tart dessert. I've also used raspberries, strawberries and blueberries instead of cranberries with great results. —Carol Miller, Northumberland, New York

      3 cups fresh *or* frozen cranberries, thawed
1-3/4 cups sugar, *divided*
  1/2 cup chopped pecans
      2 eggs
  1/2 cup butter *or* margarine, melted
      1 cup all-purpose flour
Whipped cream *or* vanilla ice cream, optional

Place cranberries in a greased 8-in. square baking dish. Sprinkle with 3/4 cup sugar and pecans. In a mixing bowl, beat eggs, butter, flour and remaining sugar until smooth. Spread over cranberry mixture. Bake at 325° for 1 hour or until a toothpick inserted near the center of cake comes out clean. Run knife around edges of dish; immediately invert onto a serving plate. Serve with whipped cream or ice cream if desired. **Yield:** 8 servings.

Pear Melba Dumplings

(Pictured below)

I substituted pears in a favorite apple dumpling recipe, then added a raspberry sauce. Yum! —Doreen Kelly
Roslyn, Pennsylvania

        2 cups all-purpose flour
1-1/4 teaspoons salt
    1/2 teaspoon cornstarch
    2/3 cup butter-flavored shortening
        4 to 5 tablespoons cold water
        6 small ripe pears, peeled and cored
        6 tablespoons brown sugar
    1/4 teaspoon ground cinnamon
        2 tablespoons milk
        1 tablespoon sugar
RASPBERRY SAUCE:
        1 tablespoon sugar
        1 tablespoon cornstarch
        2 tablespoons water
        1 package (10 ounces) frozen raspberries, thawed
    1/4 teaspoon almond extract
Ice cream, optional

In a bowl, combine flour, salt and cornstarch. Cut in shortening until mixture resembles coarse crumbs. Stir in water until pastry forms a ball. On a floured surface, roll into a 21-in. x 14-in. rectangle. Cut into six squares. Place one pear in center of each square. Pack pear centers with brown sugar; sprinkle with cinnamon. Brush edges of squares with milk; fold up corners to center and pinch to seal. Place in a greased 15-in. x 10-in. x 1-in. baking pan. Brush with milk; sprinkle with sugar.

Bake at 375° for 35-40 minutes or until golden brown. Meanwhile, in a saucepan, combine sugar, cornstarch and water until smooth. Add raspberries. Bring to a boil; cook and stir for 2 minutes or until thickened. Remove from the heat; stir in extract. Serve warm over warm dumplings with ice cream if desired. **Yield:** 6 servings.

Melon Ambrosia

(Pictured on page 164)

Each time I serve this light and refreshing dessert, it gets wonderful reviews. With three kinds of melon, it's lovely and colorful but so simple to prepare.
—Edie DeSpain, Logan, Utah

✓ Uses less fat, sugar or salt. Includes Nutritional Analysis and Diabetic Exchanges.

        1 cup watermelon balls *or* cubes
        1 cup cantaloupe balls *or* cubes
        1 cup honeydew balls *or* cubes
    1/3 cup lime juice
        2 tablespoons sugar
        2 tablespoons honey
    1/4 cup flaked coconut, toasted
Fresh mint, optional

In a bowl, combine melon balls. In another bowl, combine the lime juice, sugar and honey; pour over melon and toss to coat. Cover and refrigerate for at least 1 hour. Sprinkle with coconut. Garnish with mint if desired. **Yield:** 4 servings.
    Nutritional Analysis: One serving (3/4 cup) equals 137 calories, 4 g fat (3 g saturated fat), 0 cholesterol, 12 mg sodium, 29 g carbohydrate, 2 g fiber, 1 g protein. **Diabetic Exchange:** 2 fruit.

Tiny Cherry Cheesecakes

(Pictured above right)

I prepare these mini cheesecakes every Christmas and for many weddings. I've received countless compliments and recipe requests. When I send these along in my husband's lunch, I have to be sure to pack extras because the men he works with love them, too.
—Janice Hertlein, Esterhazy, Saskatchewan

        1 cup all-purpose flour
    1/3 cup sugar
    1/4 cup baking cocoa
    1/2 cup cold butter *or* margarine
        2 tablespoons cold water
FILLING:
        2 packages (3 ounces *each*) cream cheese, softened
    1/4 cup sugar
        2 tablespoons milk
        1 teaspoon vanilla extract
        1 egg
        1 can (21 ounces) cherry *or* strawberry pie filling

In a small bowl, combine flour, sugar and cocoa; cut in butter until crumbly. Gradually add water,

2 eggs
1 teaspoon vanilla extract
1/3 cup chopped pecans *or* almonds
TOPPING:
2-1/2 cups fresh *or* frozen pitted tart cherries
    or 1 can (15 *or* 16 ounces) pitted tart
    cherries
1/3 cup sugar
2 tablespoons cornstarch
1 tablespoon butter *or* margarine
1/8 teaspoon almond extract
1/8 teaspoon red food coloring
Whipped cream and fresh mint, optional

In a bowl, combine flour and baking powder; cut in butter and shortening until mixture resembles coarse crumbs. Gradually add water, tossing with a fork until dough forms a ball. Roll out into a 14-in. circle. Place on an ungreased 12-in. pizza pan. Flute edges to form a rim; prick bottom of crust. Bake at 350° for 15 minutes.

In a mixing bowl, beat cream cheese and sugar until smooth. Beat in eggs and vanilla. Stir in nuts. Spread over crust. Bake 10 minutes longer. Cool.

Drain cherries, reserving 1/3 cup juice. Set the cherries and juice aside. In a saucepan, combine sugar and cornstarch; stir in reserved juice until smooth. Add cherries. Cook and stir over medium heat until mixture comes to a boil. Cook and stir 2 minutes longer. Remove from the heat; stir in butter, almond extract and food coloring. Cool to room temperature; spread over cream cheese layer. Garnish with whipped cream and mint if desired. **Yield:** 10-12 slices.

tossing with a fork until dough forms a ball. Shape into 24 balls. Place in greased miniature muffin cups; press dough onto the bottom and up the sides of each cup. In a mixing bowl, beat cream cheese and sugar until smooth. Beat in milk and vanilla. Add egg; beat on low just until combined.

Spoon about 1 tablespoonful into each cup. Bake at 325° for 15-18 minutes or until set. Cool on a wire rack for 30 minutes. Carefully remove from pans to cool completely. Top with pie filling. Store in the refrigerator. **Yield:** 2 dozen.

— 🥄 🥄 🥄 —

Cherry Cheese Pizza

(Pictured at right)

This dessert pizza is a great way to use cherries—my family likes it better than cherry pie. Each bite just melts in your mouth. People who sample it rave about this "sweet" pizza.". —Elaine Darbyshire
Golden, British Columbia

1 cup all-purpose flour
1/8 teaspoon baking powder
1/4 cup cold butter *or* margarine
2 tablespoons shortening
3 to 4 tablespoons water
1 package (8 ounces) cream cheese, softened
1/2 cup sugar

Raspberry White Chocolate Mousse

(Pictured below)

This dessert is surprisingly easy and a delightful change of pace from heavier cakes and pies.
—*Mary Lou Wayman, Salt Lake City, Utah*

1 package (10 ounces) sweetened frozen
  raspberries, thawed
2 tablespoons sugar
1 tablespoon orange juice concentrate
2 cups whipping cream

6 ounces white baking chocolate
1 teaspoon vanilla extract
1/4 cup milk chocolate chips
1 teaspoon vegetable oil

In a blender, combine the raspberries, sugar and orange juice concentrate; cover and process until smooth. Press through a sieve; discard seeds. Refrigerate sauce.

For mousse, in a saucepan over low heat, cook and stir cream and white chocolate until chocolate is melted. Stir in vanilla. Transfer to a mixing bowl.

FESTIVE TREATS. Valentine Berries and Cream, Raspberry White Chocolate Mouse and True Love Truffles (shown above, clockwise from top) will be savored by sweethearts.

Cover and refrigerate for 6 hours or until thickened, stirring occasionally.

Beat cream mixture on high speed until light and fluffy, about 1-1/2 minutes (do not overbeat). Just before serving, melt chocolate chips and oil in a microwave or saucepan. Spoon 2 tablespoons of raspberry sauce on each plate. Pipe or spoon 1/2 cup chocolate mousse over sauce; drizzle with melted chocolate. Store leftovers in the refrigerator. **Yield:** 8 servings.

True Love Truffles

(Pictured at left)

Years ago, I began giving these minty truffles in tins as Christmas gifts. Now I can't go a year without sharing them. —Kim Weiesnbach, Claremore, Oklahoma

1-1/2 cups sugar
3/4 cup butter (no substitutes)
1 can (5 ounces) evaporated milk
2 packages (4.67 ounces *each*) mint Andes candies (56 pieces total)
1 jar (7 ounces) marshmallow creme
1 teaspoon vanilla extract
22 ounces white baking chocolate, *divided*
1/2 cup semisweet chocolate chips
Green food coloring, optional

In a heavy saucepan, combine sugar, butter and milk. Bring to a boil over medium heat, stirring constantly. Reduce heat; cook and stir until a candy thermometer reads 236° (soft-ball stage). Remove from the heat. Stir in candies until melted and mixture is well blended. Stir in marshmallow creme and vanilla until smooth. Spread into a buttered 15-in. x 10-in. x 1-in. pan; cover and refrigerate for 1 hour. Cut into 96 pieces; roll each into a ball (mixture will be soft). Place on a waxed paper-lined baking sheet.

In a heavy saucepan or microwave-safe bowl, melt 18 oz. of the white chocolate and chocolate chips. Dip balls in melted chocolate; place on waxed paper to harden. Melt the remaining white chocolate; add food coloring if desired. Drizzle over the truffles. Store in an airtight container. **Yield:** 8 dozen.

Valentine Berries and Cream

(Pictured at left and on page 164)

Everyone was so impressed with this scrumptious filled chocolate heart served at a banquet held by our adult Sunday school class. I got the recipe, and now I enjoy

rave reviews from family and friends when I serve it. —Tamera O'Sullivan, Apple Valley, Minnesota

8 squares (1 ounce *each*) semisweet chocolate
1 tablespoon shortening
2 packages (3 ounces *each*) cream cheese, softened
1/4 cup butter *or* margarine, softened
1-1/2 cups confectioners' sugar
1/3 cup baking cocoa
2 tablespoons milk
1 teaspoon vanilla extract
2-1/2 cups whipping cream, whipped, *divided*
1-1/2 cups fresh strawberries, halved

Line a 9-in. heart-shaped or square baking pan with foil; set aside. In a heavy saucepan over low heat, melt chocolate and shortening; stir until smooth. Pour into prepared pan, swirling to coat the bottom and 1-1/2 in. up the sides, Refrigerate for 1 minute, then swirl the chocolate to reinforce sides of heart or box. Refrigerate for 30 minutes or until firm. Using foil, lift from pan; remove foil and place chocolate heart on a serving plate.

In a mixing bowl, beat the cream cheese and butter until smooth. Combine confectioners' sugar and cocoa; add to creamed mixture with milk and vanilla. Beat until smooth. Gently fold two-thirds of the whipped cream into cream cheese mixture. Spoon into heart. Insert star tip No. 32 into a pastry or plastic bag; fill with the remaining whipped cream. Pipe around the edge of heart. Garnish with strawberries. **Yield:** 8-10 servings.

Chocolate Sauce

I make different toppings so we can enjoy our favorite dessert—ice cream sundaes. This smooth, creamy sauce is always a big hit. —Nancy McDonald Burns, Wyoming

1/2 cup butter (no substitutes)
2 squares (1 ounce *each*) unsweetened chocolate
2 cups sugar
1 cup half-and-half cream *or* evaporated milk
1/2 cup light corn syrup
1 teaspoon vanilla extract

In a saucepan, melt the butter and chocolate. Add the sugar, cream, corn syrup and vanilla. Bring to a boil, stirring constantly. Boil for 1-1/2 minutes. Remove from the heat. Serve sauce warm or cold over ice cream or pound cake. Refrigerate leftovers. **Yield:** about 3-1/3 cups.

Raspberry Delight

(Pictured above)

I knew this cool, fruity and creamy dessert was a winner the first time I tasted it. I confirmed that fact when I entered the recipe in a contest at work—it won first place! —Mary Olson, Albany, Oregon

2-1/4 cups all-purpose flour
   2 tablespoons sugar
  3/4 cup butter *or* margarine, softened
FILLING:
   1 package (8 ounces) cream cheese,
     softened
   1 cup confectioners' sugar
   1 teaspoon vanilla extract
 1/4 teaspoon salt
   2 cups whipped topping
TOPPING:
   1 package (6 ounces) raspberry gelatin
   2 cups boiling water
   2 packages (10 ounces *each*) sweetened
     frozen raspberries
Additional whipped topping and fresh mint,
  optional

In a bowl, combine flour and sugar; blend in butter with a wooden spoon until smooth. Press into an ungreased 13-in. x 9-in. x 2-in. baking pan. Bake at 300° for 20-25 minutes or until set (crust will not brown). Cool.

In a mixing bowl, beat cream cheese, confectioners' sugar, vanilla and salt until smooth. Fold in whipped topping. Spread over crust. For topping, dissolve gelatin in boiling water; stir in raspberries. Chill for 20 minutes or until mixture begins to thicken. Spoon over filling. Refrigerate until set. Cut into squares; garnish with whipped topping and mint if desired. **Yield:** 12-16 servings.

Heart's Delight Eclair

(Pictured below)

This lovely and luscious treat is rumored to have been the favorite dessert of European royalty long ago. I know it's won the hearts of everyone I've made it for. —Lorene Milligan, Chemainus, British Columbia

   1 package (17-1/4 ounces) frozen puff
     pastry, thawed
   3 cups cold milk
   1 package (5.1 ounces) instant vanilla
     pudding mix
   2 cups whipping cream
   1 teaspoon vanilla extract, *divided*
   1 cup confectioners' sugar
   1 tablespoon water
 1/4 teaspoon almond extract
 1/2 cup semisweet chocolate chips
   1 teaspoon shortening

On a lightly floured surface, roll each puff pastry sheet into a 12-in. square. Using an 11-in. heart pattern, cut each pastry into a heart shape. Place on greased baking sheets. Bake at 400° for 12-15 minutes or until golden brown. Remove to wire racks to cool. In a bowl, combine milk and pudding mix until thickened.

In a mixing bowl, beat cream and 1/2 teaspoon of vanilla until stiff peaks form. Carefully fold into pudding. Split hearts in half. Place one layer on a serving plate. top with a third of the pudding mixture. Repeat twice. Top with remaining pastry.

In a bowl, combine confectioners' sugar, water, almond extract and the remaining vanilla until smooth. Spread over top pastry. Melt chocolate chips and shortening; pipe in diagonal lines in one direction over frosting. Beginning 1 in. from side of heart, use a sharp knife to draw right angles across the piped lines. Refrigerate until set. **Yield:** 10-12 servings.

Chocolate Bavarian Torte

(Pictured above)

Whenever I take this torte to a potluck, I get many requests for the recipe. People especially enjoy the light, creamy filling. The recipe calls for a convenient cake mix, so it's easy to make. —Edith Holmstrom *Madison, Wisconsin*

1 package (18-1/4 ounces) devil's food cake mix without pudding
1 package (8 ounces) cream cheese, softened
2/3 cup packed brown sugar
1 teaspoon vanilla extract
1/8 teaspoon salt
2 cups whipping cream, whipped
2 tablespoons grated semisweet chocolate

Mix and bake cake according to package directions, using two 9-in. round pans. Cool for 15 minutes; remove from pans and cool completely on wire racks. In a mixing bowl, beat cream cheese, brown sugar, vanilla and salt until fluffy. Fold in cream. Split each cake into two horizontal layers; place one on a serving plate. Spread with a fourth of the cream mixture. Sprinkle with a fourth of the chocolate. Repeat layers. Cover and refrigerate for 8 hours or overnight. **Yield:** 12 servings.

Chocolate Eclairs

(Pictured at right and on page 164)

With creamy filling and fudgy frosting, these eclairs are extra special. People are thrilled when these finger-licking-good treats appear on the dessert table.
—Jessica Campbell, Viola, Wisconsin

1 cup water
1/2 cup butter *or* margarine
1 cup all-purpose flour

1/4 teaspoon salt
4 eggs
FILLING:
1 package (5.1 ounces) instant vanilla pudding mix
2-1/2 cups cold milk
1 cup whipping cream
1/4 cup confectioners' sugar
1 teaspoon vanilla extract
FROSTING:
2 squares (1 ounce *each*) semisweet chocolate
2 tablespoons butter *or* margarine
1-1/4 cups confectioners' sugar
2 to 3 tablespoons hot water

In a saucepan, bring water and butter to a boil, stirring constantly until butter melts. Reduce heat to low; add the flour and salt. Stir vigorously with a wooden spoon until mixture leaves sides of pan and forms a smooth ball. Remove from the heat; add eggs, one at a time, beating well after each addition until batter becomes smooth.

Using a tablespoon or a pastry tube with a No. 10 or larger tip, form dough into 4-in. x 1-1/2-in. strips on a greased baking sheet. Bake at 400° for 35-40 minutes or until puffed and golden. Immediately cut a slit in each to allow steam to escape. Cool on a wire rack.

In a mixing bowl, beat pudding mix and milk according to package directions. In another mixing bowl, whip the cream until soft peaks form. Beat in sugar and vanilla; fold into pudding. Split eclairs; remove soft dough from inside. Fill eclairs (refrigerate any remaining filling for another use).

For frosting, melt the chocolate and butter in a saucepan over low heat. Stir in sugar and enough hot water to achieve a smooth consistency. Cool slightly. Frost eclairs. Store in the refrigerator. **Yield:** 9 servings.

White Chocolate Mousse

(Pictured below)

Since almost any fresh fruit may be used, this elegant dessert can grace special meals throughout the year.
—Susan Herbert, Aurora, Illinois

- 1 **cup whipping cream**
- 2 **tablespoons sugar**
- 1 **package (3 ounces) cream cheese, softened**
- 3 **squares (1 ounce *each*) white baking chocolate, melted**
- 2 **cups blueberries, raspberries *or* strawberries**

Additional berries, optional

In a mixing bowl, beat cream until soft peaks form. Gradually add the sugar, beating until stiff peaks form; set aside. In another mixing bowl, beat cream cheese until fluffy. Add chocolate and beat until smooth. Fold in whipped cream. Alternate layers of mousse and berries in parfait glasses, ending with mousse. Garnish with additional berries if desired. Serve immediately or refrigerate for up to 3 hours. **Yield:** 4-6 servings.

Lemon Trifle

(Pictured above and on back cover)

The lemony filling and fresh berries in this tempting trifle make it as tasty as it is beautiful. I like to serve it in a clear glass dish. *—Pat Stevens, Granbury, Texas*

- 1 **can (14 ounces) sweetened condensed milk**
- 1 **carton (8 ounces) lemon yogurt**
- 1/3 **cup lemon juice**
- 2 **teaspoons grated lemon peel**
- 2 **cups whipped topping**
- 1 **angel food cake (10 inches), cut into 1-inch cubes**
- 2 **cups fresh raspberries**
- 1/2 **cup flaked coconut, toasted**

Fresh mint, optional

In a bowl, combine the first four ingredients. Fold in whipped topping. Place half of the cake cubes in a trifle bowl or 2-qt. serving bowl. Top with half of the lemon mixture. Repeat layers. Top with raspberries. Garnish with coconut and mint if desired. **Yield:** 14 servings.

🍃 🍃 🍃

Rich Chocolate Pudding

Creamy, smooth and fudgy, this dessert is a true chocolate indulgence. With just four ingredients, it might be the easiest from-scratch pudding you'll ever make.
—Verna Hainer, Aurora, Colorado

- 2 **cups semisweet chocolate chips**
- 1/3 **cup confectioners' sugar**

1 cup milk
1/4 cup butter *or* margarine
**Whipped topping and miniature semisweet
chocolate chips, optional**

Place chocolate chips and confectioners' sugar in a blender; cover and process until chips are coarsely chopped. In a saucepan over medium heat, bring milk and butter to a boil. Add to blender; cover and process until the chips are melted and mixture is smooth. Pour into six individual serving dishes. Refrigerate. Garnish with whipped topping and miniature chips if desired. **Yield:** 6 servings.

Custard Bread Pudding

This is an economical dessert that has real down-home appeal. I sometimes drizzle it with confectioners' sugar icing for added sweetness. —Barbara Little
Bedford, Indiana

2 eggs
2 cups milk
1 cup sugar
1 tablespoon butter *or* margarine, melted
1 teaspoon ground cinnamon
10 slices day-old bread (crusts removed), cut into 1/2-inch cubes
1 cup raisins
SAUCE:
2/3 cup sugar
2 tablespoons all-purpose flour
1 cup water
7 tablespoons butter *or* margarine
1 teaspoon vanilla extract

In a large bowl, combine the eggs, milk, sugar, butter and cinnamon. Add the bread cubes and raisins; mix well. Pour into a greased 11-in. x 7-in. x 2-in. baking dish. Bake at 350° for 50-60 minutes or until a knife inserted near the center comes out clean.

Meanwhile, in a saucepan, combine the sugar, flour and water until smooth. Add the butter. Bring to a boil over medium heat; cook and stir for 2 minutes. Remove from the heat; stir in vanilla. Serve warm sauce over the warm pudding. Refrigerate leftovers. **Yield:** 8 servings.

Classic Combination

The next time you make cook-and-serve chocolate pudding, stir in some creamy peanut butter after removing the pudding from the heat.

Fruit Pizza

(Pictured below)

This pretty dessert is a hit every time I serve it for dinner guests. —Janet O'Neal, Poplar Bluff, Missouri

1 package (20 ounces) refrigerated sugar cookie dough
1/4 cup sugar
1/4 cup orange juice
2 tablespoons water
1 tablespoon lemon juice
1-1/2 teaspoons cornstarch
Pinch salt
1 package (8 ounces) cream cheese, softened
1/4 cup confectioners' sugar
1 carton (8 ounces) frozen whipped topping, thawed
2 to 3 kiwifruit, peeled and thinly sliced
1 to 2 firm bananas, sliced
1 can (11 ounces) mandarin oranges, drained
1/2 cup seedless red grape halves

Pat cookie dough onto an ungreased 14-in. pizza pan. Bake at 375° for 10-12 minutes or until browned; cool. For glaze, combine the sugar, orange juice, water, lemon juice, cornstarch and salt in a saucepan. Bring to a boil; cook and stir for 2 minutes or until thickened. Cool.

In a mixing bowl, beat the cream cheese and confectioners' sugar until smooth. Fold in whipped topping. Spread over cooled crust. Arrange fruit on top. Brush with glaze. Chill until serving. **Yield:** 16-20 servings.

Chocolate Caramel Candy

(Pictured below)

This prize-winning treat tastes like a Snickers bar but has homemade flavor beyond compare. —Jane Meek
Pahrump, Nevada

   1 cup milk chocolate chips
1/4 cup butterscotch chips
1/4 cup creamy peanut butter
FILLING:
1/4 cup butter *or* margarine
   1 cup sugar
1/4 cup evaporated milk
1-1/2 cups marshmallow creme
1/4 cup creamy peanut butter
   1 teaspoon vanilla extract
1-1/2 cups chopped salted peanuts
CARAMEL LAYER:
   1 package (14 ounces) caramels
1/4 cup whipping cream
ICING:
   1 cup milk chocolate chips
1/4 cup butterscotch chips
1/4 cup creamy peanut butter

Line a 13-in. x 9-in. x 2-in. pan with foil; butter the foil and set aside. Combine the first three ingredients in a small saucepan; stir over low heat until melted and smooth. Spread into prepared pan. Chill until set.

For filling, melt the butter in a heavy saucepan over medium heat. Add sugar and milk; bring to a gentle boil. Reduce heat to medium-low; boil and stir for 5 minutes. Remove from the heat; stir in marshmallow creme, peanut butter and vanilla. Add peanuts. Spread over first layer. Chill until set. Combine caramels and cream in a saucepan;

stir over low heat until melted and smooth. Cook and stir 4 minutes longer. Spread over filling. Chill until set.

In a saucepan, combine icing ingredients; stir over low heat until melted and smooth. Pour over the caramel layer. Chill for at least 4 hours. Remove from the refrigerator 20 minutes before cutting. Using the foil, lift candy out of pan; cut into 1-in. squares. **Yield:** about 8 dozen.

Candy Bar Fudge

(Pictured above)

I created this recipe to duplicate a delightful rich fudge I tried in a shop while visiting our daughter.
—*Mary Lou Bridge, Taylor Ridge, Illinois*

6 Snickers candy bars (2.07 ounces *each*)
3 cups sugar
3/4 cup butter (no substitutes)
2/3 cup evaporated milk
2 cups (12 ounces) semisweet chocolate chips
1 jar (7 ounces) marshmallow creme
1 teaspoon vanilla extract

Line a 9-in. square pan with foil. Butter the foil and set pan aside. Cut candy bars into 1/2-in. slices; set aside. In a heavy saucepan, bring sugar, butter and milk to a boil over medium heat. Cook and stir until a candy thermometer reads 234° (soft-ball stage), about 3 minutes. Remove from the heat.

Stir in chocolate chips, marshmallow creme and vanilla until smooth. Pour half into prepared pan. Sprinkle with candy bar slices. Top with remaining chocolate mixture and spread evenly. Let stand at room temperature to cool. Lift out of pan and remove foil. Cut into squares. **Yield:** 4 pounds (about 7 dozen).

Three-Chip English Toffee

(Pictured below)

With its melt-in-your-mouth texture and scrumptiously rich flavor, this is the ultimate toffee! Drizzled on top are three kinds of melted chips, plus a sprinkling of walnuts. —Lana Petfield, Richmond, Virginia

> 1/2 teaspoon plus 2 cups butter (no substitutes), *divided*
> 2 cups sugar
> 1 cup slivered almonds
> 1 cup milk chocolate chips
> 1 cup chopped walnuts
> 1/2 cup semisweet chocolate chips
> 1/2 cup vanilla *or* white chips
> 1-1/2 teaspoons shortening

Butter a 15-in. x 10-in. x 1-in. baking pan with 1/2 teaspoon butter; set aside. In a heavy saucepan over medium-low heat, bring sugar and remaining butter to a boil, stirring constantly. Cover and cook for 2-3 minutes.

Uncover; add almonds. Cook and stir with a clean spoon until a candy thermometer reads 300° (hard-crack stage) and mixture is golden brown. Pour into prepared pan (do not scrape sides of saucepan). Surface will be buttery. Cool for 1-2 minutes. Sprinkle with milk chocolate chips. Let stand for 1-2 minutes; spread chocolate over the top. Sprinkle with walnuts; press down gently with the back of a spoon. Chill for 10 minutes.

In a microwave or heavy saucepan, melt semisweet chips; stir until smooth. Drizzle over walnuts. Refrigerate for 10 minutes. Melt vanilla chips and shortening; stir until smooth. Drizzle over walnuts. Cover and refrigerate for 1-2 hours. Break into pieces. **Yield:** about 2-1/2 pounds.

Editor's Note: We recommend that you test your candy thermometer before each use by bringing water to a boil; the thermometer should read 212°. Adjust your recipe temperature up or down based on your test. If toffee separates during cooking, add 1/2 cup hot water and stir vigorously. Bring back up to 300° and proceed as recipe directs.

Maine Potato Candy

(Pictured above)

Years ago, folks in Maine ate potatoes daily and used leftovers in bread, doughnuts and candy. —Barbara Allen, Chelmsford, Massachusetts

> 4 cups confectioners' sugar
> 4 cups flaked coconut
> 3/4 cup cold mashed potatoes (prepared without milk or butter)
> 1-1/2 teaspoons vanilla extract
> 1/2 teaspoon salt
> 1 pound dark chocolate candy coating

In a large bowl, combine sugar, coconut, potatoes, vanilla and salt; mix well. Line a 9-in. square pan with foil; butter foil. Spread coconut mixture into pan. Cover and refrigerate overnight. Cut into 2-in. x 1-in. rectangles. Cover and freeze.

In a microwave or double boiler, melt candy coating. Dip bars in coating; place on waxed paper to harden. Store in an airtight container. **Yield:** 2 pounds.

Decorating Candies

To easily drizzle melted chocolate over candies, pour the melted chocolate into a heavy-duty resealable plastic bag. Cut off a very small corner of the bag; drizzle chocolate in an "S" shape or circular pattern.

Chocolate Peanut Sweeties

(Pictured below and on page 164)

*Inspired by my passion for peanut butter and choco-
late, I combined a trusted recipe for peanut butter eggs
with the salty crunch of pretzels. Now our kids have fun
helping me make and eat these sweet treats.*
—Gina Kintigh, Connellsville, Pennsylvania

     1 **cup peanut butter***
   1/2 **cup butter (no substitutes), softened**
     3 **cups confectioners' sugar**
     5 **dozen miniature pretzel twists (about 3
         cups)**
 1-1/2 **cups milk chocolate chips**
     1 **tablespoon vegetable oil**

In a mixing bowl, beat peanut butter and butter until smooth. Beat in confectioners' sugar until combined. Shape into 1-in. balls; press one on each
pretzel. Place on waxed paper-lined baking sheets.
Refrigerate until peanut butter mixture is firm,
about 1 hour.

In a microwave-safe bowl or heavy saucepan,
melt the chocolate chips and oil. Dip each peanut
butter ball into chocolate. Return to baking sheet,
pretzel side down. Refrigerate for at least 30 minutes before serving. Store in the refrigerator. **Yield:**
5 dozen.

*Editor's Note: Reduced-fat or generic brands
of peanut butter are not recommended for use in
this recipe.

Orange Chocolate Meltaways

(Pictured above)

*The terrific combination of chocolate and orange
makes these some of the best truffles I've ever had.
As holiday gifts, they're showstoppers. I have little
time to cook, but when I do, I like to "get fancy". In this
case, "fancy" doesn't have to be difficult.*
—Lori Kostecki, Wausau, Wisconsin

     1 **package (11-1/2 ounces) milk chocolate
         chips**
     1 **cup semisweet chocolate chips**
   3/4 **cup whipping cream**
     1 **teaspoon grated orange peel**
 2-1/2 **teaspoons orange extract**
 1-1/2 **cups finely chopped toasted pecans**
COATING:
     1 **cup milk chocolate chips**
     2 **tablespoons shortening**

Place chocolate chips in a mixing bowl; set aside.
In a saucepan, bring cream and orange peel to a
gentle boil; immediately pour over chips. Let stand
for 1 minute; whisk until smooth. Add the extract.
Cover and chill for 35 minutes or until mixture
begins to thicken. Beat for 10-15 seconds or just
until mixture lightens in color (do not overbeat).
Spoon rounded teaspoonfuls onto waxed paper-
lined baking sheets. Cover and chill for 5 minutes.

Gently shape into balls; roll half in pecans. In a
microwave or double boiler, melt chocolate and
shortening; stir until smooth. Dip remaining balls
in chocolate. Place on waxed paper to harden.
Store in the refrigerator. **Yield:** 6 dozen.

In a saucepan, combine sugar, corn syrup and water; bring to a boil, stirring constantly, until sugar is dissolved. Cook, without stirring, over medium heat until a candy thermometer reads 300° (hard-crack stage). Remove from the heat; stir in butter, vanilla and baking soda. Add cashews. Pour into a greased 15-in. x 10-in. x 1-in. baking pan. Cool before breaking into pieces. **Yield:** about 2 pounds.

Editor's Note: Test your candy thermometer before each use by bringing water to a boil; the thermometer should read 212°. Adjust your recipe temperature up or down based on your test.

——— 🥄 🥄 🥄 ———

Old-Fashioned Whoopie Pies

These irresistible treats feature a fluffy white filling sandwiched between chocolate cake-like cookies.
—Maria Costello, Monroe, North Carolina

      1/2 cup baking cocoa
      1/2 cup hot water
      1/2 cup shortening
  1-1/2 cups sugar
        2 eggs
        1 teaspoon vanilla extract
  2-2/3 cups all-purpose flour
        1 teaspoon baking powder
        1 teaspoon baking soda
      1/4 teaspoon salt
      1/2 cup buttermilk
FILLING:
        3 tablespoons all-purpose flour
Dash salt
        1 cup milk
      3/4 cup shortening
  1-1/2 cups confectioners' sugar
        2 teaspoons vanilla extract

In a small bowl, combine cocoa and water; mix well. Cool for 5 minutes. In a mixing bowl, cream shortening and sugar. Add cocoa mixture, eggs and vanilla; mix well. Combine dry ingredients. Add to creamed mixture alternately with buttermilk; mix well. Drop by rounded tablespoonfuls 2 in. apart onto greased baking sheets. Flatten slightly with a spoon. Bake at 350° for 10-12 minutes or until firm to the touch. Remove to wire racks to cool.

In a saucepan, combine flour and salt. Gradually whisk in milk until smooth; cook and stir over medium-high heat until thick, about 5-7 minutes. Remove from the heat. Cover and refrigerate until completely cool. In a mixing bowl, cream shortening, sugar and vanilla. Add chilled milk mixture; beat for 7 minutes or until fluffy. Spread filling on half of the cookies; top with remaining cookies. Store in the refrigerator. **Yield:** 2 dozen.

Mocha Fondue

(Pictured above)

People have such fun dipping pieces of cake and fruit into this heavenly melted chocolate mixture. It's great at special gatherings. —*Gloria Jarrett*
Loveland, Ohio

        3 cups milk chocolate chips
      1/2 cup whipping cream
        1 tablespoon instant coffee granules
        2 tablespoons hot water
        1 teaspoon vanilla extract
      1/8 teaspoon ground cinnamon
        1 prepared pound cake (16 ounces), cut
          into 1-inch cubes
Strawberries, kiwi *and/or* other fresh fruit

In a heavy saucepan, melt chocolate chips with cream over low heat, stirring constantly. Dissolve coffee in water; add to chocolate mixture with vanilla and cinnamon. Mix well. Serve warm, using cake pieces and fruit for dipping. **Yield:** 2 cups.

——— 🥄 🥄 🥄 ———

Cashew Crickle

Instead of traditional brickle that calls for peanuts, this recipe uses cashews. Everyone agrees this holiday candy is excellent. —*Kathy Kittell, Lenexa, Kansas*

        2 cups sugar
        1 cup corn syrup
      1/2 cup water
        3 tablespoons butter (no substitutes)
        1 teaspoon vanilla extract
      1/2 teaspoon baking soda
        2 cups salted cashews

Mocha Ice Cream

(Pictured above)

I've enjoyed this recipe for chocolate ice cream for over 40 years. Coffee really enhances the flavor.
—Dick McCarty, Lake Havasu City, Arizona

2-1/4 cups sugar
  3/4 cup baking cocoa
  1/3 cup all-purpose flour
    1 tablespoon instant coffee granules
Dash salt
    3 cups milk
    4 eggs, beaten
    4 cups half-and-half cream
    2 cups whipping cream
    3 tablespoons vanilla extract

In a large heavy saucepan, combine the sugar, cocoa, flour, coffee and salt. Gradually add milk and eggs; stir until smooth. Cook and stir over medium-low heat until mixture is thick enough to coat a metal spoon and reaches 160°, about 15 minutes.

Refrigerate until chilled. Stir in the remaining ingredients. Fill ice cream freezer cylinder two-thirds full; freeze according to manufacturer's instructions. Refrigerate remaining mixture until ready to freeze. Remove from the freezer 10 minutes before serving. **Yield:** about 2-1/2 quarts.

Banana Split Supreme

(Pictured at right and on back cover)

This lovely and delightful dessert has the classic flavor of a banana split. It's a cool, creamy treat with no last-minute fuss since you just pull it from the freezer. It always solicits praise from our big family.
—Marye Franzen, Gothenburg, Nebraska

  3/4 cup butter *or* margarine, *divided*
    2 cups confectioners' sugar
    1 cup evaporated milk
  3/4 cup semisweet chocolate chips
  24 cream-filled chocolate sandwich cookies, crushed
    3 to 4 medium firm bananas, cut into 1/2-inch slices
    2 quarts vanilla ice cream, softened, *divided*
    1 can (20 ounces) crushed pineapple, drained
    1 jar (10 ounces) maraschino cherries, drained and halved
  3/4 cup chopped pecans
Whipped topping, optional

In a saucepan, combine 1/2 cup of butter, sugar, milk and chocolate chips. Bring to a boil over medium heat; boil and stir for 8 minutes. Remove from the heat and cool completely. Meanwhile, melt the remaining butter; toss with cookie crumbs. Press into a greased 13-in. x 9-in. x 2-in. pan. Freeze for 15 minutes.

Arrange banana slices over crust; spread with 1 quart of ice cream. Top with 1 cup of chocolate sauce. Freeze for 1 hour. Refrigerate remaining chocolate sauce. Spread the remaining ice cream over dessert; top with pineapple, cherries and pecans. Cover and freeze for several hours or overnight. Remove from the freezer 10 minutes before serving. Reheat the chocolate sauce. Cut dessert into squares; serve with chocolate sauce and whipped topping if desired. **Yield:** 12-15 servings.

1/4 teaspoon peppermint extract
4 drops green food coloring, optional
1/2 cup miniature semisweet chocolate chips

In a saucepan, combine eggs, milk, sugar and salt. Cook and stir over medium heat until mixture reaches 160° and coats a metal spoon. Cool to room temperature. Stir in cream, vanilla, peppermint extract and food coloring if desired. Refrigerate for 2 hours.

Stir in chocolate chips. Fill ice cream freezer cylinder two-thirds full; freeze according to the manufacturer's directions. Refrigerate remaining mixture until ready to freeze. **Yield:** 1-1/2 quarts.

Refreshing Lime Sherbet

(Pictured above)

One spoonful of this fresh-tasting and delicious treat and you'll never eat store-bought lime sherbet again!
—Lorraine Searing, Colorado Springs, Colorado

4-1/4 cups sugar
1-1/2 cups lime juice
3 tablespoons lemon juice
2 tablespoons grated lime peel
7-1/2 cups milk
1/2 cup buttermilk
1 drop green food coloring, optional

In a bowl, combine sugar, lime juice, lemon juice and lime peel until well blended. Gradually stir in milk, buttermilk and food coloring if desired; mix well. Pour into the cylinder of an ice cream freezer and freeze according to manufacturer's directions. Refrigerate remaining mixture until ready to freeze. Remove from the freezer 10 minutes before serving. **Yield:** about 2-1/2 quarts.

Mint Chip Ice Cream

(Pictured on page 164)

We have a milk cow, so homemade ice cream has become a regular treat for our family. This version is very creamy with a mild mint flavor that goes well with the mini chocolate chips. It was an instant hit.
—Farrah McGuire, Springdale, Washington

3 eggs, lightly beaten
1-3/4 cups milk
3/4 cup sugar
Pinch salt
1-3/4 cups whipping cream
1 teaspoon vanilla extract

Cranberry Orange Sundaes

(Pictured below)

I always keep a supply of cranberries in the freezer to cook up this refreshing sauce year-round.
—Rita Goshaw, South Milwaukee, Wisconsin

1 cup sugar
2/3 cup water
2 cups fresh *or* frozen cranberries
2/3 cup orange juice
1/2 teaspoon grated orange peel
1/2 teaspoon vanilla extract
Vanilla ice cream
Additional orange peel, optional

In a saucepan over medium heat, bring sugar and water to a boil; cook for 5 minutes. Add cranberries, orange juice and peel. Return to a boil. Reduce heat; simmer for 8-10 minutes or until berries pop. Remove from the heat; stir in vanilla. Serve warm or chilled over ice cream. Garnish with orange peel if desired. Sauce can also be served over angel food or pound cake. **Yield:** 2 cups sauce.

Potluck Pleasers

***In this chapter, experienced cooks share a host of large-quantity recipes
that you can rely on when planning menus for a crowd.***

— 🍮 🍮 🍮 —

SUPER FOR GROUPS. Clockwise from upper left:
Sandwich for a Crowd (p. 193), Summer Squash
Salad (p. 188), Crunchy Peanut Butter Bars (p.
201), No-Fuss Lasagna (p. 196) and Cranberry
Oatmeal Cookies (p. 201).

Feather-Light Doughnuts
(Pictured below)

When I was growing up, our farm family always had an abundance of mashed potatoes at the supper table. We loved to use leftovers in these fluffy doughnuts.
—*Darlene Alexander, Nekoosa, Wisconsin*

      2 packages (1/4 ounce *each*) active dry yeast
1-1/2 cups warm milk (110° to 115°)
      1 cup cold mashed potatoes
1-1/2 cups sugar, *divided*
   1/2 cup vegetable oil
      2 teaspoons salt
      2 teaspoons vanilla extract
   1/2 teaspoon baking soda
   1/2 teaspoon baking powder
      2 eggs
5-1/2 to 6 cups all-purpose flour
   1/2 teaspoon ground cinnamon
Oil for deep-fat frying

In a large mixing bowl, dissolve yeast in warm milk. Add potatoes, 1/2 cup sugar, oil, salt, vanilla, baking soda, baking powder and eggs; mix well. Add enough of the flour to form a soft dough. Place in a greased bowl, turning once to grease top. Cover and let rise in a warm place until doubled, about 1 hour.

Punch dough down; roll out on a floured surface to 1/2-in. thickness. Cut with a 3-in. doughnut cutter. Place on greased baking sheets; cover and let rise until almost doubled, about 45 minutes.

Combine cinnamon and remaining sugar; set aside. Heat oil in an electric skillet or deep-fat fryer to 350°; fry doughnuts until golden on both sides. Drain on paper towels; roll in cinnamon-sugar while still warm. **Yield:** about 2-1/2 dozen.

Sausage Egg Bake
(Pictured above)

This hearty egg dish is wonderful for any meal of the day. I fix it frequently for special occasions, too, because it's easy to prepare and really versatile. For a change, use spicier sausage or substitute a flavored cheese blend.   —*Molly Swallow, Blackfoot, Idaho*

   1 pound bulk Italian sausage
   2 cans (10-3/4 ounces *each*) condensed
      cream of potato soup, undiluted
   9 eggs
3/4 cup milk
1/4 teaspoon pepper
   1 cup (4 ounces) shredded cheddar cheese

In a skillet, cook sausage over medium heat until no longer pink; drain. Stir in soup. In a mixing bowl, beat eggs, milk and pepper; stir in sausage mixture. Transfer to a lightly greased 11-in. x 7-in. x 2-in. baking dish. Sprinkle with cheese. Bake, uncovered, at 375° for 40-45 minutes or until a knife inserted near the center comes out clean. **Yield:** 12 servings.

Holiday Hash Brown Bake

With the chopped red and green peppers, this dish is perfect for Christmastime. And you don't have to worry about leftovers—there never seem to be any!
—*Russell Moffett, Irvine, California*

   2 packages (2 pounds *each*) frozen cubed
      hash brown potatoes, thawed
   5 cups (20 ounces) shredded cheddar
      cheese
   2 cans (10-3/4 ounces *each*) condensed
      cream of chicken soup, undiluted
   4 cups (32 ounces) sour cream
   2 small green peppers, chopped

2 small sweet red peppers, chopped
1 medium onion, chopped

In a large bowl, combine all ingredients; mix well. Transfer to two greased 13-in. x 9-in. x 2-in. baking dishes. Cover and bake at 350° for 40 minutes. Uncover; bake 25-30 minutes longer or until heated through. **Yield:** 24 servings.

Editor's Note: Recipe can be prepared ahead and refrigerated. Remove from the refrigerator 30 minutes before baking.

Potluck Eggs Benedict

(Pictured below)

Asparagus spears give this saucy breakfast dish big springtime flavor. It's super served over warm fluffy biscuits.   —Pauline vanBreemen, Franklin, Indiana

1 pound fresh asparagus, trimmed
3/4 cup butter *or* margarine
3/4 cup all-purpose flour
4 cups milk
1 can (14-1/2 ounces) chicken broth
1 pound cubed fully cooked ham
1 cup (4 ounces) shredded cheddar cheese
8 hard-cooked eggs, quartered
1/2 teaspoon salt
1/8 teaspoon cayenne pepper
10 to 12 biscuits, warmed

Cut asparagus into 1/2-in. pieces. Cook in a small amount of boiling water until tender, about 5 minutes; drain. Cool. Melt butter in a saucepan; stir in flour until smooth. Add milk and broth; bring to a boil. Cook and stir for 2 minutes. Add ham and cheese; stir until the cheese is melted. Add eggs, salt, cayenne and asparagus; heat though. Serve over biscuits. **Yield:** 10-12 servings.

Cherry Punch

(Pictured above)

In 1952, a co-worker gave me the recipe for this versatile punch. It's not too sweet, so it really refreshes.
—Davlyn Jones, San Jose, California

1 can (6 ounces) frozen lemonade
   concentrate, thawed
1 can (6 ounces) frozen limeade
   concentrate, thawed
1 can (20 ounces) pineapple chunks,
   undrained
2 cups water
2 liters cherry soda, chilled
2 liters ginger ale, chilled
Lemon and lime slices, optional

In a blender, combine concentrates and pineapple; cover and blend until smooth. Pour into a gallon-size container; stir in water. Store in the refrigerator. To serve, pour the mixture into a punch bowl; add cherry soda and ginger ale. Garnish with lemon and lime slices if desired. **Yield:** about 6 quarts.

Proven Potluck Tip

Here's a handy way to serve deviled eggs. Put them in paper cupcake liners and set them in muffin tins. The eggs stay upright and neat and won't slide around on people's plates.

Creamy Fruit Salad

(Pictured above)

With crowd-pleasing fruits plus crunchy pecans, this wonderful salad doesn't last long on potluck buffets. I never bring home leftovers—just an empty bowl.
—*Bernice Morris, Marshfield, Missouri*

✓ Uses less fat, sugar or salt. Includes Nutritional Analysis and Diabetic Exchanges.

- 1/3 cup orange juice
- 1/3 cup unsweetened pineapple juice
- 1/4 cup sugar
- 1 egg, beaten
- 1 tablespoon plus 1/4 cup lemon juice, *divided*
- 1 cup whipping cream, whipped *or* 2 cups whipped topping
- 6 medium red apples, diced
- 6 medium firm bananas, sliced
- 3 cups halved green grapes
- 1/4 cup chopped pecans

In a heavy saucepan, combine orange and pineapple juices, sugar, egg and 1 tablespoon of lemon juice. Bring to a boil over medium-high heat, stirring constantly. Remove from the heat. When cool, fold in the whipped cream.

In a large serving bowl, toss the apples with remaining lemon juice. Add bananas and grapes. Add the dressing; stir to coat. Refrigerate. Fold in pecans just before serving. **Yield:** 20 servings.

Nutritional Analysis: One serving (prepared with egg substitute equivalent to 1 egg and reduced-fat whipped topping) equals 111 calories, 7 mg sodium, trace cholesterol, 23 g carbohydrate, 1 g protein, 2 g fat, 2 g fiber. **Diabetic Exchanges:** 1-1/2 fruit, 1/2 fat.

Peach-Cranberry Gelatin Salad

Harvest colors and flavors give this refreshing salad a delightful twist that's just right for Thanksgiving or any special meal. For Christmas, I use lime gelatin instead of peach for a green and red salad.
—*Patty Kile, Greentown, Pennsylvania*

- 1 package (6 ounces) peach gelatin
- 4 cups boiling water, *divided*
- 1 cup orange juice
- 2 cans (15 ounces *each*) sliced peaches, drained
- 1 package (6 ounces) cranberry *or* raspberry gelatin
- 1 cup cranberry juice
- 2 large oranges, peeled
- 2 cups fresh *or* frozen cranberries
- 1 cup sugar

In a bowl, dissolve peach gelatin in 2 cups boiling water. Add orange juice; mix well. Chill until partially set. Fold in peaches. Pour into a 3-qt. serving bowl. Chill until firm.

In a bowl, dissolve the cranberry gelatin in remaining boiling water. Add cranberry juice and mix well. In a blender or food processor, combine oranges, cranberries and sugar; process until fruit is coarsely chopped. Add to cranberry gelatin. Carefully spoon over peach gelatin. Chill until set. **Yield:** 14-18 servings.

Lime Gelatin Salad

I've made this refreshing recipe hundreds of times over the past 20 years! It can be a salad or dessert.
—*Louise Harding, Newburgh, New York*

- 1 package (6 ounces) lime gelatin
- 1 cup boiling water
- 1 package (8 ounces) cream cheese, softened
- 1/2 teaspoon vanilla extract
- 1 can (15 ounces) mandarin oranges, drained
- 1 can (8 ounces) crushed pineapple, drained
- 1 cup lemon-lime soda
- 1/2 cup chopped pecans
- 1 carton (8 ounces) frozen whipped topping, thawed, *divided*

Dissolve gelatin in water. In a mixing bowl, beat cream cheese until fluffy. Add gelatin mixture; beat until smooth. Stir in vanilla, fruit, soda and pecans. Chill until mixture mounds slightly when dropped from a spoon. Fold in three-fourths of whipped topping. Pour into a 13-in. x 9-in. x 2-in. dish. Chill for 4 hours or until firm. Cut into squares; garnish with remaining whipped topping. **Yield:** 16-20 servings.

— 🏆 🏆 🏆 —

Festive Fruit Salad

(Pictured below)

This refreshing beautiful salad has become a favorite of everyone who's tried it. When I take this salad to a party or cookout, it disappears quickly! This recipe is a great way to take advantage of fresh fruit at its best.
—Gail Sellers, Savannah, Georgia

- 1 medium fresh pineapple
- 3 medium apples (1 red, 1 yellow and 1 green), cubed
- 1 small cantaloupe, cubed
- 1 large firm banana, sliced
- 1 pint strawberries, halved
- 1 pint blueberries
- 4 cups seedless red and green grapes
- 3 kiwifruit, peeled and sliced

DRESSING:
- 1 package (3 ounces) cream cheese, softened
- 1/2 cup confectioners' sugar
- 2 teaspoons lemon juice
- 1 carton (8 ounces) frozen whipped topping, thawed

Additional berries for garnish, optional

Peel and core pineapple; cut into cubes. Place in a 3- or 4-qt. glass serving bowl. Add remaining fruit and stir to mix. In a mixing bowl, beat the cream cheese until smooth. Gradually add sugar and lemon juice; mix well. Fold in whipped topping. Spread over fruit. Garnish with additional berries if desired. Store leftovers in the refrigerator. **Yield:** 16-20 servings.

Peachy Tossed Salad

(Pictured above)

I serve this great salad when the lettuce in my garden is fresh.   —April Neis, Lone Butte, British Columbia

✓ Uses less fat, sugar or salt. Includes Nutritional Analysis and Diabetic Exchanges.

- 1/4 cup orange juice
- 2 tablespoons cider vinegar
- 2 tablespoons plain yogurt
- 1 tablespoon grated orange peel
- 2 teaspoons sugar
- 1/2 teaspoon garlic powder
- 1/2 teaspoon salt
- 1/4 teaspoon pepper
- 1/2 to 3/4 cup olive *or* canola oil
- 8 cups torn fresh spinach
- 8 cups torn Bibb *or* Boston lettuce
- 4 medium fresh peaches, peeled and sliced
- 4 bacon strips, cooked and crumbled

In a blender or food processor, combine the first eight ingredients. While processing, gradually add oil in a steady stream. Process until sugar is dissolved. In a salad bowl, combine spinach, lettuce, peaches and bacon. Drizzle with dressing; toss to coat. Serve immediately. **Yield:** 16 servings.

Nutritional Analysis: One 1-cup serving (prepared with 1/2 cup oil) equals 92 calories, 8 g fat (1 g saturated fat), 1 mg cholesterol, 113 mg sodium, 5 g carbohydrate, 1 g fiber, 2 g protein. **Diabetic Exchanges:** 1 vegetable, 1 fat.

Rice Dressing

To make this a meal in itself, I sometimes add finely chopped cooked chicken and a little more broth before baking. —Linda Emery, Tuckerman, Arkansas

      4 cups chicken broth, *divided*
1-1/2 cups uncooked long grain rice
      2 cups chopped onion
      2 cups chopped celery
   1/2 cup butter *or* margarine
      2 cans (4 ounces *each*) mushroom stems
         and pieces, drained
      3 tablespoons minced fresh parsley
1-1/2 to 2 teaspoons poultry seasoning
   3/4 teaspoon salt
   1/2 teaspoon pepper
Fresh sage and thyme, optional

In a saucepan, bring 3-1/2 cups of broth and rice to a boil. Reduce heat; cover and simmer for 20 minutes or until tender. Meanwhile, in a skillet, saute onion and celery in butter until tender. Stir in rice, mushrooms, parsley, poultry seasoning, salt, pepper and the remaining broth. Pour into a greased 13-in. x 9-in. x 2-in. baking dish. Bake, uncovered, at 350° for 30 minutes. Garnish with sage and thyme if desired. **Yield:** 10-12 servings.

— ☕ ☕ ☕ —

Make-Ahead Potatoes

There's no need to slave away making mashed potatoes at the last minute, not when this creamy, comforting potato side dish is so handy to prepare well in advance. —Margaret Twitched, Danbury, Iowa

   10 large potatoes, peeled and quartered
    1 cup (8 ounces) sour cream
    1 package (8 ounces) cream cheese, softened
    6 tablespoons butter *or* margarine, *divided*
    2 tablespoons dried minced onion
  1/2 to 1 teaspoon salt
Paprika

Place potatoes in a Dutch oven or large kettle; cover with water and bring to a boil. Reduce heat; cover and cook for 20-25 minutes or until the potatoes are tender. Drain and place in a bowl; mash. Add sour cream, cream cheese, 4 tablespoons butter, onion and salt; stir until smooth and the cream cheese and butter are melted. Spread in a greased 13-in. x 9-in. x 2-in. baking dish.

Melt remaining butter; drizzle over potatoes. Sprinkle with paprika. Refrigerate or bake, covered, at 350° for 40 minutes; uncover and bake 20 minutes longer. If potatoes are made ahead and refrigerated, let stand at room temperature for 30 minutes before baking. **Yield:** 12 servings.

Garden Bean Salad

(Pictured above)

My mother gave me this crunchy bean salad recipe many years ago, and I often take it to covered-dish dinners. It looks especially attractive served in a glass bowl to show off the colorful vegetables.
—Bernice McFadden, Dayton, Ohio

    2 cans (17 ounces *each*) lima beans
    1 can (16 ounces) cut green beans
    1 can (16 ounces) kidney beans
    1 can (16 ounces) wax beans
    1 can (15 ounces) garbanzo beans
    1 large green pepper, chopped
    3 celery ribs, chopped
    1 jar (2 ounces) sliced pimientos, drained
    1 bunch green onions, sliced
    2 cups vinegar
    2 cups sugar
  1/2 cup water
    1 teaspoon salt

Drain all six cans of beans; place in a large bowl. Add green pepper, celery, pimientos and green onions; set aside. In a heavy saucepan, bring remaining ingredients to a boil; boil for 5 minutes. Remove from the heat and immediately pour over vegetables. Refrigerate for several hours or overnight. **Yield:** 12-16 servings.

— ☕ ☕ ☕ —

Summer Squash Salad

(Pictured on page 182)

This dish is inexpensive to prepare and a great way to put fresh produce to use. —Diane Hixon
Niceville, Florida

    4 cups julienned zucchini
    4 cups julienned yellow squash

2 cups sliced radishes
1 cup vegetable oil
1/3 cup cider vinegar
2 tablespoons Dijon mustard
2 tablespoons snipped fresh parsley
1-1/2 teaspoons salt
1 teaspoon dill weed
1/2 teaspoon pepper

In a bowl, toss the zucchini, squash and radishes. In a jar with a tight-fitting lid, combine all remaining ingredients; shake well. Pour over vegetables. Cover and refrigerate for at least 2 hours. **Yield:** 12-16 servings.

— 🍲 🍲 🍲 —

Mexican Corn Casserole

(Pictured below)

This satisfying side dish resembles an old-fashioned spoon bread with zip. It's a convenient dish to transport to a potluck.
—Laura Kadlec
Maiden Rock, Wisconsin

4 eggs
1 can (15-1/4 ounces) whole kernel corn, drained
1 can (14-3/4 ounces) cream-style corn
1-1/2 cups cornmeal
1-1/4 cups buttermilk
1 cup butter *or* margarine, melted
2 cans (4 ounces *each*) chopped green chilies
2 medium onions, chopped
1 teaspoon baking soda
3 cups (12 ounces) shredded cheddar cheese, *divided*
Jalapeno pepper and sweet red pepper rings, optional

Beat eggs in a large bowl; add the next eight ingredients and mix well. Stir in 2 cups of cheese.

Pour into a greased 13-in. x 9-in. x 2-in. baking dish. Bake, uncovered, at 325° for 1 hour. Top with remaining cheese. Let stand for 15 minutes before serving. Garnish with peppers if desired. **Yield:** 12-15 servings.

Mushroom Green Bean Casserole

(Pictured above)

The fresh mushrooms, sliced water chestnuts and slivered almonds make this casserole special.
—Pat Richter, Lake Placid, Florida

1 pound fresh mushrooms, sliced
1 large onion, chopped
1/2 cup butter *or* margarine
1/4 cup all-purpose flour
1 cup half-and-half cream
1 jar (16 ounces) process cheese sauce
2 teaspoons soy sauce
1/2 teaspoon pepper
1/8 teaspoon hot pepper sauce
1 can (8 ounces) sliced water chestnuts, drained
2 packages (16 ounces *each*) frozen French-style green beans, thawed, drained
Slivered almonds

In a skillet, saute mushrooms and onion in butter. Stir in flour until blended. Gradually stir in cream. Bring to a boil; cook and stir for 2 minutes. Stir in cheese sauce, soy sauce, pepper and hot pepper sauce until cheese is melted. Remove from the heat; stir in water chestnuts.

Place beans in an ungreased 3-qt. baking dish. Pour cheese mixture over top. Sprinkle with almonds. Bake, uncovered, at 375° for 25-30 minutes or until bubbly. **Yield:** 14-16 servings.

Slow-Cooked Beans

(Pictured above)

This flavorful bean dish adds nice variety to any buffet because it's a bit different than traditional baked beans. It's a snap to prepare, since it uses convenient canned beans and prepared barbecue sauce and salsa.
—Joy Beck, Cincinnati, Ohio

    4 cans (15-1/2 ounces *each*) great northern beans, rinsed and drained
    4 cans (15 ounces *each*) black beans, rinsed and drained
    2 cans (15 ounces *each*) butter beans, rinsed and drained
2-1/4 cups barbecue sauce
2-1/4 cups salsa
    3/4 cup packed brown sugar
    1/2 to 1 teaspoon hot pepper sauce

In a 5-qt. slow cooker, gently combine all ingredients. Cover and cook on low for 2 hours or until heated through. **Yield:** 16 servings.

—— 🍳 🍳 🍳 ——

Corn Bread for a Crowd

These sunny squares are a terrific accompaniment for chili or any savory dish with gravy or sauce.
—Samuel Warnock, Union, Ohio

3-1/2 cups cornmeal
2-1/2 cups all-purpose flour
    2 tablespoons baking powder
1-1/2 teaspoons baking soda
1-1/2 teaspoons salt
    4 eggs
    3 cups buttermilk
    1 cup vegetable oil

In a large bowl, combine cornmeal, flour, baking powder, baking soda and salt. Combine eggs, buttermilk and oil; stir into dry ingredients just until moistened. Pour into a greased 13-in. x 9-in. x 2-in. baking pan and a greased 9-in. square baking pan. Bake at 425° for 20-25 minutes or until a toothpick inserted near the center comes out clean. Serve warm. **Yield:** 30-36 servings.

—— 🍳 🍳 🍳 ——

Lemon-Curry Deviled Eggs

(Pictured below)

I enjoy prettying up a potluck or brunch buffet with a platter of these zippy eggs. You might also consider adding this dish to a salad plate or a soup-and-salad lunch.   *—Judith Miller, Walnut, California*

  16 hard-cooked eggs
1/3 to 1/2 cup sour cream
    2 tablespoons lemon juice
 1/2 teaspoon salt
 1/2 teaspoon paprika
 1/2 teaspoon ground mustard
 1/2 teaspoon curry powder
Dash Worcestershire sauce

Cut eggs in half lengthwise. Remove yolks; set whites aside. In a bowl, mash yolks. Add the remaining ingredients; mix well. Spoon into egg whites. Refrigerate until serving. **Yield:** 16 servings.

Rainbow Pasta Salad

(Pictured below)

This refreshing, colorful salad is my mother's recipe. It features an uncommon but tempting mixture of vegetables. Mother always cooks with wonderful flair, and everything she makes is delicious as well as lovely on the table. —Barbara Carlucci, Orange Park, Florida

  1 package (16 ounces) tricolor spiral pasta
  2 cups broccoli florets
  1 cup chopped carrots
1/2 cup chopped tomato
1/2 cup chopped cucumber
1/4 cup chopped onion
  1 can (15-1/4 ounces) whole kernel corn, drained
  1 jar (6-1/2 ounces) marinated artichoke hearts, drained and halved
  1 bottle (8 ounces) Italian salad dressing

Cook the pasta according to package directions; drain and rinse in cold water. Place in a large bowl; add remaining ingredients and toss to coat. Cover and refrigerate for 2 hours or overnight. **Yield:** 12-14 servings.

Broccoli Rice Casserole

(Pictured above)

This hearty casserole is my favorite dish to make for a potluck. With the green of the broccoli and the rich cheese sauce, it's pretty to serve, and it makes a tasty side dish for almost any kind of meat.
          —Margaret Mayes, La Mesa, California

  1 small onion, chopped
1/2 cup chopped celery
  1 package (10 ounces) frozen chopped broccoli, thawed
  1 tablespoon butter *or* margarine
  1 jar (8 ounces) process cheese sauce
  1 can (10-3/4 ounces) condensed cream of mushroom soup, undiluted
  1 can (5 ounces) evaporated milk
  3 cups cooked rice

In a large skillet over medium heat, saute onion, celery and broccoli in butter for 3-5 minutes. Stir in cheese sauce, soup and milk until smooth. Place rice in a greased 8-in. square baking dish. Pour cheese mixture over; do not stir. Bake, uncovered, at 325° for 25-30 minutes or until hot and bubbly. **Yield:** 8-10 servings.

Classic Beef Stew
(Pictured below)

Here's a good old-fashioned stew with rich beef gravy that lets the flavor of the potatoes and carrots come through. This is the perfect hearty dish for a blustery winter day. I make it often when the weather turns cooler. —Alberta McKay, Bartlesville, Oklahoma

    2 pounds beef stew meat, cut into 1-inch
      cubes
    1 to 2 tablespoons vegetable oil
1-1/2 cups chopped onion
    1 can (14-1/2 ounces) diced tomatoes,
      undrained
    1 can (10-1/2 ounces) condensed beef
      broth, undiluted
    3 tablespoons quick-cooking tapioca
    1 garlic clove, minced
    1 tablespoon dried parsley flakes
    1 teaspoon salt
  1/4 teaspoon pepper
    1 bay leaf
    6 medium carrots, cut into 2-inch pieces
    3 medium potatoes, peeled and cut into
      2-inch pieces
    1 cup sliced celery (1-inch pieces)

In a Dutch oven, brown the beef, half at a time, in oil. Drain. Return all meat to pan. Add onion, tomatoes, beef broth, tapioca, garlic, parsley, salt, pepper and bay leaf. Bring to a boil; remove from the heat. Cover and bake at 350° for 1-1/2 hours.

Stir in the carrots, potatoes and celery. Bake 1 hour longer or until meat and vegetables are tender. Remove bay leaf before serving. **Yield:** 6-8 servings.

Minestrone Soup
(Pictured above)

Here's the perfect summertime soup to put all those fresh garden vegetables to good use. It's great for a light meal served with a salad and warm bread. —Lana Rutledge, Shepherdsville, Kentucky

    1 beef chuck roast (4 pounds)
    1 gallon water
    2 bay leaves
    2 medium onions, diced
    2 cups sliced carrots
    2 cups sliced celery
    1 can (28 ounces) diced tomatoes,
      undrained
    1 can (15 ounces) tomato sauce
  1/4 cup chopped fresh parsley
Salt and pepper to taste
    4 teaspoons dried basil
    1 teaspoon garlic powder
    2 packages (9 ounces *each*) frozen Italian
      or cut green beans
    1 package (16 ounces) frozen peas
    2 cans (16 ounces *each*) kidney beans,
      rinsed and drained
    2 packages (7 ounces *each*) shell macaroni,
      cooked and drained
Grated Parmesan cheese

Place roast, water and bay leaves in a stockpot; bring to a boil. Reduce heat; cover and simmer until meat is tender, about 3 hours. Remove meat; cool. Add onions, carrots and celery to broth; cook for 20 minutes or until vegetables are tender.

Cut meat into bite-size pieces; add to broth. Add tomatoes, tomato sauce, parsley, seasonings, beans, peas and kidney beans. Cook until vegetables are done, about 10 minutes. Add macaroni; heat through. Remove bay leaves. Serve with cheese. **Yield:** 40 servings (10 quarts).

Sloppy Joe Sandwiches

This recipe comes from a well-known local woman who was the lunchroom cook when my husband, Boyd, went to grade school. We use it every summer at the city's Old Settlers Day celebration. These from-scratch sloppy joes have a tangy sauce that makes them very popular. —*Karen Ann Bland, Gove, Kansas*

  20 pounds lean ground beef
   3 cups chopped onions
 1/4 cup Worcestershire sauce
   1 pound brown sugar
   1 cup prepared mustard
   2 tablespoons chili powder
   1 gallon ketchup
Salt and pepper to taste
Hamburger buns

In several large kettles or Dutch ovens, brown beef; drain. In a large bowl, combine the next seven ingredients; divide evenly between pans. Simmer for 1 hour. Stir occasionally. Serve on buns. **Yield:** 100 servings.

——— 🍴 🍴 🍴 ———

Sandwich for a Crowd

(Pictured on page 182)

My husband and I live on a 21-acre horse ranch and are pleased to invite friends to enjoy it with us. When entertaining, I rely on no-fuss make-ahead entrees like this satisfying sandwich. The blend of flavors from the savory spread, meats and pickles makes for an interesting sandwich. —*Helen Hougland, Spring Hill, Kansas*

   2 unsliced loaves (1 pound *each*) Italian
     bread
   1 package (8 ounces) cream cheese,
     softened
   1 cup (4 ounces) shredded cheddar cheese
 3/4 cup sliced green onions
 1/4 cup mayonnaise
   1 tablespoon Worcestershire sauce
   1 pound thinly sliced fully cooked ham
   1 pound thinly sliced roast beef
  12 to 14 thin slices dill pickle

Cut the bread in half lengthwise. Hollow out top and bottom of loaves, leaving a 1/2-in. shell (discard removed bread or save for another use). Combine cheeses, onions, mayonnaise and Worcestershire sauce; spread over cut sides of bread. Layer ham and roast beef on bottom and top halves; place pickles on bottom halves.

  Gently press halves together. Wrap in plastic wrap and refrigerate for at least 2 hours. Cut into 1-1/2-in. slices. **Yield:** 12-14 servings.

Italian Sausage Sandwiches

(Pictured below)

When my wife and I have friends over, we love to serve these sandwiches. This is a convenient recipe, since it can be prepared the day before and reheated.
            —*Mike Yaeger, Brookings, South Dakota*

  20 Italian sausages
   4 large green peppers, thinly sliced
 1/2 cup chopped onion
   1 can (12 ounces) tomato paste
   1 can (15 ounces) tomato sauce
   1 cup water
   1 tablespoon sugar
   4 garlic cloves, minced
   2 teaspoons dried basil
   1 teaspoon dried oregano
   1 teaspoon salt
  20 sandwich buns
Shredded mozzarella cheese, optional

In a large Dutch oven, brown sausages a few at a time; discard all but 2 tablespoons drippings. Saute peppers and onion in drippings until crisp-tender; drain. Return sausages to pan; add tomato paste, tomato sauce, water, sugar, garlic, basil, oregano and salt; bring to a boil. Reduce heat; cover and simmer for 30 minutes. Serve on buns. Top with cheese if desired. **Yield:** 20 servings.

Fudgy Toffee Bars

(Pictured at far right)

Sweet treats always go over well in my family, especially during the holidays. We think these rich bars are better than candy! They're nice to share with a group.
—Diane Bradley, Sparta, Michigan

1-3/4 cups all-purpose flour
  3/4 cup confectioners' sugar
  1/4 cup baking cocoa
  3/4 cup cold butter *or* margarine
    1 can (14 ounces) sweetened condensed milk
    1 teaspoon vanilla extract
    2 cups (12 ounces) semisweet chocolate chips, *divided*
    1 cup coarsely chopped walnuts
  1/2 cup flaked coconut
  1/2 cup English toffee bits *or* almond brickle chips

In a bowl, combine flour, sugar and cocoa. Cut in butter until mixture resembles coarse crumbs. Press firmly into a greased 13-in. x 9-in. x 2-in. baking pan. Bake at 350° for 10 minutes.

In a saucepan, heat milk, vanilla and 1 cup of chocolate chips, stirring until smooth. Pour over the crust. Sprinkle with nuts, coconut, toffee bits and remaining chocolate chips; press down firmly. Bake for 18-20 minutes. Cool on a wire rack. **Yield:** 3 dozen.

———— 🍷 🍷 🍷 ————

Topknot Rolls

(Pictured at far right)

These golden dinner rolls have a fine texture and a delightful buttery flavor. They brighten any meal. Even though they look special, they're not difficult to make.
—Bernadine Stine, Roanoke, Indiana

    2 packages (1/4 ounce *each*) active dry yeast
    2 teaspoons plus 1/2 cup sugar, *divided*
1-1/4 cups warm water (110° to 115°)
    3 eggs, beaten
  3/4 cup butter *or* margarine, melted, cooled, *divided*
5-1/2 cups all-purpose flour
    2 teaspoons salt
Softened butter *or* margarine

In a mixing bowl, dissolve yeast and 2 teaspoons of sugar in water. Let stand for 5 minutes. Add eggs, 1/2 cup melted butter, 2 cups flour, salt and remaining sugar. Beat until smooth. Add enough remaining flour to form a soft dough. Turn onto a

floured surface; knead until smooth and elastic, about 6-8 minutes. Place in a greased bowl, turning once to grease top. Cover and let rise in a warm place for 1-1/2 to 2 hours or until doubled.

Punch dough down; divide in half. On a floured surface, roll each portion into a 15-in. x 8-in. rectangle. Spread generously with softened butter. Roll up, jelly-roll style, starting with a long side. Using a sharp knife, cut into 1-in. slices. Place cut side up in greased muffin cups. Cover and let rise until doubled, about 45 minutes. Bake at 375° for 8-10 minutes or until golden brown. Brush with remaining melted butter. **Yield:** 2-1/2 dozen.

———— 🍷 🍷 🍷 ————

Lettuce Salad with Warm Dressing

(Pictured at right)

It's fun to share a different kind of tossed salad. The warm, tangy dressing wilts the greens in the most delicious way. Almonds provide a bit of crunch.
—Diane Hixon, Niceville, Florida

✓ Uses less fat, sugar or salt. Includes Nutritional Analysis and Diabetic Exchanges.

    1 large bunch green leaf lettuce, torn (about 12 cups)
    1 large bunch red leaf lettuce, torn (about 12 cups)
  1/2 pound fresh mushrooms, sliced
    3 green onions, sliced
    4 bacon strips, cooked and crumbled, optional
DRESSING:
  1/2 cup cider vinegar *or* red wine vinegar
  1/2 cup olive *or* vegetable oil
  1/4 cup water
    1 tablespoon sugar
    2 teaspoons lemon juice
    1 teaspoon Dijon mustard
    1 teaspoon Worcestershire sauce
  3/4 teaspoon garlic salt *or* 1/8 teaspoon garlic powder
  1/4 teaspoon pepper

In a large salad bowl, toss lettuce, mushrooms, onions and bacon if desired. In a small saucepan, combine the dressing ingredients. Cook and stir over medium heat until heated through. Just before serving, drizzle warm dressing over the salad; toss to coat. **Yield:** 18 servings.

Nutritional Analysis: One serving with 1 tablespoon dressing (prepared with garlic powder and without bacon) equals 68 calories, 14 mg sodium, 0 cholesterol, 3 g carbohydrate, 1 g protein, 6 g fat, 1 g fiber. **Diabetic Exchanges:** 1 vegetable, 1 fat.

'TIS THE SEASON. When you need a host of holiday helpings, reach for Topknot Rolls, Confetti Spaghetti, Fudgy Toffee Bars and Lettuce Salad with Warm Dressing (shown above, clockwise from top).

Confetti Spaghetti

(Pictured above)

Folks will go back for seconds of this hearty main dish.
—Katherine Moss, Gaffney, South Carolina

    1 package (12 ounces) spaghetti
1-1/2 pounds ground beef
    1 medium green pepper, chopped
    1 medium onion, chopped
    1 can (14-1/2 ounces) diced tomatoes,
      undrained
    1 can (8 ounces) tomato sauce
    1 tablespoon brown sugar
    1 teaspoon salt
    1 teaspoon chili powder
  1/2 teaspoon pepper
  1/4 teaspoon garlic powder
  1/8 teaspoon cayenne pepper
  3/4 cup shredded cheddar cheese

Cook spaghetti according to package directions. Meanwhile, in a large skillet, cook beef, green pepper and onion over medium heat until meat is no longer pink; drain. Stir in the tomatoes, tomato sauce, brown sugar, salt, chili powder, pepper, garlic powder and cayenne.

Drain spaghetti; add to the beef mixture. Transfer to a greased 13-in. x 9-in. x 2-in. baking dish. Cover and bake at 350° for 30 minutes. Uncover; sprinkle with cheese. Bake 5 minutes longer or until the cheese is melted. **Yield:** 12 servings.

No-Fuss Lasagna

(Pictured below and on page 182)

I like this recipe because it can be prepared a day ahead and baked just before serving.
—Denise Goedeken, Platte Center, Nebraska

1-1/2 pounds lean ground beef
1 can (12 ounces) tomato paste
3 cups water
2 packages (1-1/2 ounces *each*) spaghetti sauce mix
1 tablespoon sugar
4 teaspoons dried parsley flakes
1/2 teaspoon salt
1/2 teaspoon garlic powder
1/4 teaspoon pepper
2 eggs, beaten
2 cups (16 ounces) small-curd cottage cheese, drained
2 cups (8 ounces) shredded cheddar cheese, *divided*
2 cups (8 ounces) shredded mozzarella cheese, *divided*
1 package (16 ounces) lasagna noodles, uncooked

In a large saucepan, brown ground beef; drain. Add tomato paste, water, spaghetti sauce mix, sugar, parsley, salt, garlic powder and pepper. Simmer, partially covered, for 20 minutes. Stir occasionally. In a bowl, combine eggs, cottage cheese, half of the cheddar cheese and half of the mozzarella. Set aside. Spoon a third of the meat sauce into a 13-in. x 9-in. x 2-in. baking pan. Place half of the uncooked noodles over sauce. Top with a third of meat sauce and press down. Spoon cottage cheese mixture over all. Top with remaining noodles and meat sauce. Cover and refrigerate overnight.

Remove from the refrigerator 30 minutes before baking. Bake, covered, at 350° for 1 hour. Uncover; sprinkle with remaining cheddar and mozzarella cheeses. Bake 15 minutes longer. Let stand 10 minutes before cutting. **Yield:** 8 servings.

Ham-Stuffed Manicotti

Here's a fun and different use for ham. It's unexpected combined with the manicotti, yet delicious. The creamy cheese sauce makes this casserole perfect for chilly days. —Dorothy Anderson, Ottawa, Kansas

8 manicotti shells
1/2 cup chopped onion
1 tablespoon vegetable oil
3 cups (1 pound) ground fully cooked ham
1 can (4 ounces) sliced mushrooms, drained
1 cup (4 ounces) shredded Swiss cheese, *divided*
3 tablespoons grated Parmesan cheese
1/4 to 1/2 cup chopped green pepper
3 tablespoons butter *or* margarine
3 tablespoons all-purpose flour
2 cups milk
Paprika
Chopped fresh parsley

Cook manicotti according to package directions; set aside. In a large skillet, saute onion in oil until tender. Remove from the heat. Add ham, mushrooms, half of the Swiss cheese and Parmesan; set aside. In a saucepan, saute green pepper in butter until tender. Stir in flour until thoroughly combined. Add milk; cook, stirring constantly, until thickened and bubbly. Mix a quarter of the sauce into ham mixture.

Stuff each shell with about 1/3 cup of filling. Place in a greased 11-in. x 7-in. x 2-in. baking dish. Top with remaining sauce; sprinkle with paprika. Cover and bake at 350° for 30 minutes or until heated through. Sprinkle with parsley and remaining Swiss cheese before serving. **Yield:** 8 servings.

Editor's Note: Recipe can easily be doubled for a larger group.

Slow-Cooked Chicken and Stuffing

(Pictured above)

Prepared in a slow cooker, this tasty, no-fuss main dish has a flavorful blend of seasonings and the irresistible duo of tender chicken and moist stuffing. It's nice enough for the holidays and easy enough to fix year-round. —Angie Marquart, New Washington, Ohio

2-1/2 cups chicken broth
    1 cup butter *or* margarine
  1/2 cup chopped onion
  1/2 cup chopped celery
    1 can (4 ounces) mushroom stems and pieces, drained
  1/4 cup dried parsley flakes
1-1/2 teaspoons rubbed sage
    1 teaspoon poultry seasoning
    1 teaspoon salt
  1/2 teaspoon pepper
   12 cups day-old bread cubes (1/2-inch pieces)
    2 eggs
    1 can (10-3/4 ounces) condensed cream of chicken soup, undiluted
   5 to 6 cups cubed cooked chicken

In a saucepan, combine the first 10 ingredients. Simmer for 10 minutes; remove from the heat. Place bread cubes in a large bowl. Combine eggs and soup; stir into broth mixture until smooth. Pour over bread; toss well. In a 5-qt. slow cooker, layer half of the dressing and chicken; repeat layers. Cover and cook on low for 4-1/2 to 5 hours or until a meat thermometer inserted into stuffing reads 160°. **Yield:** 14-16 servings.

Dinner in a Dish

(Pictured below)

I haven't found anyone yet who can resist this saucy beef casserole topped with mashed potatoes. The frozen peas and canned tomatoes add color and make a helping or two a complete meal. —Betty Sitzman Wray, Colorado

  2 pounds ground beef
  1 medium onion, chopped
  2 teaspoons beef bouillon granules
  2 cans (14-1/2 ounces *each*) diced tomatoes, undrained
  3 cups frozen peas
2/3 cup ketchup
1/4 cup chopped fresh parsley
  2 tablespoons all-purpose flour
  2 teaspoons dried marjoram
  1 teaspoon salt
1/2 teaspoon pepper
  6 cups hot mashed potatoes (prepared with milk and butter)
  2 eggs

In a saucepan over medium heat, brown beef and onion; drain. Add the next nine ingredients; mix well. Bring to a boil; cook and stir for 2 minutes. Pour into an ungreased shallow 3-qt. baking dish. Combine potatoes and eggs; mix well. Drop by 1/2 cupfuls onto the beef mixture. Bake, uncovered, at 350° for 35-40 minutes or until bubbly and potatoes are lightly browned. **Yield:** 12 servings.

Turkey Tetrazzini

(Pictured below)

This recipe comes from a cookbook our church compiled. It's convenient because it can be made ahead and frozen. After the holidays, we use leftover turkey to prepare a meal for university students. They clean their plates!
—Gladys Waldrop
Calvert City, Kentucky

    1 package (7 ounces) spaghetti, broken into
        2-inch pieces
    2 cups cubed cooked turkey
    1 cup (4 ounces) shredded cheddar cheese
    1 can (10-3/4 ounces) condensed cream of
        mushroom soup, undiluted
    1 medium onion, chopped
    2 cans (4 ounces *each*) sliced mushrooms,
        drained
  1/3 cup milk
  1/4 cup chopped green pepper
    1 jar (2 ounces) chopped pimientos, drained
  1/4 teaspoon salt
  1/8 teaspoon pepper
Additional shredded cheddar cheese, optional

Cook spaghetti according to package directions; drain. Transfer to a large bowl; add the next 10 ingredients and mix well. Spoon into a greased 2-1/2-qt. casserole; sprinkle with cheese if desired. Bake, uncovered, at 375° for 40-45 minutes or until heated through. **Yield:** 6-8 servings.

Tangy Meatballs

(Pictured above)

These hearty meatballs are a family favorite and a big hit wherever they go. In their delicious barbecue sauce, they're a perfect dish to pass and also work well as hors d'oeuvres for a party. —Jane Barta
St. Thomas, North Dakota

    2 eggs
    2 cups quick-cooking *or* old-fashioned oats
    1 can (12 ounces) evaporated milk
    1 cup chopped onion
    2 teaspoons salt
  1/2 teaspoon pepper
  1/2 teaspoon garlic powder
    3 pounds lean ground beef
SAUCE:
    2 cups ketchup
1-1/2 cups packed brown sugar
  1/2 cup chopped onion
    1 to 2 teaspoons liquid smoke, optional
  1/2 teaspoon garlic powder

In a large bowl, beat eggs. Add oats, milk, onion, salt, pepper and garlic powder. Add the ground beef; mix well. Shape into 1-1/2-in. balls. Place in two 13-in. x 9-in. x 2-in. baking pans. Bake, uncovered, at 375° for 30 minutes.

Drain; place all of the meatballs in one of the pans. In a saucepan, bring the sauce ingredients to a boil. Pour over meatballs. Bake, uncovered, 20 minutes longer or until meat is no longer pink. **Yield:** 4 dozen.

Slow-Cooked Short Ribs

(Pictured below)

Smothered in a mouth-watering barbecue sauce, these meaty ribs are a popular entree wherever I serve them. The recipe is great for a busy cook—after everything is combined, the slow cooker does all the work.
—Pam Halfhill, Medina, Ohio

- 2/3 cup all-purpose flour
- 2 teaspoons salt
- 1/2 teaspoon pepper
- 4 to 4-1/2 pounds boneless beef short ribs
- 1/4 to 1/3 cup butter *or* margarine
- 1 large onion, chopped
- 1-1/2 cups beef broth
- 3/4 cup cider vinegar *or* red wine vinegar
- 3/4 cup packed brown sugar
- 1/2 cup chili sauce
- 1/3 cup ketchup
- 1/3 cup Worcestershire sauce
- 5 garlic cloves, minced
- 1-1/2 teaspoons chili powder

In a large resealable plastic bag, combine the flour, salt and pepper. Add ribs in batches and shake to coat. In a large skillet, brown ribs in butter. Transfer to a 5-qt. slow cooker. In the same skillet, combine the remaining ingredients. Cook and stir until mixture comes to a boil; pour over ribs (slow cooker will be full). Cover and cook on low for 9-10 hours or until meat is tender. **Yield:** 12-15 servings.

No-Fuss Chicken

(Pictured above)

This recipe could hardly be simpler to prepare. No one will know you used convenient ingredients like a bottle of salad dressing and onion soup mix.
—Marilyn Dick, Centralia, Missouri

- 1 bottle (16 ounces) Russian *or* Catalina salad dressing
- 2/3 cup apricot preserves
- 2 envelopes onion soup mix
- 16 boneless skinless chicken breast halves
Hot cooked rice

In a bowl, combine salad dressing, preserves and soup mix. Place chicken in two ungreased 11-in. x 7-in. x 2-in. baking pans; top with dressing mixture. Cover and bake at 350° for 20 minutes; baste. Bake, uncovered, 20 minutes longer or until chicken juices run clear. Serve over rice. **Yield:** 16 servings.

Lasagna Lessons

Try replacing a quarter of the mozzarella cheese in your lasagna recipe with shredded sharp cheddar.

When covering cheese-topped lasagna with foil before baking, coat the underside of the foil with nonstick cooking spray. That way the melted cheese won't come off with the foil.

Freeze individual pieces of leftover lasagna in an airtight container for a quick lunch or dinner later.

Sweet Peanut Treats

(Pictured below)

We sold tempting bars almost like these at the refreshment stand at a Minnesota state park where I worked in the '70s, and they were a favorite of employees and visitors alike. Now I make this recipe when I want to serve a special treat. —Phyllis Smith
Olympia, Washington

- 2 cups (12 ounces) semisweet chocolate chips
- 2 cups (12 ounces) butterscotch chips
- 1 jar (18 ounces) creamy peanut butter
- 1 cup butter *or* margarine
- 1 can (5 ounces) evaporated milk
- 1/4 cup vanilla cook-and-serve pudding mix
- 1 bag (2 pounds) confectioners' sugar
- 1 pound salted peanuts

In the top of a double boiler over simmering water, melt chips and peanut butter; stir until smooth. Spread half into a greased 15-in. x 10-in. x 1-in. baking pan. Chill until firm.

Meanwhile, in a saucepan, bring butter, milk and pudding mix to a boil. Cook and stir for 2 minutes. Remove from the heat; add confectioners' sugar and beat until smooth. Spread over chocolate mixture in pan. Stir peanuts into remaining chocolate mixture; mix well. Carefully spread over pudding layer. Refrigerate. Cut into 1-in. squares. **Yield:** 10 dozen.

Lemon Cheesecake Squares

(Pictured above)

Whether I'm hosting friends or sending a plate to work with my husband, these creamy elegant cheesecake squares are always a hit. It's a wonderful make-ahead dessert that easily serves a large group.
—Peggy Reddick, Cumming, Georgia

- 3/4 cup shortening
- 1/3 cup packed brown sugar
- 1-1/4 cups all-purpose flour
- 1 cup rolled oats
- 1/4 teaspoon salt
- 1/2 cup seedless raspberry jam

FILLING:
- 4 packages (8 ounces *each*) cream cheese, softened
- 1-1/2 cups sugar
- 1/4 cup all-purpose flour
- 4 eggs
- 1/3 cup lemon juice
- 4 teaspoons grated lemon peel

In a mixing bowl, cream shortening and brown sugar. Combine the flour, oats and salt; gradually add to the creamed mixture. Press dough into a greased 13-in. x 9-in. x 2-in. baking dish. Bake at 350° for 15-18 minutes or until golden brown. Spread with jam.

For filling, beat the cream cheese, sugar and flour until fluffy. Add the eggs, lemon juice and peel just until blended. Carefully spoon over jam. Bake at 350° for 30-35 minutes or until center is almost set. Cool on a wire rack. Cover and store in the refrigerator. **Yield:** 20 servings.

Cranberry Oatmeal Cookies

(Pictured on page 182)

Dotted with cranberries, orange peel and vanilla chips, these cookies are so colorful and fun to eat.
—Pat Habiger, Spearville, Kansas

1 cup butter (no substitutes), softened
1-1/2 cups sugar
2 eggs
1 teaspoon vanilla extract
2 cups all-purpose flour
1 teaspoon baking powder
1/2 teaspoon salt
1/4 teaspoon baking soda
2 cups quick-cooking oats
1 cup raisins
1 cup coarsely chopped fresh *or* frozen cranberries
1 tablespoon grated orange peel
1 package (12 ounces) vanilla chips

In a mixing bowl, cream butter and sugar. Add eggs, one at a time, beating well after each addition. Beat in vanilla. Combine flour, baking powder, salt and baking soda; add to the creamed mixture. Stir in oats, raisins, cranberries and orange peel. Stir in vanilla chips. Drop by rounded teaspoonfuls 2 in. apart onto greased baking sheets. Bake at 375° for 10-12 minutes or until edges are lightly browned. Cool on wire racks. **Yield:** 6 dozen.

———— 🝳 🝳 🝳 ————

Crunchy Peanut Butter Bars

(Pictured on page 182)

These delicious bars are great holiday treats, but the kids like them all year long. I used this recipe for my five children. Now I bake them for my grandkids.
—Geraldine Grisdale, Mt. Pleasant, Michigan

2-3/4 cups all-purpose flour
1-1/4 cups packed brown sugar
1 egg
1/2 cup butter *or* margarine, softened
1/2 cup shortening
1/3 cup chunky peanut butter
1 teaspoon vanilla extract
1/2 teaspoon salt
TOPPING:
1 cup (6 ounces) semisweet chocolate chips, melted
1/2 cup chunky peanut butter
1-1/2 cups crushed cornflakes

In a mixing bowl, combine the first eight ingredients and mix well (batter will be thick). Press into an ungreased 15-in. x 10-in. x 1-in. baking pan.

Bake at 350° for 15-20 minutes or until set. Cool for 5 minutes. Combine the chocolate chips and peanut butter in a bowl; stir in cornflakes. Carefully spread on top. Cut into bars. **Yield:** 4 dozen.

———— 🝳 🝳 🝳 ————

Mocha Walnut Brownies

(Pictured below)

These rich cake-like brownies are generously topped with a scrumptious mocha frosting. They're an excellent dessert when you need a dish to pass.
—Jill Bonanno, Prineville, Oregon

4 squares (1 ounce *each*) unsweetened chocolate
1 cup butter (no substitutes)
2 cups sugar
4 eggs
1 teaspoon vanilla extract
1-1/4 cups all-purpose flour
1/2 teaspoon baking powder
1/2 teaspoon salt
1 cup chopped walnuts
MOCHA FROSTING:
4 cups confectioners' sugar
1/2 cup butter, melted
1/3 cup baking cocoa
1/4 cup strong brewed coffee
2 teaspoons vanilla extract

In a saucepan over low heat, melt chocolate and butter; stir until smooth. Remove from the heat. Add sugar and mix well. Add eggs, one at a time, beating well after each. Stir in vanilla. Combine flour, baking powder and salt; add to chocolate mixture just until combined. Stir in walnuts. Pour into a greased 13-in. x 9-in. x 2-in. baking pan.

Bake at 375° for 30 minutes or until a toothpick inserted near the center comes out clean. Cool on a wire rack. Combine frosting ingredients; mix well. Spread over brownies. **Yield:** about 2 dozen.

Creamy Mocha Frozen Dessert

(Pictured above)

Light as a feather, this cool dessert is delicious and impressive to serve. It's a great dessert to take to a potluck because it can be made ahead and stored in the freezer. —Launa Shoemaker, Midland City, Alabama

    2 **teaspoons instant coffee granules**
    1 **tablespoon hot water**
    1 **cup cream-filled chocolate cookie crumbs**
 3/4 **cup chopped pecans,** *divided*
 1/4 **cup butter** *or* **margarine, melted**
    2 **packages (8 ounces** *each***) cream cheese, softened**
    1 **can (14 ounces) sweetened condensed milk**
 1/2 **cup chocolate syrup**
    1 **carton (8 ounces) frozen whipped topping, thawed**

In a small bowl, dissolve coffee granules in hot water; set aside. In another bowl, combine the cookie crumbs, 1/2 cup pecans and butter. Pat into the bottom of a 13-in. x 9-in. x 2-in. baking pan. In a mixing bowl, beat cream cheese until light and fluffy. Blend in coffee mixture, milk and chocolate syrup. Fold in whipped topping; spread over crust. Sprinkle remaining pecans on top. Freeze. **Yield:** 24 servings.

Cream-Filled Cupcakes

(Pictured below)

Folks who enjoy homemade chocolate cupcakes are even more impressed when they bite into these treats and find a fluffy filling. —Edie DeSpain, Logan, Utah

    3 **cups all-purpose flour**
    2 **cups sugar**
 1/3 **cup baking cocoa**
    2 **teaspoons baking soda**
    1 **teaspoon salt**
    2 **eggs**
    1 **cup milk**
    1 **cup vegetable oil**
    1 **cup water**
    1 **teaspoon vanilla extract**
FILLING:
 1/4 **cup butter** *or* **margarine, softened**
 1/4 **cup shortening**
    2 **cups confectioners' sugar**
    3 **tablespoons milk**
    1 **teaspoon vanilla extract**
Pinch salt
Chocolate frosting

In a mixing bowl, combine the first five ingredients. Add eggs, milk, oil, water and vanilla. Beat until smooth, about 2 minutes. Fill *paper-lined* muffin cups half full. Bake at 375° for 15-20 minutes or until a toothpick inserted near the center comes out clean. Remove from pans to wire racks to cool completely.

In a mixing bowl, combine butter, shortening, confectioners' sugar, milk, vanilla and salt; beat until fluffy, about 5 minutes. Insert a very small tip into a pastry or plastic bag; fill with cream filling. Push the tip through the bottom of paper liner to fill each cupcake. Frost tops with chocolate frosting. **Yield:** 3 dozen.

White Texas Sheet Cake

This cake gets better the longer it sits, so I try to make it a day ahead. My mother-in-law introduced this deliciously rich cake to me. No one can stop at just one piece! —Joanie Ward, Brownsburg, Indiana

    1 cup butter *or* margarine
    1 cup water
    2 cups all-purpose flour
    2 cups sugar
    2 eggs, beaten
 1/2 cup sour cream
    1 teaspoon almond extract
    1 teaspoon salt
    1 teaspoon baking soda
FROSTING:
 1/2 cup butter *or* margarine
 1/4 cup milk
4-1/2 cups confectioners' sugar
 1/2 teaspoon almond extract
    1 cup chopped walnuts

In a large saucepan, bring butter and water to a boil. Remove from the heat; stir in flour, sugar, eggs, sour cream, almond extract, salt and baking soda until smooth. Pour into a greased 15-in. x 10-in. x 1-in. baking pan. Bake at 375° for 20-22 minutes or until cake is golden brown and tests done. Cool for 20 minutes.

Meanwhile, for frosting, combine butter and milk in a saucepan. Bring to a boil. Remove from the heat. Add confectioners' sugar and almond extract; mix well. Stir in the walnuts; spread over warm cake. **Yield:** 16-20 servings.

— ☕ ☕ ☕ —

Pistachio Ambrosia

For a fruity, satisfying dessert, we like this smooth and creamy pudding. Since the recipe makes a big batch, it's nice for a potluck. —Carol Lynn Chizzoniti Holbrook, New York

    2 cans (17 ounces *each*) fruit cocktail
    2 cans (20 ounces *each*) pineapple chunks
    2 cans (11 ounces *each*) mandarin oranges
    4 packages (3.4 ounces *each*) instant pistachio pudding mix
    2 cups (16 ounces) sour cream
    1 carton (12 ounces) frozen whipped topping, thawed
Chopped pecans, optional

Drain fruit cocktail, pineapple and oranges, reserving 3 cups juice. Set fruit aside; pour juice into a 4-qt. bowl. Add pudding mix and mix until smooth. Stir in sour cream. Add whipped topping and mix until smooth. Fold in fruit; chill for several hours. Just before serving, top with pecans if desired. **Yield:** 16-20 servings.

Butterscotch Pecan Dessert

(Pictured above)

The fluffy cream cheese layer topped with cool butterscotch pudding is a lip-smacking combination. —Becky Harrison, Albion, Illinois

 1/2 cup cold butter *or* margarine
    1 cup all-purpose flour
 3/4 cup chopped pecans, *divided*
    1 package (8 ounces) cream cheese, softened
    1 cup confectioners' sugar
    1 carton (8 ounces) frozen whipped topping, thawed, *divided*
3-1/2 cups milk
    2 packages (3.4 or 3.5 ounces *each*) instant butterscotch *or* vanilla pudding mix

In a bowl, cut butter into flour until crumbly; stir in 1/2 cup pecans. Press into an ungreased 13-in. x 9-in. x 2-in. baking pan. Bake at 350° for 20 minutes or until lightly browned. Cool.

In a mixing bowl, beat cream cheese and sugar until fluffy. Fold in 1 cup whipped topping; spread over crust. Combine milk and pudding mix until smooth; pour over cream cheese layer. Refrigerate for 15-20 minutes or until set. Top with remaining whipped topping and pecans. Refrigerate for 1-2 hours. **Yield:** 16-20 servings.

Cooking for One or Two

These small-serving recipes—featuring tasty entrees, side dishes and more—prove good things really do come in small packages.

PERFECT PORTIONS. Clockwise from upper left: Apple Turnover and Baked Eggs and Ham (p. 208); Special Citrus Salad, Roasted Potatoes and Baked Fish (pp. 212 and 213); Sesame Chicken Stir-Fry (p. 217); Dan's Peppery London Broil and Italian Herb Salad Dressing (p. 214).

Chicken Monterey

(Pictured at right)

I buy chicken when it's on sale and freeze the pieces individually. Then I can use them one at a time for delicious recipes like this. —Melanie DuLac
Northboro, Massachusetts

- 1 **boneless skinless chicken breast half**
- Dash **salt and pepper**
- 1/2 **teaspoon chopped fresh parsley**
- 1/8 **teaspoon dried tarragon**
- 1 **ounce Monterey Jack *or* cheddar cheese (cut into a 2-1/2- x 1/2-inch stick)**
- 2 **tablespoons all-purpose flour**
- 1 **egg, beaten**
- 2 **tablespoons seasoned *or* plain dry bread crumbs**
- 1 **tablespoon butter *or* margarine**
- 1 **tablespoon vegetable oil**

Pound chicken to 1/4-in. thickness. Season the inside with salt, pepper, parsley and tarragon. Place cheese in the center and fold chicken around it. Roll in flour; dip into egg, then roll in crumbs. Place seam side down on a plate; refrigerate for 30 minutes. In a skillet, saute chicken in butter and oil until golden. Place in a small shallow baking dish. Bake, uncovered, at 375° for 15 minutes or until juices run clear. **Yield:** 1 serving.

— 🍵 🍵 🍵 —

No-Cook Cranberry Relish

(Pictured at right)

This relish is a tangy addition served with chicken or ham and makes a plate look so pretty! It's so important to do something nice for yourself, and a good meal is an easy way to do that. —Eleanor Slimak
Chicago, Illinois

- 1/2 **cup fresh *or* frozen cranberries**
- 1/4 **medium orange, peeled**
- 1 **tablespoon sugar**

In a blender or food processor, process all ingredients until coarsely chopped. Cover and chill for 30 minutes or until ready to serve. **Yield:** 1 serving.

— 🍵 🍵 🍵 —

Mashed Potato for One

(Pictured above right)

With two dance classes, bowling and crafting each week, I sometimes want an out-of-the-ordinary side dish but have little time. This easy recipe is perfect. It's

a treat to have rich-tasting mashed potatoes with a hint of dill. —Winifred Chesborough
Truth or Consequences, New Mexico

✓ Uses less fat, sugar or salt. Includes Nutritional Analysis and Diabetic Exchanges.

- 1 **medium potato, peeled and cooked**
- 2 **tablespoons milk**
- 1 **tablespoon cream cheese, softened**
- 1 **teaspoon butter *or* margarine**
- 1/8 **teaspoon snipped fresh dill *or* pinch dill weed**

**1/4 teaspoon salt, optional
Dash pepper**

In a small microwave-safe dish, mash all ingredients until smooth. Cook on high for 1 minute or until heated through. **Yield:** 1 serving.

Nutritional Analysis: One serving (prepared with fat-free milk, margarine and reduced-fat cream cheese and without salt) equals 163 calories, 134 mg sodium, 9 mg cholesterol, 22 g carbohydrate, 5 g protein, 6 g fat. **Diabetic Exchanges:** 1-1/2 starch, 1 fat.

Single Serving Suggestions

Cooking for one can be just as fun and satisfying as cooking for a group.

A pretty setting with a colorful napkin from some past festive occasion or a cherished gift mug promotes happy memories and a pleasant state of mind when having a meal alone.

Fresh colorful meals will not only do your body good, but your spirit as well.

Baked Eggs and Ham

(Pictured at right and on page 204)

My breakfast is never ho-hum when I fix this egg dish. I give this savory entree Southwestern flair and zip by using cheese flavored with jalapeno peppers. But regular cheddar cheese also produces tasty results.
—Carolyn Crump, Center, Texas

  1/4 **cup seasoned croutons**
   2 **tablespoons chopped fully cooked ham**
   1 **tablespoon butter** *or* **margarine, melted**
   2 **eggs**
   1 **tablespoon shredded cheddar cheese**
Fresh fruit, optional

In a greased shallow 2-cup baking dish, toss the croutons, ham and butter. Break the eggs carefully on top. Sprinkle with cheese. Bake, uncovered, at 350° for 15-18 minutes or until eggs reach desired doneness. Serve with fresh fruit if desired. **Yield:** 1 serving.

——— 🥤 🥤 🥤 ———

Apple Turnover

(Pictured at right and on page 204)

Plain toast and day-old doughnuts can't compare to this old-fashioned apple pastry without all the leftovers. My mother used to make this morning treat all the years she lived alone. Now I make it for myself or my husband as a sweet treat. —Phyllis Fahey
Fergus Falls, Minnesota

  1/4 **cup all-purpose flour**
Pinch salt
   4 **teaspoons shortening**
   1 **tablespoon ice water**
   1 **medium tart apple, peeled and sliced**
   1 **teaspoon sugar**
  1/8 **teaspoon ground cinnamon**
Milk
GLAZE:
   2 **tablespoons confectioners' sugar**
   1 **teaspoon corn syrup**
Pinch salt
  1/2 **teaspoon hot water**

In a small bowl, combine flour and salt; cut in shortening until mixture resembles coarse crumbs. Sprinkle with ice water and toss with a fork. Form into a ball. On a lightly floured surface, roll dough into a 7-in. circle. Place apple slices on half of the circle; sprinkle with sugar and cinnamon.

Fold dough over filling, sealing edges with fingers or pressing with a fork. Brush with milk. Prick top with a fork. Place on a greased baking sheet. Bake at 375° for 25-30 minutes or until golden

brown. Combine glaze ingredients until smooth; drizzle over turnover. **Yield:** 1 serving.

——— 🥤 🥤 🥤 ———

Cinnamon-Raisin Oatmeal

(Not pictured)

A satisfying alternative to cold cereal that isn't much more fuss is this hot hearty oatmeal. This simple break-

fast is my favorite on cool mornings. I love that it's so easy to prepare. —Rita Winterberger, Huson, Montana

☑ Uses less fat, sugar or salt. Includes Nutritional Analysis and Diabetic Exchanges.

1/4 cup quick-cooking oats
1/4 cup Grape-Nuts cereal
1/4 cup raisins
1 tablespoon brown sugar
1 teaspoon ground cinnamon
1 cup milk
Cream *or* additional milk, optional

In a microwave-safe cereal bowl, combine the first six ingredients. Microwave on high for 3 minutes. Serve with cream or milk if desired. **Yield:** 1 serving.

Nutritional Analysis: One serving (prepared with fat-free milk and 1 teaspoon brown sugar) equals 395 calories, 325 mg sodium, 4 mg cholesterol, 83 g carbohydrate, 15 g protein, 3 g fat. **Diabetic Exchanges:** 3 starch, 2 fruit, 1 skim milk.

Beef Tenderloin in Mushroom Sauce

(Pictured at right)

It doesn't take much fuss to make a special meal for two. When our kids are visiting Grandma, I make this delicious entree just for my husband, Derek, and me. It's a recipe my mother-in-law has been using for more than 30 years.
— Denise McNab
Warrington, Pennsylvania

>   1 teaspoon vegetable oil
>   4 tablespoons butter *or* margarine, *divided*
>   2 beef tenderloin steaks *or* fillets
>   (1 inch thick)
>   1/2 cup chopped fresh mushrooms
>   1 tablespoon chopped green onion
>   1 tablespoon all-purpose flour
>   1/8 teaspoon salt
> Dash pepper
>   2/3 cup chicken *or* beef broth
>   1/8 teaspoon browning sauce, optional

In a skillet, heat oil and 2 tablespoons of butter over medium-high heat. Cook steaks for 6-7 minutes on each side or until meat is done as desired (for rare, a meat thermometer should read 140°; medium, 160°; well-done, 170°). Remove to a serving platter and keep warm.

To pan juices, add mushrooms, onions and remaining butter; saute until tender. Add flour, salt and pepper; gradually stir in broth until smooth. Add browning sauce if desired. Bring to a boil; boil and stir for 2 minutes. Spoon over the steaks. Serve immediately. **Yield:** 2 servings.

Vegetable Ramekins

(Pictured at right)

Our children and grandchildren live far away, so my husband, Jim, and I frequently plan a quiet dinner by candlelight. We have this side dish often since we can pull fresh things from our garden all year. With a creamy cheese sauce , it's colorful and tasty.
— Dona Alsover, Upland, California

>   1 small zucchini *or* yellow summer squash,
>   halved and cut into 1/2-inch slices
>   1/4 cup chopped green pepper
>   1/3 cup broccoli florets
>   1 medium carrot, julienned
>   1 medium potato, peeled, cooked and
>   cubed
>   2 tablespoons butter *or* margarine
>   2 tablespoons all-purpose flour
>   3/4 cup milk
>   1/4 teaspoon garlic salt

>   1/8 teaspoon coarse black pepper
>   1/4 cup shredded cheddar cheese
>   1 tablespoon minced fresh parsley
>   1 tablespoon chopped walnuts

In a saucepan over medium heat, cook squash, green pepper, broccoli and carrot in boiling water until crisp-tender; drain. Stir in the potato. Spoon into two greased ovenproof 10-oz. custard cups or casseroles.

In a saucepan, melt the butter; stir in flour, milk, garlic salt and pepper until smooth. Cook for 2-3 minutes, gradually adding the cheese in small amounts; cook and stir until cheese is melted. Pour over vegetables. Sprinkle with parsley and

walnuts. Bake, uncovered, at 350° for 20-25 minutes or until sauce is bubbly. **Yield:** 2 servings.

——— 🍵 🍵 🍵 ———

Little Dixie Pound Cake

(Pictured above)

This is a moist quick-to-fix cake with a mild orange flavor. When my great-grandson and I eat dinner together, we're always happy to share this delightful dessert.
—Ruby Williams, Bogalusa, Louisiana

3 tablespoons butter (no substitutes), softened

6 tablespoons sugar
1 egg
6 tablespoons all-purpose flour
Pinch baking soda
7 teaspoons buttermilk
1/4 teaspoon vanilla extract
1/8 teaspoon orange extract

In a small mixing bowl, cream the butter and sugar. Beat in egg. Combine flour and baking soda; add alternately with buttermilk to creamed mixture. Blend in extracts. Pour into a greased 5-3/4-in. x 3-in. x 2-in. loaf pan. Bake at 350° for 30-35 minutes or until cake tests done. Cool for 10 minutes; remove from the pan to cool on a wire rack. **Yield:** 1 mini loaf.

Baked Fish
(Pictured at right and on page 204)

*I created this quick recipe after enjoying a seafood dish
with Parmesan cheese sprinkled on top at a restaurant.*
—*Lynn Mathieu, Great Mills, Maryland*

✓ Uses less fat, sugar or salt. Includes Nutritional Analysis
and Diabetic Exchanges.

**1/2 pound panfish fillets (perch, trout *or*
       whitefish)**
** 4 teaspoons grated Parmesan cheese**
1/2 teaspoon dill weed

Place fish in a 10-in. pie plate that has been coated with nonstick cooking spray. Sprinkle with
Parmesan cheese and dill. Bake, uncovered, at
350° for 8-10 minutes or until fish flakes easily with
a fork. **Yield:** 2 servings.
   Nutritional Analysis: One serving (prepared with
perch) equals 119 calories, 131 mg sodium, 104
mg cholesterol, 0 carbohydrate, 23 g protein, 2 g
fat. **Diabetic Exchange:** 3 very lean meat.

Special Citrus Salad
(Pictured at right and on page 204)

*A tangy dressing makes this salad taste as impressive
as it looks.*   —*Janice Ubaldi, Petaluma, California*

** 1 can (11 ounces) mandarin oranges**
1/4 cup minced fresh parsley
** 3 tablespoons French *or* Italian salad
       dressing**
** 1 teaspoon dried basil**
** 1 teaspoon lemon juice**
1/2 teaspoon brown sugar
1/4 teaspoon pepper
Pinch dried tarragon
Leaf lettuce, optional
1/2 grapefruit, peeled and sectioned
1/2 small cucumber, sliced
1/2 small red onion, sliced
** 1 small tomato, sliced**

Drain juice from oranges into a small bowl; set
oranges aside. To the juice, add the parsley, salad
dressing, basil, lemon juice, brown sugar, pepper
and tarragon; mix well. Line individual salad plates
with lettuce if desired; arrange oranges, grapefruit, cucumber, onion and tomato on lettuce. Serve
with dressing. **Yield:** 2 servings.

Roasted Potatoes
(Pictured above right and on page 204)

*I like trying out new recipes. The lemon juice and
thyme give these golden potatoes fabulous flavor.*
—*Sally Sue Campbell, Greenville, Tennessee*

✓ Uses less fat, sugar or salt. Includes Nutritional Analysis
and Diabetic Exchanges.

** 2 tablespoons lemon juice**
** 4 teaspoons olive *or* vegetable oil**
1/2 teaspoon dried thyme
1/2 teaspoon garlic salt
1/8 teaspoon pepper

6 small red potatoes (about 1 pound), quartered

In a medium bowl, combine lemon juice, oil, thyme, garlic salt and pepper. Add potatoes; toss to coat. Place in an 8-in. square baking dish coated with nonstick cooking spray. Bake, uncovered, at 450° for 40 minutes or until potatoes are tender, stirring occasionally. **Yield:** 2 servings.

Nutritional Analysis: One serving equals 173 calories, 335 mg sodium, 0 cholesterol, 22 g car-bohydrate, 2 g protein, 9 g fat. **Diabetic Exchanges:** 2 fat, 1 starch.

"Orange" You Curious?

Mandarin orange is a term for several varieties of loose-skinned oranges. The skins slip easily off the fruit. Among the more well-known are tangerine, clementine and Japanese satsuma oranges. Most of the canned mandarin oranges are satsumas.

Dan's Peppery London Broil

(Pictured at right and on page 204)

I was bored making the usual London broil, so I got a little creative and sparked up the flavor with crushed red pepper flakes, garlic and Worcestershire sauce. This is a special entree for two that's easy to prepare.
—Dan Wright, San Jose, California

    1 beef flank steak (about 3/4 pound)
    1 garlic clove, minced
  1/2 teaspoon seasoned salt
  1/8 teaspoon crushed red pepper flakes
  1/4 cup Worcestershire sauce

With a meat fork, poke holes in both sides of meat. Make a paste with garlic, seasoned salt and red pepper flakes; rub over both sides of meat. Place the steak in a resealable gallon-size plastic bag. Add Worcestershire sauce and close bag. Refrigerate for at least 4 hours, turning once. Remove meat; discard marinade. Broil or grill over hot heat until meat reaches desired doneness, about 4-5 minutes on each side. To serve, slice thinly across the grain. **Yield:** 2 servings.

Italian Herb Salad Dressing

(Pictured at right and on page 204)

Dan also shares his recipe for this simple yet savory Italian dressing. It's a delicious blend with home-made goodness that he likes to keep on hand to taste-fully top all sorts of salad greens. Garlic and Parmesan cheese give irresistible flavor.

  3/4 cup olive *or* vegetable oil
  1/2 cup red wine vinegar *or* cider vinegar
    1 tablespoon grated Parmesan *or* Romano
      cheese
    1 garlic clove, minced
  1/2 teaspoon salt
  1/2 teaspoon sugar
  1/2 teaspoon dried oregano
Pinch pepper

In a jar with a tight-fitting lid, combine all ingredients; shake well. Refrigerate. Shake well again before serving over greens. **Yield:** 1-1/4 cups.

Mini White Breads

(Pictured above right)

These small loaves of white bread, perfectly portioned to serve two, have a wonderful flavor and tex- ture. *It's a great way to enjoy fresh bread with a meal.* *—Nila Tower, Baird, Texas*

✓ Uses less fat, sugar or salt. Includes Nutritional Analysis and Diabetic Exchanges.

        1 package (1/4 ounce) active dry yeast
        1 tablespoon sugar
      1/3 cup warm water (110° to 115°)
2-1/4 to 2-1/2 cups all-purpose flour
        1 teaspoon salt
      1/2 cup milk

2 teaspoons butter *or* margarine, melted
Additional melted butter *or* margarine

Combine yeast, sugar and water in a large mixing bowl. Add 1-1/2 cups of flour, salt, milk and butter. Mix for 3 minutes on medium speed. Add enough remaining flour to form a soft dough. Turn onto a floured board; knead until smooth and elastic, 6-8 minutes.

Place in a greased bowl, turning once to grease top. Cover and let rise in a warm place until doubled, about 45 minutes.

Punch dough down. Divide in half; shape into two loaves and place in greased 5-3/4-in. x 3-in. x 2-in. pans. Cover and let rise until doubled, about 30 minutes. Bake at 375° for 30 minutes or until golden brown. Remove from pans; cool on wire racks. Brush tops with melted butter. **Yield:** 2 mini loaves.

Nutritional Analysis: One 1/2-inch slice (prepared with margarine) equals 75 calories, 156 mg sodium, 0 cholesterol, 14 g carbohydrate, 2 g protein, 1 g fat. **Diabetic Exchange:** 1 starch.

square baking pan. Bake at 350° for 30-35 minutes or until a toothpick inserted in the center comes out clean. Cool completely.

For frosting, combine the first six ingredients in a saucepan; bring to a boil. Boil for 1-1/2 minutes; remove from the heat. Set pan in a larger pan of ice water. Beat for 1 minute. Add butter and vanilla. Beat 10 minutes longer or until frosting is desired spreading consistency. Frost cake. **Yield:** 4 servings.

*Editor's Note: To sour milk, place 1 teaspoon white vinegar in a measuring cup; add milk to equal 1/4 cup.

Little Chocolate Cake

(Pictured above)

A small chocolate cake can be just as good as a large one. Plus, none of it goes to waste. My husband, Loren, and I love the terrific from-scratch taste and rich chocolate frosting. —Paula Anderson
Springfield, Illinois

  2 squares (1 ounce *each*) unsweetened chocolate
1/2 cup boiling water
  1 cup sugar
1/4 cup shortening
  1 egg
1/2 teaspoon vanilla extract
  1 cup all-purpose flour
1/2 teaspoon baking soda
1/2 teaspoon salt
1/4 cup sour milk*
FROSTING:
1-1/2 cups sugar
1/3 cup milk
  2 squares (1 ounce *each*) unsweetened chocolate, melted
  2 tablespoons shortening
  1 tablespoon light corn syrup
1/4 teaspoon salt
  2 tablespoons butter *or* margarine
  1 teaspoon vanilla extract

In a mixing bowl, stir chocolate and water until blended. Cool. Add the sugar, shortening, egg and vanilla; mix well. Combine flour, baking soda and salt; gradually add to the chocolate mixture alternately with sour milk. Pour into a greased 8-in.

Pot Roast for Two

(Pictured below)

A satisfying pot roast dinner doesn't have to feed an army, as this recipe proves. I love the bold combination of spices in this moist, flavorful meal-in-one dish. —Judy Armstrong, Norwell, Massachusetts

  2 beef eye of round steaks
  2 small carrots, cut into 3/4-inch chunks
  2 small potatoes, peeled and cut into 1/2-inch slices
  1 celery rib, coarsely chopped
  1 small onion, sliced
  1 can (14-1/2 ounces) diced tomatoes, undrained
1/4 cup beef broth
  2 garlic cloves, thinly sliced
  2 teaspoons onion soup mix

1 teaspoon salt
1/2 teaspoon Italian seasoning
1/4 teaspoon pepper
1/8 teaspoon aniseed
1/8 teaspoon *each* ground cinnamon, ginger
    and nutmeg
Dash ground cloves

Place steaks in an ungreased 2-1/2-qt. baking dish. Top with carrots, potatoes, celery and onion. Combine the tomatoes, broth, garlic, soup mix and seasonings; pour over vegetables. Cover and bake at 350° for 1-1/2 to 1-3/4 hours or until meat and vegetables are tender. **Yield:** 2 servings.

— 🗩 🗩 🗩 —

Autumn Pork Chop Dinner

I like to cook for two and try to make just the right amount so I don't have leftovers. With its golden pork chops, tasty green beans and tangy cabbage, this meal-in-one is a favorite of my husband, William.
                    —Cecelia Wilson, Rockville, Connecticut

1 tablespoon vegetable oil
2 loin pork chops (1 inch thick)
2 cups shredded cabbage
1 tablespoon chopped fresh parsley
2 tablespoons brown sugar
2 medium potatoes, peeled and sliced 1/4
    inch thick
1 cup fresh *or* frozen green beans
1 to 1-1/2 teaspoons lemon-pepper
    seasoning
3/4 cup apple juice
1/4 cup seasoned bread crumbs
1 tablespoon butter *or* margarine, melted

In a large skillet, heat the oil over high. Brown chops on both sides; remove and set aside. Toss cabbage with parsley and brown sugar; place in an 11-in. x 7-in. x 2-in. baking dish. Top with potatoes and beans. Arrange chops over vegetables. Sprinkle with lemon-pepper. Pour apple juice over all.

Cover and bake at 350° for 45 minutes or until the pork chops and vegetables are tender. Combine the bread crumbs and butter; sprinkle on top. Bake 15 minutes longer. **Yield:** 2 servings.

Simple Salad

If you're looking for a tasty side dish for dinner, try this pretty change from traditional tossed salad ingredients: lettuce greens with chopped carrot, celery and apple, plus raisins and sliced almonds.

Sesame Chicken Stir-Fry

(Pictured above and on page 204)

When our children were little, my husband frequently worked late. This eye-catching stir-fry was a satisfying dinner for me and the kids.
                    —Michelle McWilliams, Fort Lupton, Colorado

1 boneless skinless chicken breast half, cut
    into thin strips
2 teaspoons vegetable oil
7 snow peas
1 cup broccoli florets
1/3 cup julienned sweet red pepper
3 medium fresh mushrooms, sliced
3/4 cup chopped onion
1 tablespoon cornstarch
1 teaspoon sugar
1/2 cup cold water
3 to 4 tablespoons soy sauce
Hot cooked rice
1 teaspoon sesame seeds, toasted

In a skillet or wok, stir-fry chicken in oil for 6-8 minutes or until juices run clear. Remove chicken and set aside. In the same skillet, stir-fry peas, broccoli and red pepper for 2-3 minutes. Add mushrooms and onion; stir-fry for 3-4 minutes.

Combine cornstarch and sugar; stir in water and soy sauce until smooth. Add to the pan. Bring to a boil; cook and stir for 1-2 minutes or until thickened. Return chicken to the pan; cook until mixture is heated through and vegetables are tender. Serve over rice. Sprinkle with sesame seeds. **Yield:** 1 serving.

'My Mom's Best Meal'

Many delicious memories have been shared by Taste of Home readers who fondly recall their mothers' cooking. Here are eight such stories and the tempting recipes so you, too, can create these treasured meals.

—— 🍳 🍳 🍳 ——

THANKS, MMM-MOM! Clockwise from upper left: Feast Fit for a King (p. 224), Flavorful Fish Dinner (p. 236), Meat-and-Potatoes Meal (p. 228) and Birthday Celebration (p. 240).

*Lively dinnertime
discussions around
the family table
paired perfectly with
Mom's delicious
down-home cooking.*

By Michelle Beran, Claflin, Kansas

I HAVE fond memories of enjoying dinner at home
when I was growing up. There was fun conversation
between my parents, two sisters, brother and me…and
Mom served delectable food.

Mom (Linda Engemann, above) worked hard as a
schoolteacher. So during her busy weeks, she often
prepared casseroles ahead or had dinner simmering in
the slow cooker.

The meal that's still my favorite starts with Mom's
Meat Loaf. Mom frequently fixed this main dish on the
weekend when she had time to put something in the
oven. It's tender and flavorful with a tangy topping
we love.

Cheesy Potato Bake is an excellent, hearty side dish
that goes perfectly with meat loaf. Of course, we loved
these potatoes so much that Mom served them with a
variety of main courses.

A summertime staple on Mom's table is her Cucumbers with Dressing. Now my family asks me to
prepare this dish for our meals together.

Dessert is out of the ordinary and has wonderful old-
fashioned goodness. Purple Plum Pie is one of Mom's
specialties. A big slice of this sweet-tart pie takes me
back to those carefree days at home.

I gained kitchen confidence helping Mom. And
she's inspired me to make dinners for my family special by presenting great food and having good conversation. There are 16 around Mom's table these days,
and dinner there is still a treat!

—— 🥄 🥄 🥄 ——

PICTURED AT LEFT: Mom's Meat Loaf, Cucumbers
with Dressing, Cheesy Potato Bake and Purple
Plum Pie (recipes are on the next page).

Mom's Meat Loaf

Mom made this scrumptious main dish frequently when I was growing up. When I first met my husband, he wasn't fond of meat loaf. This is the first meal I prepared for him, and now he requests it often.

    2 eggs
3/4 cup milk
2/3 cup finely crushed saltines
1/2 cup chopped onion
    1 teaspoon salt
1/2 teaspoon rubbed sage
Dash pepper
1-1/2 pounds lean ground beef
    1 cup ketchup
1/2 cup packed brown sugar
    1 teaspoon Worcestershire sauce

In a large bowl, beat the eggs. Add milk, saltines, onion, salt, sage and pepper. Add beef and mix well. Shape into an 8-1/2-in. x 4-1/2-in. loaf in an ungreased shallow baking pan. Combine remaining ingredients; spread 3/4 cup over meat loaf. Bake at 350° for 60-65 minutes or until no pink remains; drain. Let stand 10 minutes before slicing. Serve with remaining sauce. **Yield:** 6-8 servings.

Cucumbers with Dressing

It wouldn't be summer if Mom didn't make lots of these creamy cucumbers. Just a few simple ingredients—mayonnaise, sugar, vinegar and salt—dress up slices of this crisp garden vegetable.

    1 cup mayonnaise
1/4 cup sugar
1/4 cup cider vinegar
1/4 teaspoon salt
    4 cups sliced cucumbers

In a bowl, combine mayonnaise, sugar, vinegar and salt. Add cucumbers; stir to coat. Cover and refrigerate for 2 hours. **Yield:** 6-8 servings.

Sensational Sugar Tips

Sugar will last almost indefinitely if stored in an airtight container in a cool dry place.

One pound of granulated sugar is equal to 2-1/4 cups.

Make your own colored sugar by putting granulated sugar in a resealable plastic bag with a few drops of food coloring. Knead the sugar in the bag to disperse the color. For a darker color, add a few more drops and repeat the process.

Purchasing Plums

Select plums that are free of blemishes like cracks, soft spots and brown discoloration. The skin's light gray cast is natural and doesn't affect the quality of the fruit.

Cheesy Potato Bake

This saucy side dish satisfies even hearty appetites. It's easy to fix since there's no need to peel the potatoes. The mild, comforting flavor goes nicely with any meat—I especially like it with meat loaf.

    4 large unpeeled baking potatoes
1/4 cup butter *or* margarine
    1 tablespoon grated onion
    1 teaspoon salt
1/2 teaspoon dried thyme
1/8 teaspoon pepper
    1 cup (4 ounces) shredded cheddar cheese
    1 tablespoon chopped fresh parsley

Thinly slice the potatoes and place in a greased shallow 2-qt. baking dish. In a small saucepan, heat butter, onion, salt, thyme and pepper until the butter is melted. Drizzle over potatoes. Cover and bake at 425° for 45 minutes or until tender. Sprinkle with cheese and parsley. Bake, uncovered, 15 minutes longer or until the cheese melts. **Yield:** 6-8 servings.

Purple Plum Pie

I can never resist a tart, tempting slice of this beautiful pie. It's a down-home dessert that makes any meal special. This pie is a terrific way to put bountiful summer plums to good use.

    4 cups sliced fresh plums (about 1-1/2 pounds)
1/2 cup sugar
1/4 cup all-purpose flour
1/4 teaspoon salt
1/4 teaspoon ground cinnamon
    1 tablespoon lemon juice
    1 unbaked deep-dish pastry shell (9 inches)
TOPPING:
1/2 cup sugar
1/2 cup all-purpose flour
1/4 teaspoon ground cinnamon
1/4 teaspoon ground nutmeg
    3 tablespoons cold butter *or* margarine

In a bowl, combine the first six ingredients; pour into the pastry shell. For topping, combine sugar, flour, cinnamon and nutmeg in a small bowl; cut in butter until the mixture resembles coarse crumbs. Sprinkle over filling. Bake at 375° for 50-60 minutes or until bubbly and golden brown. Cover edges of crust with foil during the last 20 minutes to prevent overbrowning. Cool on a wire rack. **Yield:** 8 servings.

***Down-home foods
Mom cooked
on the old
wood-burning
stove made her family
feel just like royalty.***

By Willa Govoro, St. Clair, Missouri

I'M in my 80's, but I still remember so clearly the delicious meals Mom prepared on her old wood-burning stove.

Sunday dinner was always special. Mom (Ellen Gibson, above) set out her good dishes and flatware on the big oak table.

My brother, sister and I couldn't wait to dig into her comforting Chicken and Dumplings, which filled the house with a wonderful aroma while simmering on the back of the stove.

Tender chicken and succulent dumplings are covered with a creamy gravy, while carrots and celery add a little bit of color.

A big bowl of her Old-Fashioned Green Beans got passed around until it was scraped clean. Bacon adds a little zip and brown sugar adds a touch of sweetness. You'll appreciate the short list of ingredients in this reliable recipe.

To round out the meal, Mother's Dinner Rolls were set on the table fresh from the oven. With their wonderfully light texture and slightly sweet dough, we could never eat just one.

For dessert, Mom would present a lovely Orange Dream Cake featuring citrus and coconut. Even full from the hearty meal, we'd still manage to devour thick slices of this refreshing sweet delight.

Although our family didn't have much money back then, Mom always made satisfying and balanced meals. And she instilled in me the joy of cooking for others, which I never lost.

—— 🥄 🥄 🥄 ——

PICTURED AT LEFT: Chicken and Dumplings, Old-Fashioned Green Beans, Mother's Dinner Rolls and Orange Dream Cake (recipes are on the next page).

brown chicken in oil; drain. Place in an 8-qt. Dutch oven. Add celery, carrots, parsley and seasonings. Add enough water to cover chicken; bring to a boil. Reduce heat; cover and simmer until chicken is almost tender, about 45-50 minutes. Remove 1 cup of broth to use for dumplings; cool, then add flour, baking powder and eggs. Mix well to form a stiff batter; drop by tablespoonfuls into simmering broth. Cover and simmer for 15-20 minutes.

Remove chicken and dumplings to a serving dish and keep warm. For gravy, remove 4 cups broth and vegetables to a large saucepan; bring to a boil. Combine flour and water; mix well. Stir into vegetable mixture. Cook over medium heat, stirring constantly, until thickened and bubbly. Pour over chicken and dumplings. Serve immediately. **Yield:** 6-8 servings.

Editor's Note: Any remaining chicken broth can be frozen for future use.

—— 🍷 🍷 🍷 ——

Old-Fashioned Green Beans

Mom would prepare homegrown green beans using this recipe, and did they taste good. The bacon adds rich flavor and the brown sugar a touch of sweetness.

   6 **bacon strips, cut into 1/2-inch pieces**
   2 **pounds fresh green beans**
   3 **tablespoons brown sugar**
1/2 **cup water**

In a large skillet, cook bacon over medium heat until crisp-tender, about 5 minutes. Add beans, brown sugar and water. Stir gently; bring to a boil. Reduce heat; cover and simmer for 15 minutes or until beans are crisp-tender. Remove to a serving bowl with a slotted spoon. **Yield:** 6-8 servings.

Chicken and Dumplings

On Sundays, Mom set our big round oak table with a snowy white cloth and her fine dishes and tableware. On the old woodstove, pushed way back to simmer slowly, was a big pot of chicken and dumplings in a thick gravy. I can still taste it.

   1 **cup all-purpose flour**
   2 **broiler/fryer chickens (2-1/2 to 3 pounds** *each***), cut up**
   2 **tablespoons vegetable oil**
   3 **celery ribs, cut into 1-inch pieces**
   3 **medium carrots, cut into 1-inch pieces**
1/4 **cup chopped fresh parsley**
   2 **teaspoons salt**
   1 **teaspoon garlic powder**
   1 **teaspoon dried thyme**
1/2 **teaspoon pepper**
   8 to 12 **cups water**
DUMPLINGS:
   2 **cups all-purpose flour**
   2 **teaspoons baking powder**
   2 **eggs, beaten**
GRAVY:
1/4 **cup all-purpose flour**
1/2 **cup water**

Place flour in a bowl or bag; add the chicken pieces and dredge or shake to coat. In a large skillet,

Orange Dream Cake

We tried to save room for a big slice of this pretty cake. The flavor of orange and lemon really comes through. This cake is a delightful end to a terrific meal.

> 2/3 cup butter *or* margarine, softened
> 1-1/3 cups sugar
> 2/3 cup fresh orange juice
> 3 tablespoons fresh lemon juice
> 1 teaspoon grated orange peel
> 1 teaspoon grated lemon peel
> 2 eggs
> 2 cups cake flour
> 2 teaspoons baking powder
> 1 teaspoon salt

FROSTING:

> 1 cup flaked coconut
> 1/4 cup sugar
> 2 tablespoons fresh orange juice
> 1 tablespoon fresh lemon juice
> 4 teaspoons grated orange peel, *divided*
> 1 cup whipping cream, whipped

In a large mixing bowl, cream butter and sugar. Add juices and peel; mix well (mixture may appear curdled). Add eggs, one at a time, beating well after each addition. Sift flour with baking powder and salt; add to creamed mixture and mix well. Pour into two greased and floured 8-in. cake pans. Bake at 375° for 25-30 minutes or until cake tests done. Cool in pans for 10 minutes before removing to a wire rack to cool completely.

For frosting, combine coconut, sugar, juices and 3 teaspoons orange peel; mix well. Let stand for 10-15 minutes or until sugar is dissolved. Fold in whipped cream. Spread between cake layers and over the top. Sprinkle with remaining orange peel. Chill for at least 1 hour. Store in the refrigerator. **Yield:** 10-12 servings.

Mother's Dinner Rolls

These tender rolls will melt in your mouth. Mom would set out her big square-footed honey bowl with them— some sweet butter and a drizzle of honey on these rolls is a special treat.

> 2 packages (1/4 ounce *each*) active dry yeast
> 1 cup warm water (110° to 115°)
> 1 cup boiling water
> 1 cup shortening
> 3/4 cup sugar
> 1 teaspoon salt
> 2 eggs, beaten
> 7-1/2 to 8 cups all-purpose flour

In a small bowl, dissolve yeast in warm water. Meanwhile, in a large mixing bowl, combine boiling water, shortening, sugar and salt. Let stand 3-4 minutes or until shortening is melted and sugar is dissolved. Add yeast mixture and eggs; mix well. Add 2 cups of flour; beat until smooth. Add enough remaining flour to form a soft dough (do not knead). Place in a greased bowl, turning once to grease top. Cover and refrigerate overnight.

Turn dough onto a floured surface. Pinch off a piece and form a 2-1/2-in. ball. Roll into a 5-in. rope; shape into a knot. Repeat with remaining dough. Place on a greased baking sheet. Cover and let rise in a warm place until doubled, about 30 minutes. Bake at 350° for 20-25 minutes or until golden brown. **Yield:** 2-1/2 dozen.

Her mom's reputation among family and friends for making terrific beef roasts has been relished—and unrivaled —for decades.

By Linda Gaido, New Brighton, Pennsylvania

FOR YEARS, Mom has had a reputation among family and friends for making the very best roast beef. And that honor still stands today.

Mom was one of those people born to be a good cook. She rarely measures anything, and everything she makes tastes wonderful.

When my two older sisters and I were growing up, the house smelled simply heavenly on those chilly fall days when Mom's Roast Beef was cooking on the stovetop.

People always ask Mom what her secret ingredients are. And they're surprised to hear that the rich flavor comes from brewed coffee! Hard as I try to follow Mom's recipe step-by-step, I can never make it taste exactly like hers.

To make Country Green Beans, Mom added garlic, chopped ham and onion. These additions blend so well with the beans and really complement the beef.

The melt-in-your-mouth Oven-Roasted Potatoes round out this meat-and-potatoes meal. They're also convenient because they can share the oven with the Baked Apples Slices.

Mom enjoyed serving this updated version of baked apples over cool, creamy vanilla ice cream. But you could also top individual servings with whipped cream. It's an easy recipe to double when cooking for more people.

Mom and I are now thrilled to pass on the treasured family recipes for this warm, satisfying meal to you and your family. Why not give these dishes a try when cooler weather has you craving hearty old-fashioned foods?

— ☕ ☕ ☕ —

PICTURED AT LEFT: Mom's Roast Beef, Oven-Roasted Potatoes, Country Green Beans and Baked Apple Slices (recipes are on the next page).

Mom's Roast Beef

Everyone loves slices of this fork-tender roast beef and its savory gravy. This well-seasoned roast is Mom's specialty. People always ask what her secret ingredients are. Now you know the secret of what makes this our favorite meat dish!

     1 tablespoon vegetable oil
     1 eye of round beef roast (about 2-1/2 pounds)
     1 medium onion, chopped
     1 cup brewed coffee
     1 cup water, *divided*
     1 beef bouillon cube
     2 teaspoons dried basil
     1 teaspoon dried rosemary, crushed
     1 garlic clove, minced
     1 teaspoon salt
   1/2 teaspoon pepper
   1/4 cup all-purpose flour

Heat oil in a Dutch oven; brown roast on all sides. Add onion and cook until transparent. Add coffee, 3/4 cup water, bouillon, basil, rosemary, garlic, salt and pepper. Cover and simmer for 2-1/2

hours or until meat is tender. Combine flour and remaining water until smooth; stir into pan juices. Cook and stir until thickened and bubbly. Remove roast and slice. Pass the gravy. **Yield:** 8 servings.

— ☕ ☕ ☕ —

Oven-Roasted Potatoes

These golden, melt-in-your-mouth potatoes go perfectly with roast beef. With only five ingredients, they're easy to make. They make a homey side dish that's also convenient because they can share the oven with the baked apple slices Mom serves for dessert.

     4 baking potatoes (about 2 pounds)
     2 tablespoons butter *or* margarine, melted
     2 teaspoons paprika
     1 teaspoon salt
   1/2 teaspoon pepper

Peel potatoes and cut into large chunks; place in a shallow 2-qt. baking pan. Pour butter over and toss until well coated. Sprinkle with paprika, salt and pepper. Bake, uncovered, at 350° for 45-60 minutes or until potatoes are tender. **Yield:** 4 servings.

Good Gravy

To avoid lumps in your gravy, whisk the hot liquid rapidly as you gradually add the flour-based paste to the hot liquid.

For a little richer color and flavor, stir in a teaspoon or two of instant coffee granules or unsweetened baking cocoa.

When preparing a big family dinner, make your gravy as usual and then keep it warm on the low setting in a slow cooker. With this simple strategy, it's easy to refill the gravy boat with hot gravy throughout the meal.

Country Green Beans

This deliciously different way to dress up green beans is sure to become a family favorite at your house, too. The garlic, chopped ham and onion blend so well with the beans. It's a beautiful and tasty side dish that has real country appeal.

      1 pound fresh green beans, trimmed
  1/4 cup chopped onion
  1/4 cup chopped fully cooked ham
  1/4 cup butter *or* margarine
  1/4 cup water
      1 garlic clove, minced
  1/2 teaspoon salt
  1/4 teaspoon pepper

In a saucepan, combine all ingredients. Cover and simmer for 15-20 minutes or until beans are tender. **Yield:** 4 servings.

— 🏺 🏺 🏺 —

Baked Apple Slices

Nothing beats these warm tender apple slices over ice cream for satisfying harvest flavor. This old-fashioned treat gives a new twist to traditional baked apples. They are also excellent served over waffles or with ham. I make sure to save room for dessert when this is the featured finale!

      3 large baking apples, peeled and sliced
  3/4 cup sugar
      1 tablespoon ground cinnamon
  1/4 teaspoon ground nutmeg
  1/4 teaspoon ground ginger
  1/4 cup apple cider
  1/2 cup butter *or* margarine
  1/2 cup walnuts *or* raisins
Vanilla ice cream

Place apples in a greased 1-qt. baking dish. Combine sugar, cinnamon, nutmeg, ginger and apple cider; pour over apples. Dot with butter. Sprinkle with nuts or raisins. Bake, uncovered, at 350° for 45-60 minutes or until apples are tender. Serve warm over ice cream. **Yield:** 4 servings.

A love of cooking—and of each other's company—led to some special moments in the kitchen for a mother and her teenage daughter.

By Gina Squires, Salem, Oregon

MY MOM is a terrific cook who has inspired me to love working in the kitchen, too.

Ever since I was little, I've enjoyed being with Mom (Shirlee, above) when she's cooking. Over the years, she's patiently shared her skills with me. Now I enjoy making and serving complete meals for her, Dad, my older sister and brother-in-law.

Mom's Lasagna has always been my favorite main dish. It's a meaty and cheesy entree with a rich flavor and lots of zip. This is the best lasagna I've ever tasted and my mother's most-requested recipe.

For as long as I can remember, she has served her hearty lasagna with crisp Three-Green Salad and zesty homemade Italian dressing. This salad is chock-full of crisp and colorful vegetables. The dressing is wonderfully fresh tasting.

She also serves Cheesy Garlic Bread. These crunchy tempting slices have a bold garlic flavor. I can never eat just one piece!

For dessert, Fluffy Pineapple Torte is a light treat that's a nice balance to this meaty main course—the perfect end to this satisfying meal. The best part is you can make it the night before, since it needs time to chill anyway.

I think Mom and I make a great team in the kitchen these days. We're excited to share our special meal with you. We hope your family will enjoy this memorable down-home menu as much as ours does.

— 🍴 🍴 🍴 —

PICTURED AT LEFT: Mom's Lasagna, Three-Green Salad, Cheesy Garlic Bread and Fluffy Pineapple Torte (recipes are on the next page.)

In a large kettle or Dutch oven, cook beef, sausage and onion until the meat is browned and onion is tender; drain. Stir in the next 10 ingredients. Simmer, uncovered, for 3 hours, stirring occasionally.

Meanwhile, cook lasagna noodles according to package directions; drain and rinse in cold water. In a greased 13-in. x 9-in. x 2-in. baking dish, layer a third of the noodles and meat sauce, half of the cottage cheese, a third of the mozzarella and a third of the Parmesan. Repeat layers. Top with remaining noodles, meat sauce, mozzarella and Parmesan. Cover and bake at 350° for 45 minutes; uncover and bake for 20 minutes. Let stand 20 minutes before cutting. **Yield:** 12 servings.

Mom's Lasagna

We can hardly wait to dig into this cheesy, meaty lasagna. It smells great when baking and tastes even better! Watching Mom carefully make this wonderful main dish and hearing the raves she gets inspired me to learn to cook.

- 1/2 **pound ground beef**
- 1/2 **pound bulk Italian sausage**
- 1 **large onion, chopped**
- 3 **garlic cloves, minced**
- 1 **can (28 ounces) crushed tomatoes, undrained**
- 1 **can (6 ounces) tomato paste**
- 1-1/2 **cups water**
- 1 **cup salsa**
- 2 **teaspoons sugar**
- 1 to 2 **teaspoons chili powder**
- 1 **teaspoon fennel seed**
- 1 **teaspoon dried oregano**
- 1 **teaspoon dried basil**
- 9 **lasagna noodles**
- 1 **carton (16 ounces) cottage cheese**
- 4 **cups (1 pound) shredded mozzarella cheese**
- 3/4 **cup grated Parmesan cheese**

Three-Green Salad

For a crisp, refreshing side dish, this tasty salad can't be beat. The bold flavor and crunch really wake up your taste buds. It goes perfectly with lasagna or any hearty main dish.

- 4 **cups torn iceberg lettuce**
- 4 **cups torn leaf lettuce**
- 4 **cups torn fresh spinach**
- 1 **medium cucumber, sliced**
- 2 **carrots, sliced**
- 2 **celery ribs, sliced**
- 6 **broccoli florets, sliced**
- 3 **cauliflowerets, sliced**
- 6 **radishes, sliced**
- 4 **green onions, sliced**
- 5 **fresh mushrooms, sliced**

ITALIAN DRESSING:
- 2/3 **cup olive *or* vegetable oil**
- 1/4 **cup plus 2 tablespoons red wine vinegar *or* cider vinegar**

  2 tablespoons grated Parmesan cheese
  1 teaspoon sugar
  1 to 2 garlic cloves, minced
  1/4 teaspoon dried oregano
  1/4 teaspoon dried basil
Pinch salt and pepper

In a large salad bowl, toss the greens and vegetables. Cover and chill. Combine all dressing ingredients in a blender; process for 30 seconds. Pour into a jar with tight-fitting lid; chill for at least 30 minutes. Shake dressing before serving; pour desired amount over salad and toss. **Yield:** 12 servings (about 1 cup dressing).

Cheesy Garlic Bread

Some garlic breads taste more like buttered toast. Not this one—the fresh garlic flavor really comes through. Parmesan cheese on top turns golden brown in the broiler. I enjoy the crunch of the crisp crust.

  1/2 cup butter *or* margarine, softened
  4 garlic cloves, minced
  1/4 teaspoon dried oregano
  1 loaf (1 pound) French bread, halved
    lengthwise
  3 tablespoons grated Parmesan cheese

In a small bowl, combine the butter, garlic and oregano; spread on cut sides of bread. Sprinkle with Parmesan cheese. Place on an ungreased baking sheet. Broil for 3 minutes or until golden brown. Slice and serve hot. **Yield:** 12 servings.

Fluffy Pineapple Torte

This fluffy dessert is so good after a hearty meal because even a big slice is as light as a feather. The cream cheese-pineapple combination makes it absolutely irresistible.

1-1/2 cups graham cracker crumbs
  1/4 cup butter *or* margarine, melted
    2 tablespoons sugar
FILLING:
    1 can (12 ounces) evaporated milk
    1 package (3 ounces) lemon gelatin
    1 cup boiling water
    1 package (8 ounces) cream cheese, softened
  1/2 cup sugar
    1 can (8 ounces) crushed pineapple, drained
    1 cup chopped walnuts, *divided*

Combine crumbs, butter and sugar; press into the bottom of a 13-in. x 9-in. x 2-in. baking dish. Bake at 325° for 10 minutes; cool. Pour evaporated milk into a metal mixing bowl. Add the mixer beaters. Cover and chill bowl and beaters for at least 2 hours. Meanwhile, in a small bowl, dissolve gelatin in water; chill until syrupy, about 30 minutes. Remove milk from refrigerator and beat until stiff peaks form.

In a large mixing bowl, beat cream cheese and sugar until smooth. Add gelatin; mix well. Stir in pineapple and 3/4 cup walnuts. Fold in milk. Pour over crust. Chill for at least 3 hours or overnight. Sprinkle remaining walnuts over the top before filling is completely firm. **Yield:** 12 servings.

Compliments on her own meals are credited to Mom—a welcoming cook who draws folks into the best spot in the house...the kitchen.

By Lisa Kivirist, Browntown, Wisconsin

WHEN GUESTS in our home compliment me on a great meal, I share some of the credit with my mom (Aelita Kivirist, above, of Glenview, Illinois). She's my inspiration in the kitchen.

I could put together a cookbook of all Mom's recipes we enjoy, but this savory and satisfying meal is my personal favorite.

When my husband, John Ivanko, and I visit my parents, Mom often prepares her light and flaky Lemon Grilled Salmon.

In the 1950s, Mom emigrated from Latvia, where dill is a popular seasoning. It certainly tastes wonderful on this salmon. We savor every bite.

Cottage Cheese Spinach Salad is a unique take-off on a traditional spinach salad. Everyone who tries it comments on the unusual (and pleasing) combination of ingredients.

Herbed Oven Potatoes have a delightful onion and herb flavor. These seasoned potatoes are easy to make since there's no peeling required. I'm always sure to help myself to a big serving.

We all save room for a creamy slice of Frozen Mocha Torte. It's surprisingly simple to make and never lasts long at gatherings.

Mom has a talent for making guests feel welcome. She's warm and cheerful as she dances around the kitchen putting the finishing touches on a meal.

She laughs when everyone crowds around the counter as she works instead of sitting in comfortable living room chairs just a few steps away.

They've discovered what I've known for many years—the best spot in the house is the kitchen when Mom's cooking.

PICTURED AT LEFT: Lemon Grilled Salmon, Cottage Cheese Spinach Salad, Herbed Oven Potatoes and Frozen Mocha Torte (recipes are on the next page).

arrange lemon and onion slices over the top. Cover and cook for 15-20 minutes or until fish flakes easily with a fork. **Yield:** 6 servings.

Nutritional Analysis: One serving (prepared with salt-free lemon-pepper seasoning and light soy sauce and without salt) equals 199 calories, 181 mg sodium, 68 mg cholesterol, 7 g carbohydrate, 22 g protein, 9 g fat. **Diabetic Exchanges:** 3 lean meat, 1 vegetable.

Editor's Note: Salmon can be broiled instead of grilled. Place the fillet on a greased broiler pan. Broil 3-4 in. from the heat for 6-8 minutes or until fish flakes easily with a fork.

Lemon Grilled Salmon

Mom proudly serves this tender, flaky fish to family and guests. A savory marinade that includes dill gives the salmon mouth-watering flavor. Since it can be grilled or broiled, we enjoy it year-round.

✓ Uses less fat, sugar or salt. Includes Nutritional Analysis and Diabetic Exchanges.

- 2 **teaspoons snipped fresh dill** *or* **3/4 teaspoon dill weed**
- 1/2 **teaspoon lemon-pepper seasoning**
- 1/2 **teaspoon salt, optional**
- 1/4 **teaspoon garlic powder**
- 1 **salmon fillet (1-1/2 pounds)**
- 1/4 **cup packed brown sugar**
- 3 **tablespoons chicken broth**
- 3 **tablespoons vegetable oil**
- 3 **tablespoons soy sauce**
- 3 **tablespoons finely chopped green onions**
- 1 **small lemon, thinly sliced**
- 2 **onion slices, separated into rings**

Sprinkle dill, lemon-pepper, salt if desired and garlic powder over salmon. Place in a large resealable plastic bag or shallow glass container. Combine brown sugar, broth, oil, soy sauce and green onions; pour over salmon. Cover and refrigerate for 1 hour, turning once. Drain and discard marinade. Place salmon skin side down on grill over medium heat;

Cottage Cheese Spinach Salad

Even folks who don't care for spinach enjoy this distinctive salad. The creamy dressing is slightly sweet, and cottage cheese assures that this dish is extra hearty and satisfying.

- 1 **package (10 ounces) fresh spinach, torn**
- 1-1/2 **cups (12 ounces) small-curd cottage cheese**
- 1/2 **cup chopped pecans, toasted**
- 1/2 **cup sugar**
- 3 **tablespoons vinegar**
- 2 **teaspoons prepared horseradish**
- 1/2 **teaspoon salt**
- 1/2 **teaspoon ground mustard**

In a large serving bowl, layer half of the spinach, cottage cheese and pecans. Repeat layers. In a small bowl, combine the remaining ingredients. Drizzle over salad and toss to coat. Serve immediately. **Yield:** 10 servings.

Herbed Oven Potatoes

Mom loves to use the fresh new potatoes my husband, John, and I share from our garden for this yummy recipe. The well-seasoned potato chunks are an excellent side dish for fish, poultry or meat. It's easy to make since there's no peeling required.

- 1/2 cup olive *or* vegetable oil
- 1/4 cup butter *or* margarine, melted
- 1 envelope onion soup mix
- 1 teaspoon dried thyme
- 1 teaspoon dried marjoram
- 1/4 teaspoon pepper
- 2 pounds red potatoes, quartered

Minced fresh parsley

In a shallow bowl, combine the first six ingredients. Add potatoes, a few at a time; toss to coat. Place in a single layer in a greased 15-in. x 10-in. x 1-in. baking pan. Drizzle with remaining oil mixture. Bake, uncovered, at 450° for 50-55 minutes or until tender, stirring occasionally. Sprinkle with parsley. **Yield:** 6 servings.

Frozen Mocha Torte

For an easy, make-ahead dessert that's elegant and luscious, try this recipe that Mom has used for years. The perfect blend of mocha and chocolate is in each cool refreshing slice. It never lasts long in the freezer.

- 1-1/4 cups chocolate wafer crumbs (about 24 wafers), *divided*
- 1/4 cup sugar
- 1/4 cup butter *or* margarine, melted
- 1 package (8 ounces) cream cheese, softened
- 1 can (14 ounces) sweetened condensed milk
- 2/3 cup chocolate syrup
- 2 tablespoons instant coffee granules
- 1 tablespoon hot water
- 1 cup whipping cream, whipped

Chocolate-covered coffee beans, optional

Combine 1 cup wafer crumbs, sugar and butter. Press onto the bottom and 1 in. up the sides of a greased 9-in. springform pan; set aside. In a mixing bowl, beat cream cheese, milk and chocolate syrup until smooth. Dissolve coffee granules in hot water; add to cream cheese mixture. Fold in whipped cream. Pour over crust. Sprinkle with remaining crumbs. Cover and freeze for 8 hours or overnight.

Uncover and remove from the freezer 10-15 minutes before serving. Garnish with coffee beans if desired. **Yield:** 10-12 servings.

Memorable birthday meal Mom prepared has become a much-requested supper throughout the year in her daughter's family.

By Karen Wingate, Coldwater, Kansas

WHEN I think of my mom's cooking, one specific menu pops into my mind.

It's the meal I requested for my birthday in my teen years…and the spread I missed most when graduate school took me 2,000 miles from home.

The meal, still a standby, starts with Crispy Baked Chicken, which Mom (Arlene Wise, above) serves with baked potatoes. The golden coating keeps this chicken remarkably moist as it bakes. It's also wonderfully seasoned.

Her Zucchini Santa Fe, a zippy side dish made with garden vegetables, is so good with the chicken. This recipe and others Mom makes reflect her background as a third-generation Arizonian. Her cooking style revolves around the hot climate and influences from pioneer and Mexican cultures.

A frugal cook, Mom has a knack for making plain foods taste wonderful using fresh ingredients and whole grains, like her flavorful Wholesome Wheat Bread. These tall lovely loaves have delicious old-fashioned flavor and a tender texture.

Mom's Strawberry Shortcake is the best. We love the sweet spongy cake, rather than the typical dry shortcake.

Now I make this memorable meal, too, for husband Jack, a minister, and our two daughters, Katherine and Christine.

I hope you enjoy this meal as much as we do. It's truly a taste of home.

🥄 🥄 🥄

PICTURED AT LEFT: Crispy Baked Chicken, Wholesome Wheat Bread, Zucchini Santa Fe and Mom's Strawberry Shortcake (recipes are on the next page).

Crispy Baked Chicken

My siblings and I couldn't wait to sit down to supper when Mom was making this delicious chicken. The cornmeal in the coating gives each juicy golden piece a wonderful crunch.

- 1/2 **cup cornmeal**
- 1/2 **cup all-purpose flour**
- 1-1/2 **teaspoons salt**
- 1-1/2 **teaspoons chili powder**
- 1/2 **teaspoon dried oregano**
- 1/4 **teaspoon pepper**
- 1 **broiler/fryer chicken (3 to 3-1/2 pounds), cut up**
- 1/2 **cup milk**
- 1/3 **cup butter** *or* **margarine, melted**

Combine the first six ingredients. Dip chicken in milk, then roll in the cornmeal mixture. Place in a greased 13-in. x 9-in. x 2-in. baking pan. Drizzle with butter. Bake, uncovered, at 375° for 50-55 minutes or until juices run clear. **Yield:** 4-6 servings.

Wholesome Wheat Bread

My sister and I were in 4-H, and Mom was our breads project leader for years. Because of that early training, fresh homemade bread like this is a staple in my own kitchen.

✓ Uses less fat, sugar or salt. Includes Nutritional Analysis and Diabetic Exchanges.

- 2 **packages (1/4 ounce** *each***) active dry yeast**
- 2-1/4 **cups warm water (110° to 115°)**
- 3 **tablespoons sugar**
- 1/3 **cup butter** *or* **margarine, softened**
- 1/3 **cup honey**
- 1/2 **cup instant nonfat dry milk powder**
- 1 **tablespoon salt**
- 4-1/2 **cups whole wheat flour**
- 2-3/4 **to 3-1/2 cups all-purpose flour**

In a large mixing bowl, dissolve yeast in water. Add sugar, butter, honey, milk powder, salt and whole wheat flour; beat until smooth. Add enough all-purpose flour to form a soft dough. Turn onto a floured board; knead until smooth and elastic, about 10 minutes. Place in a greased bowl, turning once to grease top. Cover and let rise in a warm place until doubled, about 1 hour.

Punch down. Shape dough into traditional loaves or divide into fourths and roll each portion into a 15-in. rope. Twist two ropes together. Place in greased 9-in. x 5-in. x 3-in. loaf pans. Cover and let rise until doubled, about 30 minutes. Bake at 375° for 25-30 minutes. Remove from pans to cool on wire racks. **Yield:** 2 loaves (32 slices).

Nutritional Analysis: One slice (prepared with margarine) equals 144 calories, 239 mg sodium, 0 cholesterol, 27 g carbohydrate, 4 g protein, 2 g fat. **Diabetic Exchange:** 2 starch.

— 🍴 🍴 🍴 —

Zucchini Santa Fe

This summer side dish gets lots of zip from chopped green chilies—a popular flavor around Mom's Arizona home. It's a tasty way to use up garden vegetables.

☑ Uses less fat, sugar or salt. Includes Nutritional Analysis and Diabetic Exchanges.

    3 cups sliced zucchini
    1/2 cup chopped onion
    1 tablespoon vegetable oil
    1 can (4 ounces) chopped green chilies,
      drained
    1 medium tomato, chopped
    1/2 teaspoon salt, optional
    1/4 teaspoon pepper
    1/4 teaspoon garlic powder
    1/2 cup shredded cheddar *or* Monterey Jack
      cheese

In a large skillet, saute the zucchini and onion in oil for 3-4 minutes or until crisp-tender. Add chilies, tomato, salt if desired, pepper and garlic powder. Cook and stir for 3-4 minutes. Spoon into a serving bowl and sprinkle with cheese. **Yield:** 6 servings.

Nutritional Analysis: One 1/2-cup serving (prepared without salt) equals 58 calories, 60 mg sodium, 2 mg cholesterol, 5 g carbohydrate, 3 g protein, 3 g fat. **Diabetic Exchanges:** 1 vegetable, 1 fat.

Mom's Strawberry Shortcake

When I was growing up, Mom sometimes experimented with different dessert recipes, but this tried-and-true spongy shortcake was always great just the way it was. It melted in my mouth!

    2 eggs
    1-1/2 cups sugar, *divided*
    1 cup all-purpose flour
    1 teaspoon baking powder
    1/4 teaspoon salt
    1/2 cup milk
    1 tablespoon butter *or* margarine
    1 teaspoon vanilla extract
    1 to 1-1/2 quarts fresh strawberries, sliced
Whipped cream
Mint leaves, optional

In a mixing bowl, beat the eggs on medium speed for 3 minutes. Gradually add 1 cup sugar, beating until thick and lemon-colored. Combine the flour, baking powder and salt; beat into egg mixture. Heat the milk and butter just until butter begins to melt. Beat into batter with vanilla (batter will be thin). Pour into a greased 8-in. square baking pan. Bake at 350° for 25 minutes or until a toothpick inserted near the center comes out clean. Cool for at least 10 minutes.

Just before serving, cut cake into serving-size pieces; cut each slice in half horizontally. Combine strawberries and remaining sugar. Spoon strawberries between cake layers and over the top of each serving. Top with whipped cream; garnish with mint leaves if desired. **Yield:** 9 servings.

After working hard on the farm each Saturday morning, kids looked forward to Mom's home-style menu featuring a hearty meatball stew.

By Teresa Ingebrand, Perham, Minnesota

GROWING UP on a farm, we never were afforded the luxury of sleeping in on Saturday mornings. Instead, they meant a lot of hard work both inside and out.

But one thing all seven of us looked forward to was this fit-for-a-king midday meal prepared by Mom (Odilia Riestenberg, above, of Elizabeth, Minnesota).

Her Meatball Stew was a favorite main dish at our house, especially during the cold winter months. We delighted in the aroma of the stew simmering on the stove as we came in for dinner. Mom liked that it was simple to prepare and that it satisfied all of our hearty appetites.

Like most cooks of her day, Mom was always looking for ways to use up leftovers. Older bread was never thrown away...it got recycled into Quick Garlic Toast. It never seemed like a leftover to us—we thought it was a special treat!

Sweet and tangy, Mom's Coleslaw went so well with the stew and bread. It can be made in advance, giving you more time to complete other chores around the house or cook up another treat in the kitchen.

We didn't have dessert at every meal, but when Mom asked for suggestions, Chocolate Marshmallow Cake is what we usually requested. It was very difficult to stop at one piece.

Now Mom and Dad are semi-retired (I don't think farmers ever really retire). Mom grows flowers for dried floral arrangements, and she still invites us to dinner once in a while.

I learned most of what I know about cooking from her. As a homemaker with three children, I frequently turn to Mom's recipes like these. We hope your family will enjoy them, too.

PICTURED AT LEFT: Meatball Stew, Quick Garlic Toast, Mom's Coleslaw and Chocolate Marshmallow Cake (recipes are on the next page).

Meatball Stew

The combination of tender meatballs plus potatoes, carrots and pearl onions in a golden gravy really hit the spot on chilly days after we'd worked up an appetite doing our morning chores. Mom served it with pride for Saturday dinners when I was growing up on the farm.

       1 egg, beaten
       1 cup soft bread crumbs
   1/4 cup finely chopped onion
       1 teaspoon salt
       1 teaspoon dried marjoram
   1/2 teaspoon dried thyme
1-1/2 pounds ground beef
       2 tablespoons vegetable oil
       2 cans (14-1/2 ounces *each*) beef broth
       2 cans (10-3/4 ounces *each*) condensed
           golden mushroom soup, undiluted
       4 medium potatoes, peeled and
           quartered
       4 medium carrots, cut into chunks
       1 jar (16 ounces) whole pearl onions,
           drained
   1/4 cup minced fresh parsley

In a bowl, combine egg, bread crumbs, chopped onion, salt, marjoram and thyme. Add beef and mix well. Shape into 48 meatballs. In a Dutch oven, brown meatballs in oil; drain. Add broth, soup, potatoes, carrots and pearl onions; bring to a boil. Reduce heat; simmer for 30 minutes or until the vegetables are tender. Sprinkle with parsley. **Yield:** 8 servings.

Mom's Coleslaw

Year-round, our family always goes for this crisp, refreshing salad. With a tangy vinegar and oil dressing, it has wonderful homemade flavor. When Mom made it years ago for our family of seven, it was rare to have leftovers.

       1 large head cabbage, shredded
       2 medium carrots, shredded
       1 teaspoon celery seed
       1 cup vegetable oil
       1 cup sugar
   1/2 cup white vinegar
       1 teaspoon salt
       1 teaspoon ground mustard
       1 medium onion, quartered

In a large bowl, toss cabbage, carrots and celery seed. Place the remaining ingredients in a blender or food processor; cover and process until combined. Pour over cabbage mixture and toss to coat. Cover and refrigerate for at least 2 hours. Serve with a slotted spoon. **Yield:** 10-12 servings.

Quick Garlic Toast

Mom knew how to easily round out a meal with this crisp, cheesy garlic toast. We gobbled it up when she served it alongside slaw or salad...and used it to soak up gravy from her stew, too.

- **1/3 cup butter *or* margarine, softened**
- **12 slices bread**
- **1/2 teaspoon garlic salt**
- **3 tablespoons grated Parmesan cheese**

Spread butter on one side of each slice of bread. Cut each slice in half; place plain side down on a baking sheet. Sprinkle with garlic salt and Parmesan cheese. Broil 4 in. from the heat for 1-2 minutes or until lightly browned. **Yield:** 12 slices.

— ▼ ▼ ▼ —

Chocolate Marshmallow Cake

When Mom wanted to treat us to something special, she made this awesome dessert. We could never resist the tender chocolate cake, the fluffy marshmallow layer or the fudge topping.

- **1/2 cup butter (no substitutes)**
- **2 squares (1 ounce *each*) unsweetened chocolate**
- **1 cup all-purpose flour**
- **1/2 teaspoon baking powder**
- **1/4 teaspoon baking soda**
- **1/4 teaspoon salt**
- **2 eggs**
- **1 cup sugar**
- **1/2 cup unsweetened applesauce**
- **1 teaspoon vanilla extract**
- **1 package (10-1/2 ounces) miniature marshmallows, *divided***

GLAZE:
- **1/2 cup sugar**
- **2 tablespoons milk**
- **2 tablespoons butter**
- **1/4 cup semisweet chocolate chips**

In a microwave or double boiler, melt butter and chocolate; cool for 10 minutes. Combine the flour, baking powder, baking soda and salt; set aside. In a mixing bowl, beat eggs, sugar, applesauce and vanilla. Stir in chocolate mixture. Add dry ingredients; mix well. Pour into a greased 13-in. x 9-in. x 2-in. baking pan. Bake at 350° for 20-30 minutes or until cake tests done.

Set aside 1/2 cup marshmallows for glaze. Sprinkle remaining marshmallows over cake. Return to the oven for 2 minutes or until marshmallows are softened. In a saucepan, combine sugar, milk and butter. Bring to a boil; boil for 1-1/2 minutes. Remove from the heat; stir in chocolate chips and reserved marshmallows until melted. Quickly drizzle over the cake (glaze will harden as it cools). **Yield:** 12-16 servings.

Marvelous Marshmallows

To keep marshmallows from turning hard, store them in the freezer. If marshmallows are already hard, tightly seal them in a plastic bag with a few slices of fresh white bread and let stand for 3 days. They'll be like fresh.

*The feeling of being
in Mom's kitchen is
recaptured, though
she lives far away,
by preparing these
special recipes.*

By Becky Brunette, Minneapolis, Minnesota

I TREASURE the memory of growing up and having a home-cooked meal every evening...and enjoying extravagant feasts for the holidays.

My mom, Julie Brunette (above, of Green Bay, Wisconsin), is well-known as a wonderful cook and baker. Her talent has long been appreciated by more than just my dad, my brother, Nick, and me. She is a super hostess and shares wonderful foods for many gatherings.

Mom often used to make a little extra for supper in case our friends just happened to stop by. When I went away to college, her cooking was one of the things I missed the most.

Our Christmas dinners have always been a collection of our family's favorite recipes, including Rice-Stuffed Cornish Hens.

The golden hens are stuffed with a flavorful dressing made from scratch with wild rice and savory pork sausage (just as Mom learned from her mother) and topped with a fruity glaze.

Christmas Wreath Salad is a festive and colorful gelatin side dish that looks as good as it tastes.

Green beans are one of the most-requested vegetables in our family...and Mom's recipe for Crunchy Green Beans makes them taste even better.

But we make sure to save room for dessert when Mom is baking her yummy Pistachio Cake.

Since I live a distance away now, I can't just pop in for one of my mom's dinners. Recipes like these are truly a taste of home for me. Mom and I hope you enjoy them, too.

PICTURED AT LEFT: Rice-Stuffed Cornish Hens, Christmas Wreath Salad, Crunchy Green Beans and Pistachio Cake (recipes are on next page).

In a small saucepan, bring preserves and remaining water to a boil. Pour over hens. Bake 35-40 minutes longer, basting occasionally, until a meat thermometer reads 180° for hens and 160° for stuffing. Place baking dish of stuffing in the oven for the last 35-40 minutes of hens' baking time. **Yield:** 6 servings.

Christmas Wreath Salad

It's a jolly holiday when Mom makes this cool eye-catching gelatin salad. Pecans, pineapple and maraschino cherries are sweet surprises in every serving of this side dish. It looks so pretty on the table, we can't wait to dig in.

    1 package (6 ounces) strawberry gelatin
    1 cup boiling water
    1 can (20 ounces) crushed pineapple
    1 cup (8 ounces) plain yogurt
    1 cup chopped pecans, optional
  1/2 cup red maraschino cherries, halved
Lettuce leaves and additional cherries, optional

In a bowl, dissolve gelatin in boiling water. Refrigerate until partially set, about 30 minutes. Drain pineapple, reserving juice; set pineapple aside. Add enough cold water to juice to measure 1-3/4 cups; stir into gelatin mixture. Whisk in yogurt until smooth. Fold in nuts if desired, cherries and reserved pineapple.

Pour into a 2-qt. ring mold coated with nonstick cooking spray. Refrigerate until set. Unmold onto a lettuce-lined serving plate and garnish with additional cherries if desired. **Yield:** 6 servings.

Rice-Stuffed Cornish Hens

My mom prepares this impressive-looking entree for the holidays and for other "company's coming" occasions. The savory rice stuffing goes wonderfully with the moist golden hens and sweet apricot glaze.

5-1/2 cups water, *divided*
    2 teaspoons chicken bouillon granules
1-1/2 teaspoons salt
  3/4 cup uncooked wild rice
1-1/2 cups uncooked long grain rice
    1 pound bulk pork sausage
1-1/2 cups chopped celery
  3/4 cup chopped onion
    6 Cornish game hens (20 ounces *each*)
    1 jar (12 ounces) apricot preserves

In a large saucepan, bring 5 cups water, bouillon and salt to a boil. Add wild rice. Reduce heat; cover and simmer for 20 minutes. Add long grain rice; cover and simmer 25-30 minutes longer or until rice is tender and water is absorbed.

Meanwhile, in a large skillet, cook the sausage, celery and onion over medium heat until meat is no longer pink and vegetables are tender; drain. Stir in rice mixture. Spoon about 3/4 cup stuffing into each hen. Place remaining stuffing in a greased 2-qt. baking dish; cover and set aside. Place hens breast side up on a rack in a shallow baking pan; tie drumsticks together. Bake, uncovered, at 350° for 45 minutes.

Crunchy Green Beans

Green beans taste terrific all by themselves, but my mom has managed to improve on Mother Nature! She adds mushrooms, celery and crisp slivered almonds to dress up the popular green vegetable.

4 cups fresh *or* frozen green beans, cut into 2-inch pieces
1-1/2 cups diced celery
1-1/3 cups sliced fresh mushrooms
3 tablespoons vegetable oil
1 tablespoon cornstarch
1 cup cold water
1 tablespoon soy sauce
1 teaspoon beef bouillon granules
1/2 cup slivered almonds

Place the beans in a large saucepan and cover with water. Bring to a boil; cook, uncovered, for 8-10 minutes or until crisp-tender.

Meanwhile, in a skillet, saute celery and mushrooms in oil until tender. Combine cornstarch, cold water and soy sauce until smooth; stir into celery mixture. Stir in bouillon. Bring to a boil over medium heat; cook and stir for 1 minute or until thickened. Drain beans and add to the celery mixture. Stir in almonds. **Yield:** 6 servings.

— 🍷 🍷 🍷 —

Pistachio Cake

Mom is well-known for her holiday cookies, candies and cakes. This delicious dessert starts conveniently with a cake mix and instant pudding. You're sure to get requests for second helpings when you serve it.

1 package (18-1/4 ounces) white cake mix
1 package (3.4 ounces) instant pistachio pudding mix
1 cup lemon-lime soda
1 cup vegetable oil
3 eggs
1 cup chopped walnuts
FROSTING:
1-1/2 cups cold milk
1 package (3.4 ounces) instant pistachio pudding mix
1 carton (8 ounces) frozen whipped topping, thawed
1/2 cup chopped pistachios, toasted
Whole red shell pistachios and fresh mint, optional

In a mixing bowl, combine the first five ingredients. Beat on medium speed for 2 minutes; stir in walnuts. Pour into a greased 13-in. x 9-in. x 2-in. baking pan. Bake at 350° for 45-50 minutes or until a toothpick inserted near the center comes out clean. Cool on a wire rack.

For frosting, in a mixing bowl, beat the milk and pudding mix on low speed for 2 minutes. Fold in the whipped topping. Spread over cake. Sprinkle with pistachios. Refrigerate for about 30 minutes before cutting. Garnish with whole pistachios and mint if desired. Refrigerate leftovers. **Yield:** 12-15 servings.

Editors' Meals

*Members of Taste of Home's unique staff of 1,000 field editors,
made up of great cooks from across the country,
are thrilled to share their favorite meals with our readers.
Here are some of the best from the first 10 years.*

FIELD EDITORS' FAVORITES. Clockwise from
upper left: Down-Home Ham Dinner (p. 262), Fresh
Farm Foods (p. 266), Easter Morning Brunch (p. 258)
and Holiday Make-Ahead Menu (p. 282).

**She welcomes family
with a holiday feast
of traditional
favorites—some
from recipes over
100 years old!**

By Dorothy Smith, El Dorado, Arkansas

"WE'RE COMING for Christmas!" proclaimed one of our great-grandchildren—long before the holiday. "Of course you are," I confirmed heartily.

For my husband, Hershel, and me, Christmas is a wonderful time to get together with family—30 of us in all, including our three children and 10 grandchildren with their mates, plus eight great-grandchildren!

My Christmas menu reflects the way I like to cook, using recipes that have been passed down in the family or shared by friends.

We start out with rosy Cranberry Quencher. I got the recipe while visiting Hawaii, so it's no surprise pineapple juice is a main ingredient.

With the punch, we munch on Crisp Caraway Twists. These flaky appetizer sticks always go quickly, so I'm sure to have plenty on hand. Hershel's mother sent me the recipe the year we were married.

Turkey with Corn Bread Stuffing has a delicious, rich gravy that my mama taught me to make.

The flavorful corn bread stuffing recipe—Mama's version of a Southern favorite—is more than a century old. Our two daughters and son still request it for Christmas dinner.

Hershel says Sweet Potato Apple Salad from my Grandmother Dumas is also a "must" for the occasion. The poppy seed dressing has a citrus tang and really brings out the flavor.

Another of her treasures is Apple Cream Pie. A fancy and festive treat, it has sauteed apples arranged atop a creamy, delicious custard. Guests tell me they've never tasted anything quite like it.

It's a joy to share my Christmas dinner recipes, all tried and tested. I hope you'll enjoy them, too.

PICTURED AT LEFT: Turkey with Corn Bread Stuffing, Sweet Potato Apple Salad, Crisp Caraway Twists, Cranberry Quencher and Apple Cream Pie (recipes are on the next page).

For gravy, dissolve bouillon in water; set aside. Transfer turkey to a warm platter. Remove stuffing. Pour 1/4 cup pan drippings into a saucepan; whisk in flour until smooth. Gradually add bouillon mixture. Bring to a boil; cook and stir for 2 minutes or until thickened and bubbly. Serve with turkey and stuffing. **Yield:** 6-8 servings.

Turkey with Corn Bread Stuffing

For Christmas dinner, Dorothy Smith of El Dorado, Arkansas carves a succulent turkey. She and her family savor the stuffing, which gets its color and zip from olives and chilies. The following recipes are also from Dorothy.

- 1 can (14-3/4 ounces) cream-style corn
- 2 cans (4 ounces *each*) chopped green chilies
- 1 can (4-1/2 ounces) sliced ripe olives, finely chopped
- 1/2 cup shredded Co-Jack cheese
- 1/2 cup finely chopped onion
- 1/2 cup chopped green *or* sweet red pepper
- 1 tablespoon minced fresh parsley
- 1 egg, lightly beaten
- 1 package (16 ounces) crushed corn bread stuffing *or* 6 cups crumbled corn bread
- 1 turkey (8 to 10 pounds)
- Melted butter *or* margarine
- 2 chicken bouillon cubes
- 2 cups boiling water
- 1/4 to 1/3 cup all-purpose flour

In a large bowl, combine the first eight ingredients. Add stuffing and toss lightly. Just before baking, loosely stuff the turkey. Place remaining stuffing in a greased 1-1/2-qt. baking dish; refrigerate. Skewer openings of turkey; tie drumsticks together. Place on a rack in a roasting pan. Brush with melted butter. Bake, uncovered, at 325° for 2-3/4 to 3 hours or until a meat thermometer reads 180° for turkey and 165° for stuffing. Bake additional stuffing, covered, for 40-50 minutes or until heated through. When the turkey begins to brown, baste if needed; cover lightly with foil.

——— 🎺 🎺 🎺 ———

Sweet Potato Apple Salad

Pairing a seasonal fruit and vegetable makes for a pretty and tasty salad to accompany a turkey dinner.

- 6 medium sweet potatoes (about 2-1/2 pounds)
- 1/2 cup olive *or* vegetable oil
- 1/4 cup orange juice
- 1 tablespoon sugar
- 1 tablespoon cider vinegar *or* white wine vinegar
- 1 tablespoon Dijon mustard
- 1 tablespoon finely chopped onion
- 1-1/2 teaspoons poppy seeds
- 1 teaspoon grated orange peel
- 1/2 teaspoon grated lemon peel
- 2 medium tart apples, chopped
- 2 green onions, thinly sliced

In a large saucepan, cook sweet potatoes in boiling salted water until just tender, about 20 minutes. Cool completely. Meanwhile, in a jar with a tight-fitting lid, combine the next nine ingredients; shake well. Peel potatoes; cut each in half lengthwise, then into 1/2-in. slices. In a 4-qt. bowl, layer a fourth of the sweet potatoes, apples and onions; drizzle with a fourth of the salad dressing. Repeat layers three times. Refrigerate for 1-2 hours. Toss before serving. **Yield:** 8-10 servings.

Crisp Caraway Twists

When a big family gets together, make two batches of these flaky cheese-filled twists, which start with convenient frozen puff pastry.

    1 egg
    1 tablespoon water
    1 teaspoon country-style Dijon mustard
    3/4 cup shredded Swiss cheese
    1/4 cup finely chopped onion
    2 teaspoons minced fresh parsley
1-1/2 teaspoons caraway seeds
    1/4 teaspoon garlic salt
    1 sheet frozen puff pastry, thawed

In a small bowl, beat egg, water and mustard; set aside. In another bowl, combine the cheese, onion, parsley, caraway seeds and garlic salt. Unfold pastry sheet; brush with egg mixture. Sprinkle cheese mixture lengthwise over half of the pastry.

Fold pastry over filling; press edges to seal. Brush top with remaining egg mixture. Cut widthwise into 1/2-in. strips; twist each strip several times. Place 1 in. apart on greased baking sheets, pressing ends down. Bake at 350° for 15-20 minutes or until golden brown. Serve warm. **Yield:** 1-1/2 dozen.

— 🎄 🎄 🎄 —

Cranberry Quencher

(Pictured on page 255)

Fruity and tart, this refreshing beverage brings the color of Christmas to your table.

    1 bottle (1 gallon) cranberry-apple juice, chilled
    1 can (46 ounces) pineapple juice, chilled

    3/4 cup (6 ounces) lemonade *or* orange juice concentrate
    Pineapple rings *or* tidbits, fresh cranberries *and/or* mint, optional

Combine cranberry-apple and pineapple juices in a large container or punch bowl. Stir in lemonade concentrate. Garnish glasses with pineapple, cranberries and/or mint if desired. **Yield:** 6 quarts.

— 🎄 🎄 🎄 —

Apple Cream Pie

Arranging apple slices in a pretty design gives this pie the appearance of a fancy tart. Its rich custard-like filling has an elegant flavor but is easy to prepare.

    4 cups thinly sliced peeled tart apples
    2 tablespoons sugar
    2 tablespoons lemon juice
    1/4 cup butter *or* margarine
    1 package (8 ounces) cream cheese, softened
1-1/2 cups cold milk, *divided*
    1 package (3.4 ounces) instant vanilla pudding mix
    1 teaspoon grated lemon peel
    1 pastry shell (9 inches), baked
    1/4 cup apricot preserves *or* strawberry jelly, melted

In a large skillet, saute apples, sugar and lemon juice in butter until apples are tender. Cool. In a mixing bowl, beat the cream cheese until smooth; gradually beat in 1 cup milk, dry pudding mix and lemon peel. Add remaining milk; beat until thickened. Spread into pastry shell. Arrange apples over filling. Brush with preserves. Refrigerate for 1 hour before serving. Brush with additional preserves if desired. **Yield:** 6-8 servings.

Her crowd-pleasing brunch can be prepared a day ahead to brighten Easter or any special morning.

By Mary Anne McWhirter, Pearland, Texas

AFTER CHURCH on Easter Sunday, my family likes to sit down to a leisurely brunch, to which we invite relatives or special friends.

The greatest thing about this economical menu is that most of the dishes can be made ahead of time.

The aroma of ham and green onions sauteing for my Scrambled Egg Casserole creates a savory sneak preview of this delicious dish, which is assembled entirely the night before.

In the morning, I simply pop it into the oven and then enjoy time with family and guests.

Wrapping the Pigs in a Blanket can be done in a jiffy using handy convenience foods.

The fruity base for refreshing Banana Brunch Punch is also made ahead and frozen. Just take it out of the freezer an hour before serving and blend the soda and pineapple juice with the thawing mixture.

Cream Cheese Coffee Cake is so delicious and looks impressive...but don't be fooled—it's quick and easy to make. In fact, you simply cut "X" shapes across the top of the cheese-filled yeast-dough loaves to create the attractive braided effect.

Fresh or frozen berries add fruity festivity to my Blueberry Streusel Muffins, light-textured and pretty with their sweet golden topping. They can be made several days ahead and frozen.

To complete the meal, I serve fresh fruit such as grapefruit halves topped with strawberries. You can use a variety of fruits in season, arranging a colorful plate for the buffet.

I hope to one day own and operate a bed-and-breakfast...I'll certainly treat guests to my Easter brunch. In the meantime, I hope our favorite-meal menu will soon become a favorite of yours!

— 🥄 🥄 🥄 —

PICTURED AT LEFT: Pigs in a Blanket, Scrambled Egg Casserole, Banana Brunch Punch, Cream Cheese Coffee Cake and Blueberry Streusel Muffins (recipes are on the next page).

Pigs in a Blanket

(Pictured on page 259)

This simple recipe uses refrigerated crescent rolls and pre-cooked breakfast links.

**1 tube (8 ounces) refrigerated crescent rolls
1 package (12 ounces) smoked sausage links**

Separate the dough into eight triangles. Place a sausage on wide end of each triangle and roll up. Place, point down, on an ungreased baking sheet. Bake at 400° for 10-15 minutes or until golden brown. **Yield:** 8 servings.

———— 🍷 🍷 🍷 ————

Scrambled Egg Casserole

There's nothing nicer than a delicious egg dish you can prepare the night before.

**1/2 cup butter *or* margarine, *divided*
2 tablespoons all-purpose flour
1/2 teaspoon salt
1/8 teaspoon pepper
2 cups milk
1 cup (4 ounces) shredded process American cheese
1 cup cubed fully cooked ham
1/4 cup sliced green onions
12 eggs, beaten
1 can (4 ounces) sliced mushrooms, drained
1-1/2 cups soft bread crumbs
Additional sliced green onions, optional**

In a medium saucepan, melt 2 tablespoons butter. Add flour, salt and pepper; cook and stir until bubbly. Gradually stir in milk; cook until thickened and bubbly, stirring constantly. Remove from the heat. Add cheese; mix well and set aside.

In a skillet, saute ham and onions in 3 table-spoons butter until onions are tender. Add eggs;

cook and stir until they begin to set. Add mush-rooms and cheese sauce; mix well. Pour into a greased 11-in. x 7-in. x 2-in. baking dish. Melt re-maining butter; toss with bread crumbs. Sprinkle over casserole. Cover and refrigerate for 2-3 hours or overnight.

Remove from the refrigerator 30 minutes before baking. Bake, uncovered, at 350° for 25-30 min-utes or until top is golden brown. Sprinkle with onions if desired. **Yield:** 6-8 servings.

Banana Brunch Punch

A cold glass of refreshing punch really brightens a brunch. It's nice to serve a crisp beverage like this.

**6 medium ripe bananas
1 can (12 ounces) frozen orange juice concentrate, thawed
3/4 cup lemonade concentrate
3 cups warm water, *divided*
2 cups sugar, *divided*
1 can (46 ounces) pineapple juice
3 bottles (2 liters *each*) lemon-lime soda
Orange slices, optional**

In a blender or food processor, cover and process bananas and concentrates until smooth. Remove half of the mixture and set aside. Add 1-1/2 cups of warm water and 1 cup sugar to mixture in blender; blend until smooth. Place in a large freez-er container. Repeat with remaining banana mix-ture, water and sugar; add to container.

Cover and freeze until solid. One hour before serv-ing, remove from freezer. Just before serving, place in a large punch bowl. Add pineapple juice and soda; stir until well blended. Garnish with orange slices if desired. **Yield:** 60-70 servings (10 quarts).

Cream Cheese Coffee Cake

These impressive loaves really sparkle on the buffet. You can't just eat one slice of this treat.

- 1 cup (8 ounces) sour cream
- 1/2 cup sugar
- 1/2 cup butter *or* margarine
- 1 teaspoon salt
- 2 packages (1/4 ounce *each*) active dry yeast
- 1/2 cup warm water (110° to 115°)
- 2 eggs, beaten
- 4 cups all-purpose flour

FILLING:
- 2 packages (8 ounces *each*) cream cheese, softened
- 3/4 cup sugar
- 1 egg, beaten
- 2 teaspoons vanilla extract
- 1/8 teaspoon salt

GLAZE:
- 2-1/2 cups confectioners' sugar
- 1/4 cup milk
- 1 teaspoon vanilla extract
Toasted sliced almonds, optional

In a saucepan, combine sour cream, sugar, butter and salt. Cook over medium-low heat, stirring constantly, for 5-10 minutes or until well blended. Cool to room temperature. In a mixing bowl, dissolve yeast in water. Add sour cream mixture and eggs; mix well. Gradually stir in flour (dough will be very soft). Cover and refrigerate overnight.

Next day, combine filling ingredients in a mixing bowl until well blended. Turn dough onto a floured surface; knead 5-6 times. Divide into four equal portions. Roll each portion into a 12-in. x 8-in. rectangle. Spread 1/4 of the filling on each to within 1 in. of edges. Roll up jelly-roll style from

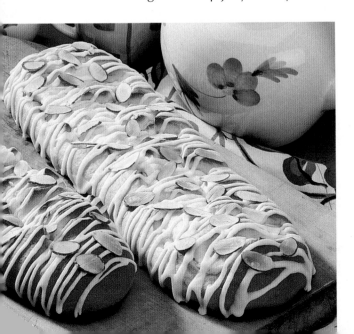

long side; pinch seams and ends to seal. Place, seam side down, on greased baking sheet. Cut six X's on top of loaves. Cover and let rise until nearly doubled, about 1 hour. Bake at 375° for 20-25 minutes or until golden brown. Cool on wire racks.

Combine sugar, milk and vanilla; drizzle over loaves. Sprinkle with almonds if desired. Store in the refrigerator. **Yield:** 20-24 servings.

Blueberry Streusel Muffins

It's a joy to set out a basket of these moist muffins!

- 1/4 cup butter *or* margarine, softened
- 1/3 cup sugar
- 1 egg, beaten
- 2-1/3 cups all-purpose flour
- 4 teaspoons baking powder
- 1/2 teaspoon salt
- 1 cup milk
- 1 teaspoon vanilla extract
- 1-1/2 cups fresh *or* frozen blueberries*

STREUSEL:
- 1/2 cup sugar
- 1/3 cup all-purpose flour
- 1/2 teaspoon ground cinnamon
- 1/4 cup cold butter *or* margarine

In a mixing bowl, cream butter and sugar. Add egg; mix well. Combine flour, baking powder and salt; add to the creamed mixture alternately with milk. Stir in vanilla. Fold in blueberries. Fill 12 greased or paper-lined muffin cups two-thirds full. Combine streusel ingredients until crumbly; sprinkle over batter. Bake at 375° for 25-30 minutes or until browned. **Yield:** 1 dozen.

Editor's Note: If using frozen blueberries, do not thaw before adding to batter.

When spring makes its debut, this farm wife welcomes the season with a fresh-tasting feast.

By Eunice Stoen, Decorah, Iowa

EVERYDAY MEALS can be hurried here on the dairy and grain farm husband Wilbur and I (everyone calls me "Euny") operate with our son, Bill. But now and then, I enjoy preparing a special feast.

My farm background, Norwegian heritage and love of sharing recipes all come through in this mouth-watering menu. Ham is my meat of choice—we used to raise hogs, and I'm a big promoter of Iowa farm products.

Not only is my Baked Ham with Cumberland Sauce easy to prepare, but it looks so impressive. When you've fixed a beautiful roast like this, I think it's nice to put it on your largest platter and take it to the table before carving it. Then pass around a platter with thick slices of the ham and a bowl of the fruity sauce.

My Asparagus with Sesame Butter recipe retains the color and shape of the spears, accentuating the fresh flavor and adding some crunch.

And a delicious simple side dish like Norwegian Parsley Potatoes goes well with the ham and honors my heritage. I also like to serve warm rolls, a relish tray and a make-ahead salad.

Hawaiian Dessert is a perfect refreshing end to this meal. It makes two large pans, so there's one to serve and another to freeze—or better yet—to share with your neighbor.

Preparing as much of my meal as possible the day before allows me to enjoy our guests and the food, too. I dish up all the food, then sit where I can reach the bowls and platters and pass them for "seconds".

Our guests often say that I make putting on a meal like this look easy. I gratefully respond that my secret to success is planning and preparing ahead of time... and, of course, using these never-fail recipes!

— ▼ ▼ ▼ —

PICTURED AT LEFT: Baked Ham with Cumberland Sauce, Norwegian Parsley Potatoes, Asparagus with Sesame Butter and Hawaiian Dessert (recipes are on the next page).

Baked Ham with Cumberland Sauce

The centerpiece of a beautiful spring family dinner, this golden ham with tangy jewel-toned sauce is impressive to serve.

>   1/2 **fully cooked ham with bone (4 to 5**
>   **pounds)**
>   1/2 **cup packed brown sugar**
>   1 **teaspoon ground mustard**
> **Whole cloves**
> **CUMBERLAND SAUCE:**
>   1 **cup red currant *or* apple jelly**
>   1/4 **cup orange juice**
>   1/4 **cup lemon juice**
>   1/4 **cup red wine *or* apple juice**
>   2 **tablespoons honey**
>   1 **tablespoon cornstarch**

Remove skin from ham; score the surface with shallow diagonal cuts, making diamond shapes. Mix brown sugar and mustard; rub into fat of ham. Insert a whole clove in center of each diamond. Place ham in a roaster with a baking rack. Bake, uncovered, at 325° for 20-22 minutes per pound or until ham is heated through and thermometer reads 140°.

For sauce, combine all of the ingredients in a medium saucepan. Cook over medium heat until thickened, stirring often. Serve over the sliced ham. (Sauce recipe can be doubled if desired.) **Yield:** 8-10 servings (1-3/4 cups sauce).

Norwegian Parsley Potatoes

I love to use parsley in many dishes, and it suits the fresh taste of small red potatoes well. Even though they're easy to prepare, they look fancy and go great with baked ham.

>   2 **pounds small red new potatoes**
>   1/2 **cup butter *or* margarine**
>   1/4 **cup chopped fresh parsley**
>   1/4 **teaspoon dried marjoram**

Cook potatoes in boiling salted water for 15 minutes or until tender. Cool slightly. With a sharp knife, remove one narrow strip of skin around the middle of each potato. In a large skillet, melt butter; add parsley and marjoram. Add the potatoes and stir gently until coated and heated through. **Yield:** 6-8 servings.

Asparagus with Sesame Butter

The first fresh asparagus is a delightful springtime treat. This light butter sauce lets the asparagus flavor come through, and the sprinkling of sesame seeds adds a delicate crunch. This is a simple yet delicious dish.

>   2 **pounds fresh asparagus**
>   1 **cup boiling water**

1/2 teaspoon salt
  1 tablespoon cornstarch
1/4 cup cold water
1/4 cup butter *or* margarine
  3 tablespoons sesame seeds, toasted

Place asparagus spears in a large skillet; add boiling water and salt. Cook for 5-7 minutes or until tender. Remove asparagus and keep warm. Drain the cooking liquid, reserving 1/2 cup in a small saucepan. Combine cornstarch and cold water; stir into liquid. Cook and stir over medium heat until thickened and bubbly; cook and stir 1 minute longer. Stir in butter until melted. Spoon over asparagus; sprinkle with sesame seeds and serve immediately. **Yield:** 6-8 servings.

Asparagus Tips

When buying asparagus, look for stalks that are brittle enough to snap and fairly uniform in circumference. The tips should be tightly closed.

Store the spears loose in a plastic bag in the crisper compartment of your refrigerator.

When fresh asparagus is plentiful, blanch some and freeze it for later. Keep asparagus frozen until you're ready to use it. Don't defrost before cooking. If the asparagus thaws, cook it right away and don't refreeze. Frozen asparagus should be used within 8 months.

Hawaiian Dessert

I got this recipe from a woman I happened to meet in a department store one day. Leftovers taste just as good the next day, and this dessert can also be frozen. I like to keep a pan in the freezer to take to a last-minute potluck.

      1 package (18-1/4 ounces) yellow cake mix
      3 packages (3.4 ounces *each*) instant vanilla pudding mix
      4 cups cold milk
1-1/2 teaspoons coconut extract
      1 package (8 ounces) cream cheese, softened
      1 can (20 ounces) crushed pineapple, well drained
      2 cups whipping cream, whipped and sweetened
      2 cups flaked coconut, toasted

Mix cake batter according to package directions. Pour into two greased 13-in. x 9-in. x 2-in. baking pans. Bake at 350° for 15 minutes or until the cakes test done. Cool completely.

In a large mixing bowl, combine pudding mixes, milk and coconut extract; beat for 2 minutes. Add cream cheese; beat well. Stir in pineapple. Spread over cooled cakes. Top with whipped cream; sprinkle with coconut. Chill for at least 2 hours. **Yield:** 24 servings.

Editor's Note: Prepared dessert can be covered and frozen for up to 1 month.

A visit to the family farm means fresh air, fun and great food when she prepares these dishes to satisfy hungry appetites.

By Page Alexander, Baldwin City, Kansas

EACH SUMMER, my husband, Monte, and I plan a weekend when our two grown children, their families and a few other relatives can come out to our farm for some fun and good food.

With the crops maturing, flowers blooming and our garden bearing fresh produce, there couldn't be a better time for a family gathering!

Barbecued Brisket is cooked slowly to its tender best. The meat absorbs the delicious sweet-tart flavor from the sauce as it tenderizes.

A friend told me how to roast the brisket, but the sauce is my own concoction. While it's easy to use bottled sauce in a recipe like this, you can make your own with just a little extra effort.

With the beef, I serve Special Potato Salad, a recipe shared by daughter-in-law Lisa. This salad is a little different from any other I'd made and has a wonderful creamy dressing. Red onion and celery add color and crunch. My nieces say it's a perfect addition to any picnic or barbecue.

Layered Fruit Salad goes well with any meat entree and is especially refreshing on a hot day. Its simple citrus dressing seems to bring out the flavor of each fruit in the medley. Be sure to serve this colorful salad in a clear glass bowl or trifle dish if you have one.

After a big meal, a slice of Meringue Berry Pie really hits the spot. This dessert's crispy nutty crust, ice cream filling, tangy fruit and sweet sauce make it a summer delight.

As we all sit back after dinner, everyone says how glad they are to come to our place for a visit. I'll often send each family home with a jar of blackberry jelly I've made using wild fruit growing on our property.

The next time your family's coming, I hope you'll consider trying one of my favorite recipes.

━━━ ⦾ ⦾ ⦾ ━━━

PICTURED AT LEFT: Barbecued Brisket, Special Potato Salad, Layered Fruit Salad and Meringue Berry Pie (recipes are on the next page).

Barbecued Brisket

Baked slowly, this brisket gets nice and tender, and picks up the sweet and tangy flavor of the sauce.

      1 beef brisket (3 to 4 pounds)*
1-1/4 cups water, *divided*
   1/2 cup chopped onion
      3 garlic cloves, minced
      1 tablespoon vegetable oil
      1 cup ketchup
      3 tablespoons cider vinegar *or* red
        wine vinegar
      2 tablespoons lemon juice
      2 tablespoons brown sugar
      1 tablespoon Worcestershire sauce
      2 teaspoons cornstarch
      1 teaspoon paprika
      1 teaspoon chili powder
   1/4 teaspoon salt
   1/4 teaspoon pepper
   1/4 teaspoon liquid smoke

Place brisket in a large Dutch oven. Add 1/2 cup water. Cover and bake at 275° for 2 hours. Meanwhile, in a medium saucepan, saute onion and garlic in oil until tender. Add ketchup, vinegar, lemon juice, brown sugar, Worcestershire sauce, cornstarch, paprika, chili powder, salt, pepper and remaining water. Simmer, uncovered, for 1 hour, stirring occasionally. Add liquid smoke; mix well.

  Drain drippings from Dutch oven. Pour sauce over meat. Cover and bake 1-2 hours longer or until meat is tender. **Yield:** 6-8 servings.

  *Editor's Note: This is a fresh beef brisket, not corned beef.

Special Potato Salad

Vinegar and yogurt give this salad a refreshing tang that's unlike typical potato salads with heavy creamy dressings. My family loves the crispness of the onion and celery, and the heartiness that comes from the eggs and crumbled bacon.

2-1/2 pounds red potatoes
      2 tablespoons cider vinegar *or* red
        wine vinegar
      1 tablespoon olive *or* vegetable oil
      1 tablespoon Dijon mustard
   1/2 teaspoon dried basil
   1/2 teaspoon pepper
   1/4 teaspoon salt
   1/2 cup plain yogurt
   1/4 cup sour cream
      1 teaspoon garlic salt
   3/4 cup chopped red onion
   1/2 cup diced celery
      4 bacon strips, cooked and crumbled
      2 hard-cooked eggs, chopped

In a saucepan, cook potatoes in boiling salted water until tender. Meanwhile, in a large bowl, combine vinegar, oil, mustard, basil, pepper and salt; mix well. Drain potatoes; cut into 1-in. chunks and add to vinegar and oil mixture while still warm. Toss to coat; cool completely.

  In a bowl, combine yogurt, sour cream and garlic salt. Add onion, celery, bacon and eggs; mix well. Add to potato mixture; toss gently. Cover and chill for several hours. **Yield:** 6-8 servings.

Layered Fruit Salad

This colorful salad is a real eye-catcher, and it tastes as good as it looks. Fresh fruit is always a welcome side dish with a summer meal. The addition of oranges and grapefruit gives this salad a different twist.

    1/2 cup orange juice
    1/4 cup lemon juice
    1/4 cup packed brown sugar
    1/2 teaspoon grated orange peel
    1/2 teaspoon grated lemon peel
      1 cinnamon stick
      2 cups pineapple chunks
      1 cup seedless red grapes
      2 medium bananas, sliced
      2 medium oranges, peeled and sectioned
      1 medium grapefruit, peeled and sectioned
      1 pint strawberries, sliced
      2 kiwifruit, peeled and sliced

In a medium saucepan, combine the first six ingredients; bring to a boil. Reduce heat; simmer, uncovered, for 5 minutes. Remove from the heat; cool completely. Meanwhile, layer fruit in a glass serving bowl. Remove cinnamon stick from the sauce; pour sauce over fruit. Cover and chill for several hours. **Yield:** 6-8 servings.

— 🍴 🍴 🍴 —

Meringue Berry Pie

A hot day calls for a cool dessert like this tempting pie. Fresh berries and a sweet raspberry sauce over ice cream in a meringue crust make each slice absolutely irresistible.

    1/2 cup sugar, *divided*
    1/4 cup toasted slivered almonds, ground
      2 tablespoons cornstarch
      2 egg whites
    1/8 teaspoon cream of tartar
SAUCE AND TOPPING:
    1/2 cup sugar
      1 tablespoon cornstarch
    1/3 cup water
      1 pint fresh *or* frozen raspberries
      1 quart vanilla ice cream
      2 cups fresh mixed berries

In a small bowl, combine 1/4 cup sugar, almonds and cornstarch; mix well. In a small mixing bowl, beat egg whites on high speed until foamy. Add cream of tartar; continue beating until soft peaks form. Gradually add remaining sugar, beating until stiff peaks form. Fold in almond mixture. Spread over the bottom and sides of a greased 9-in. pie plate. Bake at 275° for 1 to 1-1/2 hours or until light golden brown. Turn off oven; do not open door. Let meringue cool in oven for 1 hour. Remove from oven and cool completely.

Meanwhile, for sauce, combine sugar and cornstarch in a medium saucepan. Gradually stir in water until smooth. Add raspberries; bring to a boil over medium heat, stirring constantly. Boil for 1 minute or until thickened; cool.

To serve, scoop ice cream onto meringue; top with berries and sauce. Serve immediately. Freeze leftovers. **Yield:** 6-8 servings.

Pairing up on preparation, this cooking couple turns out memorable meals like this bountiful barbecue supper.

By Anne and Jesse Foust, Bluefield, West Virginia

TWO is never too many cooks in our kitchen! We share a special interest in recipes and food. It's been a tasty tie that binds.

Anne: In the early years of our marriage and as we raised our five children, Jesse helped with the cooking. He has a knack of knowing what to add to make a good dish taste even better.

Jesse: I learned to cook in the Navy while stationed at Moffitt Field Naval Air Station near San Francisco. There, I did a little of everything, from running a grill to serving on the "mess line". Cooking for a few thousand was a formidable task, to say the least!

Over the years, I've refined my cooking skills in our own kitchen. I'm always on the lookout for good food that's easy to fix.

We've served this special barbecue supper at many casual get-togethers with family and friends. With its wonderful aroma and slightly smoky taste, Shredded Barbecued Beef always wins raves. I adapted the recipe from one I'd seen, adjusting ingredients to make the sauce just right for our tastes.

Anne: Old-Fashioned Baked Beans are the kind of down-home food I grew up on in Kentucky. Hearty and savory, the beans go hand in hand with the barbecue.

Two heads are better than one for menu planning... and four hands make chores, like peeling the hard-cooked eggs for our Best Deviled Eggs, go more quickly.

Jesse: Besides serving it often at home, we frequently take a big dish of colorful Picnic Slaw by request to potluck dinners. It complements so many foods.

Anne: I'm the dessert-maker in the family. Folks have said my Peanut Butter Cream Pie is a perfect ending for this meal. We hope you like our recipes and will prepare them sometime soon.

Jesse: Yes, do try them! I'm sure there are others of you who have strengthened your family ties by sharing the role of "cook"!

— 🍴 🍴 🍴 —

PICTURED AT LEFT: Shredded Barbecued Beef, Old-Fashioned Baked Beans, Best Deviled Eggs, Picnic Slaw and Peanut Butter Cream Pie (recipes are on the next page).

Shredded Barbecued Beef

Once family and friends have dug into this tender and tangy barbecued beef, you'll be making it again and again. It takes a little time to prepare, but it's well worth the effort for a picnic or dinner anytime.

- 1 boneless beef chuck roast (about 4 pounds)
- 3 tablespoons vegetable oil, *divided*
- 2 large onions, chopped
- 1 cup ketchup
- 1 cup beef broth
- 2/3 cup chili sauce
- 1/4 cup cider vinegar
- 1/4 cup packed brown sugar
- 3 tablespoons Worcestershire sauce
- 2 tablespoons prepared mustard
- 2 tablespoons molasses
- 2 tablespoons lemon juice
- 1 teaspoon salt
- 1/4 teaspoon cayenne pepper
- 1/8 teaspoon pepper
- 1 tablespoon liquid smoke, optional
- 12 to 16 kaiser rolls *or* hamburger buns

In a Dutch oven, brown roast on all sides in 1 tablespoon of oil. Meanwhile, in a large saucepan, saute onions in remaining oil until tender. Add the next 13 ingredients; bring to a boil. Reduce heat; simmer, uncovered, for 15 minutes, stirring occasionally. Pour over roast.

Cover and bake at 325° for 2 hours; turn the roast. Bake 2 hours longer or until meat is very tender. Remove roast; shred with a fork and return to sauce. Serve on rolls. **Yield:** 12-16 servings.

Old-Fashioned Baked Beans

These hearty beans are a super side dish for a casual meal. The ingredients blend perfectly for a wonderful from-scratch taste.

- 1 pound dried navy beans
- 1-1/2 teaspoons salt
- 4 quarts cold water, *divided*
- 1 cup chopped red onion
- 1/2 cup molasses
- 6 bacon strips, cooked and crumbled
- 1/4 cup packed brown sugar
- 1 teaspoon ground mustard
- 1/4 teaspoon pepper

In a large saucepan, bring beans, salt and 2 qts. water to a boil; boil for 2 minutes. Remove from the heat; let stand for 1 hour. Drain beans; discard liquid. Return beans to pan. Cover with remaining water; bring to a boil. Reduce heat; cover and simmer for 1-1/2 to 2 hours or until beans are tender. Drain, reserving liquid. In a greased 2-1/2-qt. baking dish, combine beans, 1 cup liquid, onion, molasses, bacon, brown sugar, mustard and pepper.

Cover and bake at 325° for 3 to 3-1/2 hours or until beans are as thick as desired, stirring occasionally. Add more of the reserved cooking liquid if needed. **Yield:** 12-16 servings.

— 🛒 🛒 🛒 —

Best Deviled Eggs
(Pictured on page 270)

Herbs lend a nice zest to these pick-up-and-eat accompaniments to our easy menu.

12 hard-cooked eggs
1/2 cup mayonnaise
1 teaspoon dried parsley flakes
1/2 teaspoon dried chives
1/2 teaspoon ground mustard
1/2 teaspoon dill weed
1/4 teaspoon salt
1/4 teaspoon paprika
1/8 teaspoon pepper
1/8 teaspoon garlic powder
2 tablespoons milk
Fresh parsley and additional paprika

Slice eggs in half lengthwise; remove yolks and set whites aside. In a small bowl, mash yolks. Add the next 10 ingredients; mix well. Evenly fill the whites. Garnish with parsley and paprika. **Yield:** 2 dozen.

2 tablespoons lemon juice
1 tablespoon white vinegar
1/2 teaspoon salt
1/2 teaspoon celery seed
Dash pepper

In a large bowl, combine the first seven ingredients. Combine dressing ingredients in a blender; process until smooth. Pour over vegetables; toss to coat. Cover and refrigerate overnight. Stir before serving. **Yield:** 12-16 servings.

Picnic Slaw

Everyone loves this festive, colorful coleslaw. It not only looks good, it tastes great, too. Crisp vegetables covered with a light creamy dressing make a refreshing side dish you'll be proud to serve.

1 medium head cabbage, shredded
1 large carrot, shredded
1 medium green pepper, julienned
1 medium sweet red pepper, julienned
1 medium onion, finely chopped
1/3 cup sliced green onions
1/4 cup chopped fresh parsley
DRESSING:
1/4 cup milk
1/4 cup buttermilk
1/2 cup mayonnaise
1/3 cup sugar

Peanut Butter Cream Pie

During the warm months, it's nice to have a fluffy, no-bake dessert that's a snap to make. Packed with peanut flavor, this pie gets gobbled up even after a big meal!

1 package (8 ounces) cream cheese, softened
3/4 cup confectioners' sugar
1/2 cup creamy peanut butter
6 tablespoons milk
1 carton (8 ounces) frozen whipped topping, thawed
1 graham cracker crust (9 inches)
1/4 cup chopped peanuts

In a mixing bowl, beat cream cheese until fluffy. Add sugar and peanut butter; mix well. Gradually add the milk. Fold in whipped topping; spoon into the crust. Sprinkle with peanuts. Chill overnight. **Yield:** 6-8 servings.

⌡ *Upper Crust*

If you have chocolate lovers in your family, use a chocolate crumb crust in the Peanut Butter Cream Pie instead of the standard graham cracker crust. It's a delicious substitution.

Her three-generation Sunday dinners are making memories as the family gathers for delicious food like this fall feast.

By Bertha Johnson, Indianapolis, Indiana

SUNDAY DINNER after church is a long-standing tradition in our family. Our four sons and their families have a standing invitation to join my husband, Granville (his nickname's "Buster"), and me for the noon meal.

When autumn arrives with the harvest of pumpkins and other offerings, this is a well-loved Sunday menu at Grandma's.

Autumn Pork Chops are special but not time-consuming. This skillet entree simmers for just an hour, and the fruit sauce is easy to make. Its combination of prunes, apricots and cider is delightful with the chops.

Our grandchildren think you can't have a meal without macaroni and cheese. My creamy Deluxe Macaroni 'n' Cheese meets the approval of everyone at the table. Put together ahead of time, the dish is ready for the oven after church.

It bakes along with Butternut Squash Bake, another make-ahead dish that's so appealing. We first tasted this recipe when visiting my brother in Huntsville, Alabama several years ago.

It was a big hit and has become one of my preferred ways to fix winter squash. I put it together and refrigerate it the night before or early Sunday morning. Then I remove it from the refrigerator 30 minutes before baking as directed.

Also perfect for my time frame is Make-Ahead Lettuce Salad. This favorite is made up of crispy lettuce, fresh colorful vegetables and a tangy dressing.

The recipe for Streusel Pumpkin Pie was sent to me by a very dear friend. Since she shared it, I've never made another kind of pumpkin pie. A nutty crust and streusel topping make it unique.

I just love to cook and have everyone enjoy what they are eating. This menu has been a Sunday success at our house. We hope your family will like it, too.

— 🍷 🍷 🍷 —

PICTURED AT LEFT: Autumn Pork Chops, Butternut Squash Bake, Deluxe Macaroni 'n' Cheese, Make-Ahead Lettuce Salad and Streusel Pumpkin Pie (recipes are on the next page).

Autumn Pork Chops

A delicious fruit sauce makes this easy pork chop dish Sunday-special. It's an autumn favorite when the children and grandchildren gather at our place for dinner after church. The chops simmer to a wonderful tenderness in just an hour.

- 6 bone-in pork loin chops (1/2 inch thick)
- 1 tablespoon butter *or* margarine
- 12 dried apricots
- 6 dried pitted prunes
- 1-1/2 cups apple cider *or* juice
- 1 tablespoon sugar
- 1 teaspoon salt
- 1/4 teaspoon curry powder
- 2 tablespoons cornstarch
- 2 tablespoons cold water

In a large skillet, brown pork chops in butter for 1-2 minutes on each side. Arrange the apricots and prunes over pork. Combine the cider, sugar, salt and curry; pour over fruit. Cover and simmer for 1 hour. Remove pork and fruit and keep warm. Combine cornstarch and water until smooth; add to pan juices. Bring to a boil; cook and stir for 2 minutes or until thickened. Serve with the pork chops and fruit. **Yield:** 6 servings.

— 🍴 🍴 🍴 —

Butternut Squash Bake

For a side dish with special harvesttime appeal, you can't go wrong with this savory squash bake. It's creamy, comforting and looks delectable, thanks to the yellow butternut squash and golden crumb topping.

- 1 small butternut squash, peeled, seeded and cubed (about 2 cups)

- 1/2 cup mayonnaise*
- 1/2 cup finely chopped onion
- 1 egg, lightly beaten
- 1 teaspoon sugar

Salt and pepper to taste

- 1/4 cup crushed saltines (about 8 crackers)
- 2 tablespoons grated Parmesan cheese
- 1 tablespoon butter *or* margarine, melted

Place squash in a saucepan and cover with water; bring to a boil. Reduce heat; cover and simmer for 20-25 minutes or until very tender. Drain well and place in a large bowl; mash squash. In another bowl, combine the mayonnaise, onion, egg, sugar, salt and pepper; add to squash and mix well.

Transfer to a greased 1-qt. baking dish. Combine cracker crumbs, cheese and butter; sprinkle over top. Bake, uncovered, at 350° for 30-40 minutes or until heated through and top is golden brown. **Yield:** 6 servings.

***Editor's Note:** Light or fat-free mayonnaise may not be substituted for regular mayonnaise.

Deluxe Macaroni 'n' Cheese

(Pictured on page 274)

Our six grandchildren, who don't think a meal is complete without macaroni and cheese, love this creamy from-scratch version featuring cheddar and cottage cheese.

- 2 cups small-curd cottage cheese
- 1 cup (8 ounces) sour cream
- 1 egg, lightly beaten
- 3/4 teaspoon salt

Garlic salt and pepper to taste

- 2 cups (8 ounces) shredded sharp cheddar cheese

1 package (7 ounces) elbow macaroni, cooked and drained
Paprika, optional

In a large bowl, combine the cottage cheese, sour cream, egg, salt, garlic salt and pepper. Add cheddar cheese; mix well. Add macaroni and stir until coated. Transfer to a greased 2-1/2-qt. baking dish. Bake, uncovered, at 350° for 25-30 minutes or until heated through. Sprinkle with paprika if desired. **Yield:** 8-10 servings.

— 🍳 🍳 🍳 —

Make-Ahead Lettuce Salad

"Make-ahead" is a magic word when you're planning a hearty meal and trying to minimize last-minute preparation.

✓ Uses less fat, sugar or salt. Includes Nutritional Analysis and Diabetic Exchanges.

    1 head iceberg lettuce, torn
    1 large onion, chopped
1/2 cup chopped celery
1/2 cup chopped green pepper
    1 can (8 ounces) sliced water chestnuts, drained
    1 package (10 ounces) frozen peas, thawed
    2 cups mayonnaise
    1 tablespoon sugar
1/4 cup shredded Parmesan cheese
    4 bacon strips, cooked and crumbled, optional

In a 6-qt. bowl, layer half of the lettuce, onion, celery, green pepper, water chestnuts and peas. Combine mayonnaise and sugar; spread half over the salad. Repeat layers. Sprinkle with cheese and bacon if desired. Cover; refrigerate for 12-24 hours. **Yield:** 14-16 servings.
Nutritional Analysis: One 1-cup serving (prepared with fat-free mayonnaise and nonfat Parme-

san cheese topping and without bacon) equals 54 calories, 262 mg sodium, trace cholesterol, 11 g carbohydrate, 2 g protein, trace fat. **Diabetic Exchanges:** 1/2 starch, 1/2 vegetable.

— 🍳 🍳 🍳 —

Streusel Pumpkin Pie

Basic pumpkin pie is good, but we think this dressed-up version is even better. Plenty of pecans add a nutty crunch.

    2 cups all-purpose flour
1/4 cup finely chopped pecans
    1 teaspoon salt
2/3 cup plus 1 tablespoon vegetable shortening
    4 to 5 tablespoons water
FILLING:
    1 can (30 ounces) pumpkin pie mix
    1 can (14 ounces) sweetened condensed milk
    1 egg, lightly beaten
STREUSEL TOPPING:
1/2 cup packed brown sugar
1/4 cup all-purpose flour
1/4 cup chopped pecans
1/2 teaspoon ground cinnamon
    3 tablespoons cold butter *or* margarine

In a bowl, combine flour, pecans and salt; cut in shortening until crumbly. Gradually add water, tossing with a fork until a ball forms. Divide dough in half. Roll out each portion to fit a 9-in. pie plate; place pastry in pie plates. Flute edges; set aside.

Combine pie mix, milk and egg; pour into pastry shells. For topping, combine sugar, flour, pecans and cinnamon in a small bowl; cut in butter until crumbly. Sprinkle over filling. Cover edges loosely with foil. Bake at 375° for 40-45 minutes or until a knife inserted near the center comes out clean. Cool on a wire rack for 2 hours. Refrigerate until serving. **Yield:** 2 pies (6-8 servings each).

Make-ahead recipes assure a delicious Thanksgiving dinner this veteran cook serves with ease. She shares her savory secrets!

By Ruby Williams, Bogalusa, Louisiana

FOR ME, the perfect "recipe" for enjoying Thanksgiving Day is to serve a mouth-watering meal without a lot of last-minute fuss. The secret is planning.

My children, grandchildren and great-grandchildren gather at my home for holidays—it's such fun to be together. Each family brings a dish for the buffet, but I cook much of the food. I prepare all of the recipes at least partially the day before or earlier.

I make the Whole Wheat Dinner Rolls a week ahead. They bake to a pretty golden color, have a pleasant texture and slightly sweet taste. I freeze them, thaw the rolls the day of the party and pop them into the oven to warm before serving.

Family members often comment that no holiday meal would be complete without my Mushroom Corn Bread Dressing. They praise its good flavor and the crunch from the almonds, mushrooms, green onions and celery.

I also prepare the corn bread for the dressing in advance. When it cools, I crumble the bread and freeze it until the day before Thanksgiving, when I thaw and combine it with the other ingredients.

I bake the Holiday Pound Cake 2 days early. My family always asks for this tender, delicate-tasting cake. I dress it up with strawberry topping.

Even the Herbed Turkey Breast can be cooked the day before! Since our family prefers white meat, I roast a turkey breast rather than a whole bird, reserving the remaining herb-butter sauce to reheat with the meat the next day.

Seasoned with sage, thyme, marjoram and a little soy sauce, the mixture keeps the turkey moist and tasty.

Overnight Vegetable Salad is a convenient, colorful medley with a tangy marinade. It's always a hit.

———— 🍂 🍂 🍂 ————

PICTURED AT LEFT: Herbed Turkey Breast, Overnight Vegetable Salad, Whole Wheat Dinner Rolls and Holiday Pound Cake (recipes are on the next page).

Herbed Turkey Breast

If I cook the turkey the day before, I can spend the actual holiday visiting with my family.

- 1/2 **cup butter *or* margarine**
- 1/4 **cup lemon juice**
- 2 **tablespoons soy sauce**
- 2 **tablespoons finely chopped green onions**
- 1 **tablespoon rubbed sage**
- 1 **teaspoon dried thyme**
- 1 **teaspoon dried marjoram**
- 1/4 **teaspoon pepper**
- 1 **bone-in whole turkey breast (5-1/2 to 6 pounds)**

In a small saucepan, combine the first eight ingredients; bring to a boil. Remove from the heat. Place turkey in a shallow roasting pan; baste with butter mixture. Bake, uncovered, at 325° for 1-1/2 to 2 hours or until a meat thermometer reads 170°, basting every 30 minutes. **Yield:** 10-12 servings.

— 🍴 🍴 🍴 —

Mushroom Corn Bread Dressing

(Not Pictured)

This family-pleasing dressing is moist and flavorful.

- 2 **cups cornmeal**
- 3 **teaspoons sugar**
- 3 **teaspoons baking powder**
- 1 **teaspoon salt**
- 5 **eggs**
- 1 **can (12 ounces) evaporated milk**
- 1/4 **cup vegetable oil**
- 2 **cups chopped fresh mushrooms**

- 1 **cup chopped celery**
- 1/2 **cup chopped green onions**
- 3 **tablespoons butter *or* margarine**
- 2 **cans (14-1/2 ounces *each*) chicken broth**
- 1 **can (10-3/4 ounces) condensed cream of chicken soup, undiluted**
- 1/4 **cup sliced almonds, toasted**
- 1 **teaspoon poultry seasoning**
- 1/4 **teaspoon pepper**

For corn bread, combine the first four ingredients in a bowl. Combine 2 eggs, milk and oil; stir into dry ingredients just until moistened. Pour into a greased 9-in. square baking pan. Bake at 400° for 18-20 minutes or until a toothpick comes out clean. Cool on a wire rack. In a skillet, saute mushrooms, celery and onions in butter until tender.

In a large bowl, beat remaining eggs; add broth, soup, almonds, poultry seasoning, pepper and vegetables. Crumble corn bread over mixture; stir well. Pour into a greased 13-in. x 9-in. x 2-in. baking dish. Bake, uncovered, at 350° for 45-50 minutes or until a knife inserted near the center comes out clean. **Yield:** 10-12 servings.

— 🍴 🍴 🍴 —

Overnight Vegetable Salad

This side dish goes well with almost any meal, and we never seem to tire of it.

✓ Uses less fat, sugar or salt. Includes Nutritional Analysis and Diabetic Exchanges.

- 2-1/2 **cups cauliflowerets**
- 2 **cups sliced fresh mushrooms**
- 1-1/2 **cups *each* broccoli florets, sliced carrots and yellow summer squash**
- 1/2 to 3/4 **cup vegetable oil**
- 1/2 **cup cider vinegar**
- 2 **teaspoons sugar**
- 1 **teaspoon dill weed**

3/4 **teaspoon salt, optional**
1/2 **teaspoon garlic salt *or* garlic powder**
1/2 **teaspoon pepper**

In a bowl, combine the vegetables; set aside. In a jar with a tight-fitting lid, combine the remaining ingredients; shake well. Pour over vegetables; toss gently. Cover and refrigerate for 8 hours or overnight. **Yield:** 12 servings.
   Nutritional Analysis: One serving (prepared with garlic powder and 1/2 cup oil and without salt) equals 105 calories, 15 mg sodium, 0 cholesterol, 6 g carbohydrate, 1 g protein, 9 g fat, 2 g fiber. **Diabetic Exchanges:** 2 fat, 1 vegetable.

Whole Wheat Dinner Rolls

Even from the freezer, these rolls taste fresh and good.

   2 **packages (1/4 ounce *each*) active dry yeast**
2-1/4 **cups warm water (110° to 115°)**
1/4 **cup shortening**
   2 **eggs**
1/2 **cup plus 1 tablespoon sugar**
   2 **teaspoons salt**
   3 **cups whole wheat flour**
3-1/2 to 4 **cups all-purpose flour**
1/4 **cup butter *or* margarine, melted**

In a large mixing bowl, dissolve yeast in warm water; let stand for 5 minutes. Add the shortening, eggs, sugar, salt and whole wheat flour; beat until smooth. Add enough all-purpose flour to form a soft dough. Turn onto a floured surface; knead until smooth and elastic, about 6-8 minutes. Place in a greased bowl, turning once to grease top. Cover and let rise in a warm place until doubled, about 1 hour. Punch dough down.

Divide into four portions; shape each into 12 balls. Place 1 in. apart on greased baking sheets. Cover and let rise until doubled, about 25 minutes. Bake at 375° for 11-15 minutes or until browned. Brush with butter. **Yield:** 4 dozen.

———— 🎺 🎺 🎺 ————

Holiday Pound Cake

I bake this moist cake 2 days before our family dinner. Its flavor mellows with a little time.

   1 **cup butter (no substitutes), softened**
1/2 **cup shortening**
   1 **package (3 ounces) cream cheese, softened**
2-1/2 **cups sugar**
   5 **eggs**
   3 **cups cake flour**
   1 **teaspoon baking powder**
1/2 **teaspoon salt**
   1 **cup buttermilk**
   1 **teaspoon lemon extract**
   1 **teaspoon vanilla extract**
Strawberry ice cream topping
Sliced fresh strawberries, optional

In a large mixing bowl, cream butter, shortening and cream cheese. Gradually add sugar, beating until light and fluffy. Add the eggs, one at a time, beating well after each addition. Combine the dry ingredients; add to creamed mixture alternately with buttermilk. Stir in extracts. Pour into a greased and floured 10-in. fluted tube pan.
   Bake at 325° for 1 hour and 20 minutes or until a toothpick inserted near the center comes out clean. Cool for 10 minutes; remove from pan to a wire rack. Serve with strawberry topping and fresh strawberries if desired. **Yield:** 12-16 servings.

A fragrant roast is in the oven...the rest of her delightful dinner is already prepared ...and she's ready to relish Christmas Day with her family!

By Audrey Thibodeau, Gilbert, Arizona

I LOOK FORWARD to having a relaxed Christmas—thanks to a mostly make-ahead dinner.

My husband, Roger, and I often celebrate at home with a few of our children and grandchildren. (We have two daughters and three sons, 10 grandchildren and one great-grandson.)

The rosemary gives off a wonderful aroma while the Rosemary Pork Roast is cooking. This is an herb I use often in breads, cookies and vegetables. Sometimes I'll use fresh rosemary sprigs and bright red crab apples to garnish the roast.

Fancy Baked Potatoes have long been my favorite way to prepare double-baked potatoes for guests. They can be made the day before and kept in the refrigerator. (It's best to remove them from the fridge a half hour before reheating.)

This recipe saves the hassle of mashing potatoes at the last minute. I'll add pimientos as a colorful touch for my holiday dinner.

Apple Sweet Potato Bake is another delicious do-ahead dish I often depend on.

Cranberry Shiver has just the right tart flavor after a rich dinner. You can make it well ahead, since it will keep up to a month in the freezer.

Of course, there's always a tray of Christmas cookies to pass. Holly Berry Cookies star in my assortment, and I make extra to give as gifts. Spicy and fruity, they're holiday-special!

I also serve a green vegetable or crunchy salad and hot rolls or biscuits for our Christmas repast. It's a gratifying meal, but one that I can manage quite easily and still have time to enjoy with my family.

Perhaps you'll want to put some of my make-ahead holiday recipes to the test!

PICTURED AT LEFT: Rosemary Pork Roast, Fancy Baked Potatoes, Apple Sweet Potato Bake, Holly Berry Cookies and Cranberry Shiver (recipes are on the next page).

kle with salt if desired. Bake, uncovered, at 350° for 2 to 2-1/2 hours or until a meat thermometer reads 160°-170°.

Remove roast to a warm serving platter; let stand for 10 minutes before slicing. Meanwhile, skim fat from pan juices. Combine cornstarch and water until smooth; stir into juices. Bring to a boil over medium heat; boil and stir for 2 minutes. Serve with roast. **Yield:** 8 servings.

Nutritional Analysis: One serving (prepared with low-sodium broth and without salt) equals 305 calories, 117 mg sodium, 102 mg cholesterol, 4 g carbohydrate, 36 g protein, 15 g fat. **Diabetic Exchanges:** 5 lean meat, 1 vegetable.

— 🍳 🍳 🍳 —

Fancy Baked Potatoes

(Pictured on page 283)

I can't count the times I've turned to this tried-and-true recipe when company is coming.

    4 large baking potatoes
Vegetable oil
    2 tablespoons butter *or* margarine
    1/2 cup sour cream
    1/4 cup milk
    1/2 teaspoon salt
    1/4 teaspoon pepper
    1 jar (2 ounces) diced pimientos, drained, *divided*
    2 tablespoons minced chives, *divided*

Rub potatoes with oil; place in a shallow baking pan. Bake at 400° for 1 hour or until tender. Cool. Cut in half lengthwise. Scoop out pulp, leaving a 1/4-in. shell; set shells aside.

In a mixing bowl, combine pulp, butter, sour cream and milk; beat until creamy. Stir in salt, pepper and half of the pimientos and chives. Spoon or pipe filling into shells. Return to the baking pan. Bake at 350° for 35-40 minutes or until lightly browned. Sprinkle with the remaining pimientos and chives. **Yield:** 8 servings.

— 🍳 🍳 🍳 —

Apple Sweet Potato Bake

(Pictured on page 283)

Grandmother always served sweet potatoes and apples with pork, so I know she'd approve of this dish I created to combine the two.

    3 cups sliced peeled cooked sweet potatoes
    3 cups sliced peeled tart apples

Rosemary Pork Roast

(Also pictured on front cover)

Tender and full of flavor, this lovely roast is an impressive main dish for a Christmas dinner.

☑ Uses less fat, sugar or salt. Includes Nutritional Analysis and Diabetic Exchanges.

    1 boneless pork loin roast (3 to 3-1/2 pounds)
    1/2 cup chopped green onions
2-1/4 cups chicken broth, *divided*
    1/4 cup cider vinegar *or* red wine vinegar
    2 tablespoons olive *or* vegetable oil
    4 garlic cloves, minced
    1 tablespoon minced fresh rosemary *or* 1 teaspoon dried rosemary, crushed
    1/4 teaspoon pepper
    1 teaspoon salt, optional
    2 tablespoons cornstarch
    1/4 cup cold water

Place roast in a large resealable plastic bag. Combine onions, 1/4 cup broth, vinegar, oil, garlic, rosemary and pepper; pour over roast. Cover and refrigerate for 4-8 hours, turning occasionally.

Remove roast and place with fat side up in an ungreased shallow roasting pan. Combine marinade with remaining broth; pour over roast. Sprin-

3/4 **cup packed brown sugar**
3/4 **teaspoon ground nutmeg**
1/4 **teaspoon ground allspice**
1/4 **teaspoon salt**
Dash pepper
3 **tablespoons butter *or* margarine**

In a greased 1-1/2-qt. baking dish, layer half of the sweet potatoes and apples. Combine brown sugar, nutmeg, allspice, salt and pepper; sprinkle half over apples. Dot with half of the butter. Repeat layers. Cover and bake at 350° for 15 minutes. Baste with pan juices. Bake, uncovered, 15 minutes longer or until the apples are tender. **Yield:** 8 servings.

— ▼ ▼ ▼ —

Holly Berry Cookies

(Pictured on page 282)

These festive filled cookies are the all-time favorites of my family. Back when our children were small, we began baking them the day after Halloween and put them in the freezer.

2 **cups all-purpose flour**
1 **cup sugar**
1 **teaspoon ground cinnamon**
3/4 **teaspoon baking powder**
1/4 **teaspoon salt**
1/2 **cup cold butter (no substitutes)**
1 **egg**
1/4 **cup milk**
2/3 **cup seedless raspberry jam**
GLAZE:
2 **cups confectioners' sugar**
2 **tablespoons milk**
1/2 **teaspoon vanilla extract**
Red-hot candies
Green food coloring

In a large bowl, combine the first five ingredients. Cut in butter until the mixture resembles coarse crumbs. In a small bowl, beat egg and milk. Add to crumb mixture just until moistened. Cover and refrigerate for 1 hour or until easy to handle.

On a lightly floured surface, roll out dough to 1/8-in. thickness. Cut with a 2-in. round cookie cutter. Place on ungreased baking sheets. Bake at 375° for 8-10 minutes or until edges are lightly browned. Cool on wire racks.

Spread jam on half of the cookies; top each with another cookie. In a small mixing bowl, combine sugar, milk and vanilla until smooth; spread over cookies. Decorate with red-hots before glaze is set. Let dry. Using a small new paintbrush and green food coloring, paint holly leaves on cookies. **Yield:** 2 dozen.

Cranberry Shiver

Cool and refreshing, this pretty dessert is delightfully sweet-tart. You can make it ahead.

✓ Uses less fat, sugar or salt. Includes Nutritional Analysis and Diabetic Exchanges.

1 **package (12 ounces) fresh *or* frozen cranberries**
3 **cups water, *divided***
1-3/4 **cups sugar**
1/4 **cup lemon juice**
1 **teaspoon grated orange peel**
Fresh mint, optional

In a saucepan, bring the cranberries and 2 cups of water to a boil. Reduce heat; simmer for 5 minutes. Press through a strainer to remove skins; discard skins. To the juice, add sugar, lemon juice, orange peel and remaining water; mix well. Pour into an 8-in. square pan. Cover and freeze until ice begins to form around edges of pan, about 1-1/2 hours; stir. Freeze until mushy, about 30 minutes.

Spoon into a freezer container; cover and freeze. Remove from the freezer 20 minutes before serving. Scoop into small dishes; garnish with mint if desired. **Yield:** 10 servings.

Nutritional Analysis: One serving (1/2 cup) equals 154 calories, 1 mg sodium, 0 cholesterol, 40 g carbohydrate, trace protein, trace fat. **Diabetic Exchange:** 2-1/2 fruit.

Meals in Minutes

In a hurry? Mix and match these favorite recipes from fellow busy cooks to make countless meals that are ready to eat in 30 minutes or less.

SPEEDY SOLUTIONS. Clockwise from upper left: Hearty Ham Dinner's Ready in a Hurry (p. 294), Summer Meal Adds Sizzle to Supper (p. 302), Fall Feast Will Harvest Compliments (p. 290) and Flavors Blend to Make Chicken Special (p. 292).

Delicious Dinner Warms Heart and Soul

IF HOLIDAY hustle and bustle keeps your time in the kitchen to a minimum, a satisfying fast-to-fix meal is the perfect gift to give yourself and your family!

The complete-meal menu here is made up of favorite recipes shared by three great cooks. You can have everything ready to serve in about 30 minutes.

Salisbury Steak is shared by Carol Callahan of Rome, Georgia. "This meat dish can be made in 25 minutes," she assures, "or made ahead and reheated with the gravy in the microwave.

"I often double the recipe and freeze one batch of cooked steaks and gravy for an even faster meal on an especially busy night," she adds.

Quick Carrots is a versatile colorful side dish from Florence Jacoby. This Granite Falls, Minnesota cook says the carrots and green onions make a flavorful combination that your family is sure to enjoy.

Banana Pudding Dessert comes from Hazel Merrill of Greenville, South Carolina. "This creamy dessert with mild banana taste is 'comfort food' that tastes like you fussed," Hazel says.

— ☕ ☕ ☕ —

Salisbury Steak

✓ Uses less fat, sugar or salt. Includes Nutritional Analysis and Diabetic Exchanges.

　1　egg white, lightly beaten
1/3　cup chopped onion
1/4　cup crushed saltines
　2　tablespoons milk
　1　tablespoon prepared horseradish
1/4　teaspoon salt, optional
1/8　teaspoon pepper
　1　pound lean ground beef
　1　jar (12 ounces) beef gravy
1-1/4 to 1-1/2 cups sliced fresh mushrooms
　2　tablespoons water
Hot cooked noodles, optional

In a bowl, combine the egg white, onion, cracker crumbs, milk, horseradish, salt if desired and pepper. Add beef; mix well. Shape into four oval patties. Fry in a skillet over medium heat for 10-12 minutes or until meat is no longer pink, turning once. Remove and keep warm. Add gravy, mushrooms and water to skillet; heat for 3-5 minutes. Serve over patties and noodles if desired. **Yield:** 4 servings.

Nutritional Analysis: One serving (prepared with low-fat gravy and fat-free milk and without salt; calculated without noodles) equals 248 calories, 205 mg sodium, 66 mg cholesterol, 9 g carbohydrate, 25 g protein, 12 g fat. **Diabetic Exchanges:** 3 meat, 1/2 starch, 1/2 vegetable.

— ☕ ☕ ☕ —

Quick Carrots

　2　cups fresh *or* frozen sliced carrots
　1　tablespoon butter *or* margarine
　2　tablespoons sliced green onion
　1　tablespoon water
1/4　teaspoon salt
Chopped fresh parsley

In a saucepan, combine the first five ingredients. Cover and simmer for 8-10 minutes or until the carrots are crisp-tender. Sprinkle with parsley. **Yield:** 4 servings.

— ☕ ☕ ☕ —

Banana Pudding Dessert

1-1/4　cups cold water
　1　can (14 ounces) sweetened condensed milk
　1　package (3.4 ounces) instant vanilla pudding mix
　2　cups whipped topping
　24 to 32 vanilla wafers
　3　large firm bananas, sliced

In a large bowl, combine water, milk and pudding mix; beat on low speed for 2 minutes. Chill for 5 minutes. Fold in the whipped topping. In individual dessert dishes, layer vanilla wafers, pudding, bananas and remaining pudding. Top each with a wafer. Chill until serving. **Yield:** 6-8 servings.

Vivid Veggies

For lovely looking vegetable dishes, add a bit of vinegar to the water when cooking. This trick helps all vegetables keep their fresh, bright color.

Fall Feast Will Harvest Compliments

WHEN COOLER DAYS signal the start of the busy pre-holiday season, even dedicated cooks can't always spend as much time as usual in the kitchen. Then hearty, fast-to-fix meals come in handy.

The complete-meal menu here is made up of favorites from three busy cooks, combined in our Test Kitchen. You can have everything ready to serve in only half an hour!

Turkey in Curry Sauce is a delicious fall entree with a hint of curry flavor and crunchy nuts. "You can whip up this main dish in just minutes using leftover turkey," relates Lucile Proctor of Panguitch, Utah.

Peas with Mushrooms, from Mary Dennis of Bryan, Ohio, is a savory side dish with a fresh taste, even though it calls for convenient frozen peas.

Rich Chocolate Mousse will get raves for its big chocolate taste. The recipe comes from Florence Palmer of Marshall, Illinois, who says, "I love to serve this impressive dessert because people think I went to a lot of trouble. Actually, it's easy to make."

—— ☕ ☕ ☕ ——

Turkey in Curry Sauce

1/2 cup chopped onion
1/4 cup butter *or* margarine
1/4 cup all-purpose flour
 1 can (14-1/2 ounces) chicken broth
 1 cup half-and-half cream
 2 to 3 teaspoons curry powder
 2 cups cubed cooked turkey
 2 tablespoons chopped pimientos
Hot cooked rice
1/2 cup chopped peanuts

In a saucepan, saute onion in butter until tender. Add flour to form a smooth paste. Gradually stir in broth; bring to a boil. Boil for 1-2 minutes or until thickened. Reduce heat. Add the cream and curry; mix well. Add turkey; heat through. Stir in pimientos. Serve over rice; sprinkle with peanuts. **Yield:** 4 servings.

—— ☕ ☕ ☕ ——

Peas with Mushrooms

✓ Uses less fat, sugar or salt. Includes Nutritional Analysis and Diabetic Exchanges.

1/2 pound fresh mushrooms, sliced
 2 tablespoons sliced green onion
 1 tablespoon butter *or* margarine
1/4 teaspoon dried marjoram
1/4 teaspoon salt, optional
1/8 teaspoon pepper
Dash ground nutmeg
 1 package (10 ounces) frozen peas, cooked

In a skillet over medium heat, saute the mushrooms and onions in butter for 3-5 minutes. Add marjoram, salt if desired, pepper and nutmeg; mix well. Add peas and heat through. **Yield:** 4 servings.

Nutritional Analysis: One serving (prepared with margarine and without salt) equals 95 calories, 117 mg sodium, 0 cholesterol, 10 g carbohydrate, 4 g protein, 3 g fat. **Diabetic Exchanges:** 1 vegetable, 1/2 starch, 1/2 fat.

—— ☕ ☕ ☕ ——

Rich Chocolate Mousse

8 squares (1 ounce *each*) semisweet chocolate
3 tablespoons confectioners' sugar
3 tablespoons hot strong coffee
3 egg yolks
1 carton (8 ounces) frozen whipped topping, thawed, *divided*

In a double boiler over simmering water, melt chocolate. Remove top pan from heat; stir in sugar and coffee. Add one yolk at a time, stirring until smooth. Place top pan over boiling water; cook and stir for 3-4 minutes or until thick. Pour into a bowl; chill for 6-8 minutes. Fold in 3 cups whipped topping. Spoon into serving dishes. Top with remaining whipped topping. **Yield:** 4 servings.

Poultry Pointers

The next time you roast a whole turkey or turkey breast, set aside 2 cups cubed cooked meat for this meal. Cool completely and place in an airtight container. To prevent the turkey from drying out, cover with a damp paper towel; refrigerate for 3 to 4 days. For longer storage, freeze up to 3 months.

Flavors Blend to Make Chicken Special

SPENDING TIME preparing an elaborate meal is no problem for those who like to cook *and* have time to spend in the kitchen. But some days, speed can be the crucial ingredient in what foods you whip up for your hungry clan.

The complete-meal menu here is comprised of family favorites from three great cooks. The ingredients are readily available any time of year, plus you can have the entire meal ready to serve in just 30 minutes or less!

Baked Garlic Chicken is a quick oven entree for lovely golden breaded chicken breasts. "The coating keeps the meat moist and well-seasoned," assures Mary Lou Wayman of Salt Lake City, Utah. "It's a simple recipe that tastes like it took a lot more work than it really did."

Salad with Buttermilk Dressing is suggested by Vivian Haen of Menomonee Falls, Wisconsin. "My family has requested this creamy dressing over garden-fresh salad greens for years," she says, "and I haven't had to disappoint them yet! Peppers provide added color and crunch."

Raspberry Pear Delight is a fast-to-fix yet fancy-looking dessert that's a perfect ending to just about any type of meal—from simple to special-occasion, says Marion Tipton of Phoenix, Arizona. "This is one dessert my family just adores. Chocolate and raspberries were made for each other!"

— 🥄 🥄 🥄 —

Baked Garlic Chicken

  1/3 cup mayonnaise*
  1/4 cup grated Parmesan cheese
  3 to 4 tablespoons savory herb with garlic soup mix
  4 boneless skinless chicken breast halves
  2 tablespoons dry bread crumbs

In a bowl, combine mayonnaise, Parmesan cheese and soup mix. Place the chicken in a greased 11-in. x 7-in. x 2-in. baking dish. Spread with the mayonnaise mixture. Sprinkle with bread crumbs. Bake, uncovered, at 400° for 20-25 minutes or until juices run clear and a meat thermometer reads 170°. **Yield:** 4 servings.

  *Editor's Note: Light or fat-free mayonnaise may not be substituted for regular mayonnaise.

Salad with Buttermilk Dressing

  3/4 cup buttermilk
  3/4 cup mayonnaise
  1 tablespoon minced fresh parsley
  1/2 teaspoon sugar
  1/2 teaspoon ground mustard
  1/4 teaspoon onion powder
  1/4 teaspoon garlic powder
  1/4 teaspoon pepper
Assorted salad greens, sweet yellow pepper strips and sliced cucumbers *or* vegetables of your choice

In a bowl, whisk together the buttermilk, mayonnaise, parsley, sugar, mustard, onion powder, garlic powder and pepper. Serve over salad greens and fresh vegetables. Refrigerate leftover dressing. **Yield:** 1-1/2 cups.

— 🥄 🥄 🥄 —

Raspberry Pear Delight

  1 package (10 ounces) frozen sweetened raspberries, thawed
  1 can (15 ounces) pear halves, drained
  1 pint raspberry sorbet *or* sherbet
Hot fudge ice cream topping
Fresh raspberries and mint, optional

In a blender or food processor, puree the raspberries; strain the seeds. Pour onto four dessert plates or into shallow bowls. Top with pears and a scoop of sorbet. Drizzle with hot fudge topping. Garnish with fresh berries and mint if desired. **Yield:** 4 servings.

Cooking Chicken

Reduce shrinkage in boneless chicken breasts by removing the clearly visible white tendon.

Add fiber to the coating of fried or baked chicken by mixing oat bran with the seasonings.

To spark the flavor of a mild dish, rub the whole chicken or pieces with a paste of fresh herbs (tarragon, rosemary and/or thyme are classic choices), minced garlic and olive oil.

Hearty Ham Dinner's Ready in a Hurry

FOR THOSE who love to cook, spending time in the kitchen preparing an elaborate meal is a joy. Still, there are some days when you need to pull together a satisfying meal in just minutes.

The fast and flavorful meal here is made up of tried-and-true favorites from three busy cooks. You can have everything on the table in just half an hour!

Hurry-Up Ham 'n' Noodles is a rich-tasting entree created by Lucille Howell of Portland, Oregon. "This basic hearty dish is ready to serve in almost the time it takes to cook the noodles," she says. "I make it often for luncheons and potlucks. Mostly I make it on days when I'm in a hurry to get something on the table."

Continues Lucille, "This stovetop specialty is a great way to use up leftover ham from Easter, Christmas or any other dinner."

Tangy Carrot Coins give a popular nutritious vegetable a new twist, writes Lois Stephen from Mt. Morris, Michigan. "This colorful side dish is as easy to fix as plain carrots, but the light, creamy coating makes them extra yummy," she adds. "Even folks who don't usually care for carrots gobble them up in no time…then ask for more!"

Peachy Sundaes are a treat that grandmother Betty Claycomb has enjoyed since she was a teenager. "Years ago, a friend worked at a fancy hotel where this delicious dessert was served," recalls the Alverton, Pennsylvania cook. "These sundaes are very simple to prepare but look and taste elegant."

— 🥄 🥄 🥄 —

Hurry-Up Ham 'n' Noodles

     5 to 6 cups uncooked wide egg noodles
 1/4 cup butter *or* margarine
     1 cup whipping cream
1-1/2 cups julienned fully cooked ham
 1/2 cup grated Parmesan cheese
 1/4 cup thinly sliced green onions
 1/4 teaspoon salt
 1/8 teaspoon pepper

Cook noodles according to package directions. Meanwhile, in a skillet over medium heat, melt butter. Stir in cream. Bring to a boil; cook and stir for 2 minutes. Add ham, cheese, onions, salt and pepper; heat through. Drain noodles; add to ham mixture and heat through. **Yield:** 4 servings.

— 🥄 🥄 🥄 —

Tangy Carrot Coins

 1 pound carrots, sliced
 3 tablespoons butter *or* margarine
 1 tablespoon brown sugar
 1 tablespoon Dijon mustard
1/8 teaspoon salt

Place 1 in. of water and carrots in a saucepan. Bring to a boil. Reduce heat; cover and simmer for 7-9 minutes or until crisp-tender. Drain. Add the butter, brown sugar, mustard and salt; cook and stir over medium heat for 1-2 minutes or until sauce is thickened and carrots are coated. **Yield:** 4 servings.

— 🥄 🥄 🥄 —

Peachy Sundaes

 1 pint vanilla ice cream
1/2 to 1 cup peach preserves, warmed
1/4 cup chopped almonds, toasted
1/4 cup flaked coconut, toasted, optional

Divide ice cream among four serving dishes. Top with preserves; sprinkle with almonds and coconut if desired. **Yield:** 4 servings.

A Bunch of Carrot Tips

The best carrots are young and slender. Look for those that are firm and smooth; avoid any with cracks or that have begun to soften and wither.

If buying carrots with their greenery, make sure the leaves are moist and bright green. Carrot greens rob the roots of moisture and vitamins, so remove them as soon as you get home.

Store carrots in a plastic bag in the refrigerator for up to 2 weeks.

Stir-Fry Is Simple Way To Serve Supper

AFTER SPRING has "sprung" where you live, you can't wait to start enjoying the flavors of the season. There's no better way to do that than by serving foods that feature plenty of refreshing, colorful produce.

Here three country cooks share family-favorite recipes for delightful dishes showcasing peppers, peas and pineapple! Together, these foods create a complete-meal menu that goes from start to serving in 30 minutes or less.

With peppers, onion and celery, Curried Beef Stir-Fry is a flavorful eye-catching entree. "I created this hearty recipe myself and prepare it often when time is short," relates Karen Munn from St. Francois Xavier, Manitoba.

Dilly Pea Salad dresses up peas in a deliciously different way. "I got the recipe for this refreshing salad from my best friend when I was a young bride," recalls Rita Applegate of La Mesa, California. "I've shared it with many people over the years."

Broiled Pineapple Dessert is a sweet and tangy treat that looks impressive but is very little fuss, assures Karen Owen of Rising Sun, Indiana. "People frequently request seconds of this fruity dessert."

Curried Beef Stir-Fry

3 tablespoons soy sauce
3 garlic cloves, minced
1 tablespoon minced fresh gingerroot *or* 1 teaspoon ground ginger
4 tablespoons vegetable oil, *divided*
1 pound boneless sirloin steak, cut into 1/8-inch strips
1 large onion, cut into 1-inch pieces
1 medium green pepper, cut into 1-inch pieces
1 medium sweet red pepper, cut into 1-inch pieces
2 large celery ribs, sliced
1 cup cold water
5 teaspoons cornstarch
1 to 2 teaspoons curry powder
Hot cooked rice *or* noodles

In a bowl, combine soy sauce, garlic, ginger and 2 tablespoons oil. Add beef; toss to coat. Cover and refrigerate for 15-20 minutes. In a large skillet or wok, heat remaining oil. Stir-fry beef over medium-high heat for 2-3 minutes. Remove beef and set aside. In the same skillet, stir-fry onion for 1 minute. Add peppers and celery; stir-fry for 2 minutes. Return beef to the skillet. Combine water, cornstarch and curry until smooth; add to skillet. Bring to a boil; boil and stir for 1 minute. Serve over rice or noodles. **Yield:** 4 servings.

Dilly Pea Salad

✓ Uses less fat, sugar or salt. Includes Nutritional Analysis and Diabetic Exchanges.

1 cup (8 ounces) sour cream
4 teaspoons lemon juice
4 teaspoons sliced green onion
2 teaspoons sugar
1 teaspoon dill weed
1/2 teaspoon curry powder
1/2 teaspoon salt, optional
1/4 teaspoon pepper
2 packages (10 ounces *each*) frozen peas, thawed

In a medium bowl, combine the first eight ingredients. Add peas; toss. Chill until ready to serve. **Yield:** 6 servings.
Nutritional Analysis: One 1/2-cup serving (prepared with nonfat sour cream and without salt) equals 123 calories, 111 mg sodium, 3 mg cholesterol, 23 g carbohydrate, 7 g protein, trace fat. **Diabetic Exchange:** 1-1/2 starch.

Broiled Pineapple Dessert

4 pineapple slices
8 teaspoons brown sugar
2 tablespoons butter *or* margarine
4 slices pound cake
4 scoops vanilla ice cream
Ground cinnamon

Place pineapple slices on a broiler pan. Top each with 2 teaspoons brown sugar and 1-1/2 teaspoons butter. Broil 4 in. from the heat for 3-5 minutes or until the sugar is bubbly. Place each slice on a piece of pound cake; top with ice cream and sprinkle with cinnamon. Serve immediately. **Yield:** 4 servings.

Chicken Salad Brings Cool Refreshment

THE SEASON helps determine how much time is spent in the kitchen. A clear summer day tempts even the most avid cooks to minimize time there.

This menu will give you plenty of time to garden, swim or enjoy a host of other outdoor activities. Its cool and creamy components will provide a welcome chill on a scorching day. Truly, though, it's a refreshing meal any time of year.

The menu was created in our Test Kitchen using tried-and-true recipes from three seasoned cooks. You can put together this complete meal—including dessert—in 30 minutes or less.

Dijon Chicken Salad is a tasty combination from Raymond Sienko of Hawleyville, Connecticut. "This is, by far, my most requested recipe," he says. "In addition to the traditional grapes, this chicken salad also features sweet apricots."

Buttermilk Rosemary Muffins have a delicate herb flavor that's special alongside any entree. Here, it complements the chicken salad especially well. The recipe is from Debbie Smith of Crossett, Arkansas, who suggests using fresh rosemary for best flavor.

Butterscotch Parfaits, from Judi Klee of Nebraska City, Nebraska, are pretty confections that are impossible to turn down. "You can change the pudding flavor to suit your tastes," notes Judi.

— 🍴 🍴 🍴 —

Dijon Chicken Salad

    4 cups cubed cooked chicken
    1 cup sliced celery
    1 cup seedless green grapes, halved
    1 cup seedless red grapes, halved
  1/4 cup chopped dried apricots
  1/4 cup sliced green onions
  3/4 cup mayonnaise
    2 tablespoons honey
    1 tablespoon Dijon mustard
  1/2 teaspoon salt
  1/8 teaspoon pepper
Lettuce leaves
  1/2 cup sliced almonds

In a bowl, combine the first six ingredients. In a small bowl, combine the mayonnaise, honey, mustard, salt and pepper; mix well. Stir into chicken mixture. Cover and refrigerate until serving. Serve on a lettuce-lined plate. Sprinkle with the almonds. **Yield:** 6 servings.

— 🍴 🍴 🍴 —

Buttermilk Rosemary Muffins

2-1/4 cups all-purpose flour
    2 tablespoons sugar
    1 tablespoon baking powder
    2 teaspoons minced fresh rosemary *or* 3/4 teaspoon dried rosemary, crushed
  3/4 teaspoon salt
  1/2 cup plus 1 tablespoon shortening
  3/4 cup buttermilk
  1/4 cup butter *or* margarine, melted

In a large bowl, combine the first five ingredients. Cut in shortening until mixture resembles coarse crumbs. Stir in buttermilk just until moistened (mixture will be dry). Fill greased muffin cups two-thirds full; brush with butter. Bake at 400° for 10-13 minutes or until a toothpick comes out clean. Cool for 5 minutes before removing from pan to a wire rack. Serve warm. **Yield:** 1 dozen.

— 🍴 🍴 🍴 —

Butterscotch Parfaits

✓ Uses less fat, sugar or salt. Includes Nutritional Analysis and Diabetic Exchanges.

    2 cups cold milk
    1 package (3.4 ounces) instant butterscotch pudding mix
   18 vanilla wafers, coarsely crushed
    1 carton (8 ounces) frozen whipped topping, thawed
    6 maraschino cherries, optional

In a mixing bowl, beat milk and pudding mix for 2 minutes or until thickened. In six parfait glasses, alternate layers of pudding, wafer crumbs and whipped topping. Garnish with a cherry if desired. Refrigerate until serving. **Yield:** 6 servings.

Nutritional Analysis: One serving (prepared with fat-free milk, sugar-free pudding mix and reduced-fat whipped topping and without cherries) equals 194 calories, 289 mg sodium, 2 mg cholesterol, 25 g carbohydrate, 4 g protein, 7 g fat, 0 fiber. **Diabetic Exchanges:** 2 starch, 1/2 fat.

No More Fishing For Fast Foods

DO YOU find yourself fishing for quick-to-fix dishes, especially during the hectic holiday season?

The homemade meal here, shared by Jean Ann Perkins of Newburyport, Maryland, goes from start to serving in about 30 minutes!

"I use this mouth-watering meal for my family and for guests, too," says Jean Ann. "It's a wonderful combination of colors and flavors—and no fuss.

"With a seasoned bread-crumb coating, Baked Lemon Haddock is my husband's favorite dish. It bakes while I prepare the rest of the meal."

She continues, "Harvard Beets make a pretty accompaniment to this or any meal and have wonderful flavor. Even those who normally shy away from beets will gobble these up.

"Almonds give Orange and Onion Salad special flair. It's a refreshing salad I serve year-round," she relates. "For dessert, Chocolate Mint Delight is especially nice for the holidays."

Baked Lemon Haddock

✓ Uses less fat, sugar or salt. Includes Nutritional Analysis and Diabetic Exchanges.

2 pounds haddock fillets
1 cup seasoned dry bread crumbs
1/4 cup butter *or* margarine, melted
2 tablespoons dried parsley flakes
2 teaspoons grated lemon peel
1/2 teaspoon garlic powder

Cut fish into serving-size pieces. Place in a greased 11-in. x 7-in. x 2-in. baking dish. Combine remaining ingredients; sprinkle over fish. Bake, uncovered, at 350° for 25 minutes or until fish flakes easily with a fork. **Yield:** 6 servings.

Nutritional Analysis: One serving (prepared with margarine) equals 266 calories, 706 mg sodium, 86 mg cholesterol, 15 g carbohydrate, 31 g protein, 9 g fat. **Diabetic Exchanges:** 4 lean meat, 1 starch.

Harvard Beets

1 can (13-1/4 ounces) sliced beets
1/4 cup sugar
1-1/2 teaspoons cornstarch
2 tablespoons cider vinegar
2 tablespoons orange juice
1 tablespoon grated orange peel

Drain beets, reserving 2 tablespoons juice; set beets and juice aside. In a saucepan, combine sugar and cornstarch. Add vinegar, orange juice and beet juice; bring to a boil. Reduce heat and simmer for 3-4 minutes or until thickened. Add beets and orange peel; heat through. **Yield:** 4-6 servings.

Orange and Onion Salad

1 head Boston lettuce, separated into leaves
1 medium red onion, thinly sliced into rings
1 can (11 ounces) mandarin oranges, drained
Sliced almonds
Bottled poppy seed dressing

Arrange lettuce leaves, onion and oranges on salad plates. Chill. Just before serving, sprinkle with almonds. Serve with poppy seed dressing. **Yield:** 4-6 servings.

Chocolate Mint Delight

1 package (3.9 ounces) instant chocolate pudding mix
2 cups cold milk
28 miniature cream-filled chocolate cookies, crushed, *divided*
1/4 cup crushed candy canes *or* peppermint candy
Frozen chocolate-flavored whipped topping, thawed
Additional peppermint candy *or* miniature candy canes

Prepare pudding with milk according to package directions. Divide among individual dessert dishes. Reserve 2 tablespoons crushed cookies; sprinkle the remaining cookies over pudding. Top with crushed candy. Spoon whipped topping over candy. Sprinkle with reserved crushed cookies. Garnish with peppermint candy. **Yield:** 4-6 servings.

Summer Meal Adds Sizzle to Supper

SPICE UP your cooking without turning up the heat in the kitchen. With this Southwestern-style meal, you'll be out of the kitchen in less than 30 minutes!

It's a complete-meal menu made up of favorites from three great cooks, combined in our test kitchen.

Chicken Quesadillas have an impressive look and taste with little preparation. "Leftover chicken gets Mexican flair from cumin in this fun main dish," says Linda Wetzel of Woodland Park, Colorado.

"Zippy Beans and Rice is a super side dish, and we also enjoy it as a light entree with corn bread and salad," relates Darlene Owen, Reedsport, Oregon.

Berry Pineapple Parfaits from Ruth Andrewson of Peck, Idaho are lovely and refreshing.

— ▭ ▭ ▭ —

Chicken Quesadillas

2-1/2 cups shredded cooked chicken
2/3 cup salsa
1/3 cup sliced green onions
3/4 to 1 teaspoon ground cumin
1/2 teaspoon salt
1/2 teaspoon dried oregano
6 flour tortillas (8 inches)
1/4 cup butter *or* margarine, melted
2 cups (8 ounces) shredded Monterey Jack cheese
Sour cream and guacamole

In a skillet, combine the first six ingredients. Cook, uncovered, over medium heat for 10 minutes or until heated through, stirring occasionally. Brush one side of tortillas with butter. Spoon 1/3 cup chicken mixture over half of unbuttered side of each tortilla. Sprinkle with 1/3 cup cheese; fold plain side of tortilla over cheese.

Place on a lightly greased baking sheet. Bake at 475° for 10 minutes or until crisp and golden brown. Cut into wedges; serve with sour cream and guacamole. **Yield:** 6 servings.

— ▭ ▭ ▭ —

Zippy Beans and Rice

✓ Uses less fat, sugar or salt. Includes Nutritional Analysis and Diabetic Exchanges.

1 can (15 ounces) black beans, rinsed and drained

1 can (10 ounces) diced tomatoes and green chilies, undrained
1 cup frozen corn
3/4 cup water
1 medium jalapeno pepper, seeded and chopped*
1 teaspoon salt, optional
1 cup uncooked instant white *or* brown rice
1 green onion, sliced

In a skillet, combine the beans, tomatoes, corn, water, jalapeno and salt if desired. Bring to a boil; stir in rice. Cover and remove from the heat. Let stand for 5 minutes or until liquid is absorbed. Sprinkle with onion. **Yield:** 6 servings.

Nutritional Analysis: One 3/4-cup serving (prepared with brown rice and without salt) equals 197 calories, 414 mg sodium, 0 cholesterol, 40 gm carbohydrate, 8 gm protein, 2 gm fat. **Diabetic Exchanges:** 2 starch, 1 vegetable, 1/2 fat.

***Editor's Note:** When cutting or seeding hot peppers, use rubber or plastic gloves to protect your hands. Avoid touching your face.

— ▭ ▭ ▭ —

Berry Pineapple Parfaits

3 cups whole fresh strawberries
3 to 4 tablespoons sugar
12 scoops vanilla ice cream
1 can (8 ounces) crushed pineapple
Whipped topping

Reserve six strawberries for garnish. Slice the remaining strawberries and toss with sugar; let stand for 10 minutes. Spoon half of the sliced berries into six parfait glasses. Top with half of the ice cream and half of the pineapple. Repeat layers. Top with whipped topping and reserved strawberries. **Yield:** 6 servings.

⌡ *Easy Equivalents*

If you need 2 cups of shredded cooked chicken for a recipe, start with 3/4 pound of boneless skinless chicken breasts or about 1-1/2 pounds of bone-in chicken breasts.

Italian Dinner Comes Together in a Jiffy

TAKING THE TIME to prepare an elaborate dinner can be a pleasure—if you enjoy cooking and have the time to do it.

Sometimes, though, even the most accomplished cook has to make a speedy meal to feed a hungry, on-the-go family. There's no time for fuss—just good food. The time-saving dinner here has a tangy Italian taste that's both hearty and satisfying.

Quick Italian Spaghetti has been a standby for Ruth Peterson of Jenison, Michigan for more than 40 years. "I can make it in a snap," says Ruth, "and there's no other spaghetti recipe my husband is even interested in trying!"

Norma Erne of Albuquerque, New Mexico shares her recipe for Celery Seed Bread. "This quick, easy bread is a family favorite with just about any Italian meal," she says. "And it's a great way to use up extra hot dog buns."

Crunchy Vegetable Salad is colorful and tasty, plus it's a good way to get kids to eat their veggies, says Linda Russell of Exeter, Ontario. "I put it on my dinner table frequently because the kids just love it!"

Taffy Apple Dip is a fun and speedy dessert. "My mother-in-law gave me this recipe," notes Sue Gronholz of Beaver Dam, Wisconsin. "It's simple to make, and it tastes just like the real thing!"

Quick Italian Spaghetti

- 1/2 pound ground beef
- 3/4 cup thinly sliced green onions
- 1/2 teaspoon salt
- 1/8 teaspoon pepper
- 2 teaspoons sugar
- 1 teaspoon Worcestershire sauce
- 3 cans (8 ounces *each*) tomato sauce
- 1 can (2-1/4 ounces) sliced ripe olives, drained

Hot cooked spaghetti
Grated Parmesan *or* Romano cheese
Real bacon bits, optional

In a skillet, brown ground beef and onions. Add the next five ingredients; cover and simmer for 10 minutes. Add olives; simmer 5 minutes longer. Spoon over spaghetti; sprinkle with cheese and bacon bits if desired. **Yield:** 4 servings.

Celery Seed Bread

- 6 tablespoons butter *or* margarine, softened
- 1/2 teaspoon celery seed
- 1/4 teaspoon paprika
- 1/4 teaspoon dried parsley flakes
- 4 hot dog buns, sliced

In a bowl, blend the butter, celery seed, paprika and parsley. Spread on cut sides of each roll. Place on a baking sheet; broil until golden brown. **Yield:** 4 servings.

Crunchy Vegetable Salad

- 2 cups cauliflowerets
- 2 cups broccoli florets
- 2 medium carrots, thinly sliced
- 1 small zucchini, sliced
- 1 small red onion, sliced
- 1 to 1-1/2 cups Italian salad dressing

Combine vegetables in a large mixing bowl. Pour salad dressing over and toss to coat evenly. Refrigerate until serving. **Yield:** 4-6 servings.

Taffy Apple Dip

- 1 package (8 ounces) cream cheese, softened
- 3/4 cup packed brown sugar
- 1 tablespoon vanilla extract
- 1/2 cup chopped peanuts
- 6 medium apples, cut into wedges

In a small mixing bowl, beat cream cheese, brown sugar and vanilla until smooth. Spread on a small serving plate; sprinkle with peanuts. Serve with apple wedges. **Yield:** 6 servings.

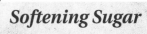

Softening Sugar

If your brown sugar has hardened, put it in a resealable plastic bag with an apple wedge; seal. Remove the apple in 1 to 2 days when the sugar is soft.

From-Scratch 'Fast Food' Is Fit for Fall

ON THE GO with your children's after-school practices and other fall activities? Forget the drive-thru—you can make satisfying fast food at home. Ready to serve in just 30 minutes, the menu here combines recipes from three super cooks.

Skillet Pork Chops cook up moist and tender with a sauce seasoned with ginger and grape jelly. "We enjoyed this main dish while visiting our son and his family," recalls June Formanek of Belle Plain, Iowa. "It was so tasty that I got the recipe from my daughter-in-law, Sandy."

Curried Celery and Apples is a delicious accompaniment for pork, suggested by Lois Miller of Bradenton, Florida. Curry powder adds a delightful zip.

Fluffy Fruit Salad, shared by Christine Halandras of Meeker, Colorado, is a simple refreshing salad. "I like this recipe since I can prepare it in advance when entertaining," Christina says. "Even people who don't care for cranberries usually like this treat."

— 🏆 🏆 🏆 —

Skillet Pork Chops

    4 pork chops (1 inch thick)
    1 tablespoon vegetable oil
    1 medium onion, chopped
    1 cup chicken broth
    2 to 3 tablespoons grape jelly
1/4 teaspoon ground ginger
4-1/2 teaspoons cornstarch
    3 tablespoons cold water
Hot cooked rice

In a skillet over medium heat, brown pork chops in oil; drain. Add onion; cook until tender. Pour broth around chops; bring to a boil. Reduce heat; cover and simmer for 12-16 minutes or until the meat is tender. Remove chops and keep warm.

Stir jelly and ginger into broth. Combine cornstarch and water until smooth; add to broth. Bring to a boil; cook and stir for 2 minutes. Serve over pork chops and rice. **Yield:** 4 servings.

— 🏆 🏆 🏆 —

Curried Celery and Apples

    2 cups thinly sliced celery
    1 small onion, chopped

1/3 cup butter *or* margarine
    1 medium tart apple, chopped
    1 tablespoon all-purpose flour
1/2 to 1 teaspoon curry powder
1/2 teaspoon salt
1/8 teaspoon pepper

In a skillet, saute celery and onion in butter until crisp-tender, about 5 minutes. Stir in apple. Cover and simmer for 3 minutes. Sprinkle with flour, curry powder, salt and pepper. Cook for 2 minutes, stirring occasionally. Serve immediately. **Yield:** 4 servings.

— 🏆 🏆 🏆 —

Fluffy Fruit Salad

✓ Uses less fat, sugar or salt. Includes Nutritional Analysis and Diabetic Exchanges.

    1 can (20 ounces) unsweetened pineapple tidbits, drained
    1 can (16 ounces) whole-berry cranberry sauce
    1 can (11 ounces) mandarin oranges, drained
    1 carton (8 ounces) frozen whipped topping, thawed
1/2 to 1 teaspoon grated orange peel
Lettuce leaves, optional
1/2 cup pecan halves, toasted

In a bowl, combine the pineapple, cranberry sauce and oranges. Fold in the whipped topping and orange peel. Serve on lettuce if desired. Top with pecans just before serving. Refrigerate leftovers. **Yield:** 14 servings.

Nutritional Analysis: One 1/2-cup serving (prepared with reduced-fat whipped topping) equals 138 calories, 10 mg sodium, 0 cholesterol, 23 g carbohydrate, 1 g protein, 5 g fat. **Diabetic Exchanges:** 1-1/2 fruit, 1 fat.

Saving Citrus Peels

Before using oranges, lemons and limes, remove the peels with a vegetable peeler or citrus zester (be sure to avoid the white pith). Store the peels in the freezer to use in a variety of recipes.

Meals on a Budget

Taste of Home has proven time and again that flavorful satisfying meals can be economical, too. Here are seven super examples.

—— 🛒 🛒 🛒 ——

PENNIES PER PERSON. Clockwise from upper left: Chicken Rice Dinner and Marinated Garden Salad (p. 322); Crunchy Chicken Salad and Rhubarb Berry Delight (p. 314); Sausage Pancakes, Cinnamon Breakfast Bites and Hot Fruit Compote (p. 318); Chili Spaghetti, Jalapeno Corn Bread and Chocolate Bundt Cake (p. 320).

Feed Your Family for $1.29 a Plate!

WHY NOT WELCOME family and friends to a casual supper featuring a country meat-and-potatoes meal? Three creative cooks show how entertaining can be simple and satisfying as well as economical. They estimate this meat-and-potatoes meal at just $1.29 per setting!

Country-Fried Steak is a longtime favorite of Betty Claycomb and her husband, Harold, who live in Alverton, Pennsylvania. It's easy to make and so delicious. This recipe makes economical cube steaks very tender.

Chive Carrots have such rich garden-fresh taste, you'd never guess how inexpensive this dish is to prepare. Wills Point, Texas cook Dorothy Pritchett says garlic gives them great flavor.

In Spencerport, New York, Theresa Evans recalls her grandmother making Dilly Mashed Potatoes for her many times over the years. You'll agree they're a perfect side dish anytime.

— 🛒 🛒 🛒 —

Country-Fried Steak

- 1/2 **cup all-purpose flour**
- 1/2 **teaspoon salt**
- 1/2 **teaspoon pepper**
- 3/4 **cup buttermilk**
- 1 **cup crushed saltines (about 30 crackers)**
- 4 **cube steaks (1 pound)**
- 3 **tablespoons vegetable oil**
- 1 **can (10-3/4 ounces) condensed cream of mushroom soup, undiluted**
- 1 **cup milk**

In a plastic bag or bowl, combine flour, salt and pepper. Place buttermilk in a shallow bowl. Place saltine crumbs in a plastic bag or bowl. Coat steaks with flour mixture, then dip into buttermilk and coat with crumbs.

In a large skillet over medium-high heat, cook steaks in hot oil for 2-3 minutes on each side or until golden and cooked to desired doneness. Remove and keep warm. Add soup and milk to skillet; bring to a boil, stirring to loosen browned bits from pan. Serve gravy with steaks. **Yield:** 4 servings.

Chive Carrots

✓ Uses less fat, sugar or salt. Includes Nutritional Analysis and Diabetic Exchanges.

- 1 **pound carrots, cut into 2-inch julienne strips**
- 1 **garlic clove, minced**
- 1 **tablespoon vegetable oil**
- 1 **tablespoon butter *or* margarine**
- 2 **tablespoons minced fresh chives *or* parsley**

In a large skillet, saute the carrots and garlic in oil and butter for 3 minutes. Reduce heat; cover and cook for 10 minutes or until carrots are crisp-ten-

der. Sprinkle with chives or parsley. Serve immediately. **Yield:** 4 servings.

Nutritional Analysis: One 1/2-cup serving (prepared with margarine) equals 106 calories, 64 mg sodium, 0 cholesterol, 12 g carbohydrate, 1 g protein, 6 g fat. **Diabetic Exchanges:** 2 vegetable, 1 fat.

—— 🍶 🍶 🍶 ——

Dilly Mashed Potatoes

2 pounds potatoes, peeled and cubed
2 tablespoons butter *or* margarine, softened
1/4 cup milk
1/4 cup sour cream
1/2 to 3/4 teaspoon dill weed
1/2 to 3/4 teaspoon salt
1/4 teaspoon pepper

In a saucepan, cook potatoes in boiling water until tender; drain. Mash with remaining ingredients. **Yield:** 4 servings.

Magical Marmalade

For fast glazed carrots, toss 1 pound of cooked carrots with 2 tablespoons of orange marmalade.

Feed Your Family for $1.37 a Plate!

AFTER A LONG DAY, there's nothing like sitting down to an old-fashioned, down-home dinner featuring flavorful "comfort" foods.

Three busy cooks show how easy it is to assemble a million-dollar meal for just $1.37 per person.

Budget Macaroni and Cheese is a quick and creamy main dish shared by Debbie Carlson of San Diego, California. "I've tried many macaroni and cheese recipes, but this is my favorite," she says.

Vegetable Salad from Pat Scott of Delray Beach, Florida is a super combination of crunchy fresh vegetables coated with a tangy marinade.

Even a budget meal can include dessert, points out Teresa Pelkey of Cherry Valley, Massachusetts, who shares her old-fashioned recipe for Great-Grandma's Ginger Cake.

— ☕ ☕ ☕ —

Budget Macaroni and Cheese

- 1 **package (7 ounces) elbow macaroni**
- 3 **tablespoons butter** *or* **margarine**
- 3 **tablespoons all-purpose flour**
- 1/4 **teaspoon salt**

Dash pepper

- 1 **cup milk**
- 1 **cup (4 ounces) shredded cheddar cheese**

Cook the macaroni according to package directions. Drain and keep warm. In a saucepan over medium-low heat, melt butter. Add flour, salt and pepper; stir to make a smooth paste. Gradually add milk, stirring constantly. Heat and stir until thickened. Remove from the heat; stir in cheese until melted. Pour over macaroni and mix well. **Yield:** 4 servings.

— ☕ ☕ ☕ —

Vegetable Salad

- 2 **cups broccoli florets**
- 2 **cups cauliflowerets**
- 4 **large mushrooms, sliced**
- 1 **celery rib, sliced**
- 1 **medium green** *or* **sweet red pepper, diced**
- 1/4 **cup chopped onion**
- 1/3 **cup vegetable oil**
- 1/4 **cup sugar**
- 1/4 **cup cider vinegar**
- 1/4 **teaspoon salt**
- 1-1/2 **teaspoons poppy seeds**

In a large bowl, combine all of the vegetables. Combine remaining ingredients in a jar with tight-fitting lid; shake well. Pour over vegetables and toss. Cover and chill 6-8 hours. **Yield:** 4 servings.

Great-Grandma's Ginger Cake

2-1/4 cups all-purpose flour
 1 teaspoon baking soda
 1 teaspoon ground ginger
 1 teaspoon ground cinnamon
 1/2 teaspoon salt
Dash ground cloves
 1/2 cup sugar
 1/2 cup shortening
 2/3 cup molasses
 1 egg

 3/4 cup boiling water
Whipped topping

Combine flour, baking soda, ginger, cinnamon, salt and cloves; set aside. In a mixing bowl, cream sugar and shortening; beat in molasses and egg. Stir in the dry ingredients alternately with water; mix well. Pour into a greased 9-in. square baking pan. Bake at 350° for 35-40 minutes. Cool completely.

Cut into squares; top with a dollop of whipped topping. Leftovers will keep for several days in an airtight container. **Yield:** 9 servings.

Feed Your Family for $1.38 a Plate!

WOULD YOU like to host a special spring luncheon without breaking your budget? Try this colorful meal with a cost per serving (including the purchased breadsticks) of only $1.38.

Crunchy Chicken Salad from Diane Hixon of Niceville, Florida features tender chicken and crunchy vegetables. With peanut oil, soy sauce and toasted sesame seeds, the dressing has a slight Oriental flair.

To save time when entertaining, you can cook the chicken and prepare the dressing the day before.

Rhubarb Berry Delight—from Joan Sieck of Rensselaer, New York—will be an instant success. This layered gelatin dish does take some time to prepare, but it's worth it.

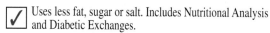

Crunchy Chicken Salad

✓ Uses less fat, sugar or salt. Includes Nutritional Analysis and Diabetic Exchanges.

- 4 cups shredded cooked chicken
- 2 cups shredded lettuce
- 1 cup julienned carrots
- 1 cup julienned cucumber
- 2/3 cup green onion strips (2-inch pieces)
- 1 cup canned bean sprouts

DRESSING:
- 2 tablespoons peanut *or* vegetable oil
- 2 tablespoons lemon juice
- 2 tablespoons sesame seeds, toasted
- 1-1/2 teaspoons soy sauce
- 1/2 teaspoon salt, optional
- 1/4 teaspoon pepper
- 1/4 teaspoon ground mustard

Hot pepper sauce to taste

In a large salad bowl, toss the chicken, lettuce, carrots, cucumber, green onions and bean sprouts. Refrigerate. In a small bowl, combine dressing ingredients. Refrigerate. Just before serving, pour dressing over salad and toss gently. **Yield:** 10 servings.

Nutritional Analysis: One 1-cup serving (prepared with vegetable oil and light soy sauce and without salt) equals 141 calories, 80 mg sodium,

48 mg cholesterol, 5 g carbohydrate, 19 g protein, 6 g fat. **Diabetic Exchanges:** 2 lean meat, 1 vegetable, 1/2 fat.

Rhubarb Berry Delight

- 4 cups diced rhubarb
- 2 cups fresh *or* frozen strawberries
- 1-1/2 cups sugar, *divided*
- 1 package (6 ounces) raspberry gelatin
- 2 cups boiling water
- 1 cup milk

1 envelope unflavored gelatin
1/4 cup cold water
1-1/2 teaspoons vanilla extract
2 cups (16 ounces) sour cream

In a saucepan, cook rhubarb, strawberries and 1 cup sugar until fruit is tender. In a large bowl, dissolve raspberry gelatin in boiling water. Stir in fruit; set aside. In another pan, heat milk and remaining sugar over low until sugar is dissolved. Meanwhile, soften unflavored gelatin in cold water. Add to hot milk mixture and stir until gelatin dissolves. Remove from the heat; add vanilla. Cool to lukewarm; blend in sour cream. Set aside at room temperature.

Pour a third of the fruit mixture into a 3-qt. bowl; chill until almost set. Spoon a third of the sour cream mixture over fruit; chill until almost set. Repeat layers twice, chilling between layers if necessary. Refrigerate until firm, at least 3 hours. **Yield:** 12 servings.

Keeping Carrots

Store carrots in a plastic bag in the refrigerator for up to 2 weeks. As they age, they'll lose flavor and firmness. Rinse and/or peel before using.

Feed Your Family for 82¢ a Plate!

HOMEMADE MEALS are always more economical —and certainly more delicious—than foods prepared in a restaurant. That's especially true when it comes to pizza and all the fixin's!

Three terrific cooks show how easy it is to put together a tempting Italian menu for just 82¢ a setting.

Pizza from Scratch is a low-budget crowd-pleaser that tastes so good. This recipe comes from Audra Dee Collins of Hobbs, New Mexico, who asks, "Why pay for takeout or pop a frozen pizza in the oven?

"You can make this tasty pizza yourself with hardly any fuss. My sister shared the recipe with me years ago. It's now a staple in our home," says Audra Dee. "Have everyone pitch in when assembling the pizzas...it's a nice way to get the family together. Mix and match topping ingredients to suit your tastes."

Italian Cucumber Salad, shared by Jane Nichols of Houston, Texas, is a snap to prepare and a great use for your garden's bounty of vegetables. "Folks enjoy this tangy, refreshing side dish," Jane shares. "I came up with the recipe after sampling a similar salad at a local cafeteria."

Chewy Peanut Butter Bars have been a favorite treat at the Milan, Ohio home of Deb DeChant for years. "With seven of us here, including two teenage boys, these bars never last long!" Deb says. "It's hard to believe how simple they are to prepare."

Pizza from Scratch

1 package (1/4 ounce) active dry yeast
1 cup warm water (110° to 115°)
2 tablespoons vegetable oil
1 teaspoon salt
1 teaspoon sugar
2-3/4 to 3-1/4 cups all-purpose flour
SAUCE:
  1 can (15 ounces) tomato sauce
1/2 cup chopped onion
3/4 teaspoon Italian seasoning
1/4 teaspoon garlic powder
1/4 teaspoon salt
1/8 teaspoon pepper

TOPPINGS:
1/2 pound bulk Italian sausage, cooked and drained
  1 can (4 ounces) mushroom stems and pieces, drained
  1 medium green pepper, sliced
1-1/2 cups (6 ounces) shredded mozzarella cheese

In a mixing bowl, dissolve yeast in water. Add oil, salt, sugar and 2 cups flour. Beat on medium speed for 3 minutes. Stir in enough remaining flour to form a soft dough. Turn onto a floured surface; knead until smooth and elastic, about 6-8 minutes. Place in a greased bowl, turning once to grease top. Cover and let rest in a warm place for 10 minutes.

Meanwhile, combine sauce ingredients; set aside. Divide dough in half. On a floured surface,

roll each portion into a 13-in. circle. Transfer to two greased 12-in. pizza pans; build up edges slightly. Bake at 375° for 15 minutes or until lightly browned. Spread sauce over hot crusts; sprinkle with toppings. Bake for 20 minutes or until cheese is melted. **Yield:** 2 pizzas (8 servings).

— 🍶 🍶 🍶 —

Italian Cucumber Salad

   2 **medium cucumbers, peeled and sliced**
   1 **cup halved cherry tomatoes**
   1 **cup sliced red onion**
  1/2 **cup chopped green pepper**
  1/2 **cup Italian salad dressing**

In a large bowl, combine all of the ingredients; cover and refrigerate until serving. Serve with a slotted spoon. **Yield:** 8 servings.

— 🍶 🍶 🍶 —

Chewy Peanut Butter Bars

  1/2 **cup butter *or* margarine**
  1/2 **cup creamy peanut butter**
1-1/2 **cups sugar**
   1 **cup all-purpose flour**
   2 **eggs, beaten**
   1 **teaspoon vanilla extract**

In a large saucepan, melt butter and peanut butter. Remove from heat; add sugar and flour. Stir in eggs and vanilla. Spread into a greased and floured 13-in. x 9-in. x 2-in. baking pan. Bake at 350° for 28-32 minutes or until lightly browned and edges start to pull away from sides of pan. **Yield:** 2 dozen.

Feed Your Family for $1.46 a Plate!

PANCAKES are a traditional breakfast favorite, but they can be served any time of day. Steaming cakes with syrup and a warm fruit salad can help start your morning or take the chill out of a cold evening.

This flavorful meal is from three frugal cooks who estimate the total cost at only $1.46 per setting.

Sausage Pancakes are a hearty entree from Barbara Downey of Preston, Iowa. "These fluffy pancakes are an easy way to fill up the kids before school," she relates.

Ruth Hastings of Louisville, Illinois recommends Cinnamon Breakfast Bites, scrumptious treats with a sweet, crispy coating.

Hot Fruit Compote is a gently spiced salad perfect for any season. "It's a pretty way to use canned fruit," says Helen Austin of Grand Rapids, Ohio.

Beverage choices could include hot tea or coffee, and cold fruit juices or milk.

— ☕ ☕ ☕ —

Sausage Pancakes

  2 **cups all-purpose flour**
  2 **teaspoons baking powder**
  1 **teaspoon salt**
1/2 **teaspoon baking soda**
  2 **eggs**
  2 **cups sour milk***
  2 **tablespoons vegetable oil**
  1 **pound bulk pork sausage, cooked and drained**
1-1/2 **cups pancake syrup**

In a bowl, combine the flour, baking powder, salt and baking soda. In another bowl, beat the eggs, milk and oil. Stir into dry ingredients just until moistened. Fold in sausage. Pour batter by 1/4 cupfuls onto a lightly greased hot griddle. Turn when bubbles form on top of pancakes. Cook until second side is golden. Serve with syrup. **Yield:** 6 servings.

*Editor's Note: To sour milk, place 2 tablespoons white vinegar in a 2-cup measuring cup. Add milk to measure 2 cups.

Cinnamon Breakfast Bites

1-1/3 **cups all-purpose flour**
  1 **cup crisp rice cereal, coarsely crushed**
  2 **tablespoons plus 1/2 cup sugar, *divided***
  3 **teaspoons baking powder**
1/2 **teaspoon salt**
1/4 **cup butter-flavored shortening**
1/2 **cup milk**
  1 **teaspoon ground cinnamon**
1/4 **cup butter *or* margarine, melted**

In a bowl, combine the flour, cereal, 2 tablespoons sugar, baking powder and salt; cut in shortening until mixture resembles coarse crumbs. Stir in milk just until moistened. Shape into 1-in. balls.

In a bowl, combine the cinnamon and remain-

ing sugar. Dip balls in butter, then roll in cinnamon-sugar. Arrange in a single layer in an 8-in. round baking pan. Bake at 425° for 15-18 minutes or until a toothpick comes out clean. **Yield:** 6 servings (2-1/2 dozen).

———— 🍵 🍵 🍵 ————

Hot Fruit Compote

1 can (20 ounces) pineapple chunks, drained
1 can (15-1/4 ounces) sliced peaches, drained
1 can (15-1/4 ounces) apricot halves, drained
1 can (15-1/4 ounces) pear halves, drained
1/4 cup maraschino cherries
1 cup orange juice
1/3 cup packed brown sugar
1/4 teaspoon ground cinnamon
4 whole cloves
1/8 teaspoon ground mace
Dash salt

In a 2-1/2-qt. baking dish, combine the pineapple, peaches, apricots, pears and cherries; set aside. In a small saucepan, combine the remaining ingredients. Bring to a boil over medium heat; pour over fruit. Bake, uncovered, at 350° for 25-30 minutes or until bubbly. Discard cloves. Serve warm. **Yield:** 6 servings.

Feed Your Family for 75¢ a Plate!

WANT TO ADD SPARK to your supper without burning cash? The cooks who shared these tasty recipes estimate the cost at a mere 75¢ per setting.

Chili Spaghetti is recommended by Pam Thompson of Girard, Illinois. "My husband often requested that his grandma make this dish," says Pam.

The recipe for Jalapeno Corn Bread comes from Anita LaRose of Benavides, Texas. "We enjoy the combination of flavors in this golden corn bread."

Chocolate Bundt Cake is a dessert from Lori Bennett's grandmother. "When I make this yummy, economical cake for my son and husband, it brings back many fond memories for me," Lori says from her Greencastle, Indiana kitchen.

— 🍽 🍽 🍽 —

Chili Spaghetti

    1 pound ground beef
1/2 cup chopped onion
    2 garlic cloves, minced
    3 cups tomato juice
    1 can (16 ounces) kidney beans, rinsed
       and drained
    6 ounces spaghetti, broken into 3-inch
       pieces
    1 tablespoon Worcestershire sauce
    2 to 3 teaspoons chili powder
    1 teaspoon salt
1/2 teaspoon pepper

In a skillet over medium heat, cook beef, onion and garlic until meat is no longer pink; drain. Transfer to a greased 2-1/2-qt. baking dish; stir in the remaining ingredients. Cover and bake at 350° for 65-70 minutes or until spaghetti is just tender. Let stand, covered, for 10 minutes. **Yield:** 6 servings.

— 🍽 🍽 🍽 —

Jalapeno Corn Bread

    1 cup cornmeal
1/2 cup shredded cheddar cheese
    2 teaspoons baking powder
3/4 teaspoon salt
    2 eggs, beaten
    1 can (8-3/4 ounces) cream-style corn
    1 cup buttermilk
1/4 cup vegetable oil
    1 to 2 tablespoons minced fresh jalapeno
       peppers*

In a bowl, combine cornmeal, cheese, baking powder and salt. Combine the remaining ingredients; stir into cornmeal mixture just until moistened. Transfer to a greased 9-in. square baking pan. Bake at 350° for 1 hour or until a toothpick inserted near the center comes out clean. **Yield:** 9 servings.

*Editor's Note: When cutting or seeding hot pep-

pers, use rubber or plastic gloves to protect your hands. Avoid touching your face.

— 🏆 🏆 🏆 —

Chocolate Bundt Cake

  1 cup salad dressing*
  1 cup water
  2 teaspoons vanilla extract
  2 cups all-purpose flour
  1 cup sugar
  2 tablespoons baking cocoa
  2 teaspoons baking soda
1/4 teaspoon salt

Confectioners' sugar, optional

In a mixing bowl, combine salad dressing, water and vanilla. Combine the flour, sugar, cocoa, baking soda and salt. Add to salad dressing mixture and beat until mixed. Transfer to a greased and floured 10-in. fluted tube pan (pan will not be full).

Bake at 350° for 35-40 minutes or until a toothpick inserted near the center comes out clean. Cool for 10 minutes; remove from pan to a wire rack. Dust with confectioners' sugar if desired. **Yield:** 12 servings.

*Editor's Note: This recipe was tested with Miracle Whip salad dressing. Light or fat-free Miracle Whip may not be substituted.

Feed Your Family for $1.50 a Plate!

AN ECONOMICAL MEAL can satisfy even the most hearty appetites. Just ask Judith Anglen. Here she shares a down-home dinner (including purchased dinner rolls) that can be put together for $1.50 a setting.

"One of our favorite meals around here is also very affordable," assures this Riverton, Wyoming cook. "I buy chicken thighs when they're on sale and freeze them for use in this meal later.

"Everyone enjoys the country-style combination of chicken, rice and mushrooms. Using chicken bouillon adds to the wonderful flavor," she says.

"Marinated Garden Salad is colorful, tangy and crunchy and complements the main dish nicely. With six simple ingredients, it's a salad I can toss together in minutes," Judith explains. "Then let it marinate for 1 hour to beautifully blend the flavors."

She adds, "Friends and family are always happy to see this meal on the table."

Leave it to a country cook like Judith to prove inexpensive foods can be flavorful, too.

— 🍴 🍴 🍴 —

Chicken Rice Dinner

- 1/2 cup all-purpose flour
- 1 teaspoon salt
- 1/2 teaspoon pepper
- 10 chicken thighs (about 3 pounds)
- 3 tablespoons vegetable oil
- 1 cup uncooked long grain rice
- 1/4 cup chopped onion
- 2 garlic cloves, minced
- 1 can (4 ounces) mushroom stems and pieces, undrained
- 2 chicken bouillon cubes
- 2 cups boiling water

Minced fresh parsley, optional

Combine flour, salt and pepper; coat chicken pieces. In a large skillet over medium heat, brown the chicken in oil. Place rice in an ungreased 13-in. x 9-in. x 2-in. baking dish. Sprinkle with onion and garlic; top with mushrooms. Dissolve bouillon in boiling water; pour over all. Place chicken pieces on top. Cover and bake at 350° for 1 hour or until chicken juices run clear and rice is tender. Sprinkle with parsley if desired. **Yield:** 5 servings.

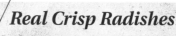

Real Crisp Radishes

For added crispness, cover radishes with water and refrigerate for 2 hours before slicing.

Marinated Garden Salad

✓ Uses less fat, sugar or salt. Includes Nutritional Analysis and Diabetic Exchanges.

1/2 cup sliced celery
1/2 cup sliced cucumber
1/2 cup sliced carrots
1/2 cup sliced radishes
1/2 cup bottled Italian salad dressing

5 cups torn salad greens

In a large bowl, combine the celery, cucumber, carrots and radishes. Add the dressing and refrigerate for 1 hour. Just before serving, add greens and toss. **Yield:** 5 servings.

Nutritional Analysis: One serving (prepared with fat-free dressing) equals 28 calories, 239 mg sodium, 0 cholesterol, 5 g carbohydrate, 1 g protein, trace fat. **Diabetic Exchange:** 1 vegetable.

Getting in the Theme of Things

These popular and fun theme-related menus include the recipes, decorating ideas and activities to make your party a success!

🍽 🍽 🍽

FESTIVE FAVORITES. Clockwise from upper left: Picnic Celebrates Red, White and Blue (p. 332), Make the Grade with Class Party (p. 334), Host a Hibernation Celebration (p. 328) and Welcome to My Pineapple Palace (p. 338).

Brunch—It's Snow Trouble at All!

By Shelly Rynearson, Dousman, Wisconsin

AS A KICKOFF to the Christmas season, my parents, my brother and his family come to our house for a theme brunch. One year's theme was snowmen and snowflakes.

My layered Potato Ham Omelet Pie can be prepared the day before, then baked the morning of the party.

Chocolate chips and pecans add a flavorful crunch to Banana Split Bread. Since finding this recipe a decade ago, I seldom make plain banana bread.

Cute as can be, Minty Snowmen have nice fresh flavor. They are easy to shape...and it's so simple to add colorful hats and earmuffs.

I also served spicy Gingerbread Snowflakes with hot spiced cider, and everyone said the party had gotten them into the holiday spirit.

Potato Ham Omelet Pie

- 1 package (17-1/4 ounces) frozen puff pastry, thawed
- 1/4 cup butter *or* margarine
- 3 cups sliced peeled red potatoes
- 1 cup thinly sliced onion
- 1/4 teaspoon salt
- 1/4 teaspoon pepper

OMELETS:
- 6 eggs
- 1/4 cup minced fresh parsley
- 2 tablespoons water

Dash *each* salt and pepper
- 2 tablespoons butter *or* margarine, *divided*

FILLING:
- 2 cups (8 ounces) shredded cheddar cheese, *divided*

1-1/2 cups cubed fully cooked ham
  1 egg, lightly beaten
  1 tablespoon water

On a floured surface, roll each puff pastry sheet into a 12-in. square. Place one square in a 10-in. quiche dish; set dish and remaining pastry aside.

In a skillet, melt butter. Add potatoes, onion, salt and pepper; cover and cook for 10-12 minutes or until potatoes are tender and golden brown, stirring occasionally. Set aside.

Beat eggs, parsley, water, salt and pepper. In a 10-in. skillet, melt 1 tablespoon butter; add half of the egg mixture. Cook over medium heat. As eggs set, lift edges, letting uncooked portion flow underneath. Continue cooking until set. Slide omelet onto a baking sheet. Repeat with remaining butter and egg mixture to make a second omelet.

Sprinkle 1 cup cheese over prepared pastry. Top with one omelet and half of the potato mixture. Layer with ham and the remaining potato mixture, cheese, omelet and puff pastry. Trim pastry to fit dish; seal and flute edges.

In a small bowl, combine beaten egg and water; brush over pastry. Bake at 375° for 30-35 minutes or until golden brown. Let stand for 10 minutes before serving. **Yield:** 8 servings.

— 🍴 🍴 🍴 —

Banana Split Bread

1/2 cup butter *or* margarine, softened
  1 cup sugar
  1 egg
  1 cup mashed ripe bananas (about 2 large)
  3 tablespoons milk
  2 cups all-purpose flour
  1 teaspoon baking powder
1/2 teaspoon baking soda
  1 cup (6 ounces) semisweet chocolate chips
1/2 cup chopped pecans

In a mixing bowl, cream butter and sugar. Beat in egg. In a small bowl, combine bananas and milk. Combine the flour, baking powder and baking soda; add to creamed mixture alternately with banana mixture. Fold in chocolate chips and pecans.

Pour into a greased 9-in. x 5-in. x 3-in. loaf pan. Bake at 350° for 60-70 minutes or until a toothpick inserted near the center comes out clean. Cool for 10 minutes before removing from pan to a wire rack. **Yield:** 1 loaf.

— 🍴 🍴 🍴 —

Minty Snowmen

  1 tablespoon butter (no substitutes), softened
  1 tablespoon light corn syrup
1/2 teaspoon mint extract
1/8 teaspoon salt
  1 cup confectioners' sugar
  1 drop *each* blue, yellow and red food coloring
Colored sprinkles and cake decorator candies

In a bowl, combine butter, corn syrup, extract and salt, mixing with a wooden spoon until blended. Gradually stir in confectioners' sugar. Knead by hand for 1-2 minutes or until mixture becomes pliable.

To 1 tablespoon of dough, add blue food coloring; knead until blended. Add yellow food coloring to another tablespoon of dough and knead. Add red food coloring to another tablespoon of dough and knead. Leave remaining dough white.

Roll white dough into a log; remove one-fourth of the log and set aside. For the snowmen's bodies, divide the remaining log into 8 pieces and roll into balls. For the snowmen's heads, divide the reserved dough into 8 pieces and roll into balls. Stack 1 smaller ball on top of each larger ball. Use the colored dough to form hats, scarves and earmuffs as desired. Used colored sprinkles and candies to make eyes, noses and buttons. **Yield:** 8 snowmen.

— 🍴 🍴 🍴 —

Gingerbread Snowflakes

  1 cup butter (no substitutes), softened
  1 cup sugar
  1 cup molasses
1/2 cup water, *divided*
  5 cups all-purpose flour
2-1/2 teaspoons ground ginger
1-1/2 teaspoons baking soda
1-1/2 teaspoons ground cinnamon
1/2 teaspoon ground allspice
1/4 teaspoon salt
3-3/4 cups (1 pound) confectioners' sugar
1-1/2 teaspoons light corn syrup
1/2 teaspoon vanilla extract

In a mixing bowl, cream butter and sugar. Beat in molasses and 1/4 cup water. Combine the flour, ginger, baking soda, cinnamon, allspice and salt; gradually add to creamed mixture. Cover and refrigerate for 1 hour or until easy to handle.

On a lightly floured surface, roll out dough to 1/4-in. thickness. Cut with 2-1/2-in. cookie cutters dipped in flour. Place 2 in. apart on ungreased baking sheets. Bake at 350° for 10-12 minutes or until edges are firm. Remove to wire racks to cool.

In a mixing bowl, combine confectioners' sugar, corn syrup, vanilla and remaining water until smooth. Transfer to a plastic bag. Cut a small hole in one corner; pipe frosting onto cookies. **Yield:** about 5 dozen.

Host a Hibernation Celebration

By Annette Ellyson, Carolina, West Virginia

IN THE MIDDLE of winter, if your "cubs" get bored with hibernation, just grin and "bear" it—with a delightful teddy bear party!

Daughters Rachel and Leah—not to mention me!—found it the perfect way to beat the blahs. We made invitations using teddy bear cookie cutters as patterns, tracing the shapes onto folded construction paper so they'd open like a card. Besides including the usual party details, we asked each guest to bring a favorite teddy bear.

My child-friendly menu for this whimsical event included finger foods—Chicken Nuggets, Teddy Bear Rolls and Valentine Cutouts, plus "cubcakes"—and a sparkling berry punch.

Quick and easy Chicken Nuggets are always a hit with kids. The coating is flavorful but not too spicy.

I remember my mom making Teddy Bear Rolls for me when I was a girl, and it's a tradition I enjoy passing on to my daughters. I always give each of them a portion of dough to shape.

If you're in a hurry, you can use hot roll mix instead of mixing the dough from scratch. The easy-to-make honey butter included with my recipe is delicious with the tiny teddy breads.

I'm often asked to share my secret for shaping Valentine Cutouts so perfectly. It's actually easy. Instead of using cookie cutters, I coat a mini heart pan with nonstick cooking spray and fill it with the gelatin mixture. After the hearts are set, they simply slide out.

For dessert, bake your favorite cupcakes, frost them with white icing and sprinkle with coconut. Then add a chocolate peppermint patty and three brown M&M's to the center to create "bear paws".

For our party table, we used a red tablecloth with a lace overlay and red heart doilies as place mats. Heart-shaped confetti (made with a heart paper punch) was strewn over the table.

Our favorite stuffed bears served as a focal point amid Victorian boxes, tins, flowers and heart-shaped trinkets. Tiny baskets brimming with chocolate hearts and teddy bear-shaped graham crackers were the favors.

Theme-related activities included a bear hunt, musical bears (musical chairs) and a reading of *Goldilocks and the Three Bears*. Lots of bear hugs at the end of the party assured me that our young guests had enjoyed themselves.

This theme could easily be adapted for a birthday or Valentine's Day party. Whatever the occasion, you can be sure your guests will have a "beary" good time!

------ 🌂 🌂 🌂 ------

Chicken Nuggets

I like to make these golden chicken nuggets because they're so quick and easy and the whole family loves them. The seasoning can also be used on chicken breast halves to make great sandwiches.

- 1 cup all-purpose flour
- 4 teaspoons seasoned salt
- 1 teaspoon paprika
- 1 teaspoon poultry seasoning
- 1 teaspoon ground mustard
- 1/2 teaspoon pepper
- 8 boneless skinless chicken breast halves
- 1/4 cup vegetable *or* olive oil

In a resealable plastic bag, combine the first six ingredients. Pound chicken to 1/2-in. thickness and cut into 1-1/2-in. pieces. Place chicken pieces, a few at a time, into bag and shake to coat. Heat oil in a skillet; cook chicken, turning frequently, until browned and juices run clear, about 6-8 minutes. **Yield:** 8-10 servings.

------ 🌂 🌂 🌂 ------

Teddy Bear Rolls

When planning the menu for this "Teddy Bear" party, I just had to include these delectable rolls and the homemade honey butter. Their oven-fresh goodness appeals to the kid in all of us.

- 2 packages (1/4 ounce *each*) active dry yeast
- 1 cup warm water (110° to 115°)
- 1 cup warm milk (110° to 115°)
- 2 tablespoons sugar
- 2 tablespoons vegetable oil
- 1 egg
- 1 teaspoon salt
- 5-1/2 to 6-1/2 cups all-purpose flour
- Raisins (2 for each roll)
- White frosting
- HONEY BUTTER:
  - 1 cup butter (no substitutes), softened
  - 1/4 cup honey
  - 1/4 cup confectioners' sugar

In a mixing bowl, dissolve yeast in water. Add the milk, sugar, oil, egg, salt and 4 cups flour; beat until smooth. Add enough remaining flour to form a soft dough. Turn onto a floured board; knead until smooth and elastic, about 6-8 minutes.

Place in a greased bowl, turning once to grease top. Cover and let rise in a warm place until doubled, about 1 hour. Punch dough down. For each bear, shape a 2-in. ball for the body. Add a 1-1/4-in. ball for the head and six 1/2-in. balls for the ears, arms and legs. Place 2 in. apart on greased baking sheets. Cover and let rise until doubled, about 20 minutes.

Bake at 400° for 17 minutes or until golden brown. Cool on wire racks. Add raisins for eyes, anchoring with a dab of frosting. Add a frosting smile. In another mixing bowl, beat honey butter ingredients until fluffy. Chill; serve with rolls. **Yield:** about 10 rolls (1-1/4 cups butter).

------ 🌂 🌂 🌂 ------

Valentine Cutouts

Cool, fruity and creamy, these gelatin treats are richer than plain gelatin since they include milk and vanilla pudding. They cut easily into whatever shape you'd like and are a fun finger food.

- 2 packages (6 ounces *each*) cherry *or* raspberry gelatin
- 2-1/2 cups boiling water
- 1 cup cold milk
- 1 package (3.4 ounces) instant vanilla pudding mix

In a bowl, dissolve gelatin in water; set aside for 30 minutes. In another bowl, whisk milk and pudding mix until smooth, about 1 minute. Quickly pour into gelatin; whisk until well blended. Pour into a 13-in. x 9-in. x 2-in. dish coated with nonstick cooking spray. Chill until set. Cut into cubes or use a heart-shaped cookie cutter. **Yield:** 8-10 servings.

'Hoops' Fan Shows Spirited Colors

By Sharon Landeen, Tucson, Arizona

TO CHEER on our favorite basketball team, the University of Arizona Wildcats, husband Don and I host a yearly party, inviting friends to come watch an out-of-town game on TV.

I decorate our whole house in the team colors, red and blue… and even our street sign is temporarily changed to "Wildcat Way".

Between 40 and 50 friends show up, so the menu must be a "grab and go" finger-food bonanza. The snack table holds annual favorites, including Slam Dunk Crab Dip, Sporty Sugar-Spice Nuts and my homemade Courtside Caramel Corn.

Folks like the curry in the zippy seafood dip, served with crackers and tortilla chips. The caramel corn, a family favorite, is a treat our children always request. Then there's the sweet and spicy nut mix—no one can stop at just one taste.

After trying a variety of desserts over the years, I've found that Butterscotch Basketball Cookies are the most popular. I use my gingerbread man cutter and then s-t-r-e-t-c-h the arms and legs into athletic positions before baking. "Suiting up" the players with icing can be a fun family project.

This casual menu is a slam dunk for the cook, since everything is easy to prepare ahead of time.

Why not plan a similar get-together to root for your home team? The crowd will love it!

Slam Dunk Crab Dip

The spirited crowd we invite is quick to dig in to this delectable dip.

    1 package (8 ounces) cream cheese,
      softened
1/4 cup milk
    1 package (8 ounces) imitation flaked
      crabmeat *or* 1 can (6 ounces) crabmeat,
      drained, flaked and cartilage removed
1/4 cup sliced green onions
1/4 cup chopped sweet red pepper
    1 teaspoon curry powder
1/2 teaspoon garlic salt
Assorted crackers

In a mixing bowl, beat cream cheese and milk until smooth. Stir in the crab, onions, red pepper, curry powder and garlic salt. Refrigerate until serving. Serve with crackers. **Yield:** 3 cups.

— 🏀 🏀 🏀 —

Sporty Sugar-Spice Nuts

To save time on the day of the big party, I mix up a batch of these nuts days in advance.

3/4 cup sugar
    3 tablespoons water
    1 egg white, lightly beaten
    1 teaspoon ground cinnamon
3/4 teaspoon salt
1/2 teaspoon ground cloves
1/4 teaspoon ground allspice
1/4 teaspoon ground nutmeg
    2 cups pecan halves
1-1/2 cups whole unblanched almonds

In a large bowl, combine the first eight ingredients; mix well. Add nuts and stir until coated. Spread evenly in a greased 15-in. x 10-in. x 1-in. baking pan. Bake at 250° for 45 minutes or until golden brown, stirring every 15 minutes. Spread on a waxed paper-lined baking sheet to cool. Store in an airtight container. **Yield:** 3-1/2 cups.

— 🏀 🏀 🏀 —

Courtside Caramel Corn

I fill up a red tin sporting the University of Arizona logo with this sweet popcorn.

    6 quarts popped popcorn
    2 cups packed brown sugar
    1 cup butter *or* margarine
1/2 cup corn syrup
    1 teaspoon salt
    1 tablespoon vanilla extract
1/2 teaspoon baking soda

Place popcorn in a large bowl and set aside. In a saucepan, combine brown sugar, butter, corn syrup and salt; bring to a boil over medium heat, stirring constantly. Boil for 5 minutes, stirring occasionally. Remove from the heat. Stir in vanilla and baking soda; mix well.

Pour over popcorn and stir until well-coated. Pour into two greased 13-in. x 9-in. x 2-in. baking pans. Bake, uncovered, at 250° for 45 minutes, stirring every 15 minutes. Cool completely. Store in airtight containers or plastic bags. **Yield:** about 5-1/2 quarts.

— 🏀 🏀 🏀 —

Butterscotch Basketball Cookies

Nope, I didn't need a special basketball player cutter to shape these sporty cookies—the gingerbread men make the team!

    1 cup butterscotch chips
    1 cup butter (no substitutes), softened
1/2 cup sugar
1/2 cup packed brown sugar
    1 egg
    2 tablespoons milk
    2 teaspoons vanilla extract
    3 cups all-purpose flour
FROSTING:
3/4 cup shortening
1/4 cup water
    2 tablespoons all-purpose flour
1-1/2 teaspoons vanilla extract
    4 cups confectioners' sugar
Paste food coloring

In a microwave, melt butterscotch chips; cool for 10 minutes. In a mixing bowl, cream butter and sugars. Add egg, milk and vanilla; mix well. Beat in melted chips. Gradually add flour; mix well. Cover and refrigerate for 1 hour.

On a floured surface, roll out dough to 1/4-in. thickness. Cut with a floured 4-1/2-in. gingerbread man cookie cutter and a 3-in. round cutter. Place 2 in. apart on greased baking sheets. Bake at 375° for 5-8 minutes or until edges are lightly browned. Cool for 1 minute; remove to wire racks to cool completely.

For frosting, combine shortening, water, flour and vanilla in a mixing bowl; mix well. Gradually beat in sugar. Place 1 cup frosting in a plastic bag; cut a small hole in corner of bag. Pipe shirt and shorts on players. Fill in outline and smooth with a metal spatula. Tint 1/4 cup frosting black; place in a plastic bag. Pipe lines on round cookies to create basketballs; pipe hair, eyes and noses on players. Tint 1/4 cup frosting red; pipe a mouth on each player. Tint remaining frosting to match team colors of your choice; pipe around shirts and shorts and add a letter on shirts if desired. **Yield:** about 2 dozen.

Picnic Celebrates Red, White and Blue

By Sue Gronholz, Beaver Dam, Wisconsin

INSPIRED BY the Stars and Stripes, I decided to go all out with red, white and blue for the Fourth of July picnic husband Todd and I host annually.

Among the lineup of delicious foods were my hearty All-American Barbecue Sandwiches and Grandma's Potato Salad, which has a cooked dressing well worth the little extra effort.

I really waved the flag when it came to Patriotic Gelatin Salad and Red, White and Blue Dessert!

We carried lunch to the lawn to cheer our community's Independence Day parade going by.

The next time you're entertaining on the Fourth, I hope you might try my ideas!

All-American Barbecue Sandwiches

I came up with this delicious recipe on my own. It's a big hit with family and friends, who say they like the way the flavors blend in the sauce.

4-1/2 pounds ground beef
1-1/2 cups chopped onion
2-1/4 cups ketchup
   3 tablespoons prepared mustard
   3 tablespoons Worcestershire sauce
   2 tablespoons vinegar
   2 tablespoons sugar
   1 tablespoon salt

1 tablespoon pepper
18 hamburger buns, split

In a Dutch oven, cook beef and onion until meat is browned and onion is tender; drain. Combine ketchup, mustard, Worcestershire, vinegar, sugar, salt and pepper; stir into beef mixture. Heat through. Serve on buns. **Yield:** 18 servings.

— 🍴 🍴 🍴 —

Grandma's Potato Salad

Our Fourth of July feast wouldn't be complete without this cool, old-fashioned potato salad. It's Grandma's treasured recipe.

1 cup water
1/2 cup butter *or* margarine
1/4 cup white vinegar
2 eggs
1/2 cup sugar
4-1/2 teaspoons cornstarch
3/4 cup salad dressing *or* mayonnaise
3/4 cup whipping cream, whipped
6 pounds red salad potatoes, cooked, peeled and sliced
1/2 cup chopped onion
1/4 cup sliced green onions
1 teaspoon salt
1/2 teaspoon pepper
3 hard-cooked eggs, sliced
Leaf lettuce and paprika, optional

In the top of a double boiler over boiling water, heat water, butter and vinegar. In a bowl, beat eggs; add sugar and cornstarch. Add to butter mixture; cook and stir constantly until thickened and a thermometer reads 160°, about 5-7 minutes. Remove from the heat and allow to cool.

Stir in the salad dressing; fold in the whipped cream. In a large bowl, toss potatoes, onion, green onions, salt and pepper. Pour dressing over and mix gently. Chill. Garnish with hard-cooked eggs. Serve in a lettuce-lined bowl and sprinkle with paprika if desired. **Yield:** 18 servings.

— 🍴 🍴 🍴 —

Patriotic Gelatin Salad

Almost as spectacular as the fireworks, this lovely salad makes quite a "bang" at our July Fourth meal.

2 packages (3 ounces *each*) berry blue gelatin
2 packages (3 ounces *each*) strawberry gelatin
4 cups boiling water, *divided*
2-1/2 cups cold water, *divided*

2 envelopes unflavored gelatin
2 cups milk
1 cup sugar
2 cups (16 ounces) sour cream
2 teaspoons vanilla extract

In four separate bowls, dissolve each package of gelatin in 1 cup boiling water. Add 1/2 cup cold water to each and stir. Pour one bowl of blue gelatin into a 10-in. fluted tube pan coated with nonstick cooking spray; chill until almost set, about 30 minutes. Set other three bowls of gelatin aside at room temperature.

Soften unflavored gelatin in remaining cold water; let stand 5 minutes. Heat milk in a saucepan over medium heat just below boiling. Stir in softened gelatin and sugar until sugar is dissolved. Remove from heat; stir in sour cream and vanilla until smooth. When blue gelatin in pan is almost set, carefully spoon 1-1/2 cups sour cream mixture over it. Chill until almost set, about 30 minutes. Carefully spoon one bowl of strawberry gelatin over cream layer. Chill until almost set.

Carefully spoon 1-1/2 cups cream mixture over strawberry layer. Chill until almost set. Repeat, adding layers of blue gelatin, cream mixture and strawberry gelatin, chilling in between each. Chill several hours or overnight. **Yield:** 16 servings.

Editor's Note: This salad takes time to prepare since each layer must be almost set before the next layer is added.

— 🍴 🍴 🍴 —

Red, White and Blue Dessert

Serving this rich, fresh-tasting dessert is a great salute to the nation's independence!

2 packages (8 ounces *each*) cream cheese, softened
1/2 cup sugar
1/2 teaspoon vanilla extract
1/2 teaspoon almond extract
2 cups whipping cream, whipped
2 quarts strawberries, halved, *divided*
2 quarts blueberries, *divided*

In a large mixing bowl, beat cream cheese, sugar and extracts until fluffy. Fold in the whipped cream. Place a third of the mixture in a 4-qt. bowl. Reserve 20 strawberry halves and 1/2 cup blueberries for garnish. Layer half of the remaining strawberries and blueberries over cream mixture. Top with another third of the cream mixture and the remaining berries. Spread the remaining cream mixture on top. Use the reserved strawberries and blueberries to make a "flag" on top. **Yield:** 18 servings.

Make the Grade with Class Party

By Leslie Miller, Butler, Pennsylvania

OUR DAUGHTER, Kayla, could hardly wait for her fifth birthday so she could start kindergarten. When the big day finally came, we wanted it to be really special for her. We invited eight of her friends to help celebrate with a school days theme.

Each guest was asked to wear a school backpack, which was used to hold goodies during a candy hunt. The eager group of new students also used colorful stickers and markers to personalize brown lunch bags, which I filled with favors and set at their places.

The braided Pepperoni Stromboli, filled with pizza-type ingredients and baked to a golden brown, received high marks from children and adults alike. For occasions like birthdays, when there are so many things to

do, this stromboli is easy to make and fun to serve.

Sprinkle Fruit Dip is light, fluffy and not too sweet. Candy sprinkles fleck the yogurt mixture, and their colors run as you scoop the dip, creating a rainbow or tie-dyed effect.

We had strawberries, red and green grapes and, of course, apples. But you could use any of your special favorites or fruits in season.

Kayla was delighted with her School Bus Cake! The other moms were impressed with its vibrant color and design, and I was quick to tell them how easy it was to bake, shape and decorate.

Since it was a beautiful day, we ate lunch outside on the picnic table. I set it with a paper birthday tablecloth, red and yellow streamers and balloons. On a little schoolhouse with a chalkboard roof, we wrote, "Happy Birthday, Kayla."

At the place settings where a knife would normally be placed, each child found a plastic stencil to keep. Their drinking cups were lined with red napkins and held new pencils, candy dispensers and shiny metallic paper party horns.

With a send-off like this, what child wouldn't be excited to go to kindergarten?

If someone in your family is ready to enroll...or if you'd like to plan a unique meal to mark the beginning of a new school year, try this theme.

— 🍴 🍴 🍴 —

Pepperoni Stromboli

There's a surprise inside this impressive golden braided loaf—a flavorful pizza-like filling. The children at our daughter's special "going to school" birthday party loved it—and adults enjoyed it, too!

 2 loaves (1 pound *each*) frozen bread
   dough, thawed
 1/2 cup spaghetti *or* pizza sauce
 1/2 teaspoon dried oregano
 4 ounces sliced pepperoni
 2 cups (8 ounces) shredded mozzarella
   cheese
 1/3 cup grated Parmesan cheese

Punch dough down. On a lightly floured surface, roll each loaf into a 20-in. x 8-in. rectangle. Place one rectangle on a greased baking sheet. Spread spaghetti sauce in an 18-in. x 4-in. strip down the center. Sprinkle with oregano, pepperoni and mozzarella. Fold sides of dough over filling; set aside.

Cut the remaining rectangle into three strips. Loosely braid the strips and pinch ends to seal. Place braid on top of the cheese and dough; pinch dough to seal. Sprinkle with Parmesan cheese. Bake at 350° for 30 minutes or until golden brown. **Yield:** 8-10 servings.

— 🍴 🍴 🍴 —

Sprinkle Fruit Dip

Bright candy sprinkles make this creamy mixture even more festive. Served with an array of fresh fruit "dippers", it was fun for Kayla's party. Apple slices were especially appropriate to go with our school theme.

1-1/2 cups strawberry yogurt
1-1/2 cups whipped topping
 1/4 cup colored sprinkles, *divided*
 4 large green apples, sliced
 4 large red apples, sliced

 2 pints fresh strawberries
 4 cups red *and/or* green grapes

In a bowl, fold together yogurt, whipped topping and half of the sprinkles. Cover and refrigerate for 20 minutes. Just before serving, top with remaining sprinkles. Serve with fruit. **Yield:** 3 cups.

— 🍴 🍴 🍴 —

School Bus Cake

Kayla could hardly wait to board a real school bus to go to kindergarten, so I made her birthday cake to look like one. Everyone at the party immediately recognized the sweet vehicle.

 1 package (18-1/4 ounces) yellow cake mix
 1 cup butter *or* margarine, softened
 1 cup shortening
 8 to 9 cups confectioners' sugar
 1/4 cup milk
 1 teaspoon vanilla extract
 1/4 teaspoon salt
 2 teaspoons black paste *or* gel food coloring
 1/2 to 3/4 teaspoon yellow paste *or* liquid
   food coloring
 2 cream-filled chocolate sandwich cookies,
   cut in half
 2 yellow gumdrops
 6 red gumdrops

Prepare cake batter according to package directions. Pour into two greased 8-in. x 4-in. x 2-in. loaf pans. Bake at 350° for 40-45 minutes or until a toothpick inserted near the center comes out clean. Cool for 10 minutes; remove from pans to a wire rack to cool completely. Place cakes end to end on a 22-in. x 8-in. covered board. Level if needed.

From the top of one end, form the front of the bus by cutting out a section 1 in. deep and 3 in. long. (Save the removed piece for another use.)

For frosting, beat butter and shortening in a mixing bowl until fluffy. Beat in 6 cups sugar, milk, vanilla and salt. Beat in enough additional sugar until frosting reaches desired spreading consistency. Remove 3/4 cup of frosting; add black food coloring. Tint remaining frosting yellow. Frost entire cake yellow. Frost cut edge of cookies with yellow frosting to form wheel wells; place two cookie halves on each side of bus.

Cut a hole in the corner of a plastic bag or insert a #5 round tip in a pastry bag; fill with black frosting. Outline windows on both sides of bus; pipe stripes under windows. Pipe windshield and back window; fill in with black frosting. Pipe lines on front for grille. Place yellow gumdrops on front of bus for headlights; place red gumdrops on front and back for lights. **Yield:** 12-16 servings.

Spooky Supper for Hungry Goblins

By Vicki Schlechter, Davis, California

AS SOON AS our son and daughter were old enough for trick-or-treating, I began serving them a special Halloween meal. (My ulterior motive was to fill them up so they wouldn't eat too much candy!) Our spooky supper became a family tradition that outlived going door-to-door for treats.

No tricks—my menu is a treat! Jack-o'-Lantern Burgers are tasty beef patties with cheesy pumpkin-style "faces".

Broccoli Boo Salad, which can be made a day ahead, is a colorful accompaniment for the burgers. As a startling garnish, I placed a fake spider (available at craft stores) in the center of each serving. If your goblins are little, you may prefer to decorate the table with plastic spiders rather than set them on the salads.

Candy gummy worms hung over the bowl of Wormy Orange Punch, inviting guests to sip some of this sparkling, frothy beverage. I also dropped a worm into each person's cup.

With its "cemetery topping", Graveyard Cake is always a hit! Cookie tombstones and whipped-topping ghosts set an eerie mood atop this haunted holiday dessert.

I made ghoulish-looking popcorn hands to set on each plate using disposable clear plastic gloves (found in a hardware store) and packed little treat bags with Halloween goodies such as fake teeth.

Years ago, my well-planned witchery to keep the kids filled up proved to be a trick on me—I caught my son sneaking out the door with a pillowcase to collect candy! Even so, the theme meal has become a time-honored treat…so try this ghostly grub on your gang!

⍟ ⍟ ⍟

Jack-o'-Lantern Burgers

It's fun to "carve" cheesy faces for these nicely seasoned burgers. Hungry trick-or-treaters welcome the hearty sandwiches. They're a can't-miss entree for a casual holiday get-together.

- 1 envelope onion soup mix
- 1/4 cup ketchup
- 2 tablespoons brown sugar
- 2 teaspoons prepared horseradish
- 2 teaspoons chili powder
- 2-1/2 pounds ground beef
- 10 slices process American cheese
- 10 hamburger buns, split

In a bowl, combine soup mix, ketchup, brown sugar, horseradish and chili powder. Add beef; mix well. Shape into 10 patties. Grill, broil or pan-fry until meat is no longer pink. Cut eyes, nose and mouth out of each cheese slice to create a jack-o'-lantern. Place cheese on burgers; cook until cheese is slightly melted, about 1 minute. Serve on buns. **Yield:** 10 servings.

⍟ ⍟ ⍟

Broccoli Boo Salad

There's nothing scary about the recipe for this popular salad—it's delightfully easy to put together. The mandarin oranges also look nice with the colors in other foods and decorations for my theme.

- 1 cup mayonnaise *or* salad dressing
- 1/4 cup sugar
- 2 tablespoons cider vinegar
- 8 cups broccoli florets
- 1 can (11 ounces) mandarin oranges, drained
- 1/2 cup chopped red onion
- 6 to 8 bacon strips, cooked and crumbled
- 1/2 cup raisins

In a small bowl, whisk mayonnaise, sugar and vinegar. Cover and refrigerate for at least 2 hours. In a large bowl, combine broccoli, oranges, onion, bacon and raisins. Add dressing and toss to coat. Cover and refrigerate for 1 hour. **Yield:** 10-12 servings.

⍟ ⍟ ⍟

Wormy Orange Punch

This simply delicious punch is great for any large gathering. No one can resist the sweet orange flavor.

- 1 gallon orange sherbet, softened
- 1 quart pineapple juice, chilled
- 1 liter lemon-lime soda, chilled
- Gummy worms

Combine sherbet and pineapple juice in a punch bowl; stir well. Add soda; stir until sherbet is almost dissolved. Decorate bowl with gummy worms. Serve immediately. **Yield:** 20 (1-cup) servings.

⍟ ⍟ ⍟

Graveyard Cake

Underneath the tasty "tombstones", ghosts, pumpkins, "worms" and "soil" that make this dessert a conversation piece, you'll find a delectable chocolate cake made from scratch in a few simple steps.

- 2 cups all-purpose flour
- 2 cups sugar
- 1 teaspoon baking soda
- 1/2 teaspoon salt
- 1 cup butter *or* margarine
- 1 cup water
- 1/4 cup baking cocoa
- 1/2 cup sour cream
- 2 eggs
- FROSTING:
- 1/4 cup butter *or* margarine
- 3 tablespoons milk
- 2 tablespoons baking cocoa
- 2 cups confectioners' sugar
- 1/2 teaspoon vanilla extract
- 18 cream-filled chocolate sandwich cookies
- 9 cream-filled oval vanilla sandwich cookies
- 1 cup whipped topping
- Green and brown decorator's icing *or* gel
- Pumpkin candies and gummy worms, optional

In a mixing bowl, combine flour, sugar, baking soda and salt; set aside. In a saucepan over medium heat, combine butter, water and cocoa; bring to a boil. Add to flour mixture; beat well. Beat in sour cream and eggs. Pour into a greased 13-in. x 9-in. x 2-in. baking pan. Bake at 350° for 35-38 minutes or until a toothpick inserted near the center comes out clean. Cool on a wire rack for 5 minutes.

Meanwhile, in a saucepan, combine butter, milk and cocoa; bring to a boil. Remove from the heat; stir in sugar and vanilla. Pour over the warm cake. Crumble chocolate cookies; sprinkle over frosting while still warm. Cool completely.

For tombstones, use icing to decorate vanilla cookies with words or faces; place on cake. For ghosts, make mounds of whipped topping; use icing to add eyes and mouths as desired. Refrigerate for at least 1 hour. Just before serving, add pumpkins and gummy worms if desired. **Yield:** 16 servings.

Welcome to My Pineapple Palace

By Jo Ann Fox, Johnson City, Tennessee

I STARTED collecting pineapple items when I learned that the pineapple is the symbol of hospitality. Plus, I love the flavor of this versatile tropical fruit. So wouldn't it be fun, I reasoned, to plan a pineapple party?

I had made many pineapple recipes for various occasions over the years, but I had never tried combining several into a complete meal. When I did, it was not only delicious, it was fun!

Baked Ham with Pineapple is an attractive but easy entree to serve company. My recipe has a pleasant sauce of pineapple juice and brown sugar that's poured over the ham and used for basting. Pineapple slices and maraschino cherries make a pretty garnish on top of the succulent ham.

Pineapple tidbits, miniature marshmallows and dried cranberries give my Pineapple Mallow Slaw special-occasion flair. I combined several recipes to come up with this popular side dish.

I also served sweet potatoes with pineapple chutney and gave guests jars of chutney as favors. Wrapped with yellow and green netting and tied with yellow ribbon, the jars even resembled little pineapples!

For dessert, I baked moist, delicious Hawaiian Cake. An acquaintance shared the recipe with me some 20 years ago, and I've used it many times since then. Toasted coconut sprinkled on the cake's wonderful fluffy topping adds another tropical flavor to this pineapple treat.

My entire kitchen is decorated with pineapple accents, which spill over into the dining room. I set the table using plenty of pineapple pieces.

For the fresh fruit centerpiece, I filled a wrought-iron basket with Golden Delicious and Granny Smith apples and placed a whole pineapple on top.

I also used pineapple-shaped candles, serving dishes and salt and pepper shakers, plus salad utensils with carved pineapple handles. My pineapple napkin rings looked very pretty with the pastel yellow tablecloth and napkins.

Of course, you don't need an extensive "pineapple patch" like mine to enjoy this party theme. You can purchase inexpensive pineapple-design paper plates and napkins and many other decorations.

My husband, Bob, is a symbol of hospitality himself! He doesn't cook much, but he loves to put on a chef's outfit and greet guests at the door. I can always count on his help when we entertain.

We had a great evening eating, talking about the pineapple menu and decorations and visiting with friends. Everyone seemed delighted by my tasty tribute to the symbol of hospitality!

— 🍵 🍵 🍵 —

Baked Ham with Pineapple

My mom used to bake ham like this. It's a simple recipe that proves the simplest things in life are best!

 1 fully cooked bone-in ham (6 to 8 pounds)
Whole cloves
 1/2 cup packed brown sugar
 1/4 cup pineapple juice
 1 can (8 ounces) sliced pineapple, drained
 5 maraschino cherries

Place ham in a roasting pan. Score the surface with shallow diagonal cuts, making diamond shapes; insert cloves into the diamonds. Cover and bake at 325° for 1-1/2 hours. Combine brown sugar and pineapple juice; pour over the ham. Arrange pineapple and cherries on the ham. Bake, uncov-

ered, 30-45 minutes longer or until a meat thermometer reads 140° and ham is heated through. **Yield:** 16-20 servings.

— 🍵 🍵 🍵 —

Pineapple Mallow Slaw

When I couldn't find a recipe I liked, I created my own. Our guests loved the mixture and commented on its appealing sweet-tart dressing.

 9 cups shredded cabbage
 1 can (20 ounces) pineapple tidbits, drained
1-1/2 cups mayonnaise
 3/4 cup cider vinegar
 1/2 cup sugar
 3/4 teaspoon salt
 3/4 teaspoon celery seed
 3 cups miniature marshmallows
1-1/2 cups dried cranberries

In a bowl, combine the cabbage and pineapple. In another bowl, combine the mayonnaise, vinegar, sugar, salt and celery seed. Stir into cabbage mixture. Cover and refrigerate for 2 hours. Fold in marshmallows and cranberries 30 minutes before serving. **Yield:** 16-20 servings.

— 🍵 🍵 🍵 —

Hawaiian Cake

Every time I take this cake to an event, someone asks for the recipe. It's moist, delicious and easy to make.

 1 package (18-1/4 ounces) yellow cake mix
1-1/4 cups cold milk
 1 package (3.4 ounces) instant vanilla pudding mix
 1 can (20 ounces) crushed pineapple, drained
 1 envelope whipped topping mix
 1 package (3 ounces) cream cheese, softened
 1/4 cup sugar
 1/2 teaspoon vanilla extract
 1/2 cup flaked coconut, toasted

Prepare and bake cake according to package directions, using a greased 13-in. x 9-in. x 2-in. baking pan. Cool. In a bowl, whisk together milk and pudding mix; let stand to thicken. Stir in pineapple. Spread over cake. Prepare whipped topping mix according to package directions; set aside.

In a mixing bowl, beat cream cheese, sugar and vanilla until smooth. Beat in 1 cup whipped topping. Fold in remaining topping. Spread over pudding. Sprinkle with coconut. Cover and chill for 3 hours or overnight. **Yield:** 12-15 servings.

General Recipe Index

This handy index lists every recipe by food category, major ingredient and/or cooking method, so you can easily locate recipes to suit your needs.

✓ *Recipe includes Nutritional Analysis and Diabetic Exchanges*

✓ *Recipe includes Nutritional Analysis and Diabetic Exchanges*

✓ *Recipe includes Nutritional Analysis and Diabetic Exchanges*

✓ Recipe includes Nutritional Analysis and Diabetic Exchanges

✓ *Recipe includes Nutritional Analysis and Diabetic Exchanges*

✓ Recipe includes Nutritional Analysis and Diabetic Exchanges

✓ *Recipe includes Nutritional Analysis and Diabetic Exchanges*

✓ *Recipe includes Nutritional Analysis and Diabetic Exchanges*

✓ Recipe includes Nutritional Analysis and Diabetic Exchanges

Alphabetical Recipe Index

This handy index lists every recipe in alphabetical order so you can easily find your favorite recipes.

✓ Recipe includes Nutritional Analysis and Diabetic Exchanges

✓ Recipe includes Nutritional Analysis and Diabetic Exchanges

✓ Recipe includes Nutritional Analysis and Diabetic Exchanges

✓ Recipe includes Nutritional Analysis and Diabetic Exchanges